Steve Jobs and the NeXT Big Thing

Steve Jobs

and the

NeXT Big Thing

RANDALL E. STROSS

ATHENEUM

NEW YORK 1993

MAXWELL MACMILLAN CANADA
TORONTO

MAXWELL MACMILLAN INTERNATIONAL
NEW YORK   OXFORD   SINGAPORE   SYDNEY

Atheneum	Maxwell Macmillan Canada, Inc.
Macmillan Publishing Company	1200 Eglinton Avenue East
866 Third Avenue	Suite 200
New York, NY 10022	Don Mills, Ontario M3C 3N1

Macmillan Publishing Company is part of the Maxwell Communication Group of Companies.

Library of Congress Cataloging-in-Publication Data
Stross, Randall E.
    Steve Jobs and the NeXT big thing / by Randall E. Stross.
        p.   cm.
    ISBN 0-689-12135-0
    1. NeXT (Computer)   2. Jobs, Steven, 1955–   .   3. NeXT Computer,
Inc.   I. Title.
QA76.5.S786   1993   93-20761   CIP
338.7'61004165—dc20

Macmillan books are available at special discounts for bulk purchases for sales promotions, premiums, fund-raising, or educational use. For details, contact:

Special Sales Director
Macmillan Publishing Company
866 Third Avenue
New York, NY 10022

10   9   8   7   6   5   4   3   2   1
Printed in the United States of America

To Gordon Cohen

Contents

Contents

Steve Jobs and the NeXT Big Thing

Introduction

E ach day brings a gentle rain of white petals, thousands and thousands of new pages of press releases, floating down upon newspaper and magazine editors. Each sheet is a compact package of glad tidings that companies hope will be noticed, even though all releases are filled with the same untrustworthy cheeriness. Here is the headline of one that wafted down on January 25, 1993:

NeXT Profitable in Q4 '92
North American Sales up 36% in 1992[1]

The news release was issued by NeXT Computer, Inc., a small computer company headed by a well-known entrepreneur, Steve Jobs, the cofounder of Apple Computer.

NeXT's existence owed much to the inspirational example of Apple. When Jobs left Apple in 1985 to start another computer company from scratch, the *next* in its name referred to Steve Jobs's next bid to shape history, to present to a grateful world the next big thing. Intermittently, the world had heard from him and his company, in press releases such as this, or in staged events for the media. But though eight years had passed, and the fire of ambition burned as brightly in Jobs as ever, another business miracle had yet to materialize. Reporters who wrote about NeXT would often forget when exactly NeXT had been founded, and as late as 1992 would still refer to NeXT as a company that was two or three years old, inadvertently lopping off years, an error that Jobs of course was happy to let stand uncorrected. The less attention paid to his failures to repeat at NeXT his earlier success at Apple, the more attention he could direct toward NeXT's future, clean and untarnished, always bright with possibility.

Better to look anywhere but to the past record, where Jobs's attempts to build a profitable rival to Apple had led him from one strategy to another, from blunder to blunder, disaster to disaster. What makes his NeXT story especially intriguing, however, is the gullibility of many others who lent money, careers, and prestige to Steve Jobs's quest. The greater portion of investment capital came not from Jobs's own pocket but from that of others. The amount of money that was sunk into the NeXT venture makes it a story for the history books, but not in the way that Jobs intended: well over *$250 million* of capital and royalties disappeared in NeXT, without a penny of net profit to show for the investment.[2] NeXT's dismal skein of business misjudgments threatened to go do down in the books as the most expensive flop in the history of entrepreneurship.

And yet Jobs remained buoyant about the prospects for his NeXT. At the moment of the press release, in late January 1993, he asked that the news media pay attention to the happy news about recent sales, which had reached an all-time record $140 million for calendar year 1992. He also boasted that the fourth quarter of 1992 marked the first profitable quarter ever for NeXT. Ordinary entrepreneurs would not be permitted the luxury of seven-plus years of struggles without a single profitable quarter, but Jobs enjoyed resources that had given him a more leisurely timetable to find his footing. On the face of such figures, the company appeared to have turned a corner indeed. Upon second glance, however, the press release concealed some important facts. It did not mention the amount of profit earned, an omission that was a curious way to trumpet a company's financial health. In fact, the profits that NeXT wanted the world to notice were an accounting phantom and excluded interest payments for loans—NeXT had a net loss for the quarter.[3] NeXT did not reveal that for the year, the company had fallen about $40 million short of break-even.[4] Nor did it disclose the number of computers sold, a statistic that similar computer companies routinely disclose when releasing quarterly and annual results. One can understand the company's decision not to call attention to the fact that the total number of computers that the company had sold, not just in 1992, but cumulatively since its founding in 1985, came to only 50,000. This seven-year-total was the number of computers that Apple in early 1993 sold in any given *six days*.[5]

If all was well at NeXT, as press releases always must say, then one was left to wonder why it was that in the past year no less than seven of Steve Jobs's nine vice-presidents had been fired or had left on their own, leaving unfilled vacancies in many cases (*Business Week* joked, "Will the last executive to leave NeXT Computer Inc. please turn out the lights?").[6] Despite an exodus of NeXT managers,[7] and other contrary evidence, Jobs was able, as he always was, to assert that his company was doing fine. He declared that "things are going better than they have in a long time."[8] The tacit assumption in his remarks was that the public need only pay attention to the selective facts (and factoids) of the press release.

Rumors were circulating at the time that NeXT might close its factory and devote all of its resources to selling the software that it had provided along with its computers. The recent departure of Rich Page, the vice president in charge of hardware, and the absence of a named successor, had served to increase speculation that the NeXT factory might be closed. When queried by reporters, Jobs denied any change was in the offing. At the end of the press release, however, a seemingly innocuous passage attracted some unwanted attention. As a way of introducing the company to those not already familiar with it, the release explained that NeXT Computer, Inc. was a company that designed and marketed something called NeXT-STEP software. This self-description was not the standard boilerplate that it had used in the past; until this moment, the company had defined itself in the same place in its press releases as the company that "designs, manufactures, and markets professional workstations," a class of computer that is more powerful—and more expensive—than ordinary personal computers. Earlier, it had even changed its name from NeXT, Inc. to NeXT *Computer*, Inc., to emphasize its principal product. All of the $140 million in revenue of which it had boasted for the past year was earned by the sale and servicing of those computers, made exclusively by NeXT itself—the NeXTSTEP software came free with the machines. Thus, hidden at the end of this seemingly unremarkable document, was the apparent disappearance of the computer that had been the company's raison d'être and its primary revenue-generating product.

When the press inquired about the meaning of the last paragraph of the press release, NeXT issued a torrent of emphatic denials: NeXT was not abandoning its hardware production, no sir, absolutely not, the company had no such plans.[9] (The spokeswoman at NeXT who issued the denials was also the same person who had on one day, denied that Rich Page was resigning, then the very next day, confirmed it.)[10] NeXT management was so persuasive in its denials of recent or imminent change and in its serene pronouncements about profits that it fooled not only the public but also the company's own employees. Hence, the news that leaked on Tuesday, February 9th, caught almost everyone by surprise: The company was immediately abandoning computer manufacturing and laying off 330 of its 500 employees, cutting not only in manufacturing and design but also in sales, marketing, and administration.[11] Many of the affected employees learned of the layoffs in a fashion that made awful news all the worse: *from the radio*. The day would be remembered by victims and survivors alike as "Black Tuesday."

One has to admire the audacity of NeXT's public relations efforts: here is a company that could claim that its business was healthy and profitable one moment, then announce the abandonment of its sole existing source of revenue and the decimation of more than 60 percent of its workforce, and then reassert with innocent equanimity that it was simply "capitalizing" on its assets. Steve Jobs offered no explanation of the discrepancy between the earlier sanguine announcements and the apparent need to change direction radically. He directed attention forward, to the future, to the beckoning opportunity of leading NeXT into the ranks of "first-tier" software companies.[12] The current line was always correct (until further notice).

According to Jobs, NeXT once again was poised on the eve of great success, now a "leaner" company, with an unspecified "pipeline of orders" in hand for its software.[13] Unfortunately for NeXT, the software was not ready for sale, and would not be for months yet. The NeXTSTEP software that the company had bundled with its own computers could not run on any other brand of computer. Its incompatibility of course was one of the principal problems that had contributed to NeXT's record of disappointing sales, but it had taken Jobs years before he was willing to recognize it as a problem instead of as a "strategic advantage." He had belatedly given his assent to the massive task of rewriting NeXTSTEP software so that it would run on IBM-compatible personal computers that were based on microprocessors made by Intel. But the task was far from complete, and the NeXTSTEP for Intel software was not going to be ready until late summer of 1993. When Jobs decided to drop computer production, he of necessity expedited the announced schedule for completing the new software, which he now said would be ready May 25, at the opening of NeXT's own trade show, NeXTWORLD Expo.

Even with an accelerated schedule, NeXT still found itself in an unenviable predicament. The company pulled out of the computer business before it had its replacement product, the Intel software, ready for sale. All it had to offer in the interim was the older version of the software that ran only on NeXT computers; the only potential customers—that is, those who owned a computer that could actually run it—already had been given the software when they had purchased their machines. NeXT was an eight-year-old company that was attempting the most awkward of all possible transitions: going months without a single revenue-producing product.

Daunting as all these difficulties might have been, Jobs remained enigmatically ebullient. Puzzled, a reporter for *Fortune* confessed that "it's hard to tell whether Steve Jobs is a snake-oil salesman or a bona fide visionary."[14] Jobs predicted that the newly transformed NeXT was going to rescue the world from what he called the "Microsoft monopoly," and his decision to concentrate exclusively on software was not merely the transformation of a single company, "it is, in all likelihood, the transformation of an entire industry."[15] When Jobs appeared at a meeting of the Bay Area NeXT Group a week after Black Tuesday, he brushed aside suggestions that NeXT should consider licensing its software to Microsoft. It made no sense, he said, to aid the enemy. And if some thought it was preposterous for tiny NeXT to compete against Microsoft, Jobs's second-in-command, Peter van Cuylenburg, derided the doubters as cowards. Van Cuylenburg pointed to his own successful experience taking on an entrenched monopoly in the British telecommunications business. He said he relished the opportunity to exploit the advantages of the underdog: "sympathy, focus, and nimbleness." Jobs echoed the same sentiment and confided that unnamed others had told him that he was erring on the side of *under*estimating NeXT's potential to steal market share away from Microsoft.

Listening to him, it was easy to forget that his was a company that had managed to gobble the $250 million in investment capital while securing only about a two percent share of the workstation market; it still had not seen a single quarter where it earned a net profit; it still had not found a viable path for itself; and a few weeks after these cataclysmic announcements, Jobs pushed van Cuylenburg, his hand-chosen president and heir apparent, out of the company.[16] For the battle against Microsoft, Jobs insisted on fighting singlehandedly, as the sole senior executive.

Such bravado invites morbid attention. Steve Jobs seems powerless to resist the temptation of exploits that will accomplish nothing if not sustaining attention to himself, even if observers remain skeptical of the face value of his pronouncements, and even if interest in Jobs originates in nothing more than the generic fascination of the most wealthy. The fascination is mixed with a beguiling mystery that we are reminded of whenever we peer at the faces of our fellows who have become rich. We will always experience a shock of recognition of the mortally ordinary, and such is the case when we look at the face of Steve Jobs, youthful though his remains. F. Scott Fitzgerald was wrong; the rich are not different, or at least appear no different, from you and me. Inspect all we wish, but we cannot actually see the power to amass an unimaginable fortune, and in Jobs's case, at a tender age no less.

How does the arrival of a monstrously large fortune during one's young adulthood influence the pristine person within? A Steve Jobs makes one wonder. So, too, Bill Gates, his archrival and the power behind the "Microsoft monopoly," who like Jobs has played an important role in bringing a personal computer industry into being in a very short period of historical time. Their personal fortunes chart changes in the landscape of the American economy, as money shifts from the solid, the bulky, the tangible, toward the transitory and rapidly obsolescent, the miniature, the cerebral. Partially offsetting this shift represented by two computer multimillionaires is the anachronistic coincidence that each dropped out of college early, and pursued business fortunes in a highly technical industry, free of formal engineering or computer science training, or the credentialism of the modern age, a quaint throwback to the rough and tumble education of the unlettered captains of industry a century ago. Other comparisons to the nineteenth century are not so quaint: Gates's ruthlessness in seeking complete domination in his industry would be compared to the robber barons of yore, and Jobs's utter lack of charitable impulse would shame even the robber barons.

Jobs's unlined face tells us little about his entry into the ranks of the extremely rich. The fortune appeared too quickly for it to have registered. The garage-to-riches story unfolded in a trice: In 1977, Steve Jobs and the other Steve, Steve Wozniak, moved their fledgling Apple Computer from the Jobs's family garage into an office; by 1980, the company's annual sales of their Apple II, the first popular personal computer, reached almost $120 million, and the company went public, making Steve Jobs, the largest shareholder, a millionaire many times over. When *Forbes* magazine in 1982 began an annual survey of the four hundred richest Americans, there was Steve Jobs with Apple stock valued at $100 million. He was twenty-seven years old, one of only three among the 400 who were under thirty.[17]

Very few of the 400 wealthiest in 1982 were under the age of forty, let alone thirty, and these were overwhelmingly inheritors of fortunes from the old industrial economy—oil, real estate, shipping, and the like. The two individuals who were under thirty aside from Jobs both were heiresses of oil fortunes. The only fortunes in the under-forty set that indicated anything of the new were those of filmmaker George Lucas and Federal Express founder Frederick Smith, both of whom then were thirty-eight and worth an estimated $100 million. Jobs was the precocious wonder of the entire elite group. Rising from modest suburban working-class origins, one is almost tempted to say he did it on his own. But of course only relatively so. First, the myth of the self-made fortune conveniently ignores the partners and all of the less visible Little People, whose contributions are at least collectively as indispensable. In the case of Apple, one particular individual, cofounder Steve Wozniak, was the technical wizard who created the hugely successful Apple II that made Apple a large company, but Wozniak was too generous and too passive to look out for his own best financial interests. It was Steve Jobs alone who emerged with a net worth that extended to nine figures.

Second, real life does not resemble the mythic drama in which the hardscrabble entrepreneur claims the mountaintop by dint of his own sweat and assertion of pure will, without financial assistance. Self-made fortunes are virtually never created without someone else providing risk capital at an early stage, and this too applies to the case of Apple. The two young Steves were able to move out of the garage only because Armas Clifford ("Mike") Markkula, Jr., who had already made a small fortune from Intel, invested in Apple with his own money, helped arrange for $600,000 in venture capital financing, and not least of all, recruited outside talents for board and executive leadership. Without the less visible backing of figures such as Markkula, the public would not have heard much about a Steve Jobs. It is telling that Wozniak was not on the 1982 *Forbes* list, but Markkula was, with a net worth estimated at $60 million.

Third, and this is most vexing of all to the rich hero who makes rather than inherits a fortune: one has difficulty quelling doubt that one's sudden business success owes much to chance, the happenstance of stumbling upon the right place at the right time, a sweet spot in the business cosmos. This suspicion troubles entrepreneurs of all ages, and many have embarked upon a succession of new ventures, self-imposed tests that could confirm that it was their own internal resources, not luck, that accounted for their first success. Almost all fail in their quest to repeat earlier history. It is hardly surprising that a preternaturally young business phenomenon like Steve Jobs would suffer from the affliction of self-doubt most of all.

For Jobs, the very different, slower, gradual, and untroubled course of Bill Gates's rise feeds consternation. In their longstanding competition, Gates originally had a slight head start, having co-founded Microsoft in 1975 with friend Paul Allen just as he was about to begin his freshman year at Harvard. He wrote programs for the first home computer, the Altair, then for other personal computers as they appeared, and secured the contract to write the basic software for IBM's new personal computer, introduced in 1981. But it would take awhile for the growth of the company to reach the point that would place Gates within the upper echelons of the most wealthy in the country. His debut on the *Forbes* list would come in 1986, at the age of thirty, after Microsoft had completed a public offering of its shares that made Gates's holdings worth $315 million.[18] This was four years after Jobs was on the list, and ironically the rise of Gates's Microsoft was owed partially to the success of Apple's Macintosh, which Gates had provided with programs before other software companies realized the potential of a market outside that defined by the standards of the IBM personal computer. With ecumenical shrewdness, Gates made Microsoft the beneficiary of growth of the entire personal computer industry, whether the computers were IBMs, clones, or Apple Macintoshes. This was to prove the most successful strategy in the industry.

It was Gates, then, not Jobs, who by 1988 was the thirty-two-year-old billionaire, who by 1991 had become, by *Forbes* reckoning, the second-richest American, with Microsoft stock valued at $4.8 billion. The 1991 listings showed that the financial arrangement between the old business partners at Microsoft was more generous to the lesser-known partner than what Apple co-founder Steve Wozniak had worked out with Steve Jobs. Microsoft cofounder Paul Allen, who had left Microsoft many years before but had retained stock, was a billionaire himself, the eleventh-richest person in the country, though at the comparatively senescent age of thirty-eight.[19]

In late 1991 and early 1992, the value of Microsoft stock turned skyward at an even steeper climb, pulling Gates's paper value up beyond $6 billion, and briefly even above $7 billion, far beyond any other individual. Gates's ascension in 1992 to the top of *Forbes*'s list of the richest Americans—and at the age of thirty-six, the youngest person ever to occupy the position—has completed what Jobs's appearance on the 1982 *Forbes* list had begun: demonstrating the new business possibilities opened up by computer technology, defying the old rules that placed a premium on inheritance, age and experience, patience measured in decades, the possession of real estate and the other massive, visible assets of an industrial age.

By anyone's measure, Steve Jobs is a financially secure multimillionaire himself, and has no material reason to be envious of Zillionaire Bill. But the Fates have not been as kind to Jobs, and though the utility value of the money may lose meaning in the hundreds-of-millions-and-up range, it stands as a measurable proxy for the difference in power that is wielded by the two. If we hear an edge of bitterness that sometimes creeps into Jobs's remarks, it can be traced to this difference and to the tribulations Jobs has gone through that Gates has not. Initially, Jobs went from rich to very rich on the *Forbes* list. In 1983, the value of his Apple stock soared from $100 to $225 million. But Apple encountered setbacks and by 1985 was in managerial disarray. Jobs, who had been increasingly at odds with John Sculley, the man he had recruited from Pepsi to be his successor, lost a final showdown. In September 1985, Jobs resigned from Apple, relinquishing a place in the company that had been the source of his adult identity. To mark his exit, he liquidated most of his Apple stock holdings, a decision that in retrospect was dearly costly; after his departure (and not a little *because* of his departure) the value of Apple stock soared. *Forbes* dropped him from the list of the richest 400.

He immediately set out to build a new company, which he ambiguously named NeXT (with the intentional mix of lower- and upper-case spelling), but his own intentions were hardly ambiguous. He had been all but literally cast out of the company that he had poured his soul into for eight years. Humiliated, he could think of little else but proving his ungrateful tormentors at Apple wrong. He would do so by building another computer company. For eight years he pursued at NeXT a Quixotic quest to conjure back the elusive magic that had borne Apple, about the same amount of time as Jobs was at Apple but with nothing like the same result. When

Jobs closed the NeXT factory in February 1993, he finally abandoned the Apple model and began to follow the Gates model for the first time in his life, an attempt to make a success of a company that made nothing but software.

Until that moment, Jobs's career differed significantly from Gates's. Snugly secure as always as head of Microsoft, Gates has been cossetted and has never had to face anything remotely similar to the coup d'état that deposed Jobs at Apple. Gates still spends his days and good portions of nights devoted to business and programming and hamburgers and little else, round the calendar, just as he has done ever since adolescence. His famous attachment to his work brings to mind another Robber Baron image: James Buchanan Duke, whose American Tobacco Company controlled tobacco markets at the beginning of the twentieth century as completely as Microsoft dominates personal computer software at the end. Duke described his attitude to work during his prime: "I was sorry to have to leave off at night and glad when morning came so I could get at it again."[20] Gates keeps Duke's spirit alive today.

Gates has never had reason to experiment with change. Jobs, on the other hand, set up the self-imposed test of himself at NeXT in such a way as to make it all but impossible for anyone to have succeeded. In the shadow of Apple (its annual revenue at the time was almost $2 billion), Jobs chose to build another personal-computer company. Pursuing the same customers. Using old friends recruited from Apple. But building a machine that could not use the software that was written for Apple, IBM, or any other personal computers.

Jobs had difficulty figuring out how his company could explain in nontechnical terms why his NeXT computer was special. Without a machine on hand to demonstrate, a NeXT spokesperson, trying to describe the machine to an ordinary prospective customer, had to refer to technical jargon, intelligible only to the cognoscenti—a *megapixel display with a 94-dpi screen, Mach Unix kernel, Display PostScript, a digital signal processor,* an *object-oriented operating sys-*

tem, preemptive multitasking, and so on. These features needed explication; and the most visible feature, the striking all-black styling
that distinguished the computer from the light colors of the competition, was hardly a compelling reason in itself to coax a wary buyer.
The NeXT computer simply did not lend itself to a snappy, one-
sentence summary. Look wherever you wished, you could not find
any clear, convincing label that said in plain English: Here's Why
You Should Buy Me.

Jobs had not been concerned, however, because he believed that
history could be commanded to repeat itself; the NeXT computer
would become successful in the same unpredictable way that the
Macintosh had. History teachers are wont to chant George Santay-
ana's famous dictum that "those who cannot remember the past are
condemned to repeat it," and we could amend what might be called
Steve Jobs's Corollary: "those who *do* remember the past are permitted to repeat it." Alas, the triumphs of the past are not so easily
commanded to return.

Repetition of the Macintosh success would have been difficult
enough to achieve even if Jobs had made the correct call on every
decision that came before him. He failed this time, however, to
appreciate fully the importance of enlisting the outside support of
Gates's Microsoft or a similar software company to ensure that
there would be plentiful software available when a new computer
standard, incompatible with existing ones, was introduced to the
public. Gates's willingness to begin work on software development
for the Macintosh prior to its introduction in 1984 had been instrumental to its eventual success, but this time Jobs did not succeed in
obtaining the assistance of Gates and Microsoft. He did not try
very hard, either. When Gates visited NeXT's offices in the summer
of 1987, while the NeXT computer was under development, Jobs
let him sit in the lobby for a half hour while Jobs moved conspicuously about the building, letting his visitor stew. Jobs's subordinates
were amused to see Jobs deliberately keep Gates waiting, which was
a way of NeXT telling Microsoft that NeXT did not really need

the software company's help, but the ploy was more than an act of discourtesy. It was the prelude of what would later become an acrimonious competition between the two men for the power to direct the personal-computer industry, which had grown manyfold since their earlier collaboration when Jobs was still at Apple.

When Jobs finally unveiled the NeXT machine to the general public in late 1988, Gates said with derision about his rival, "He put a microprocessor in a box. So what?"[21] Asked about the NeXT computer's disk drive, which was new for personal computers and used optical technology supplied by the Japanese, Gates sneered, "Anybody can write Sony a check" (for the record, the check went to Canon, not Sony).[22] The all-black design did not impress him, either. Gates: "If you want black, I'll get you a can of paint."[23] Would he develop software for Jobs's new machine? "Develop for it? I'll piss on it."[24] The industry consumed these remarks as delectable morsels; it also saw them as perfectly understandable, given the many threats that Microsoft already faced on a number of fronts, from a strained relationship with IBM and legal conflicts with Apple, to uncertain prospects for new software called Windows, and now Jobs's new machine, which invited the world to abandon the software that Microsoft provided and use a new standard. NeXT had ominously secured the imprimatur of Microsoft's most important partner, IBM, no less. In October 1988, one industry analyst went so far as to say that the new IBM-NeXT relationship "was the biggest risk that Microsoft has, and Gates is doing all he can to undermine it."[25]

The public feud between Gates and Jobs continued on through the following year. Gates dismissed the new technical features that the NeXT computer boasted of as "truly trivial,"[26] and later, when Gates and Jobs found themselves sitting on a dais at a personal-computer industry meeting, the two traded shots over the head of the hapless representative from IBM, James Cannavino, who sat between them. Cannavino said he felt like he was in Beirut.[27] It was Jobs, however, more than Gates who was most damaged by their estrangement. When Gates shunned the NeXT computer, NeXT was deprived of Microsoft's considerable resources for new software development, which it desperately needed. And Gates's cold response also sent a message to other potentially interested parties that NeXT's place in the personal-computer galaxy would be marginal. Everyone knew that Gates had been willing to take a considerable risk in backing the Macintosh when it was first introduced. Thus his refusal to back Jobs this time was read as evidence that NeXT would begin hobbled by a crippling handicap with which Apple had never had to contend.

With or without Gates's endorsement, Jobs was unconcerned: his motto then was Build It and They Will Come. But hardly anyone came when the machine was introduced in 1988. Nor did they come in 1989. Jobs was so slow to perceive just how grave was the failure that it was not until 1990 that he threw out the old plan and cobbled together a new one, and another, and another, right up to the present. For a person who seems constitutionally resistant to change, Jobs has done a remarkable job of adapting himself eventually to circumstances. Apple Computer's Bad Boy of 1985, the sworn enemy of IBM, began NeXT as the bête noire of corporate gigantism. He was determined to produce a wholly new computer standard for the following decade, and on his own terms, with his own company and own hand-picked employees. Moreover, NeXT eschewed corporate America as its customers and served only colleges and universities. Instead of pursuing profit for its own sake, NeXT was dedicated to furthering the mission of higher education by providing computers designed for the special needs of students and scholars. By 1993, Fortune 500 companies had become his favored customer prospects, and colleges and universities were relegated to the side. The push for a NeXT computer standard for the world had had to be modified to take into account the fact that 100 million personal computers were already in existence and unlikely to be dropped in the wastebasket because Jobs had a new, improved machine. Eventually, the crusade for NeXT-built computers had had to be abandoned altogether.

To get from there to here, Jobs has had to scramble, reinventing himself along the way, keeping his company alive through dark days of nonexistent sales. When asked about NeXT, many in the industry shook their heads, saying that if it had been anybody's but Jobs's, it would have had no possible chance of surviving. One could add that Bill Gates also has similar capacities for endurance, but he does not come to mind because he has never faced similar challenges. While Jobs's post-Apple venture was floundering, Gates's Microsoft was growing rapidly into the behemoth whose commanding power over the software industry gave the two largest personal computer companies, IBM and Apple, a deep fright that drove the former enemies into detente. Gates has never had to scrap like Jobs for his company's survival. So though it may be hard to discern from their unlined faces, one of them has been roughed up a bit by life, if such can be said about a multimillionaire, and the other, the multibillionaire, has not been.

Against his will though it may have been, the changes that an unappreciative world have forced upon Jobs have made him a much more interesting person. The NeXT story could well have turned out to be a short one-act play, a pallid variation of Godot, starring only Jobs, as the solipsist in black turtleneck, waiting for customers that never would appear. It has not turned out that way. From the beginning of his new venture, and despite his original intentions, Jobs had been forced to rely on outside talent, outside suppliers, outside investors, outside allies, and outside journalist supporters. Jobs, his recruits, and his varied partners comprise a colorful cast. Picture the group as a film director would. At the center, of course, is Jobs himself, with several personae, but the one that Hollywood would be most interested in is the glitzy showman who stages product introductions unlike any others (though critics have always made unflattering comparisons to P. T. Barnum). Around him stands the original NeXT crew whom he recruited, drawing from Apple and elsewhere in Silicon Valley; for the most part it was a young group, negotiating the transition from twenty-something to thirty-something. Behind them stand the outside investors, an unlikely assemblage: H. Ross Perot, first hooked by a television show about NeXT and whose legitimizing support made Jobs's youthful NeXT crew seem less young and more credible; the heads of two elite universities, Stanford and Carnegie-Mellon, who lent the prestige as well as the money of their institutions to this private venture; and an important Japanese investor, Canon, whose investment in 1989 overnight gave NeXT, when it lacked a finished product, a book value of $600 million and by so doing, temporarily restored Jobs, who then owned fifty percent of NeXT's stock, to the good graces of the *Forbes* richest 400 list. Unlike Gates, who possessed an entrenched position at the top, Jobs's mere inclusion was tenuous. When the 1992 list of the *Forbes* 400 appeared in October, the cover featured a gallery of six figures, three of whom are found in the NeXT story: Jobs, who was dropped once again from the list (the caption under his photo: "Didn't Cut It This Year"); his rival Gates; and Ross Perot, whose political ambitions and willingness to spend his own money liberally on his presidential campaign made his net worth especially newsworthy ("How Much Is Ross Really Worth").[28]

The cast has included at times a number of business allies, such as IBM, the company that Jobs had denounced so vociferously during his years at Apple, and Businessland, then the largest computer retailer in the country. And the cast extras include the fanatic "heat-seeking" early buyers, who bought the first NeXT computers and kept the company alive, until Jobs shifted his attention to their replacements, the corporate information-management professionals, displacing the T-shirted pioneer customers with their cultural enemies, the "suits." The entrances and exits of cast members are often bewildering. Jobs's engagements with all parties, within and without NeXT, have been marked by the tempestuousness one would expect when a precociously rich businessperson launches a new company, driven by existential urgency more than financial ambition. The plot line is simple: our central protagonist introduces a new product and, carrying it proudly, runs straight into the wall of customer indifference; he picks himself up, and tries again and again, each time with a new approach and a new set of supporting characters, and each staging is a bit different. An infamous temper, a mulish will, and a capacity, when needed, to apply a mesmerist's charm give Jobs numerous opportunities to dominate all scenes in which he makes an appearance.

The NeXT story, however, has more to show us than simply Jobs and company. If we use a wide-angle lens and fit a large frame around the changing personal-computer industry as a whole, we can watch how the NeXTs, the IBMs, the Apples, and the lesser-known companies vie to claim or hold on to a share of the vast market for desktop computers in the office. All have had to contend with extremely bloody competition and a precipitous decline in the price of the computer hardware that they sell—good for *our* pocketbooks, bad for *their* profits, and perhaps a portent of the future for other American industries. If we look at the competition between companies that sell computers that they make, as NeXT tried to do, and those that sell only the software, like Microsoft, we glimpse the advantage enjoyed by the software companies. The most value that a company can add to a product and charge customers for is in the arrangement of the 0's and 1's of the digital world, where a package of software that costs $10 to manufacture and package commands $500 on the store shelf. Gates's fortune from Microsoft comes from this phenomenon; it turns out that he has been more fortunate than Jobs because his company was more modest in its ambitions and has never produced the computers themselves, while Jobs, both at Apple and following the same formula at NeXT, produced both computer hardware and software. Jobs's decision in 1993 to abandon hardware was belated recognition of the advantage that Gates has long enjoyed. And if we look at the competition between NeXT and its most powerful rivals, such as Sun Microsystems, a company not well known to the general public that is located near NeXT's home office in the San Francisco Bay Area, we have an opportunity to see others in Silicon Valley who, lacking the celebrity of a Steve Jobs, exert important influence, even if in less visible fashion.

Jobs is one of a very small group of businesspeople who might be compared to a Hollywood star. His fame and personality are well-known enough to have generated fans and antifans. Like a true Hollywood celebrity, he cannot step out on the street without being recognized, and like a shrewd businessperson, he has used this same celebrity to open doors to conservative corporations that would otherwise have remained closed to other twenty- or thirty-some-thing-year-olds. To his credit, he does not carry the usual baggage that Hollywood celebrities favor, a retinue of personal factotums. He is publicly visible in commonplace ways, which for a resident of Palo Alto, California, means conveyance by expensive sports cars or roller blades.

Jobs does relish the company of fellow stars, and the one industry outside of computers in which he has demonstrated an interest is the film industry. He early made friends with George Lucas, and while building NeXT, Jobs bought Lucas's computer animation company, Pixar, well-known for excelling in technology and losing money. Initially, he did little with it, but in 1991 he began work with Disney on full-length computer-animated films. Other wealthy businesspeople had but one way to gain entrance to Hollywood: as nuisances tolerated only as sources of movie production funds. Or the very well-heeled could do as oil baron Marvin Davis had done, buying an entire studio outright. But with Pixar as his calling card, Jobs has ingeniously come up with a way that allows him to enter Hollywood not as the rich amateur who knows nothing other than how to write checks, but as a player contributing to the technical production side of filmmaking.

It would be fitting if Hollywood rather than Silicon Valley is the place where Jobs succeeds in solving what one might call his *Citizen*

Kane problem. Just as Orson Welles had had the misfortune of creating, directing, and starring in a masterwork at the age of twenty-five and spent the rest of his life trying vainly to find another outlet for his talents that would allow him to repeat what he had accomplished when so young, so too Jobs has been casting about for a way to make another Apple appear. Welles died at the age of seventy, leaving many years of bad films, failed ventures, embarrassing appearances on television commercials, and sundry disappointments behind. If Jobs remains consumed by the same quest, the spectacle of post-*Kane* Welles, a person of talents that were often described as those of a "genius," should serve as a somber reminder of the long odds in summoning the lightning strike of youthful success a second time.

Bill Gates, of course, has no need to worry about a second career when his first one continues to set records of one sort or another with every passing year. But Jobs has an advantage over Gates in being able to call upon powers of charm that have made him friends with college presidents, artists, designers, photographers, and others in positions of power who have no particular stake in the computer industry. The art world is one that Jobs feels especially close to; he often has likened his own ambitions to those of the late Edwin Land, inventor of instant photography, who spoke of Polaroid's mission as embodying the intersection of technology and art. In contrast, Gates blundered badly in his initial venture into the art world, attempting to acquire rights from art museums to reproduce fine-art and photography images in electronic form, for personal computers or for new, large digital screens that will hang on walls like flat televisions. The company that Gates had set up to acquire electronic rights to art works, Interactive Home Systems, encountered tremendous resistance from the art world, not just because the idea of yielding electronic rights was new, but also because of the painfully clear absence of an artistic bone in Gates. Museums preferred to discuss licensing with the small companies that had fewer demands and had an appreciation for art as something other than commercial garnish. When it came to venturing into the art world, Jobs was the respectful patron, Gates, the oafish Philistine.[29]

Jobs has another strength that has helped redress the imbalance of power and money that had come to separate the two boy wonders, and this was the one that was most important: Jobs was the revolutionary, the person who had staked out for himself the mission of coaxing the world along with him to take great leaps forward in computer technology. Gates, in contrast, stood by what he called an evolutionary approach, improving existing software incrementally, and permitting computer users to keep their older personal computers longer. When Microsoft introduced a new kind of software program, more often than not, it would be deeply flawed. But successive versions would eliminate the problems, and by dint of steady investment and persistence, the program would mature into a well-received product that computer owners could use on the personal computers that they already owned. Jobs's style was antithetical: first, when he brought out the Macintosh at Apple, then the NeXT computer, Jobs's customers had to buy new computers and new software and invest considerable time learning how to use both. Eventually, Gates copied in approximate fashion many of the easy-to-use features that the Macintosh had introduced, and this new wave of programs, which work on computers that are not Macintoshes, has been phenomenally successful commercially. It is fitting that Jobs and Gates be treated as a royal pair: the pattern that the two have set is this—Jobs blazes the trail, and Gates comes behind, incorporating Jobs's revolutionary leap in a more modest fashion, but one which appeals to the millions of computer users who are reluctant to jettison past investments.

When Gates and Jobs got together in 1991 at Jobs's home for a *Fortune* magazine story on the occasion of the tenth anniversary of the IBM Personal Computer, the shift in power toward those who controlled the software instead of those who made the computers themselves was already evident.[30] IBM's absence from the birthday cover story for its own Personal Computer, and the substitution of

Jobs and Gates, was an indication of how the computer industry had changed. So too was the softening of the contention between Jobs and Gates themselves. Jobs still hoped to enlist Gates in his cause, and Gates, for his part, no longer had as much reason to be concerned about losing IBM's monogamous commitment to Microsoft; the two companies' formerly close relationship had ruptured, and it looked as if Microsoft was in a much better position after the split than IBM. The Microsoft program that copied the look of Macintosh, Windows, whose future seemed questionable when it was released in an earlier version a few years before, was well on the way to selling in a revised version its ten-millionth copy. Meanwhile, IBM was still struggling to complete work on its competing software, which had not been released and was rumored to be bloated and even further behind schedule than was already evident. In 1988, when it had appeared that IBM might make NeXT software a new standard for its own computers, Gates had derisively dismissed NeXT. Three years later, which is a long, long time in the computer industry, alignments had changed to such a degree, and Microsoft's power had grown to such an extent, that Gates could afford to talk with Jobs about NeXT without the rancor and perception of personal challenge that he had felt before. Each declared to the other that the press had invented animosities and had erroneously assumed they were no longer friends. These were declarations that required historical amnesia, but were fair indications that, at least at that moment in 1991, both preferred amity to enmity. Though this private meeting was the first in a long while, the two had maintained a wary friendliness with periodic conversations by phone, which were more often than not entreaties from Jobs for Gates to reconsider his declaration that Microsoft would consider writing software only for a computer that had sold one million machines, a milestone that for NeXT was impossibly far off. At the end of their chat in 1991, however, Jobs had failed once again to enlist Gates's help, and by the next year was speaking publicly about the dire threat posed to the world by the "Microsoft monopoly."

In one sense, Jobs and Gates, and all the other members of the computer industry, are a united band of revolutionaries, all with a vested interest in seeing the rest of the society embrace computers in their lives. By watching Jobs's attempts to carry out his vision of the needed revolution, at the same time that the others have pursued theirs, we have the chance to detach ourselves from these events and reflect a bit about the computers that have appeared on some desks and not on others, that have been welcomed by some, greeted tepidly by many, and shunned by many more.

Jobs has spent a lot of time over the past ten years thinking about history and his own future place in accounts of his era, again making him a bit more complex than Gates, whose ambition seems free of existential worries. Jobs wants to reassure himself that he is making a difference in the course of history itself. He respects figures like Edwin Land and Thomas Edison, yet he knows he does not have their technical talents. Land, for example, held 533 U.S. patents, which was second only to Edison's 1,093.[31] Jobs has none. So he has defined his historical role as the matchmaker, shuttling between those who create new technology and those who will use it. While at Apple, in early 1984, he said, "Computers and society are out on a first date in this decade, and for some crazy reason, we're in the right place at the right time to make that romance blossom."[32] He likened his own introduction of the easy-to-use Macintosh computer to what Alexander Bell had done when he filed patents for the telephone in the 1870s: replacing existing technology with a new way of accomplishing the same task much more easily. Without blushing, Jobs compared Bell's breakthrough, replacing the hard-to-learn code of the telegraph with the telephone that anyone could use immediately without training, to his own replacement of the hard-to-learn commands of the IBM personal computer with his Macintosh, which anyone could also use immediately. And just as the telephone permitted greater range of expression than the dots and dashes of Morse code, even permitting one to sing, Jobs's Macintosh permitted greater expressiveness, too, incorporating picture-drawing tools that the IBM machines did not have.[33]

The historical comparisons that fill Jobs's mind are all of a grand scale. Another recurring favorite is to compare his own work with computers to that of Henry Ford when the automobile industry was in its infancy. In 1986, after he had left Apple and started NeXT, Jobs looked back to Ford and said, "It must have been the most incredible feeling to know that this was going to change America." Referring to NeXT, he said, "If we can create the kind of company I think we can, it will give me an *extreme* amount of pleasure."[34] This is what makes Jobs unusual among the business gentry, the naked chasing of not Money, per se, but a place in History, writ with a grandiose capital "H."

Jobs is correct: the computer industry is still at a young, formative stage, and if its future development is imagined as a long arc, then a single individual—like himself—can exert significant, lasting influence by nudging the industry's path at an early point. Jobs put it into the vocabulary of space shots: "You just have to move the vector a little bit in the first inch, and the swing will be enormous by the time it gets to be three miles long."[35] He had done it twice with the Apple II and Macintosh computers, and he has tried his damndest to do it again at NeXT, though the industry is much further along, the velocity much greater, the opportunity for a single person or single company to redirect its direction much diminished. His race at NeXT is not only with terrestrial competitors, it is also a race with time, before the rocketship of History pulls out of sight.

With all of his talk about contributing to History, Jobs should have known that sooner or later he might receive a knock on his door from a historian. I do not know if I am the first such, and I am certain of course I will not be the last. I thought that now would be a good time to prepare a book about NeXT because one could say that whatever the future may hold, the years of NeXT as a computer company are now complete, and a book written at this point would preserve many of the details of these years and the reflections of participants, before memories fade and the historical actors move on to new interests and disperse. My own interest in NeXT originates in Jobs's revolutionary ambitions to take the world by storm, ambitions that seemed to me to be audacious enough when one is young and has never tried before, but especially audacious when attempted when one is more experienced, worldly, and scarred. I was curious about the interplay between the apostles of computer revolution and the rest of us who are supposed to be converted. I wanted to know what might be learned by looking closely at Steve Jobs and NeXT's self-conscious attempt to pull the world along their own revolutionary path.

In 1991, when I knocked on Jobs's door, that is, following the protocol expected, sent him via a special NeXT format for electronic mail a prospectus for the book I planned to write and a request for permission to conduct interviews, I did not expect him to welcome the knock. With NeXT struggling, he would not want a historian preserving for posterity the difficulties the company had experienced or a fatal crash that potentially lay ahead. But he did not dismiss out of hand the credentials that I presented, and instead asked the head of his public relations firm to advise him what to do. Her reply was that the book should not be written at that time and I would not be permitted to interview friends and acquaintances at NeXT who were enthusiastic about the book project. She said, "*They* are not the right people." When I later met with Mike Slade, then NeXT's director of marketing, and mentioned again that NeXT employees had volunteered to use their own free time to speak with me about the history of the company, Slade mocked, "Free time? I question the concept. Everybody here needs to spend one-hundred-percent of their time pushing boxes [computers]. If anybody under me took time to speak with you, I'd know they weren't doing their job."

The company's official lack of support posed little hindrance in preparing the book. To a far greater degree than I ever would have guessed, people who had worked for NeXT or had had extensive contacts with it were happy to speak with me. Occasionally, I would stumble directly over the obstructing hand of Jobs and his minions, when a prospective interviewee would tell me of having been warned not to cooperate. The loss of these sources had no important deleterious effect. But hearing of the attempts to suppress the contributions of sources gave me a creepy feeling, similar to the one I had had when I had done research in the People's Republic of China ten years earlier and had encountered Party hacks who served the role of NeXT's public relations guardians, deciding when history could be written, what sources could be used, who were the *right* people that could be interviewed, and ultimately what the historian should say. The authorities in China, just like the authorities at NeXT, were fond of thinking that theirs would be the sole version of what the world knew about their history.

In the end, the story was built from the many individuals who were not warned off and from the publicly visible efforts of Jobs and his company to sell their vision these many years. This is not a royal history of the King and his court. My vantage point is that of an independent observer, and I have some opinions to share with readers, whom I assume are not necessarily as passionately attached to computers as the people who make them. I especially wish to engage readers who do not care for computers at all; this book is an attempt to make the emotional investments of the computer revolutionaries understandable to those who look askance. My opinions are idiosyncratic, but, I hope, not preachy, and are made plainly evident, so the reader can easily accept or reject them on their merits.

I also would like my book to call attention to our society's persistent tendency to create larger-than-life figures. Watching Steve Jobs try to live up to an outsized reputation is to be reminded of the public's voracious need for contemporary heroes. Just as we look to the technicolor of Hollywood for respite from the monochrome of ordinary life, so too we gaze upon those handful of places, such as Silicon Valley, home to NeXT and many other computer companies, or north to Redmond, Washington, home of the Microsoft empire, where we sense business life is not ordinary and gray. We project our own colorful hopes upon these bubbles, imagining that in these privileged places meritocracies recruit the talented, and the rewards that come to the winners are of a scale far beyond what one could dare dream of anywhere else. Whether seen as a possible El Dorado for the modern age, or as the last best hope for the U.S. economy, struggling to keep up with global competition, the computer industry has come to assume a special place in the national imagination. If actual work life in computer companies falls well short of the fabulous images that circulate on the outside, it seems to make little difference in dissuading waves of many of the brightest young people in the country from seeking admission. The myth creates concentrations of unnaturally dense pools of talent, and in the end serves to make these places special, no matter how idealized the images were that lured the high-tech adventurers in the first place. Hollywood has long used a similar concentration of hopeful actors and actresses, who arrive annually by the thousands, to replenish the disillusioned who leave and to perpetuate the image of Hollywood's glamour that the rest of the world expects. So too the computer industry constantly replenishes its stocks, continually reinventing itself, providing everyone with a nonstop dream machine.

Playing in the PARC

I n the beginning, there was Xerox. What would become the
most famous concentration of computer talent assembled in one
place was established in 1970 because during a talk delivered
to stock analysts one day Peter McColough, the chairman of Xerox
Corporation, found himself earnestly talking about the information
age, without being sure exactly of what he was saying. He announced Xerox's determination to confront the new "knowledge
explosion" by developing "the architecture of information." As the
story goes, he then turned to one of his senior vice-presidents and
said, "All right, go start a lab that will find out what I just meant."[1]

The Xerox Palo Alto Research Center was created to figure out
what "information architecture" meant and what the office of the
future would look like. The center became known by its acronym,
PARC, which was apt, given its location in a verdant office park
that was developed by the nearby landlord, Stanford University.
PARC looked like the science complex of a college campus. The
main building had a striking modern design; a volleyball court was
in the back. People came and went on their own schedules around
the clock, and wore T-shirts and "Question Authority" badges.[2]

Bicycles were the primary means of commuting (one staff member, Richard Shoup, would ride on his bike up to the door—and on through, pedaling down the hall to his office.)[3] But PARC was like a campus that was perpetually on summer break, empty and quiet, without undergraduate students milling about. Compared to the colossus in industrial research, Bell Laboratories, which before the AT&T breakup employed 25,000, Xerox PARC was tiny. It employed only a couple of hundred people in the 1970s. Yet like Old Testament genealogy, every important development in personal computers traces back to this same single source.

When PARC began its research, computers were anything but personal. The prevailing view was that machines are fast and people are slow, which led to one machine being shared by many people simultaneously.[4] In the 1960s, this had been an important break-through. Far better to be able to have many people use a single, expensive, centralized computer simultaneously than to have just one person use it. But "time-sharing" one computer among many people was far from ideal. The more people who were connected to the computer at the same time, the slower the machine would respond to any one person's commands. It had to split its attention among all the users, devoting a few milliseconds to Person A, then switching to Person B, then to Person C, on through the queue of waiting users until it revisited Person A again. If the central processor in the heart of the computer had to serve too many individuals at once, each would get the impression that the system had slowed to a crawl.

The software was also a source of frustration. The commands that the machine accepted demanded mastery of an arcane foreign language, and the commands had to be communicated by typing on a keyboard. The software that was responsible for what one saw on the screen assumed that all that one would ever need to see were the letters and numbers found on a typewriter. The screen was divided into an invisible grid of squares, and within each square, only a letter or number could be placed. For typing instructions to the computer, it was a satisfactory system. But it was ill-suited for displaying drawings or graphs. Even when displaying text, it was limited. One could not display letters in different sizes or typefaces. The grid imposed a limit on the size of the letters, and the machine had a canned routine that it invoked every time it received a command to display a particular letter or number. If one typed the letter "G," for example, the software could display it in one size and in one typeface only.

PARC researchers started fresh. They sought to provide "the maximum computer power in the hands of every individual who wants it."[5] Instead of forcing many individuals to share a single, centralized machine, they conceived of, and built, a machine for each individual. No more time-sharing; no more delays when too many people were using the machine simultaneously. As one of its inventors boasted, it "does not run faster at night."[6] And instead of forcing everything that the computer would display into a rigid grid of letters and numbers, the PARC Computer Science Laboratory wrote software that allowed one to "paint" the screen with an infinite variety of marks, freed from a grid of predefined boxes. By pioneering what was called a "bit-mapped display," every individual point [every *pixel*] on the screen could be changed, regardless of whether it was part of a character or not. This put much heavier demands on the computer, however. As Butler Lampson, one of the early PARC designers, explained, when the computer was asked to "play the game on the human's terms," that is, present a page of attractively formatted text or paint a screen of pictures in less than the fraction of a second that is visible to the eye, it turned the old convention upside down: people are fast, and it is *computers* that are slow. One machine could not really keep up with more than one person, so each individual should have a dedicated machine. By 1973, just three years after PARC's founding, the PARC staff had built the first truly personal computer, the Alto.

For computer scientists who had cut their teeth on large computers, it took a while to adjust to the fact that each person had his or her own machine. Jim Horning, one of the PARC veterans, spoke of how ill at ease he was when he turned his back on the machine momentarily and let it idle; it seemed an unconscionable waste (how oblivious to such sensations are we, the spoiled ones in the subsequent generations).[7] The Alto was more than a stand-alone personal computer, however. The Altos at PARC were linked together in a network, another PARC innovation, which permitted the development of electronic mail, still another. (Among the many firsts that Bert Sutherland observed when at PARC was the first electronic raffle that was held nationwide, the first electronic junk mailing, and the first electronic obituary.)[8] More followed: The first laser printer. Development of a wholly new kind of software, called "object-oriented programming," which used self-contained modules that could easily be reused in other programs. Refinement of a widget called a "mouse," which one took hold of in one's hand and rolled on a desktop to give commands to the computer instead of typing on a keyboard. This and other features would later come to be viewed as a set, what the industry would call the "WIMP" interface: Windows, Icons, Mouse, and Pull-down menus. The list of accomplishments at PARC is numbingly long. Well after having left PARC, former employees could still claim in the 1990s that they do not have to invent the future, they merely have to remember it.

The inventors at PARC were good, and they knew it. This has, however, warped our ability to see their shortcomings clearly. They and everyone else in the computer industry have collectively written what I would call the Creation Myth that obscures the history of PARC. With the imprimatur of Scriptural authority, the myth tells us that once upon a time, in a prelapsarian Eden, a group of angels presented the world with the gift of the personal computer, only to be rejected by the benighted parent of the Xerox Corporation. Bureaucratic and obtuse, Xerox did not have an inkling of the value of what the prolific inventors at PARC produced. The company decided not to bring the Alto to market, and its own derivative, the

Star, belatedly introduced in 1981, was an expensive disaster.[9] Xerox, the dumb giant, had had the future placed in its hands, then allowed it to slip through its fingers. So goes the myth.

The PARC researchers wear seraphic white; the Xerox "corpocracy" wears diabolical red. This might serve well as inspirational myth for everyone who detests the confining strictures of the large corporation, but as history, this is too Manichean to be satisfying, too selective in its assignment of blame. PARC itself should share in the responsibility for the dismal failure of Xerox in the personal-computer marketplace. Even if the computer industry chooses to ignore the facts, PARC remains the best illustration one could imagine of how collective arrogance leads to failure.

The arrogance originated in the nature of the selection process. To be hired at PARC's Computer Science Laboratory, for example, job seekers were pushed through a stressful battery of presentations and interviews that, in the words of Robert Taylor, the laboratory's associate director, were deliberately intended to test the "quality of their nervous systems." The ones who survived the ordeal and were chosen as the best were those select few who were accustomed to "dealing with lightning in both hands." Taylor was unabashed about his rejecting candidates who were regarded as merely good but not great: "You can't pile together enough good people to make a great one."[10]

One could say that all organizations strive to recruit the best from any given pool of candidates, and if PARC preferred to hire the great instead of the merely good, so too would other companies. But what is troubling is the way that the PARC staff used the stringent selection process as a means of drawing a line between two entirely distinct worlds: the inner world of PARC, the domain of the brilliant, and the outer world that lay beyond, populated by everyone else, who by definition were less intelligent. The binary simplicity of the digital world was mirrored in the binary point of view that the PARC staff used to organize the social world. You either could keep up with whatever they said and thus were qualified to be one of them, or you were "stupid" and might be told so to your face.[11]

Like an idiot savant, an exceptionally sharp computer scientist can excel in one intellectual domain, but be surprisingly weak in another. The PARC staff, for all of its collective brilliance in designing new computer systems, was not well-chosen to translate the work of a research laboratory into products for store shelves. The staff designed new computers not for hypothetical customers but for themselves. PARC's "Use What We Build" maxim was laudable because it meant that the technology that the center produced was put to immediate and constant testing. But it was testing in the hands of knowledgeable cognoscenti, not ordinary mortals. The only outside customers to whom PARC supplied the Alto were on the outside in a relative sense—other departments *within* Xerox, who ordered their own Altos and paid from $12,000 to $20,000, depending on the desired features. If the machines had been sold to the general public, with customary gross margins, they would have sold for $40,000 each.[12] This was not the path to ready products that would appeal to real customers who would be a bit more sensitive to price than were family members in a fabulously wealthy, successful Fortune 500 company, "buying" from itself. Preparation for greeting the world beyond would require the collaboration of product development and marketing people, who were not at PARC but based elsewhere within Xerox. But PARC researchers compiled an abysmal record of unsuccessful attempts to enlist the support of Xerox in moving PARC innovations through the process of product development. The Creation Myth ignores how much PARC arrogance got in the way. The rest of Xerox, which may not have been as "smart" as the elect who worked at PARC, was certainly smart enough to sense when it was being condescended to and when its technical innocence was the object of behind-the-back ridicule at PARC. Is it surprising, then, that when PARC needed the assistance of other Xerox people to help make a potential product into a real product, it received a cold reception?

Suppose we were to imagine that Xerox, the evil parent company that we hear so much about in the Creation Myth, had been more enlightened. Suppose it had told PARC, "Don't let us keep you back. Here's even more money than we have already lavished upon you; take it and spin off. You'll now be on your own, free to market your own products and stand or fall on your own merits. We'll keep an equity stake in this new company and wish you all the best." What would have happened then? Emancipated from the dim-witted parent, would PARC have gone on to fabulous business success as the preeminent personal-computer company?

It is hard to imagine how events would not have played out much the same as they did. PARC's Alto was far from ready for the masses and would not have succeeded in the marketplace. PARC culture was a research culture, too far removed from customers. Just as in a university, the research staff members were free to choose their own projects, which they did because problems were "interesting," the laconic all-purpose adjective. By "Tom Saw-yering," as it was called at PARC, one individual would start work on a problem and attract the attention of others, who might choose to join the fun and help whitewash the fence.[13] The self-directed technical expertise that was collected at PARC and which grew luxuriantly in an ideal research environment needed to be wedded to expertise in other areas as well, such as marketing, finance, marketing, manufacturing, and marketing (one can never overemphasize the importance of marketing). It needed to consider cost constraints that customers faced, even though they as researchers had been completely free of such restraints and had been given a charter to use hardware that was five to ten years ahead of everyone else, that is, the most expensive there was. (An historical aside: even at PARC, where there were essentially no budgetary limits, the researchers were limited by a lack of imagination and failed to appreciate the need to design the software to take advantage of lots of memory capacity in their personal computer—the legendary Alto had only 128,000 bytes of main memory, a paltry amount compared to the many millions, or megabytes, that come standard in personal computers today, and design limitations restricted its ability to utilize additional memory.)[14]

Several PARC alumni who left in the late 1970s and early 1980s began computer-related businesses on their own and did well, building up sizable enterprises, but in technical products, not mass consumer items. Two of the most successful companies—3Com and Adobe Systems—have yet to become household names, unless one's household has a computer expert who is familiar with computer networks or laser-printer font software, respectively. The PARC alumni have not had to explain themselves to the technically unsophisticated. Even within the computer industry, one could say that their success has been proportionate to the degree that they teamed up with or employed others who had skills that did not fit the PARC template and who helped drive home the lesson that good technology does not necessarily speak for itself unaided.

The attention that has been lavished upon PARC, by the Creation Myth and by other tributes, perpetuates the unspoken assumption that the computer game is a competition with one simple rule: the company with the highest average IQ wins. But is intelligence best thought of in general terms, as if it can be likened to horsepower ratings, as if it is fungible and readily applied to any sort of task that one chooses with equal efficacy? We always assume that this is so. Moreover, we in the United States have long preferred to attribute the most intelligence to the original inventor and to ignore those who come after, modifying and improving, sometimes in great measure. It is a tendency that has proven to be a costly one for us—in the post–World War II era, we dismissed Japanese modifications that improved upon American-born electronics technology as mere *copying*, until our consumer electronics industry was beaten bloodily. The deification of PARC invention continues this tradition.

Charles Simonyi was one of the young PARC inventors, as brilliant as they came. He was born in Hungary in 1948, defected to the West in 1966, and eventually came to the United States and picked up his bachelor's degree at Berkeley and Ph.D. at Stanford. In 1974, he joined PARC, where he developed a word-processing program for the Alto that for the first time displayed the words on the screen just as they would eventually appear when printed. It is a feature that now is taken for granted in many advanced word-processing programs—this is *WYSIWYG* (not as daunting to pronounce as it may appear: *whizzy-wig* will do), *What You See Is What You Get*—but at the time Simonyi wrote his program, Bravo, it was a pioneering feat. In 1981, Simonyi left Palo Alto and took the "PARC virus," as he called it, with him; he implanted it in Bill Gates's Microsoft, where he has worked ever since. He did not change in some fundamental ways. The sense of being one of the very best programmers in the world certainly remained. When he was interviewed for a book in the mid-1980s, and was asked if he associated with other eminent programmers, Simonyi said that when they got together, they had little to talk about:

> We feel good vibes and exchange three or four words. I know that if one of these guys opens his mouth, he knows what he is talking about. So when he does open his mouth and he does know what he is talking about, it's not a great shock. And since I tend to know what I am talking about, too, I would probably say the same thing, so why bother talking, really? It's like the joke tellers' convention where people sit around and they don't even have to tell a joke. They just say the joke number and everybody laughs.[15]

This reflects the old PARC roots in Simonyi's past, the feeling of being a Master of the Programming Universe. But there was something new, too, in Simonyi's talk of how naive he had been for thinking that the Alto computer was a computer that everyone in the world would use. He also insisted that he now programmed for reasons of business more than of pleasure. He was happy to see people use his program, but it was also nice that some of them paid for the program and some of that money found its way into his pockets, which he could then use to visit Egypt or rent a helicopter. (Simonyi had a theory that flying a helicopter was not unlike programming, as "the ride can get very tiring, and the whole thing can come apart at any time.")[16] Confessing such crass materialist motives for programming was very *un*-PARC-like.

Here we come upon one facet of the business acumen of Bill Gates. He knew the value of recruiting a PARC alumnus like Simonyi, applying the expertise of the technology-centered research park to his market-conquering agenda at Microsoft. Microsoft was still a tiny company when Simonyi joined—he was employee number 43. But his joining did not make Microsoft more like PARC; rather, the Microsoft culture remained intact, and instead it was the PARC genes that were neatly absorbed into the large organism. Simonyi's word-processing program, Bravo, was rewritten and appeared in new form as Microsoft Word. It would eventually become one of the dominant word-processing programs on personal computers, but not until it had passed through several major revisions. And not until the marketing genius of Microsoft had been skillfully deployed. In the end, though its lineage could easily be traced back to early PARC days, Microsoft Word seemed appropriately named. It was much more a creature of Microsoft than it was of PARC, and it serves to remind us that PARC technology was held back by more than a few missing signatures from the senior powers at Xerox. It needed a marketing machine like Microsoft.

Gates has hired many others like Simonyi, programmers who are legends in their field. He buys them with salaries and stock option packages that no one else can match. His motive, however, is not to re-create PARC. He puts these hired guns to work on applied problems, on *his* problems. The products that emerge from Microsoft are known for being derivative and unoriginal; the programmers, though they may never say so publicly, must come to terms with the realization that Microsoft is not an environment in which the best technical work will be done. But it is an environment that knows how to squeeze out the most commercial value of whatever does emerge from its programmers. That is the Faustian bargain that they have accepted, pursuing wide commercial acceptance of their work instead of technical accolades from a knowledgeable but small group of peers in the guild.

Perhaps because PARC was a world unto itself, it became susceptible to self-delusion. PARC's management made the mistake of believing that it had rounded up the only sharp computer scientists in the world. In 1979, Larry Tesler, one of the PARC staff members, argued with his boss, Robert Taylor, who insisted that PARC had "all the smart people" and that only it had the requisite talent to build the leading personal computers. Tesler said, no, there were smart people that could be found elsewhere.

"Hire them," Taylor said.

Tesler tried to explain the facts of life beyond the PARC campus: "We can't get them all—there are hundreds of them out there, they are all over the place!"[17] Exasperated, he decided to leave PARC and join some other "smart people" he had recently met: Steve Jobs and some engineers at Apple.

In the long view of history, Steve Jobs would seem to have profited more from the work at PARC than anyone else, inside or outside Xerox. The legend goes like this: One day in 1979, in a lapse of strategic vigilance, PARC administrators permitted Jobs and a contingent from Apple to make a brief visit to the PARC laboratories. At the very time that Xerox did not know what to do with its Alto computer and the other technology that its researchers had developed, here was Jobs, who with just a glimpse recognized the importance of the easy-to-use design of the Alto. "Why aren't you doing anything with this?" he asked his PARC hosts. "This is the greatest thing! This is revolutionary!"[18] He returned to Apple with the conviction to make a machine like the Alto, and shortly after the visit he hired Larry Tesler away from PARC. The Macintosh appeared a few years later, and Jobs thus achieved the commercial success that Xerox could have had.

Like the Creation Myth at PARC, the legendary story of Jobs

pilfering the intellectual jewels at PARC and spiriting them off to Apple does not stand as good history. It is missing important details, and it simultaneously makes Jobs undeservedly sinister—as well as undeservedly prescient.

Consider the question of intellectual theft and the cloud that hangs over the infamous 1979 visit. A few simple observations will put the matter in a different light. We should remember that PARC administrators at times were themselves ambivalent about the wisdom of keeping the laboratories closed to outside visits. In the early 1970s, PARC had been an open research center. It had been built within bicycling distance of Stanford on purpose, so that staff members at PARC could easily exchange visits with colleagues at the Stanford Artificial Intelligence Laboratory and other departments. Originally, there had been no security restrictions at PARC; it was as open as a university campus, so much so that at a supposedly internal staff meeting in 1971, someone from Stanford's AI lab, who had tagged along with a PARC friend, offered suggestions that Xerox's chief scientist Jack Goldman complimented, oblivious that he was thanking an outside visitor. The staff members who watched played innocent and did their best to suppress their laughter.[19]

Those carefree days came to an abrupt end when a 1972 article about the long-haired programmers at PARC appeared in *Rolling Stone*. Alvy Ray Smith, one of the staff members, later recalled how the article had upset the corporate headquarters of Xerox. "All these wild, hairy people out there in a research lab got written up—how embarrassing!" Jack Goldman flew to California and held an emergency staff meeting, where he warned that if anything like the *Rolling Stone* article appeared again, Xerox would permanently close the laboratory. Articles about PARC henceforth were restricted, and even technical articles by the PARC staff were severely curtailed.[20]

Denied an outlet in print, but yearning to show off their work to their professional colleagues, the staff communicated with the outside world by providing demonstrations for visitors. Alan Kay, one of the leading lights at PARC who would later become a minister-without-portfolio for Apple Computer, spoke of "demos" as a way of life at PARC; in 1975, four years before Jobs's famous visit, an estimated 2,000 people, in groups of various sizes, were provided with the standard show. Hosting so many visitors proved draining, and the number of demonstrations diminished somewhat. But some of the early visitors were inspired to try to build commercial products from what they had seen, and Jobs was far from the first. What distinguished Jobs's visit from the others' was that, in Kay's words, "we had very few visitors who were multiple-hundred-dollar millionaires, in their twenties, and heads of companies, so most of the people who visited were not able to simply go back and, by fiat, say this is what we want."[21]

Xerox permitted Jobs to visit PARC, even though Apple was an apparent competitor, because Xerox—the parent company, not little PARC—had quietly just made a major equity investment in Apple,[22] which would turn out to be the last major private financing before Apple would go public. When arranging the financing from Xerox, Jobs had asked if he could visit the PARC labs, and Xerox, viewing Jobs as a new partner, not a predator, acceded naturally enough. Apple's gain would be Xerox's gain, too. What the Apple contingent got at PARC was the standard one-hour demonstration of the Xerox Alto on two separate occasions, not one (the second visit by an Apple contingent is missing from the Legend of Steve because he was not present). Being given a peek, however, is quite a different thing than being given a set of blueprints. Bill Atkinson, one of the Apple engineers who accompanied Jobs, would claim that what he saw came as no great revelation; he had heard about what PARC was working on from the trade press. What was useful to him was seeing that the system did indeed work, that the direction that he and his colleagues had chosen on their own was the right one."[23] PARC's own director, George Pake, agreed. Pake, a physicist by training, would later denounce the decision of his superiors at Xerox to permit Jobs to visit as a "dumb thing to do." But Pake described the main damage as simply having given Jobs the opportunity to know that a radically different kind of personal computer was "doable." Pake said, "Just like the Russians and the A-bomb. They developed it very quickly once they knew it was doable."[24]

One hears in Pake and the others at PARC a tone of aggrievement, as if Apple's success after 1979 is rightfully PARC's. They neglect the fact that what PARC had been working on could not be kept secret indefinitely, that Xerox had already shown the Alto to many others, and that PARC was at that time getting permission from the parent company to disseminate to the non-Xerox world the software Smalltalk, which gave the Alto its distinguishing features such as multiple, overlapping windows and pop-down menus of commands.[25] They neglect what a long road still lay ahead of the Apple engineers when they returned to their own laboratories after visiting Xerox's. They neglect too what a long road lay ahead for Apple's marketing people. Subsequent events showed that success was anything but assured. And credit for eventual success should go to Apple, not Xerox. Jobs and the other Apple visitors at PARC had been permitted to see only surfaces— of the machine and of the software that ran on it. If the software that Apple later produced, with wholly original program code, resembled in its operation that of the Xerox Alto, the most that could be claimed was that Apple had copied its "look-and-feel," a dubiously vague concept that stretched the definition of what could be regarded as copyrightable. It would be as if one automobile manufacture claimed that because it was the first to position a steering wheel on the left-hand side of the car and below it a brake pedal on the left and a gas pedal on the right, it and only it had the rights to this unique "look-and-feel" of an automobile interior.

In fact, what Apple took away from PARC was nothing specific enough to be regarded as proprietary. When Microsoft copied the look-and-feel of Apple's Macintosh software and the shoe was on the other foot, what splendid irony it was for Apple then to take on the same aggrieved tone as Xerox had. Committing what should stand as one of the more astounding acts of hypocrisy in the modern age of litigation, Apple sued Microsoft in 1988, claiming copyright infringement for Microsoft's software called Windows, which gave an IBM personal computer a look similar to the Macintosh. Microsoft, no angel, certainly had played rough with many competitors in its rise to dominance, but stealing the primeval secret of fire from poor little Apple was not one of its transgressions. Apple's claims of theft of look-and-feel were triply absurd—first, because of the nebulousness and impracticality of the legal concept itself; second, in this case because of the complications of specific software rights that Apple had granted Microsoft in a cross-licensing agreement; and third because of Apple's own connection to Xerox PARC. For Apple to have dared to sue Microsoft required an impressive feat of willed historical amnesia.

The spectacle of silly litigiousness did not end there, however. The next year, Xerox decided it would help remind Apple of its indebtedness to PARC by filing its own $150 million copyright infringement suit against Apple.[26] Now it was hard to keep all of these suits straight. Microsoft was sued by Apple, Apple was sued by Xerox, and we might add that the daisy chain could have continued indefinitely. Xerox, in turn, could have been sued by the Stanford Research Institute for "stealing" the idea of a computer mouse— on and on the legal circus could have gone, tracing the family tree of personal-computer technology backward to the Stone Age in an unending concatenation of lawsuits.

The Xerox suit against Apple was inexplicably tardy, filed six years after Apple supposedly infringed upon Xerox's copyrights. It did not fare well in court. Judge Vaughan Walker quickly disposed of five of the six counts, and the last one was soon dismissed, too.[27] In Walker's view, Apple had created its software independently; it showed "scant similarity" to Xerox's.[28] Xerox had simply tried to use improper copyright claims to try to salvage something from its then-defunct computer, the Star, which had done so poorly when introduced in 1981, well before blame could be pinned on Apple, which then had yet to introduce any computers similar in "look-and-feel." Walker decided that all Xerox could complain of was that it had been less successful in the marketplace with its Star copyright than Apple had been with its own copyrights. He dryly noted that federal copyright laws "offer no relief for commercial disappointment."[29]

Apple may have been relieved by the judge's sympathetic reasoning, but the same words of course deserved to be applied to it, too: copyright laws were not the proper remedy for its commercial disappointment that Microsoft Windows was doing so well. The same judge who had presided in the Apple-Xerox case also presided in the Apple-Microsoft case, and he was consistent in protecting Microsoft from Apple's claims in the same way that he protected Apple's from Xerox's. Though it is no fun to cheer Microsoft, the eight-hundred-pound gorilla that always gets its way, still, when in 1992 the four-year-long legal battle virtually came to an end in a court ruling that upheld Microsoft's position on all substantive points,[30] one had to be glad that the forces of reason had won.

Jobs had left Apple well before the suit was filed against Microsoft and so was not connected directly to Apple's brazen hypocrisy, but he was not guiltless. While at Apple, he had become angry when he first saw Microsoft's Windows (Gates responded with a devilish riposte: "Hey, Steve, just because you broke into Xerox's house before I did and took the TV doesn't mean I can't go in later and take the stereo.")[31] At NeXT, Jobs was no less hypocritical when one looks back at his visit to PARC in 1979 and what came afterward. When he founded NeXT and finally had the total control over his own company that he had not had at Apple, he sealed the company up completely, keeping its interior invisible not only to prospective competitors, but even to employees it was about to hire. In Silicon Valley, companies routinely invest in elaborate security measures, but even by the local standards, Jobs made NeXT the paragon of the paranoid organization, a closed black box, like the computer that it would eventually produce. By his actions, Jobs implicitly validated all of the wrongheaded assumptions that one finds implicit in the bitter reminiscences of PARC management: that a research organization can thrive in an airless chamber; that invention is easily copied by the mere glimpse of surface appearances; that technical strength is synonymous with future marketing prowess; that competitive advantage is so fragile that permitting the wrong party even a glance will destroy the company. It is as if Jobs was saying that he would never allow someone else to make away with the jewels at NeXT as he thought he had done at Xerox PARC. One could use this material to write a psychological thriller: Jobs as an unknowing innocent who had became convinced of his guilt for a crime that never actually occurred.

If a peek at a computer demonstration was tantamount to grand larceny, then the diamonds that the Apple visitors to PARC took with them were awfully rough. Look at the dismal fate of the Star, the first computer that Xerox introduced to the market based on the work done at PARC. The Star was priced at almost $20,000, far above what customers were willing to pay. It died a wretched death in the marketplace. Look at the almost as dismal fate of Apple's Lisa, the company's first computer to resemble the ones that had been glimpsed at PARC in 1979. Work on the Lisa project had actually begun before Jobs's November 1979 visit to PARC, and yet the machine was not introduced until January 1983. The long lead time should help exonerate Apple from the charge of pilferage; clearly, a considerable amount of work at Apple had been required to produce it. Apple claimed at the time that it had spent $50 million on its development, including $20 million on the software alone.

Jobs was unapologetic about the long gestation required to bring the Lisa to market: "We could have introduced Lisa a year ago, but we wanted to make it perfect."[32] In fact, despite the many years of work, it was still far from perfect. The software that had been developed for it succeeded in making it much easier to use than the software that ran on IBM personal computers or even Apple's own Apple II and Apple III computers. By moving a mouse, one could direct the arrow on screen to the little pictures that served to represent commands. By moving the arrow to an "icon" resembling a trash can, for example, the computer user could discard an unwanted file. The machine came bundled with six programs, which were designed to be used by anyone, without recourse to arcane computer commands or bulky manuals. But this suite of software programs, designed specifically to work well with each other, required bulky program code that slowed the performance of each, and the programs did not perform as well as advertised. Furthermore, because the underlying system software was proprietary and incompatible with other personal computers on the market, the owner of a Lisa could not use any of the thousands of software packages that were available for other computers. Perhaps prospective buyers would have tolerated this as a short-lived inconvenience, until new software presumably would come onto the market, if the Lisa had not been so expensive. At $9,995, the Lisa leapt far beyond prevailing prices for computers marketed as "personal." Apple itself had no previous successful experience pitching big-ticket machines; its enormously successful Apple II sold for about $1,500 at the time.

Jobs was not concerned about the pricing or software incompatibility issues. He cared most about setting a new standard. At the time of Lisa's introduction, he said, "The industry's not had a real technical innovation in five years."[33] The Lisa provided innovation in spades, and Jobs's only regret was that he had not been more directly involved with the day-to-day details while the Lisa was in development. He had wanted to be head of the Lisa division, but he was a mere vice-president, not the president of Apple, and the decision was not his. Despite popular impression to the contrary, Apple was controlled even in these, its early years, not by the cofounders Jobs and Wozniak, but by the grown-ups, the less visible board chairman Mike Markkula and his appointees. For Jobs, though Lisa was not his own personal project, it remained his kind of computer, a machine that would stand technically far above the pack.

Just as Xerox PARC would have grandiose delusions about the commercial potential of its pioneering Alto, so too would Jobs and the other senior Apple executives about their own pioneering Lisa. Apple envisaged an enormous pool of customers for the machine, "knowledge workers," the 30 million office professionals and managers who all needed their own powerful, but easy to use, personal computers. It was a pipe dream, built without consulting the intended customers about the maximum amount of money they would consider reasonable for a single personal computer, and for a black-and-white one to boot (Lisa had no color display). Nor, apparently, did Jobs give any thought to the fact that Lisas would be expected to coexist amicably with other computers and networks in offices, and that Lisa's incompatibility with the others presented a serious obstacle to its acceptance. The PARC researchers could be excused; they belonged to a research organization, isolated from real customers in the flesh. But the marketeers at Apple had no such excuse. They had copied PARC all right: they had succeeded in creating an organization so sealed off from the commercial world as to lose touch with marketplace realities.

Jobs predicted that with Lisa "we're going to blow IBM away; there's nothing they can do when this computer comes out."[34] His confidence in the machine extended to a prediction, made at Lisa's birth, that "we're prepared to live with Lisa for the next ten years."[35] But Lisa died haplessly at the tender age of two. Its death was hastened by the interim appearance in 1984 of the much less expensive distant relative, the Macintosh, which had been in development separately also since 1979 and was slower to come to market than even the Lisa had been. In its last days, the Lisa was repackaged and renamed as a high-end Macintosh, and its price was slashed to a more reasonable $4,000. The marketplace responded positively, and sales jumped threefold.[36] But even then, sales were still only about 1,000 machines a month. It was too little, too late. Lisa: Born 1983, Died 1985. *Requiescat in pace.*

What saved Apple from financial catastrophe at the time was the primitive little Apple II. Though it belonged to the Pleistocene era of personal computers, Apple continued to sell hundreds of millions of dollars worth of the machine every quarter, long after demand had been expected to drop. How ironic that the Apple II, with a microprocessor that only gobbled data in what engineers called "8-bit" chunks, proved stalwart when the Lisa, based on a far more advanced 32-bit microprocessor, faltered and collapsed. The lessons that one could draw from the Lisa debacle include these: Keep in touch with intended customers and avoid the pitfalls of anaerobic isolation; do not assume that customers will pay any price to secure the latest computer technology; ease the way for customers to adopt a new computer standard by providing software and hardware bridges that help connect older machines to the new ones; rely upon less expensive products that have fewer features or less advanced technology to pay the bills while the top-of-the-line flagship computer establishes a secure place in the market. These are hardly profound. Yet Steve Jobs would ignore every one of these when he launched NeXT.

Due Credit

I think of two men, one British, the other American, as exemplars of what we might call the unknown almost-famous. The two would never have had any reason to have met each other but I still regard them as a pair: Peter Best was the drummer in the Beatles who preceded Ringo Starr and who was forced out on the eve of the group's fame;[37] Jef Raskin was the father of the Macintosh computer who preceded Steve Jobs and was forced out on the eve of the Macintosh's fame. By tricks of fate, Best and Raskin have had to spend their lives in the shadow of what-may-have-been, their mark on their times to be remembered, if ever, only as answers to questions of trivia.

For Raskin, the acclaim that Jobs has received for fathering the Macintosh has deeply rankled all these years. In interviews with any journalist who will listen, and in letters sent to newspaper editors to reclaim due credit, Raskin has persevered in a quest for respect that is as hopeless as if he were an unkempt crank wandering in a public park, shouting at passersby who avert their eyes. No matter how many times Raskin tries to get the world to pay attention, it will not be him but Steve Jobs who in the public mind will always be remembered as the genius to have successfully conceived the first affordable personal computer that was as easy to use as it was sophisticated. In retrospect, clarifying the genesis of the Macintosh is important not just to restore Raskin's contribution to the record, but also to better understand Jobs and what would follow at NeXT. The Macintosh is the link that connects the early ambitious visions of PARC, and the commercial failures of the Xerox Star and the Apple Lisa, to the more recent utopianism of NeXT Computer. Steve Jobs and his NeXT employees have been most influenced by this, their own history, or I should say, have been imprisoned by what they have chosen to remember as their own history, from which they generalized to produce a recipe that presumably would result in the same success.

The parentage of the Macintosh always is traced back to Jobs's famous visit to Xerox PARC in 1979, which, as we have seen already, was a visit where there was less, not more, than meets the eye. Moreover, the halo of prescience that Jobs has worn ever since that visit to PARC should not be his alone. It was Jef Raskin who first knew about the work at PARC and suggested that Jobs pay a visit.[38] Raskin was twelve years older than Jobs, and had been hired as the thirty-first employee at Apple. His eclectic interests— spanning philosophy, music, visual art, and computer science— had taken him in, then out, of an academic career at the University of California at San Diego. (He resigned from the university by flying over the university chancellor's house in a hot air balloon, in what he called a symbolically fitting gesture.) Before joining Apple he worked for a while at the Stanford Artificial Intelligence Laboratory, where he learned about research at nearby PARC.[39] Later, when he was at Apple, it took more than a year of cajoling before Raskin succeeded in persuading Jobs to visit PARC and see what its researchers were up to for himself.[40]

Raskin had begun work on the Macintosh project even before Jobs visited PARC. The idea that he proposed to Apple chairman Mike Markkula was to build a new model of personal computer that would combine pictures with regular text in an inexpensive package. Markkula asked if the machine could be designed to sell for $500. After deliberating a week, Raskin replied that realistically the future price of the machine would have to be $1,000, still an ambitious target considering that the computers that could comfortably handle picture images were specialized graphics workstations that at the time cost tens of thousands of dollars.[41] With Markkula's encouragement, Raskin set to work, inscribing design ideas in a notebook that he called the Macintosh Document. The project had no connection to Jobs, who was excited about the more advanced, and much more expensive computer, the Lisa, and who tried to scuttle the Macintosh. He was prevented from doing so by Markkula and Apple president Mike Scott, but Raskin took care to stay well away from Jobs and harm.[42]

One of the first people that Raskin recruited to work with him on the Macintosh team was an old friend, Guy ("Bud") Tribble, with whom he had worked in a theater group in San Diego. Tribble was a polymath like Raskin who could have followed any of several wildly different careers, and his joining Apple was serendipitous. At the time, in 1980, he was pursuing a joint M.D./Ph.D. program at the University of Washington in Seattle, with a specialty in neurophysiology. He had heard, however, that Raskin had been given permission to start up his own research group at Apple and was at work on a machine that would be inexpensive yet still redefine the state-of-the-art of the personal computer. When he visited Apple and saw the ideas in the Macintosh Document, which had grown to about 400 pages by then, he got so excited that he decided to take a leave from his medical studies and join the Macintosh group. At Apple, then later as one of the cofounders at NeXT, Tribble-the-neurophysiologist would exhibit nothing less than brilliance in designing software.[43] (One would never guess at such talents in someone whose doctoral dissertation, finished in 1983, would concern a study of seizures in cats.)

Tribble joined the Macintosh team specifically to work with Jef

Raskin, but his loyalty was put to the test when Raskin found himself at odds with his nemesis, Steve Jobs, who had decided to move into the Macintosh group after Mike Scott, Apple's president, spurned Jobs's request to be appointed as head of the Lisa project (Scott had no confidence in Jobs's management skills).[44] The Lisa was viewed as too important to be entrusted to Jobs, so he cast about for another project and latched on to Raskin's Macintosh. It did not take long for disagreements to arise. Raskin and Jobs fought most bitterly about the design decisions that affected the future cost of the machine. To keep the machine as inexpensive as possible, so that it could be sold profitably for $1,000, Raskin lobbied for an older microprocessor than the new one that Jobs wanted to use. Jobs prevailed, but once the new chip was chosen, then other hardware decisions necessarily had to follow: Instead of being able to use a kind of modified tape-recorder to store the computer's data, which was an inexpensive but slow method, the Mac would need a faster though more expensive medium, a floppy disk drive. The computer memory would have to be enlarged from the 64,000 bytes that had originally been planned. Other improvements, such as an expanded screen and a detached keyboard, also pushed the price higher. Raskin fought hard against the flow, trying vainly to keep the cost of the machine from escalating upward.[45] Eventually, Raskin wrote a scathing memo about Jobs, reciting a litany of complaints about him: he did not listen to others; he acted without thinking; he did not give credit where it was due; he played favorites; he missed appointments, and on and on. Raskin forced a showdown with the company's cofounder in which Raskin lacked the political capital to win.[46]

In the middle was Bud Tribble, who was pulled by his old friend Raskin to stand by him and prevent the Macintosh from edging toward the Lisa in its design and future price, and who was pulled in the opposite direction by Steve Jobs to support him in choosing more expensive hardware, which was necessary for the computer to be capable of running the software that Tribble was working on.

Tribble knew himself well enough to see his own bias as a "technological junkie," who preferred "fancier bits" in his computer. Looking back later on this episode, he would say that there had been "these bad, political things happening, kind of above my head." He was in love with the Macintosh, and wanted to see it completed, so when Jobs prevailed and Raskin left the company, Tribble told himself that he needed to be Machiavellian and support whoever could best obtain resources from Apple to support the Macintosh effort through to the end. He stuck with Jobs.[47]

When the Macintosh was eventually released three years after Raskin's unhappy departure, it was sold for $2,495, a price far higher than Raskin had wanted. Jobs and Tribble were fortunate, however, because the unexpectedly high cost of the final Macintosh was much lower than it would have been if the prices of the semiconductor chips used in the machine had not fallen dramatically in the three years since the chips had been chosen. When the Macintosh was introduced, Jobs and Tribble and the others who had leaned toward a machine of greater, rather than less, capability ironically were vindicated because even the more powerful design did not save the machine from being criticized as underpowered, too slow, too small, not up to the task. Tribble had once apologized about the decision to give the Macintosh double the 64,000 bytes that had originally been planned, but even 128,000 bytes proved to be too cramped.[48] New Macintosh software needed much more memory (for perspective, consider that in 1993 Macintoshes are purchased with a minimum of four megabytes, that is, four million bytes, of memory). It was fortunate for Apple that the Jobs-Tribble position had won out.

Not all of the Macintosh design decisions proved wise. Jobs was so enamored of using the computer mouse for moving the arrow on a computer screen that he decided that the mouse would be the *only* way to move the arrow; he decreed, over the objections of his staff, that the Macintosh keyboard would not have the arrow keys that were then standard on other computers. The same impulse to dictate what users could, and could not, do with the machine led Jobs to decide to make the Macintosh a "closed" box, which left the factory with everything that a user supposedly would want. The purchaser was not to add any equipment to it, or even peek inside. If a wayward owner were to succumb to temptation and unscrew the cover, the warranty was instantly revoked. By such measures, Apple could write Macintosh system software more easily, knowing exactly what kind of hardware it would be running on, and without having the headache of making allowances for a variety of added equipment from other manufacturers. In contrast, IBM provided its "open" IBM personal computer with empty slots inside the box, inviting the user to expand memory, add equipment from other companies, and customize the machine in any of hundreds of ways. Jobs chose to ignore the fact that the openness of the IBM PC— and the openness of the Macintosh's own predecessor, the Apple II—went a long way toward explaining why the machines thrived.

If we were to play a parlor game of What If, and ask what if Jef Raskin had remained in charge of the Macintosh project, we would have to answer that the machine would have been less expensive, but underpowered too. Jobs turned out to be right that it was better to choose power over economy in this case. But Jobs was also wrong to deny his prospective customers choices, about keyboards and add-on boards, or about other possible options that could have been offered but were not, such as a color display or a hard-disk drive for storing much more data than a floppy disk could. Upon the Macintosh's introduction, these and other design decisions contributed to buyer resistance that came dangerously close to being fatal, and without doubt would indeed have killed the Macintosh if Apple had not subsequently reversed Jobs's decisions and rectified, one by one, these problems of artificially limited choice. By then, Jobs had moved on to NeXT, and though it was others who would fix the problems his decisions had caused, and though it was Raskin who should have been credited with the original conception of the machine, it was Jobs who would appropriate the credit for the success of the Macintosh.

Playing the role of the sole designer-genius suited Jobs's needs, and it suited the media who were accomplices in fixing this simplified image in the public mind. His unwillingness to share credit with his irksome predecessor, Raskin, would leave Jobs with an inflated sense of the deftness of his own instincts. It would blind him, however, from seeing the many decisions that he insisted upon during the Macintosh's gestation that ultimately crippled the machine in an extremely competitive market. Later at NeXT, when the same sorts of design choices presented themselves, whether to favor power or economy, whether to preserve isolation from the contaminating influences of inferior software or provide convenient links to other computers, whether to wait for a major technological advance before providing a color option or instead provide a poorer-quality color option immediately, and so on, Jobs followed the choices he had made before. It had all worked out well for the Macintosh; why would it not work again?

It may be difficult now to recall that when the Macintosh was introduced, it was almost delivered stillborn, without any buyers in sight beyond the computer-mad hobbyists. Who else would want it? Not business customers, who would balk at the complete absence of business-oriented software and the lack of compatibility with IBM personal computers. Not schoolteachers, who would balk at the price. The less sophisticated Apple II was difficult enough for schools to afford, and the Macintosh, even with an educational discount on its $2,495 price, was simply beyond the means of most school budgets. Whom, then, could Apple look to? The Macintosh's prospective buyers needed to have both money and compelling reasons to own personal computers, but still be new to the market, not yet lost to the IBM camp. Ideally, they needed to be tinkerers, less concerned with the availability of older programs familiar on other machines than with the Macintosh's suitability for the creation of entirely new ones. This wish list happened to fit one group perfectly: college students.

Apple dealers would have been glad to sell the new machine to whatever college students were nearby. But as the Macintosh group at Apple made plans for the introduction, they devised an unorthodox plan that called upon enlisting universities to become Apple dealers themselves, selling to students right on campus. To entice universities to agree to such a then-novel arrangement, Apple offered to sell each computer for a flat $1,000, less than half the regular retail price. The catch was that every university that joined a proposed Apple University Consortium had to make a commitment to buy $2 million worth of machines for resale to students over a three-year period.

It was not an easy decision for university administrations. The proposal would mean a breach in the wall that universities liked to think encircled their noncommercial cloister. It also posed a threat to the neutral position that universities had been careful to maintain in relationships with the various computer companies, avoiding any appearance of favoritism. Also, the two-million-dollar commitment that Apple required was itself sufficient to make the proposal unattractive. The university mission was in higher education, not the messy business of inventory control and risk management. The campus bookstore could always return unsold textbooks to the publisher; the university took on no risk itself. But now Apple was demanding that the university itself assume the risks of selling large quantities of a product that, even with the generous discount, represented a significant purchase for each buyer, and which had yet to be released and tested in the marketplace. If the Macintosh was a flop, universities would be stuck with financial liability and, even more embarrassing, with their image of collegiate impartiality besmirched.

The Ivy League universities and other major research universities had the most prestigious names to protect, and so were the most desirable for Apple to enlist. Steve Jobs wisely figured that if Apple secured the big names, other colleges and universities would be much more willing to join in. The others would reason that the Macintosh must indeed be special if the Ivies were willing to shed their usual decorum and throw in with one computer vendor on behalf of their students. For the Apple University Consortium to have the desired impact on the nonmember colleges and universities, the Macintosh group had to persuade the elite schools to make their commitments and sign the contracts in advance, so the roster of member names would be ready on the day of the Macintosh's introduction in January 1984.

Jobs did not have a clear idea of what universities needed, nor did he understand the collective nature of university decision-making. His own inclination was to go to lunch with Donald Kennedy, the president of Stanford, lift a sheet off the Macintosh, and act as if he were selling wholesale quantities of apples, not Apples: "How would you like to buy a thousand of these for a million dollars?" Such a decision was not primarily the prerogative of a single person, however. Rather, it was a collective decision that involved varying combinations of computer-center directors, deans and associate deans, academic vice-presidents, university counsel, and faculty committees. Jobs did not have the skills or the patience for persuading the lower levels of the academic power structure, but he did have Dan'l Lewin, a young, smooth Princeton graduate who was under thirty, as Jobs was, and who had come to Jobs's attention when he knocked on the door of Apple as a district sales manager working for Sony in California. Lewin's mission at the time of their initial contact was to persuade Jobs to adopt a floppy drive made by Sony, a drive that used three-and-a-half-inch disks, an unconventional size at the time. Jobs was sold on the Sony drive, and was sold on Lewin himself, whom he persuaded to leave Sony and join Apple. Lewin's mission was to sell the Macintosh in advance to higher education, and he set off, going from campus to campus, listening and pitching. Like Tribble, Lewin is of special interest because he would later join Jobs as a cofounder of NeXT.

Lewin pitched the Macintosh as the future. True, it fell short of meeting the specifications that Pat Crecine at Carnegie-Mellon University and other leaders in academic computing had been asking of computer manufacturers, a "3M" machine, which would have a million bytes of memory, a million dots on the screen, and a speed of a million instructions per second. The Macintosh fell short on all counts. But Lewin would say that the Macintosh offered the best available path to get to an easy-to-use but powerful 3M machine. The IBM Personal Computer was too difficult to use, and the Apple II, the other possible personal-computer contender, could never be sufficiently powerful. Lewin presented the first Macintosh as the outline of a machine that would allow the university eventually to obtain the desired power. Lewin spoke of the Apple University Consortium as a group of "codevelopers," not customers, who would collaborate with Apple and with each other in developing innovative software for the Macintosh that would have a profound impact on higher education.

Stanford administrators were interested in the Macintosh, but leery of the Consortium and the required financial commitment of two million dollars. But alternatively, providing students with access to centralized computers owned by the university was expensive, too. The campus had an insatiable appetite for time-shared mainframe computers and minicomputers ("mini" only when compared to the large mainframes but actually quite bulky and expensive when compared to the personal computers). The $1,000 price of a Macintosh was actually less than the cost of providing a student with a time-shared piece of a centralized computer. Best of all, in the case of the Macintosh, the cost would be paid not by Stanford University but by the students or their parents. By joining the Consortium, the university would instantly benefit within one year from savings achieved by *not* having to invest in the equivalent in large university-owned machines. It would be as if the computing budget for the university received an overnight supplement of six or seven million dollars. This proved to be a powerful enticement, helping move the university to make a seemingly daring commitment to support one company's "revolutionary" technology, when in fact considerations of the university's financial self-interest were important, too.

On the East Coast, Stacey Bressler was the Apple representative whose territory included five Ivy League schools. Bressler was young, vivacious, and possessed of seemingly inexhaustible energy. Apple had flown her to California to have a look at the Macintosh in development, and though it had few programs at that point, she instantly felt passionately attached to it. She and others who were permitted early glimpses spoke of feeling a love for the machine, an emotional attachment that inanimate objects do not commonly excite. From that moment, her work at Apple was transformed from a sales job into a crusade. She mounted a campaign to win recruits to the Apple University Consortium by starting at the ground level.

Persuading Brown University to come aboard was easy. The Brown computer people had heard positive things about the machine through the computer-community grapevine, so when she walked in the door, they were expecting her. They grabbed the machine, and sent her on her way so that they could play with it on their own. Soon afterward they called her back and said they wanted to sign a contract.

The other Ivy League schools were a much harder sell. Initially, everyone said they were not interested. They had not even decided whether they were going to use personal computers, and if they should decide to use any computer, they explained, it would be the IBM personal-computer standard. Rebuffed, Bressler used guerrilla tactics, taking her prototype Macintosh with her on visits to dormitories and administrative offices, letting students and secretaries see what the machine could do. At Dartmouth, she set up her computer in the lobby of the computer center and occupied herself drawing pictures on the screen, without saying a proselytizing word to anybody. Crowds gathered, and as word got around, William

Arms, the director of the center, came out to see what had caused the hubbub. He became a convert on the spot, envisioning a campus in which every student and faculty member had their own individual Macintosh, all linked to the central campus center and to each other through a network. Dartmouth had pioneered in the 1960s in providing its students with free access to campus computers; now Arms helped push Dartmouth into the Consortium with ambitious plans for a campuswide network of personal computers, another coup for Apple.

Bressler learned that the intense competition among the Ivy League schools would bring the others into the era of the personal computer if for no other reason than to keep up with rivals. When Brown University expressed its strong interest in joining the Consortium, Bressler went to work on Harvard and the other footdraggers. She reassured each of the laggard schools that it could elect to remain the only member of the Ivy League not to join the Consortium. She would add that just because the school had an image problem, just because the brightest high school seniors viewed it as a research institution that ignored the needs of undergraduates, and just because those seniors might be even more attracted to a school like Brown by the abundant presence of Macintoshes, the school that already had the highest number of undergraduate applicants, this was no reason to join the Apple University Consortium. . . . These words had the desired effect. She got all of the Ivy League schools to join.

If a school like Harvard brought prestige to the Consortium, a school like Drexel University in Philadelphia brought in a headline-producing name for having announced earlier in 1982 that it would be the first college that would require *all* students to own a personal computer. Drexel's president had made the announcement as part of the university's recent decision to pursue a national pool of applicants, and by making the announcement when he did, he was consciously placing Drexel ahead of the pack of schools that were contemplating adopting a similar requirement. After attracting national publicity for the announcement, a university committee quickly had to select the one computer that the university would adopt as its standard from among 300 different kinds and prepare for implementing the requirement in fall 1983.

During these preparations, Apple called Drexel's Brian Hawkins, an assistant vice-president for academic affairs, and asked if he would be interested in seeing a machine that was *nondisclosed*, meaning that Hawkins had to agree not to disclose to anyone else anything about the machine. (In the computer industry, the term "nondisclosed" has assumed many syntactical guises that would give an English teacher a fright: for example, it could be an adjective, as here when Hawkins was asked if he'd like to see a "nondisclosed machine," or it could even be a transitive verb, as in "I have to nondisclose you.") Hawkins explained that he alone could not accept Apple's offer to show him the machine, an offer which reflected Jobs's inclination to find a single decision-maker; Hawkins insisted that the machine be shown to the full faculty committee. The arrangements required special dispensation from a reluctant Jobs.

When the Macintosh was shown to Hawkins and the Drexel faculty, it was still in primitive form, capable of showing little other than bouncing balls and a rudimentary drawing program. Nevertheless, it captured everyone's imagination. Just like Bressler, they could see what its pictorial orientation *would* be capable of. The Drexel committee was concerned, however, that whatever machine it chose, the price to the students be affordable. Other computer manufacturers had offered to make major donations of equipment to Drexel, but the donations would be to the university, not to students. Apple stood apart from the rest for its willingness to provide deep discounts expressly for students.

Hawkins and Drexel decided to adopt the Macintosh as the standard. With the machine not even finished, the decision to require its purchase of all students was a dicey one. If the Macintosh did not turn out to be what had been promised, Drexel University would find itself with an outraged student body, livid parents, and the wrong kind of national publicity. With so much on the line, it is understandable that Drexel did not simply hope for the best. It got to work immediately developing educational software for the machines. Like a scholarship student that had been admitted to an exclusive Ivy League school on the basis of wits alone, Drexel was the hungriest and hardest-working member of the Apple University Consortium.

For software development, Drexel took delivery of six prototype machines prior to the Macintosh's unveiling. Jobs insisted on elaborate cloak-and-dagger security measures. When Apple called Drexel to notify the campus that the machines were about to be shipped, the computers were cryptically referred to as "six friends" who would be arriving shortly, so that eavesdroppers would be foiled. While a "secure room" on campus was prepared for the machines, with sound and motion detection, alarms, and electronic locks, Hawkins hid the Macintoshes temporarily at home. When the secure room at Drexel was ready, the machines were moved under cover of darkness at 3:30 in the morning, escorted by campus police cruisers. Jobs had hectored everyone about security, and the Drexel people absorbed his paranoia.

While Drexel and other campuses went to work preparing software, the Macintosh group at Apple worked feverishly to have the computers ready as promised for students to take delivery at the beginning of the fall semester in 1983. But problems that the engineers discovered with the disk drive led to delays. Even though Drexel had begun to collect initial payments from students in the fall, the Macintosh was not officially unveiled until January 24, 1984. On the day of the unveiling, Jobs could point proudly to the commitment that all of the Ivy League schools, as well as Drexel, Stanford, the University of Chicago, and other institutions had made to the new machine in joining the Apple University Consortium, twenty-four schools in all. If Drexel worried about having made such a risky investment in a machine that was untested, and now was very late, at least it was one among a distinguished crowd of fellow travelers. Misgivings were swept away when trucks carrying the machines finally arrived on the campuses that spring and students excitedly took delivery of their machines.

No one at Apple or at the universities anticipated how quickly students would adopt Macintoshes. At Stanford, administrators who had been concerned about selling $2 million worth of Macintoshes over three years were pleasantly surprised to see $2.5 million worth sold within the first two weeks. They sold far too many, in fact; Apple could not keep up. Stanford had to hold a lottery to provide an equitable way of handling the delay in deliveries, and it took six months before all the students who had prepaid their $1,000 got their machines. Other schools, which were not members of the Consortium, found that their students demanded that they join. At California Polytechnical State University in San Luis Obispo, a group of one hundred students staged a protest at the president's office, backed by a petition signed by nearly 1,000 students, demanding that the university renegotiate with Apple and gain admittance to the Consortium. The university authorities explained to the students that Cal Poly had had to turn down Apple's invitation because of state laws that required competitive bidding for all contracts of any significance.[49] The Macintosh received more free publicity when newspapers carried stories of a black market in Macintoshes springing up in college towns, when some students violated the terms of their purchase agreement and resold the machines off-campus for a tidy profit. Brian Hawkins at Drexel warned these students, however, of dire consequences other than legal ones: "A student who sells his or her Macintosh is committing academic suicide."[50]

The idea that owning a Macintosh would now be indispensable to a college education, combined with the news that the Apple University Consortium included the most exclusive universities in the country, gave the Macintosh a cachet unlike any other computer. By early 1985, Jobs would boast that in less than a year the Macintosh had become *the* standard in college computing. In giddy overstatement, he claimed, "I could ship every Macintosh we make this year just to those 24 colleges."[51] But he was justified in hailing the Apple University Consortium for providing the Macintosh, at the moment of its debut, with high visibility on key campuses. There was no precedent for a group of august universities lending their names to the launch of a product that was manufactured by a for-profit company. The Consortium gave the Macintosh instant credibility. Other campuses woke up and took notice.

Students and faculty members seemed to embrace the Macintosh naturally with little prompting, but campus bookstores were initially uncomfortable in the role of computer dealer that Apple thrust upon them. The stores were accustomed to selling nothing more complicated than textbooks and sweatshirts, whose prices were fixed and whose customers were a captive market. No marketing pizzazz was required. When Apple marketing people arrived and explained how the stores could also sell computers, the bookstore management usually was uneasy, especially when the Apple representatives went on to talk about advertising campaigns and promotional pricing that the bookstores could use to increase sales. The bookstores demurred: We're nonprofit; we don't do marketing.

Well, you'll be providing a service, Apple representatives explained. Wouldn't you be doing your students a disservice if you sold these computers at a deep discount but did not let the students know about it? And if in ignorance the students went off-campus and spent their parents' money at an Apple dealer, and the parents found out that they had not gotten the educational discount they were entitled to, and called the school to complain . . . ?

This is how bookstores were signed up to deliver not just shelf space, but the full gamut of marketing efforts that a regular computer dealer would offer. They were even convinced of the need to do fall promotions and Christmas promotions and spring promotions, not to make profits per se, but for the impeccable reason of securing the best available discount by generating the highest possible volume, all in the name of better serving the students.

The campaign to sell to college students at heavily discounted prices was dependent upon excluding Apple's regular dealers from these special arrangements with universities. The dealers howled in protest. They wanted the college student business too; this was especially true when it became clear to them that the *only* customers likely to be interested in the Macintosh were college students. In at least one instance, angry Apple dealers in Michigan sued Dan'l Lewin and Apple. In New England, one of Stacey Bressler's larger Apple dealers, incensed about the Apple University Consortium, threatened that if it ruined his business, she would be physically harmed.

This was the low point of the transition. The dealer later called Bressler to apologize for his intemperate outburst. Apple won the Michigan suit. Other Apple dealers adjusted to the newly contoured landscape and reluctantly came to appreciate the presence of a thriving university market, even though they did not benefit immediately. The high volume of machines sold on campuses helped to legitimize the Macintosh in the wider marketplace and to attract the interest of software developers, who brought out new Macintosh software that benefited everyone who sold the machine. And when the students graduated, leaving campus as loyal Macintosh converts, they turned to regular dealers for their Apple purchases. For-profit dealers came to accept this *modus vivendi* with their nonprofit competition on campus.

Apple might have reaped few rewards for converting the college bookstores into personal computer dealers, if its far larger competitors had been successful in their own campaigns to sell machines to college students. The bookstores, careful not to jeopardize their nonprofit status by giving exclusive distribution rights to any one computer company, added other computer lines to their offerings. The Macintosh marketing group "plowed the street," and IBM and the others rolled in right behind them, setting up similar discount programs for students and faculty.

It hardly mattered, however, as the Macintosh outsold the IBM personal computer in wildly imbalanced ratios on campus, 15 to 1 or even 40 to 1. The Macintosh marketing people themselves were astonished at how well their machine did against the far better-financed competition. Jobs, too, was taken aback and took undisguised pleasure in the spectacle of IBM forming four-hundred-person task forces to plot a response and lavishing gifts of thousands of its personal computers on campuses, but to little avail. The students still preferred Macintoshes. And so too did university administrators, who realized that the value of hardware gifts still paled compared to the far larger, if much less visible, investment that would be necessary for developing software and providing training for the new users of IBM-compatible personal computers. If the easier-to-use Macintosh greatly reduced the necessary investment in training, then universities could view it as more economical in the long run, even if other computer manufacturers literally gave away their IBM-standard hardware. Jobs said he knew of some cases in which colleges had used IBM grant money to purchase Apple Macintoshes.[52]

Stanford, for example, was one of the principal targets of IBM's campaign to secure a beachhead on college campuses for its personal computers. The university received $18 million worth of IBM personal computers, yet it nevertheless became a Macintosh-heavy campus. Stanford administrators were relieved at this outcome because they figured that the training costs for IBM machines, extended to the entire university community, would have been prohibitive. When the first IBM personal computers had arrived, the university provided twelve hours of training for each faculty member in the arcane intricacies of the word-processing program Wordstar. No such training was needed for the Macintosh word-processing program, MacWrite. IBM tried its best to buy the allegiance of campuses like Stanford, but failed, while Apple found that its machine leapt into the hands of eager students with the help of only a bare-bones marketing organization at Apple. The Macintosh higher-education marketing group consisted of a grand total of four people at a time when annual sales on campuses were running $50 million a year.

Once the Macintosh had taken hold, Apple enjoyed the recurring benefits of a unique characteristic of the college market: twenty-five percent of the market was brand new each year, when the freshman class arrived. It was the only market that had such regular turnover. Sales to elementary and secondary schools, always a strong market for Apple, were not characterized by this kind of turnover because the sales were to the schools themselves, not to students. So, too, in the business market, turnover did not redound to the benefit of Apple because the computers were owned by the organization, not the individual. But in higher education, Apple enjoyed what it internally referred to as an "annuity market," with steady streams of income from campuses already saturated with Macintoshes, as the entering freshman class provided an inexhaustible supply of new customers.

The annuity continued to pay benefits to Apple even after the students graduated. The Macintosh was so markedly superior to the IBM personal computer that it elicited a fierce loyalty in its young owners. Students told corporate recruiters that they owned Macintoshes and would not switch to the IBM personal computer, the prevailing office standard. Once hired, they would demonstrate the machine to their superiors, which in some cases led to immediate additional sales, what Apple called the "bottom-up sale." Apple acquired more than simply happy customers when its machines were sold on campuses, and then in offices. It acquired evangelical devotees who sought to bring enlightenment to the benighted masses of the IBM world. This advantage was uniquely Apple's; owners of IBM personal computers did not have a machine that lent itself to passionate devotion. IBM owners displayed, at best, an irritated defensiveness when challenged by the Macintosh partisans about computer standards. They did not feel strongly enough, however, to try to win converts the way that Macintosh owners did.

The extraordinary success of Macintoshes on college campuses was a compound of these many elements: a new model for personal computers, in the form of the Macintosh itself; a new system of distribution, in the form of college bookstores; and a new kind of customer loyalty, in the form of evangelical Macintosh partisans. For Apple, the cost of distributing a high volume of product was extremely low because an intermediary, the Apple dealer, was circumvented entirely. For the universities, the cost of expanding computing resources across the student body was minimal because the costs were absorbed by the students and their parents. Most striking of all, the business-related aspects of the Macintosh's success were relegated to secondary place. What excited the university community and the Macintosh marketing people was the idea that the Macintosh was contributing in important ways to teaching and learning.

The idealism of Apple's Stacey Bressler illustrates the rush of adrenaline that the participants in the story experienced. Bressler, who before the Macintosh was introduced had to camp out in the lobbies of campus computer centers in order to get a hearing for the proposed Apple University Consortium, was as surprised as anyone by the extraordinary sales of Macintoshes on campuses. She worked one-hundred-hour weeks, happily possessed by the press of demands caused by the machine's success, as she tried to serve the needs of many clamoring campuses simultaneously. The work was so exciting and demanding that it pushed everything else out of her life. As a salesperson who earned a commission on the campus sales, Bressler was also becoming wealthy. But the money did not seem to matter. More important was the happy congruence of having socially useful work and customers that were clawing to get hold of the machine. At one point in the midst of the onslaught of customers, a friend noticed at Bressler's house that several commission checks, totaling more than $100,000, lay on her messy desk. She had not had time to deposit them.

For the participants, it was the early years of the Macintosh that were the most exciting, even though Apple's annual revenue from college sales would later climb from the tens of millions, to the hundreds of millions, to eventually an estimated $800 million-plus by the early 1990s. As time passed, the work became routinized, and the giddy sense of being a pioneer faded. The dominance of the Macintosh on so many campuses deprived its partisans of the pleasures of feeling outgunned and besieged. Though certainly not true off-campus, at least on campus, the Macintosh was the regal leader in volume of unit sales.

Anyone who was associated with the success of the Macintosh on campuses in the early days, before its viability had been established, earned a halo that will probably follow them for the rest of their careers. At Apple, Dan'l Lewin's future was secured for his leading role in organizing the Consortium. At Drexel University, Brian Hawkins, who had gambled on the Macintosh when it was still not yet completed, also secured an aura of preternatural vision and a blessed future. Others looked on and wondered how they could become heroes like Lewin and Hawkins when the equivalent of the next Macintosh appeared.

Steve Jobs had many reasons to be grateful for higher education's early embrace of the Macintosh. It was universities that provided early purchase commitments even before the machine was introduced to the public. It was universities that were willing to support an improved computer standard, defying the overweening muscle of the standard-bearer, IBM. It was universities that voted to support the Macintosh, even though it would be years before a wide variety of software would be available for it. Universities were flexible, appreciative of new technology, and, not incidentally, constituted a renewable market.

The one-millionth Macintosh was sold in early 1987, a mere three years after the machine's introduction (keep this in mind when we look at NeXT's subsequent history). The Apple Macintosh division—sans Steve Jobs—used the occasion to honor Jef Raskin. At a party to commemorate the sales milestone, Raskin was presented with a machine that was designated as Number One Million. It was the first and only recognition that Raskin received for his early contribution to the Macintosh's birth.[53]

Just as Raskin's contribution to the Macintosh has remained out of sight in the public mind, so too has higher education's. In the popular history of the Macintosh, the arrival of the laser printer and the use of Macintoshes for desktop publishing are always given credit for rescuing the early Macintosh from oblivion. Without quibbling with the idea that desktop publishing was a necessary condition, we might add that it was insufficient alone, and sales to higher education also should be rightfully credited as another necessary, if insufficient, factor in the equation. Universities kept the Macintosh alive until it succeeded in broadening its commercial appeal. Jobs drew one lesson above all others from this experience. If universities backed superior computer technology once, they could do it again for NeXT.

The *thirtysomething* Company

When Steve Jobs celebrated his thirtieth birthday in February 1985, he did not appear to have any inkling that his tenure at Apple would soon end, and that by the time of his next birthday, he would be engaged in building a new computer company from scratch. Before this tumult, Jobs had viewed his commanding perch in the company as threatened only by the advance of age, and he viewed even this with serenity. When an interviewer for *Playboy* noted that the average age of Apple employees was only twenty-nine and asked Jobs why the computer field was so dominated by young people, Jobs offered the observation that it was the ineluctable processes of biochemistry. "People get stuck as they get older," he said, comparing their patterns of thought to the permanently etched grooves that were impressed upon a vinyl record. He observed that it was rare that one saw "an artist in his 30s or 40s able to really contribute something amazing." For an oldster like him, the challenge was to "grow obsolete with grace."[54]

This was easy to say when Jobs felt that his central place in the computer cosmos was secure and never seriously contemplated the possibility of being viewed as dispensable. But such calm detachment proved impossible when his cosmos disintegrated into chaos: the Macintosh sold well in the first months, but excepting college campuses, demand had then dropped precipitously after the first flush of orders had been filled. Jobs suddenly found himself at odds with John Sculley, the man from Pepsi whom Jobs had brought to Apple only two years before with the famous taunt, "Do you want to spend the rest of your life selling sugared water, or do you want a chance to change the world?" The evaporation of demand for the Macintosh drove Jobs and Sculley apart. Antagonizing all who did not belong to his inner circle, Jobs held everyone else at Apple to blame for the Macintosh's problems, and busied himself with grandiose plans for new projects. In late spring of 1985, the Apple board stripped him of all operational responsibilities and banished him to the empty position of chairman and a remote office that he called Siberia.

Suddenly, he had nothing much to do. He came into the office, busied himself with a look at the mail, but whatever reports were still routed to him soon stopped. He was hit by the realization that he was now an unappreciated pariah, "there was nobody really there to miss me."[55] He soon decided it was too depressing to go where he was not wanted, and he stayed away from Apple and began casting about for ideas about what to do with the rest of his life. Now, placed in circumstances outside of his own control, his outlook about his own obsolescence changed radically. Suddenly, his thirty years seemed young, not old; he was not ready for involuntary retirement. He would rage before going gently into *that* good night.

The epiphany that revealed what he should do with himself supposedly occurred in early September during a lunch that he arranged with Paul Berg, a Stanford biochemist. The story, as Jobs later retold it, is suspiciously pat, but one cannot but notice the remarkable entrée that Jobs had into the most elevated circles of the academic world; what other thirty-year-old college dropout could entice a busy Nobel laureate like Berg to lunch at a coffee shop? The Jobs version of their luncheon encounter positions the birth of

NeXT as the blessed offspring of both Jobs and Berg. As Berg talked about the difficulty of doing wet-lab research on gene splicing, his area of specialty, Jobs asked him why he did not simulate the experiments on computer. It would help Berg's own research, Jobs suggested, and it would also make it possible for future freshmen to play with recombinant-DNA software created by the leading authority in the field. At the Kid's brilliant suggestion, the Nobel Laureate's eyes "lit up" (according to the Kid); this was the "landmark lunch" that the Kid said got his own wheels turning again.[56]

The Nobel Laureate's recollection of the encounter was a bit different, however. Berg said that Jobs had already been going around the country, asking what an ideal computer for universities would be. The ideal, Jobs had been told, would cost about $25,000 each; he wanted to market one for $500.[57] One can see why Jobs preferred in his own version of the luncheon to ignore this prior canvassing of colleges. It was much preferable to tell the world that the idea to build a computer expressly for the university market was the joint inspiration of himself and the distinguished professor.

A few days later, Jobs informed the Apple board of directors of his intention to start a new computer company, which would be complementary and would address the needs of higher education, manufacturing a machine tailored expressly for college students and faculty. He would take a few "low-level" Apple people with him, and thought it best that he resign as chairman. The board deliberated in private and returned to express an interest in buying as much as ten percent of the new company, since it would not compete with Apple directly. This would turn out, however, to be only a temporary moment of amity. The next day, Jobs sent a note to Sculley listing five individuals who would be leaving with him: Dan'l Lewin, the marketing person most closely associated with the Apple University Consortium; Bud Tribble, the Macintosh software manager; two hardware engineers, George Crow and Rich Page; and a person in finance, Susan Barnes. The founders were a youthful group; their median age was in the low thirties. But Sculley was outraged that Jobs would take individuals so "sensitive" to Apple. He told Jobs, "These are not low-level people."[58]

In the heat of panic, Sculley and the Apple executive staff perceived a deadly threat to Apple in the departure of Jobs and the five associates. The new company, NeXT, would market a computer too close to what Apple already had in the works, code-named the Big Mac, which was intended to deliver the powerful but inexpensive "3M" machine, with a million bytes of memory and the other stipulated requirements that research universities had been clamoring for and which the Macintosh had been insufficiently powerful to fulfill. While at Apple, the founders of NeXT had been privy to information about costs and marketing plans that would be valuable to them in their new venture. Sculley called in the legal heavies and filed a suit, enjoining Jobs from proceeding. After the fact, Sculley would describe the moment as a sad one, when "we sued one of the fathers of our company." With perspective, we can see that the suit was not so much a tragic act of patricide as it was a comical act of litigious silliness, attempting to stop the unstoppable.[59]

How curious that when Jobs was still at Apple, he was considered by the board to be an incompetent manager at best, but as soon as he set off on his own, he was suddenly perceived as invaluable. In the suit, Apple charged that Jobs and the others had schemed to take advantage of Apple's own plan to develop and market the "Next Generation Product." The suit also pointed to Jobs's "secret plan" to sell his Apple stock in order to finance the new venture. There was nothing illegal about such a sale, however. The most that Apple could charge was that as part of his "nefarious scheme" Jobs planned to sell the maximum number of shares of Apple stock allowed by securities law without public disclosure.[60] It was as meaningless a charge as the one that equated everything that Jobs knew about Apple as "confidential and proprietary." Though John Sculley would attempt to draw a distinction between encouraging Jobs in "starting another company and continuing to bring innovation and creativity to the industry" and forbidding him from using "Apple's confidential and proprietary information," in fact, the sweeping nature of the charges lodged against Jobs and his coconspirators revealed that Sculley had no idea of how he would actually encourage the former without invoking the latter. Sculley was relatively new to Silicon Valley, and so can be excused for his ignorance of how mitosis was a natural process in the Valley—one cell dividing into two, two into four, *ad infinitum*. Jobs suggested that Sculley, the recent immigrant to the Valley, labored under a "cultural misunderstanding."[61] But Mike Markkula and other Apple board members knew better (Markkula's own first fortune, made at the semiconductor firm Intel, was dependent upon the same process, as its founders were two rogue engineers, Robert Noyce and Gordon Moore, who had split off from the parent cell, Fairchild Semiconductor).[62] It was hypocritical for them to declare unilaterally that no more mitotic growth would be permitted.

Jobs was right when he said that Apple was free to compete against NeXT if Apple thought the idea of selling a computer made specially for the higher education market was so attractive. He mused, "It is hard to think that a $2 billion company with 4,300-plus people couldn't compete with six people in blue jeans."[63] The Apple suit created a horrible legal nightmare for tiny NeXT; the fledgling company could not count on producing its own computer until the suit was resolved. Yet psychologically it was a wonderful thing: it was as if Apple indeed was afraid of competing with this youngish group of six in blue jeans. In his last days at Apple, Jobs had been regarded as a has-been at thirty, kicked upstairs into an empty attic like an unloved octogenarian who drooled and had to be kept out of sight. But now that Jobs had left the house of Apple, he and his coconspirators were suddenly the most important of people. Why else would Apple have trained a full battery of artillery upon their departing backs? The more that Apple fulminated about their departure, the more their powers to do great things were affirmed

75

and the more their new venture was validated as a potent business. This was a precious gift that Apple unintentionally gave them.

Though Jobs wanted Apple to think of the NeXT founders as an unassuming group in blue jeans, he was not about to return to the frugal circumstances of the beginning of his business career. He had started Apple in his family's garage, and had invoked the image of the "metaphorical garage" when he later took control of the Macintosh group and managed a company-within-a-company, but this time, at NeXT, he would start off not in a garage but in a mansion, his home in Woodside, which he had purchased from the Giannini family, founders of the Bank of America. This served as the company's temporary office for four months until they could move into formal offices. The advance of age and personal fortune promoted his intolerance of anything but the absolute best. Instead of choosing the least-expensive office space available in the area, he chose some of the most expensive. NeXT leased as its first office a modern building in the Stanford University Industrial Park in Palo Alto, a stone's throw from the Xerox PARC campus, set amidst undeveloped hills and wildlife.

Jobs did not follow the customary script for a scrappy start-up that would need to husband its initial capital. He hired a full-time interior designer as one of the first ten employees of NeXT.[64] The interiors were gutted and elegantly redone, starting with the upstairs, where hardwood floors were installed to define a common area, including a kitchen area with granite counter tops and a lounge area with a U-shaped sofa that sat twelve. Walls were replaced with glass; enormous Ansel Adams prints and custom-made furniture were installed; and the bathrooms received no less costly investment than other areas. The objective was to create a comforting impression that this was a company that had already made its mark on the world. Long before a computer would be ready for unveiling, Jobs talked with architects about designing NeXT sales offices in major cities around the country. Jobs pursued his own set of priorities, and the look of the NeXT offices took precedence over most everything else. The trademark attention to appearances was most extravagantly displayed when Jobs decided, over the objections of the early employees, to spend $100,000 to commission a logo for NeXT.

One did not necessarily have to spend such a sum to obtain a logo design. Jobs had met with four designers, none of whom asked for anything close to $100,000 for their services, but all had failed to please Jobs. He decided to give the commission to Paul Rand, a Yale professor widely regarded as the grand master of American design. Someone had told Jobs that Rand was the best, so Rand he would get. Rand had done the corporate logo for IBM, and Jobs could take satisfaction in being able to buy for his own little company the same expertise that mighty IBM had hired (Rand still consulted for IBM and insisted that Jobs first obtain IBM's permission to use Rand's services, which to Jobs's surprise IBM granted). For the designer, Jobs was the perfect client. Rand abhorred the businessperson who second-guessed his own design judgment, and he abhorred the business bureaucracy that impeded access to the ultimate decision-maker.[65] In submitting his design to Jobs, Rand had direct access to the person with final say, who was also a respectful admirer, someone who would accede to Rand's demands that he be paid not a penny less than $100,000, that the amount be paid in advance, that the fee would cover one design only. Rand insisted that for the commission he would not be bound to revise or rework the design; NeXT would have to take it or leave it, unaltered. Hiring Rand would be an expensive crapshoot.

As it turned out, for his $100,000, Jobs received from Rand not just a logo but also a lengthy pamphlet in which every passing thought that had gone into the final design was explained. It was Rand who proposed *NeXT* instead of NEXT. The lower-case *e* that stood out from the other letters, Rand suggested, could stand for "education, excellence, expertise, exceptional, excitement, $e = mc^2$." Placing the four letters on the face of a black cube, tilted at a precisely stipulated angle of 28 degrees, Rand described the logo as designed to appeal to a youthful audience. "Tipped at a jaunty angle," he wrote, "it brims with the informality, friendliness, and spontaneity of a Christmas seal and the authority of a rubber stamp." Each of the four letters was assigned a carefully considered color, drawn from a palette that included vermilion and cerise.[66] Every detail was precious. When Jobs finished reading Rand's lengthy gloss, he jumped up and embraced him.[67]

The perfect logo would be the beginning of the perfect company, perfect because Jobs could start with what he called a "blank sheet of paper."[68] There was no system to be dismantled; they were starting again from scratch. As one NeXT manager who had come from Apple put it, NeXT had the chance to "do it right the first time."[69] This was an expression of the *thirtysomething* company, young enough to still aspire to perfection, yet old enough to be aware of the aspiration. By Jobs's reasoning, NeXT should become a company superior to Apple precisely because this time around he would have wisdom gained from his two previous successes, in developing the Apple II and then the Macintosh computer. He had had "good instincts" but had not consciously understood why his instincts had led him to success. "By the third time," he said, full of confidence, "you should start to get a pretty good feeling in your gut that you understand the process."[70] At NeXT, he could use his awareness of what had worked well in the past to "become a lot more productive." One of the lessons that he now felt comfortable owning up to was that he had not listened attentively to his customers. "Well, I'm not going to make the same mistakes twice," he declared in October 1985.[71]

The philosophy of a model company was formally articulated years later in NeXT's statement of its mission:

> to build computers that change the world and that our friends can afford to buy
> to build a great company, so exciting and fulfilling that we can't wait to come to work in the morning

to treat our customers so well that they will love our products and
our company
to lead the industry with vision and innovation

Admirable goals, every one of them. One can see how Jobs could become intoxicated with the purity of the vision he was conjuring for himself and his followers. He would claim that pursuit of riches was no longer what he cared about. Rather, he simply wanted to be able to say ten years later, when he turned forty, that "I spent my 30s well."[72]

One important element of Jobs's self-defined task for his thirties was crafting an ideal work environment at NeXT, an organization that would elicit the kind of affection for the company among its employees that the mission statement called for (Jobs, no less than Bill Gates, echoed James Duke's regret about "leaving off at night"). By design, then, NeXT began as a flat organization with little hierarchy. Business cards did not carry titles, only an identifying department or area. The goal was to create a "unified company," without the divisive barriers that were associated with job categories and rank. The company was literally unified by the physical arrangement of the interior—by removing the interior walls on the upper floor when his company moved in, Jobs created a large bullpen in which all desks, his as well as the others, shared the same space in egalitarian fashion. Like the Puritans who established an exemplary City on a Hill (John Winthrop: ". . . the eies of all people are uppon us . . ."),[73] Jobs gave his company on a hill its own nomenclature that differentiated the world within which the chosen worked from the profane world outside. NeXT was not a company but rather a *community*, comprised not of employees but of *members*. This was an extension of Apple culture, where new terms had also been used to set the company's culture apart from that of the humdrum others. In 1981, when Apple had decided to replace all typewriters with its own personal computers, the company marked the occasion by nominally abolishing the position of *secretary* and replacing it with the more euphonious *area associate.*[74]

One could say that West Coast dialect has its own vast vocabulary of gentle euphemisms. An anonymous guide to "Doing Business on the Opposite Coast" that circulated among computer companies provided helpful translations for those who were not bilingual:

East Coast	*West Coast*
Absolutely not	Maybe
Yes	Maybe
Do it and do it now	Can you sign up for this program?
Do it right or you're fired	I'm confident you'll get it done
Get out of my office	Let's get consensus on this one
Local bar	Offsite facility
Meet me in the parking lot	Let's take that discussion offline
Dictator	Facilitator
Oh Shit	Thanks for bringing that to my attention

At NeXT, the egalitarian ideal was encouraged by pegging salary levels to groups rather than to particular individuals. In 1985 and 1986, NeXT had an extremely simple policy on salaries: members of NeXT's senior staff earned $75,000 annually, and everyone else earned $50,000. No distinctions were drawn on the basis of previous experience, field of expertise, or individual performance. This was perhaps a unique policy among Silicon Valley firms. The most extreme contrast in the Valley was provided by Cypress Semiconductor, where the compensation of its managers was based on how well management fulfilled some 6,000 weekly goals, each tracked by computer. At NeXT, pay raises were distributed as equally as possible; at Cypress, raises were distributed in a bell-curve pattern, which dictated that as many managers did not receive raises as those that did. Cypress based compensation decisions exclusively on computer systems, believing that human error and favoritism were eliminated, while NeXT defended an old-fashioned belief in the "art" of compensation and the impossibility of fairly making distinctions among peers.[75]

An ideal company provided more than just salary and stock options; NeXT employees were also provided health club memberships, counseling services, emergency personal loans up to $5,000, and health insurance benefits extended not only to married families but also to unmarried cohabitants (initial coverage of same-sex couples had to be retracted later due to difficulties with the insurance company). In the expensive housing market of the Bay Area, NeXT's provision of housing assistance in the form of a low-interest loan, up to fifty percent of the employee's annual salary, was a great help in meeting a down payment that would otherwise have been impossible for most young employees buying a first home.

Jobs prided himself on sharing sensitive company information among employees. Initially, all employees were gathered together weekly to hear reports; as the company grew larger, the meetings became biweekly, then monthly, but the spirit of open internal communication was maintained. Jobs would say, "We'll tell you everything," on condition that the information was not to be shared with anyone outside of the company. It was a serious matter to him, and he would occasionally threaten that any leaks would mean an end to the internal disclosure of financial information and impending deals under consideration. But he lightened the threats with humor, such as demanding in a jocular tone that his employees raise their hands and swear together that no one tell even the dogs what was about to be revealed. He did not hold himself to the same strict standards expected of his employees, and he exercised his prerogatives to say what he wished to the press and to bring in visitors for "sneaks" without asking that they sign a nondisclosure agreement.

The policy of internal openness extended to that most sensitive of all categories of company information, the salaries of one's fellow employees. Another boast of NeXT's was that any employee could look up what anyone else earned. In practice, the right to investigate the juicy details had to be exercised in public view. Unlike all other information circulating within NeXT, which was available through the company computer network and could be read from the privacy of one's office, the information about salaries was available only in the human resources office. There the curious employee could look at, without copying, a listing on paper of salaries and stock grants. Many employees never did so, and were content with the knowledge that they could exercise the right to snoop politely at any time. Those that did pay a visit to satisfy their curiosity often regretted doing so. Some discovered that in their particular area of the company, salaries varied much more than anticipated, rigged according to starting dates at the company, not to varying skills or responsibilities; others learned that the salaries of close colleagues were close or identical but were dismayed to see that interdepartmental variations could be wide. Those who were demoralized by the revelations drew the conclusion that when it came to the distribution of salaries and stock packages on the other side of the company, it was better to remain blissfully ignorant.

The egalitarian spirit that had guided the initially simple two-tier salary structure had dissipated by late 1986 and early 1987, when Jobs discovered that it was difficult to convince engineers from the Midwest to move to California, where house prices were so much higher, and yet NeXT offered a salary that was less than what they were already making. When a $100,000 "sign-on" bonus was offered to one engineer to help sweeten the offer, a precedent was set that permitted flexible offers and an end to the early experiment. Once NeXT began to offer "relocation bonuses," too, prospective recruits were able to assemble financial packages that were more generous than those that existing employees had received. One new employee even received a $20,000 "relocation bonus" just to move from his home in Santa Cruz to Fremont, a relatively short distance, given that some NeXT employees commuted between the two places on a daily basis.

Jobs had adopted the policy of making all information internally available as a deliberate departure from standard operating procedure in business. He reasoned that NeXT's individual employees were like human cells: each was specialized but each one possessed the genetic code for the whole body. The organic model underlay his management philosophy: "We think NeXT will be the best possible company if every single person working here understands the whole basic master plan and can use that as a yardstick to make decisions."[76] The internal openness was virtually forced by the small size of NeXT. Starting with a handful of employees in an industry dominated by giants (when NeXT was founded, IBM's annual revenues were $50 billion), NeXT could not begin to match the resources deployed by its much larger competition. By necessity, the new company could grow only by what Jobs called "outthinking" the others.[77] If NeXT employees were to outsmart the competition, they required unimpeded access to company information. Well-armed with electronic ammunition, the NeXT infantry would be able to vanquish its much larger enemy armies. (The righteous vision of Puritan John Winthrop again comes to mind: ". . . tenn of us shall be able to resist a thousand of our enemies . . .").[78]

Small was ideal, or so at least it seemed in the heady moment when NeXT began. Jobs lured some of NeXT's first employees away from Apple with the enticement that NeXT offered respite from the impersonally large organization. NeXT would be a private company, owned solely by its employees, a company built on an intimately small scale, manufacturing a small number of very good computers, with all of the company's functions including manufacturing kept cozily in one place. If the company grew it would simply release new little companies like a ripe pea pod. By 1987 it became apparent, however, that small could never exert the major influence upon the industry that Jobs so desperately sought, so big became the necessary ideal. "Our smallest competitor is $1.75 billion these days," he explained. "The world doesn't need another

$100-million computer company. We have to get up to a certain scale if we want to play in the sandbox."[79] Nothing less than a billion-dollar company would suffice.

When Jobs switched in that first year, however, he did not pause for intermediate goals; he immediately set about building an organization suitable for the billion-dollar company. He bragged that NeXT had executives who were "overqualified" for a small start-up company. Phillip Wilson, for example, hired as the vice-president for human resources, had formerly been head of human resources for Cummins Engine, a $3 billion company with 27,000 employees (he also held a Ph.D. in English language and literature from the University of Chicago). Susan Barnes, the cofounder who was NeXT's chief financial officer, had hired as her subordinate a cost accountant who had once been the controller of a much larger company.[80] The necessary organization was already in place for the time when NeXT would be a billion-dollar company, Barnes proudly said, "so that we won't be breaking down just at the time we get that big."[81]

It was precisely this grandiosity that made NeXT such an exciting place to be. It was the mid-1980s, a time when limits were not nearly as visible in American business culture as they are today. For those who adopted the vision, there was no ceiling, only open sky. If NeXT employees willed it to be so with sufficient force, then there was no reason why the billion-dollar size would not be attainable. An internal publication that expanded upon the company's original mission statement laid out the credo that NeXT could achieve whatever it wanted to: "When the goal seems impossible, we don't lower our sights; we raise them. . . . Remember: There is no such thing as a problem, there is only work!"

Inadvertently, Jobs revealed the all-consuming nature of his investment in NeXT, and the existential investment he demanded from the others. *There is only work!* The boundaries of the real world could be simplified and reduced to the four walls of the new company. Outside was the world of the untidy, the ordinary, the profane; within, the world of true believers, who knew that anything was possible. For the chosen few invited to join, working at NeXT would be unlike working anywhere else; it would be like joining a millenarian sect, protected from the contaminating influence of the nondevout. The NeXT members would experience work not as a burden that ground them down but rather as an opportunity to escape the mundane, the chance for redemption through the transcendent accomplishments of a larger whole. *There is only work!* To change the world, however, one's dedication to the cause had to be total.

The purity of the commitment among the NeXT *members* was institutionalized by a brutal interview gauntlet through which prospective new employees had to pass. As at Apple, and as at Xerox PARC before that, the questions that peppered the candidates were unpredictable, the number of separate interrogations overwhelming. Jobs participated, reserving for himself the final interview of a candidate, whom he would put on the spot with an intentionally disarming query. It might concern personal appearance ("Why do you wear cuff links?"); it might concern self-appraisal ("Do you think you're great?"), which posed a difficult choice—should one declare humility or arrogance?—as deep traps surrounded either answer; or it might be naked provocation ("Why should I believe you know what the fuck you're doing?") At Bill Gates's Microsoft, the PARC tradition of plying candidates with intimidating questions also lived on and assumed its own distinctive character, with an emphasis on brain-teasers that has become legendary. A programmer there might be asked, How many gas stations are there in the United States? If you did not happen to have this number at your fingertips, you were permitted to reason out loud and show how an answer might be arrived at—if there are 250 million people, and one car for every four people, and 500 cars for each gas station, the answer would be 125,000. Or one might be asked why do many vending machines and jukeboxes have both letters and numbers (Answer: Too many numbers would be required if the buttons had only numbers.)[82] At NeXT, the questions ranged more widely, probing the depth of the person's willingness to invest totally in the quest. Jobs sought more than just very smart people; he required *believers.*

As progressive as NeXT's guiding philosophy was, the ancillary benefits and loans to its employees came only in 1987, when the company secured outside capital, and in its first few years, the company was relatively parsimonious in the salaries it extended. But this did not detract from building the ideal company; it merely served to insure the purity of motives of those who chose to sign on. Some of the new employees accepted pay cuts as deep as eighty percent to have the chance to join. If there was to be a material payoff, it would have to be down the road, and it would come not through salary but in "ship bonuses" promised for when the computers were shipped and in the employee-owned NeXT stock when the company went public. As in any start-up company, joining NeXT was not for those who sought a safe, predictable ride. One of the first people that NeXT recruited was Avie Tevanian, a software engineer who as a graduate student at Carnegie-Mellon University had been one of the lead designers of a new operating system, the underlying software, which Jobs wanted to use for his new computer. Flattered that Jobs said he was willing to "bet the company" on his work, Tevanian accepted Jobs's invitation to join NeXT upon finishing his Ph.D. Choosing NeXT meant that Tevanian had to turn down Microsoft, which had extended an offer that, with stock options, he valued at nearly a million dollars.[83] Such was the willingness of Jobs's recruits to strive for heavenly deliverance in the future, forgoing the rewards of the here-and-now. (By 1991, after the value of Microsoft stock had soared many-fold, Tevanian confessed that it was painful for him to check in *The Wall Street Journal* and calculate the current value of the stock options that Bill Gates had promised).[84]

As a final test of the earnestness of its prospective new hires, from 1985 until late 1988, when its first computer was publicly unveiled,

NeXT required that new employees accept employment without seeing so much as a glimpse of the product to which they were henceforth to devote all of their waking hours to. The computer remained wrapped in secrecy not just to keep details secure; it also served to reinforce the religious nature of the commitment that was asked. Denying prospective employees a prior look forced them to take what Jobs called in all seriousness a "leap of faith."[85] (As with other restrictive company policies, Jobs reserved for himself the right to make frequent exceptions and would provide previews for prospective recruits that he especially wanted to hire.)

Until the veil was lifted, the machine was not the lure so much as Jobs himself was, and all of the extraordinary history that stood behind him. NeXT employees bridled when outside observers suggested that they resembled Hare Krishna followers, and they strenuously disavowed blind allegiance to Jobs. But they did not have to swear undying fealty to him to be affected by the pull of his aura. How many rainmakers had track records like his? An unemotional review of Jobs's past successes led to the conclusion that remarkable success had befallen many people in his immediate vicinity in the past, and it was a simple step to assume that the odds favored that similar success would continue to come to those who stood by him in the future. If, when NeXT managers found that a candidate that they sought to recruit balked at the salary and benefits package that was offered, or resisted accepting the job offer for other reasons, they would resort to the ultimate weapon: "time to call in Steve." It was uncanny how deftly Jobs knew what each person most would want to hear, hitting the right buttons, with visions of greatness combined with measured dollops of flattery ("Hey, I hear you're the hottest designer on the planet").[86] To be invited to make history with Jobs was bewitching.

The educational mission of NeXT made the invitation to join exalted. One would not be making just another computer box but a machine that would be the answer to the dreams of the best and brightest on university campuses, giving the human mind the most powerful yet easy-to-use tools ever devised. The academic computer honchos who had supported the Macintosh were now even more excited about NeXT, a company that would be devoted to their needs not incidentally but exclusively. The marketing group at Apple was happily carrying out a revolution on college campuses, supplying Macintoshes; the only opportunity that could be more attractive was if another company was wholly dedicated to what Apple was already doing in higher education. That was NeXT. And the more good people that NeXT hired, the more that other good people wanted to join, too. When Kathryn Kilcoyne, a marketing person at Apple who had worked with Dan'l Lewin and Stacey Bressler in making the Apple University Consortium a success, mulled over an offer to move from Apple to NeXT, she asked the academic computer czars at several research universities for their advice. They all urged her to go to NeXT; an administrator at Stanford told her, "It's the cream of the cream who are going. If Apple is the best, then NeXT is the fucking Green Berets."

Stacey Bressler, though happy at Apple, also decided to move to NeXT. To an outside observer, Bressler would appear to have had everything that the other early NeXT employees sought: she already had made history by being an early member of the Macintosh group; she already had the satisfaction of seeing the personal computers that she sold used on college campuses in innovative ways; she already was financially secure, wealthy far beyond what a salaried employee could ever imagine. She was addicted to her work at Apple, working seven days a week, fifty-two weeks a year (except when Apple enforced a brief vacation by sending its best salespeople on a cruise). The principal reason for the otherwise contented Bressler to switch from Apple to NeXT was because she wanted to be right at ground-zero when the next Macintosh took off from the launch pad. Though others would think of her as belonging to the original Macintosh team, in her own mind she had just missed inclusion. She had been in the early group, but not *the* earliest founding group with Raskin and Tribble, and she had been on the East Coast, conducting her guerrilla marketing campaign on campuses, thousands of miles from the Macintosh group bunker in Cupertino, California. Jobs's invitation to join him, Dan'l Lewin, and the other Macintosh alumni at NeXT offered a second chance at gaining admittance to the sanctum sanctorum where history would be created. If someone like Bressler was not immune from the siren song of Jobs and the invitation to step onto the pages of the history book of the future, one can imagine how powerfully attractive the invitation was for those who had been much farther removed from the Macintosh story.

Many of the people NeXT hired first were people like Bressler and Kilcoyne, recruited from Apple. But after the initial flurry, NeXT sought to diversify the sources of its recruits and avoid replicating Apple in miniature. Taking the best practices from many companies was another way that NeXT could outsmart its far larger competition. NeXT was a tabula rasa, and Jobs and the early employees were convinced that they could selectively choose what would be inscribed. Only the best of the best would be permitted in; all others and their baggage would be left at the door.

At NeXT's birth one sees a strange paradox: the company that aspired to serve as the model for the twenty-first century resembled nothing as much as a throwback to the past, the mid-nineteenth-century American utopian community that was centered on a charismatic leader. Charisma, when used today to refer to a business leader, usually refers to some form of indefinable magnetism. The charisma that Jobs had, however, was more than this—it was the power that a leader, religious or not, possesses that derives from a perceived connection to the overarching questions of human existence.[87] Jobs was not engaged in the business of selling breakfast cereal or bathroom faucets; he was not even focused on the pursuit of profits, per se. Others could pursue the mundane. He was after the much larger quarry of *changing the world*, rescuing computer users from the existing prison of mediocrity, making a dent in the universe, carrying out revolution, claiming an enduring place in history; it was the extraordinary scope of his ambition that was the ultimate source of his appeal. Charismatic power cannot exist in isolation, however, without followers. Bryan Wilson, a student of charisma, puts the matter colorfully: "If a man runs naked down the street proclaiming that he alone can save others from impending doom, and if he immediately wins a following, then he is a charismatic leader: a social relationship has come into being. If he does not win a following, he is simply a lunatic."[88]

Once the charismatic leader secures followers, then retention must be ensured. The organization that the leader builds employs a number of mechanisms, some subtle, some not, that are designed precisely for this end, to reinforce the commitment of the followers to the mission and to preserve the leader's charisma. It should not surprise us, then, to see that many lines of correspondence can be drawn between the nineteenth-century utopian communities (like Amana, New Harmony, and Oneida) and the late twentieth-century NeXT. The same functional purposes underlay many features: demanding that members make a financial sacrifice as a condition for admission; physically isolating the commune to minimize any potential disruption of group cohesion; strictly controlling visitors and all traffic across the boundary; using special rituals and vocabularies to reinforce group identity; fanning a feeling of persecution from the outside to bind members together.[89] Perhaps most eerie of all to see in both the communes and NeXT is the frequent use of public mortification at the hands of the leader, when a member would be subjected to severe criticism and was expected to confess to failings. This would be a critical component of NeXT culture—blistering, humiliating criticism by Jobs of designated individuals that could reduce the employee to tears, but served a functional purpose in reminding all members of the primacy of group over individual interests.

If Jobs had pursued an earlier dream that he had had at Apple, he would have built a town literally like a nineteenth-century utopian settlement, a world unto itself. In the early 1980s, Jobs had directed

Apple to purchase hundreds of acres of undeveloped land in south San Jose (right across from an IBM plant) where he planned to develop Appletown, which Jobs imagined as a "much more enlightened implementation" of a company town, where no line separated work life and personal life. There Apple would provide housing, company stores, recreational facilities, complete immersion in Apple culture. His model was Disney World, a state within a state, with its own fire and police departments.[90] Appletown was never built before its sponsor, Jobs, left Apple, but at NeXT its spirit of benevolent enclosure found psychological expression in the new company's culture and limited physical expression in the hermetic office surrounded by the open space of the Stanford research park.

One could compare Steve Jobs at NeXT to other kinds of charismatic leaders in the past. The turn-of-the-century German sociologist Max Weber called attention long ago to the importance of charisma in economic life, but Weber showed that charismatic leadership was ill-suited to the management of the large, bureaucratic organization, in which success depended upon steadiness and professional expertise. Charismatic leadership, however, was often seen elsewhere, in what Weber called "booty capitalism": colonial adventures; slave trading; piracy; private financing of military ventures; risky financial transactions.[91] NeXT was innocent of planning piratical depredations, and so the comparison may seem unfair. But booty capitalism was enormously risky by its nature and thus required an extraordinary leader to attract and keep followers if the venture were to succeed, and the same held true for NeXT. To start a new computer company in the shadow of an already enormously successful one, in a market that was fast maturing, aiming for a billion-dollar size after Jobs himself had declared earlier at Apple that it was too late for another billion-dollar computer company to be hatched[92]—against such odds a charismatic leader was a necessity.

The utopian identity of NeXT, however, was fundamentally in conflict with its *thirtysomething* identity. When NeXT was founded, Jobs did something he had never done when working on the Macintosh—he acknowledged that his employees had families. So for a while he spoke about the importance of getting home to the family at the end of the day, and the company party was a picnic with the Pickle Family Circus hired to perform, instead of an evening party for adults. His confederates felt the onset of middle age, and Jobs confessed that he too was slowing down a bit ("I can't stay up four nights in a row like I used to").[93] The official line, then, was that NeXT did not expect the round-the-clock commitment that one could exact in a twentysomething group like the team that had built the Macintosh. Dan'l Lewin declared that he and the others at NeXT were not running a sprint but a marathon, which meant that the work week would be a sedate sixty or seventy hours a week, not a hundred.[94] But in practice the pressure to resume the old pace crept back, exhausting even a stalwart soldier like Stacey Bressler, who in 1987 decided to leave NeXT and the bid to repeat Macintosh history and instead chose to work at a relatively sedate company, Hewlett-Packard, where one did not have to work seven days a week. At NeXT, the employees who were held up as exemplars in company meetings were those who worked straight through weekends or had otherwise distinguished themselves by a physically extraordinary skein of hours devoted to the common cause. NeXT was tiny, the odds against it long, its mission glorious. There was really only one way to remain a happy member, and that was to renounce competing claims on one's attention and make one's dedication total. As the leader had done. As Ken Kesey had said in the 1960s, one was either on the bus or off. There were no seats held for laggards.

Perot's Magic

N eXT began its life with a major, if unrecognized, problem: it had too much money, courtesy of a single person—Steve Jobs—whose plans for the company were unformed and innocent of financial analysis. Others may have envied NeXT and the $7 million that Jobs bestowed upon it, but in fact time would show that relying upon a founding benefactor like Jobs for its financing ultimately hurt NeXT because it meant that the company did not have to face the discipline of assembling financial numbers that made sense, looking hard at itself as a business proposition, and defining milestones by which it could measure whether it was on track or not. The ordinary entrepreneur, who starts without capital and is forced by necessity to assemble a business plan for banks or other prospective investors, must give attention to such matters as surveying the existing market and justifying projections of estimated revenues and expenses. Even if the business plan turns out to be an exercise in wishful thinking, it at least can be credited with forcing the supplicant to give some thought to these matters. At NeXT, however, Jobs and the other founders gave themselves dispensation to skip the prosaic ritual of planning. They had Jobs's money and did not need outside financing. Also, their spontaneity served well in the civil suit that Apple had filed against them—the very lack of a business plan would help them establish the absence of premeditated "nefarious" schemes.

Most important of all, however, the founders proceeded by seat-of-the-pants instincts because of the underlying feeling of invincibility that their earlier success at Apple had instilled in them. At Apple, and later at NeXT, they might have liked to talk about serving ordinary people, "mere mortals," but they themselves were not mortals; they were the gods who had created a personal-computer universe out of nothingness. Jobs, for example, displayed little modesty in NeXT press releases, describing himself as the person who had overseen the growth of Apple into a two-billion-dollar company and had led the growth of Apple's Macintosh Division into a billion-dollar division. Rich Page described himself and the other cofounders as if they constituted a dream All-Star team: "When you look at the people at NeXT, you can see that all the bases are covered. Nobody has quite the track record these people do." He warned that in business the unprepared perish: "You have to have your act together. And we do."[95]

Jobs and the founders felt as if they could do no wrong, but the entire industry at the time shared a similar false feeling of invincibility. John Warnock, a PARC alumnus who cofounded his own software company, Adobe Systems, and who is a friend of Jobs, looks back upon NeXT's founding in 1985 as a product of that historical moment when everyone said, "Gee, because we're so profitable, we must be doing everything right." NeXT was born at what we now see was the twilight of the early era of the personal computer. The Apple exiles at NeXT were pumped with adrenaline and self-confidence and unaware of how the incredible growth that the industry had experienced obscured misjudgments that would have been fatal in any other setting. The market in the early 1980s had been forgiving because personal computers were in such demand. Unfortunately for NeXT, by the time it would have its own machines ready, the personal-computer industry would have entered a wholly distinct new era, in which competition was much more intense and the market much less tolerant of missteps.

Having watched Macintosh sweep rapidly across college campuses, Jobs and the others at NeXT imagined that they would be able to repeat the feat by offering a more powerful machine tailored to the needs of higher education. All that NeXT had to do was to visit campuses, listen to what professors and administrators wanted, and build the computer they requested. A consortium of twenty large research universities already had invited far larger companies—IBM, Hewlett-Packard, and Apple—to build powerful "3M" computers for universities, but no company had yet accepted the challenge of transforming a computer that then cost $15,000 to $25,000 into one that could be sold profitably for $3,000. Their timidity gave NeXT its big opportunity. Jobs believed NeXT could succeed where the other companies dared not venture because it had none of their baggage to carry along, like bloated middle management and vested interests in old technology.[96] It could travel light. This was all the planning that the new company felt it needed.

Its intended customers confirmed the company's inclination to believe in its own blessed invincibility. First, the NeXT founders were encouraged by the reception they received at Stanford, where they had meetings with a number of key administrators on the same day that Jobs and the NeXT founders also met with their lawyers about the Apple suit. By good fortune, the very next week the annual meeting of Educom, the national organization of computer administrators in higher education, was held in Austin, Texas, which gave NeXT the perfect opportunity to make its pitch to its intended customers. Jobs and his associates stood up at one of the sessions and introduced their new venture, describing what they wanted to accomplish. NeXT placed itself at the service of the universities: "You've got to tell us what to do." It was an extremely persuasive presentation. One member of the audience turned to Michael Carter, an administrator at Stanford, and said, "I saw 200

IBM engineers [at the Austin facility working on the new generation of IBM's workstation], and I've seen these six people, and I
give them an odds-on chance." By visiting a number of campuses
and repeating the same invitation, asking administrators what they
wanted, the NeXT contingent secured advice and basked in its
association with Stanford, Carnegie-Mellon, Brown, UC-Berkeley,
the University of Texas, the University of Michigan, the University of Illinois, Rice, Princeton, Duke, and MIT. In its composi-
tion, the group overlapped considerably with the Apple University
Consortium, which served to further encourage the NeXT founders
in their belief that they were well on their way to repeating the
success of the Macintosh.

The pivotal importance of Dan'l Lewin at this stage is a reminder
of how technology choices—here, the decision about what model
of personal computers universities should purchase—are affected
by personal relationships and unrelated intangible assets such as a
gregarious nature and good looks. It was Lewin much more than
Jobs who was instrumental in enlisting the immediate support of
higher education. By virtue of his chiseled features and large,
muscular frame, strengthened by years of competitive swimming
(Stanford's Michael Carter's first thought had been of Clark Kent
and Superman upon meeting him), Lewin could enter a room and
command attention. But he deployed this physical power disarm-
ingly, surprising those who met him with solicitude, listening in-
tently to prospective customers. The academics who were
responsible for computer fiefdoms on college campuses normally
disliked computer-company salespeople and kept their distance as
much as possible, but they liked and trusted Lewin and regarded
him as a friend. They had worked together—and made history
together—in the Apple University Consortium; now NeXT offered
the opportunity to team with Lewin and make history again. They
cheered NeXT onward.

The euphoria of the beginning soon evaporated, however. The
first company retreat was an occasion to voice concerns about

NeXT's master plan and timetable and was captured on film by an Emmy-winning filmmaker, John Nathan. An earlier film made by Nathan, an adaptation of the bestselling business book *In Search of Excellence*, had featured Apple Computer as one of the examples of excellence in business practice. Though a television critic had regarded the Apple philosophy as "spooky," disparaging the remarks of a young Apple sales manager who had said "Here is how we want the world to be. We want to convert people,"[97] Steve Jobs had loved the program. When Nathan called him about doing a segment on Jobs and NeXT for a program in progress on outstanding entrepreneurs, Jobs was immediately receptive. He told Nathan "you made the best film about us ever," and invited him and his film crew to come along on the company retreat. Company attorneys had told Jobs that as long as the Apple suit was pending, under no circumstances should he allow an outsider in to observe the company. Jobs's decision to disregard their advice and let Nathan film would, thanks to a stroke of luck, turn out to be fateful for the company.

Nathan intended to make what he unabashedly called a valentine. He assured each of his subjects that he was looking not for the "dark corners" of investigative journalism but rather for "exciting cultural models."[98] Jobs was also receptive because he thought that he would get to review the film before airing (he was mistaken; Public Broadcasting System rules at the time forbid it). Moreover, Jobs knew he could be the de facto codirector and could tell Nathan where to set up the cameras and when to turn them off if discussion touched on an overly sensitive issue. Given Nathan's intention to prepare a confection of inspirational puffery, and Jobs's active role in directing the filming, it is something of a miracle that the first company retreat made it into Nathan's program. The segment shows a company filled with considerable self-doubt and disagreement, which is to say it showed a real company with real people engaged in real debate. There was nothing hokey or contrived about what was captured on film.

The NeXT employees in the fall of 1985 were clear-eyed about the problems that they faced. They knew that in order to break the allegiance of university customers to established computer lines, the NeXT computer would have to be more than just marginally better, it would have to be "an order of magnitude" better. They knew that time was working against them: they had to deliver the computer to the market by the spring of 1987 in order to be considered for fall 1987 purchases. Universities usually make large purchase decisions only once a year. If NeXT was late, it would not have another chance until the following academic year's purchase cycle began again, which would be too late to prevent the company from exhausting its start-up capital and technological lead. "If we don't deliver this by spring of 1987, we're out of business," said one employee. Jobs too saw clearly—even though he would lose sight of this later—that the world was not standing still for him. If NeXT was late, even if the company could survive a little longer financially, its computer would be obsolete even before the first machine was pushed out the door.

At the retreat, Joanna Hoffman, an early member of the Macintosh team who had joined NeXT, challenged Jobs on the practicality of holding to spring 1987 as the target. She acknowledged that "reality distortion" provided a motivational spur, but she worried that paying lip-service to an unrealistic schedule would result in hasty design decisions, creating problems that would have to be addressed down the road and would result in additional delays. Jobs cut her off in midsentence: "See, I think we have to drive a stake in the ground somewhere, and I think if we miss this window, then a whole series of events come into play. We can't sell enough units in '87 to pay for our operating costs." Worse, word would get out that NeXT was not doing well. "A lot of the credibility starts to erode." George Crow, the hardware engineer who was one of the cofounders, piped up and sniped at the tardiness of the software engineers. Jobs, visibly irritated, the pitch of his voice climbing high, snapped, "Well, George, I can't change the world, you know.

What do you want me to do?" He returned to the idea of the opportunity of the present moment to deliver a machine that others could not; NeXT had an open window that provided the perfect entrée to the university market: "We've been given it, and thank god we've been given it. Nobody else's done it. It's a wonderful window. We have eighteen months." If they failed to deliver their machine on time, he said, the company would fail, due to the hard realities of the marketplace and regardless of "what I say or anybody else says."

Jobs conceded that in the past, at Apple, they had not always used their heads. He said, "We can do better, in many respects, because we are wiser, and smarter and know more." But besides using their heads, he also wanted NeXT employees to use their hearts, to build the company out of "passion," just as they had done in the early Apple days. "We're doing this," he said, "because we really care about the higher educational process; not because we want to make a buck." Devoting themselves to higher education meant that they had to stick to what university administrators had told them: the price of the machine absolutely could not go over $3,000. At the time of the retreat, Jobs fully understood the inviolability of this criterion, even if NeXT might be tempted to offer its customers better technology at a higher price. Jobs showed that he had listened to the academics: "They didn't say, if you make it three times faster, we'd pay $4,000. They didn't say that. They said, you go over $3,000, forget it. That's the magic number." Unfortunately, he suffered amnesia on this point later on.

In January 1986, NeXT and Apple reached an out-of-court settlement that finally removed the cloud of the lawsuit. NeXT agreed to a six-month moratorium on hiring away any more employees from Apple and to a noncompete stipulation that required the NeXT computer to be more powerful than any of Apple's offerings, which Jobs was delighted to agree to, aware of the ammunition such a "restriction" would provide NeXT against Apple in future marketing battles.[99] But the suit had cost NeXT valuable time; until it was resolved and the permissible legal boundaries defined, Jobs and his engineers had held off work on designing the computer and had joined Dan'l Lewin, the head of marketing, in an extended cross-country tour of campuses, listening to what their future customers had to say.[100]

By January 1986, when the legal clouds lifted and work could begin in earnest on the new machine, the company found itself already behind on its timetable. If delivering a finished machine by the spring of 1987 had seemed difficult to achieve in the fall of 1985, it seemed even more unlikely by the time the company held its second retreat in early 1986, which was also captured on film by Nathan. "The Honeymoon Is Over" was the theme that Jobs suggested to the gathering. No longer would they be able to rest on past laurels or to seek the solace of feeling victimized by the lawsuit and lost time. "Bottom line is, the world doesn't really care," he said. NeXT was now just another start-up, and would be judged henceforth by what its product was and in how timely a fashion it was delivered to market.

Not only was time slipping by too quickly, but so too was the money. Jobs complained aloud that "we're not scrounging." The company had just bought new Macintoshes instead of finding friends at Apple to buy them for NeXT at deep employee discounts. He complained, "We stopped nickel and diming for that stuff and it all adds up." Susan Barnes chimed in, saying that NeXT had not been sufficiently tough with vendors, who assumed that NeXT had $20 or $30 million in financial assets. "We signal deep pockets out there," she said.

Was it any wonder that outsiders got that impression, however? For Jobs to lounge on the sofa, berating himself and everyone else for insufficient "start-up hustle," was like an obese loudmouth lecturing others about the virtues of dieting. The pattern that Jobs had set when spending on the luxurious offices in Palo Alto, the Paul Rand logo, and all the rest, was to binge first and save remorse for later. He was absolutely right—at NeXT they had not kept the "war" in perspective: "the war is called not-run-out-of-money-until-we-get-our-product-on-the-market." He was not able, however, to take his own advice. At the end of 1986, NeXT was out of money. And their machine was not even close to being ready. Unbeholden to outside investors, Jobs had exercised the freedom to spend his own money as he wished. It is certainly strange, however, that the man whom *Inc.* magazine would later name as "Entrepreneur of the Decade" conserved his $7 million at NeXT no better than a child deposited at a candy store with a bulging piggy bank. Born too rich for its own good, NeXT was a start-up that was privileged, and crippled, with fiscal complacency; by the time Jobs and the other senior managers awakened to the limits of its founding capital and tried to practice economies, it was too little too late. The money was gone.

When NeXT had been founded, Jobs intended that the company would remain solely in the hands of himself and his employees. This was part of the pitch to the early recruits—NeXT would always be employee-owned. When the money ran out in late 1986, in theory, Jobs could have dipped again into his own money to keep NeXT capitalized. But a prudent businessperson knows that resorting to such a course would be folly. When the initial capital is exhausted, the financial risk of failure must be shared with other investors, not merely to husband the founder's personal wealth but more importantly to verify the company's viability. If no one can be found to coinvest in a going concern, then the founder knows that it would be foolish to continue putting more money in. And future customers would know it would be foolish to buy products from such a company, too. In the case of NeXT, university computer czars wanted reassurance that the company was more than an expensive hobby for Jobs. It was time for NeXT to look for outside investors and put itself to the test.

When Jobs sent out a prospectus to venture capital firms on both coasts, seeking investment for a small share of equity in NeXT, his invitation met with universal disdain.[101] Venture capitalists had been eager to invest in NeXT at the time of its founding in 1985, when the company was bathed in a magical aura from the previous success at Apple, when thirty-year-old Steve Jobs was believed to have a Midas touch, when the historical moment was so full of possibility. Then, Jobs had spurned offers from outside investors; now, in late 1986, he had to humble himself and seek their assistance. But Jobs being Jobs, he did not humble himself very much. He presented a take-it-or-leave-it proposition that was not open for negotiation, and the most critical part of any such proposition, the valuation of the company, was pegged at $30 million (for a meager ten-percent stake, then, a venture capitalist would have to put in $3 million, which was almost half of the capital that had gone into the company to date). Given that NeXT had no products and no revenue, prospective investors regarded the $30 million figure as outrageously high. Jobs could not tell these outsiders the real reason he had arrived at the $30 million—it had nothing to do with NeXT's financials and everything to do with Jobs's wish to best a local record held by a company called Trilogy, for the highest valuation to date of a Silicon Valley company before it went public. The $30 million would set a new record and Jobs would not budge from it. The venture capitalists stayed away.

Just as NeXT was in the most dire straits, rescue came from a completely unexpected source: H. Ross Perot, who had not even been approached by NeXT. Perot's interest in the company had been piqued by John Nathan's program "The Entrepreneurs," which aired nationally in November 1986. A snippy review in *The New York Times* ("Its heroes of American capitalism no longer build better mouse traps; they talk and talk and hold meetings")[102] failed to acknowledge the rarity of an intimate glimpse of internal company debates in the raw. But Perot was impressed by what he saw and was especially taken with Jobs, whom he called "Mr. Electricity." Perot said that as he watched the program "I was finishing their sentences for them"[103] (apparently unaware that finishing the other's sentences was precisely what Steve Jobs and John

Sculley had said about each other when they were in their courtship phase). The next day Perot called Jobs to compliment him on the program and added, "If you ever need an investor, call me."[104]

The timing could not have been more propitious. It seemed in fact too good to be true. When Jobs hung up, he told his colleagues, "You'd never guess who just called. This is incredible." So as not to appear desperate, Jobs waited a week before calling Perot back and asking about his offer. Perot reaffirmed his interest and sent three of his senior lieutenants to California to visit NeXT. A similar visit had taken place a few years earlier, when Jobs's Apple had invited Perot's Electronic Data Systems to become an investor. Nothing had come out of that earlier visit. But this time, after Perot's team had departed, Jobs took his pitch directly to Perot. It was clear that Perot's associates had considerable experience trolling for investment prospects in the computer industry, practicing "due diligence" and examining possible deals carefully. Jobs was adamant that NeXT not be treated like others. In this he was shrewd—close analysis of NeXT, Inc.'s financials would sink any proposed deal. So instead of permitting more rounds of scrutiny and meetings with number-crunching MBAs, Jobs wisely put the proposition to Perot as a deal that should stand or fall on the basis of personal chemistry (and impulsivity). Perot was amenable. He came out to California, as Jobs had insisted, and spent a day saying hello to each of the several dozen NeXT employees. After a few hours of exchanging pleasantries, he had made up his mind to invest, on whatever terms were proposed. He did not care about the numbers; he would let the NeXT people worry about such things. He told them, "I pick the jockeys, and the jockeys pick the horses and ride 'em. You guys are the ones I'm betting on, so you figure it out."

When a billionaire says to a tiny company that is out of money, "Here's my checkbook, you fill out the check," it is a moment to be savored, even for a multimillionaire like Jobs. Though NeXT's Susan Barnes had complained that the outside world saw nothing but deep pockets when they looked at Jobs and NeXT, Jobs himself was susceptible to the same tendency to see a dollar sign and many zeros instead of the actual person when dealing with one of the few people in the country who had pockets deeper than his own. He offered Perot a deal much less generous than the one that had been shopped around unsuccessfully to venture capitalists. It was based on a valuation of NeXT put at a cool $100 million. The very roundness of the number might have suggested to the wary that the $100 million valuation had been plucked out of the air, but Perot did not care. He cheerfully accepted. He chose to remain oblivious to the better terms that he could have had or to the future designs that NeXT had on more of his money. When Perot was in the NeXT offices for the brief negotiations, at one point, out of his presence, NeXT held its own caucus and one of the senior NeXT executives said to Jobs, "Boy, if we've got this much from Ross, maybe if things go well, we can get more later on." Jobs's eyes gleamed. "Don't let on to Ross that that's what we're trying to do."

In Perot, they had found the perfect benefactor: rich as Croesus and eager to invest without questions, placing his faith totally in the "jockeys" themselves. Jobs did not settle for the good news itself; as is his wont he insisted on giving his account of the news a little twist, just so, to make NeXT appear even more desirable and successful. He told the press that NeXT had previously spurned any outside investment in the company (no hint that the outside investors had been the ones doing the spurning), but had been favorably impressed by Perot's approach: "Rather than just looking at the numbers, he started with the most important things—looking under the hood and evaluating the quality of the idea and of the people."[105] In Jobs's version, then, NeXT had chosen *Perot* for the privilege of being permitted to invest.

The notion that investment in NeXT should not rest on the numbers and should be seen as a privilege was also the message that NeXT had broadcast to the leading research universities, who were invited to invest in the company that would be producing a product expressly for them. It is remarkable that despite the cash crunch, Jobs steadfastly maintained a take-it-or-leave-it attitude toward the offer that he extended. He made it clear that he would not put up with the standard scrutiny of due diligence, in which the university's junior accountants would visit NeXT and pore over the books. Jobs's pitch was simple and impatient: "We have built successful products in the past, and you can roll the dice on us if you want. But this remains our show and we won't stand for extended investigation." He did no better with universities than with the venture capitalists; even a cursory glance showed that the valuation, measured by any conventional ruler, was far too high.

Perot's blessing, however, convinced two universities, Stanford and Carnegie-Mellon, to join in and invest, too. Perot put in $20 million, Jobs put in another $5 million, and the two universities each put in $660,000, increasing NeXT's nominal valuation from $100 million to $126 million after the new investment. Jobs owned 63 percent of the company; Perot, 16 percent; Stanford and Carnegie-Mellon, 0.5 percent each; NeXT employees, 20 percent. The money that the two universities put in was dwarfed by the Perot investment, but their endorsement of the company was more important than the dollars they brought in. The imprimatur of two distinguished research universities, combined with the presumption that a sound business plan had passed Ross Perot's muster, conferred upon NeXT new clothes for public parade: solidity, legitimacy, bankability, a bright future. And Jobs had turned his $12 million investment in NeXT into an equity share that, thanks to Perot's willingness to sign off on the valuation, was now worth on paper more than $79 million. Not a shoddy gain for a year and a half of work. What a remarkable turn of events had followed that fateful showing of "The Entrepreneurs": from the brink of collapse, NeXT in one stroke had been saved and now could gloat that Ross Perot, with his unlimited resources, and Stanford and Carnegie-Mellon, with their prestige, were in their corner. Jobs bragged that the

$126 million valuation was the highest for "any company in Silicon Valley history without a product." And all this accomplished without any damaging publicity about the cash crisis.

Why would Ross Perot be so pleased to receive a mere 16 percent of NeXT when his $20 million investment would have secured a large majority ownership of a similar start-up, or as *Newsweek* put it, "would buy everything but the founder's firstborn child"?[106] Let us begin with the most obvious reasons. First, Perot did not belong to the venture capitalist camp, which played by a strict set of unsentimental business rules. Rather, he was an individual investor, acting on his own whims, the prototypical "angel," as they have come to be called, the name coming from the private investors who finance theatrical productions on Broadway.[107] Off-Broadway, so to speak, wealthy angels invest in promising start-ups as a pleasurable avocation, usually going in earlier, taking on greater risk, and being more patient than venture capital firms.[108] Some angels assert control over management. For example, Phillip Romano, who used the money he earned from his restaurant chain Fuddrucker's to make investments as an angel, explained his insistence on taking control this way: "It's my ball; it's my bat; we'll play my way." Ross Perot, however, purposely chose not to take a majority position in investments such as that in NeXT, reasoning that "the builders must have control."[109] A second reason that Perot was so casual about his NeXT investment was because $20 million, whether it vanished without a trace or grew manyfold, does not have much of an impact on the net worth of a billionaire. Perot said he hoped to get a tenfold return on his NeXT investment, but conceded "that don't rock the boat very much."[110]

Perot emphatically disavowed that he was a softie who had invested in NeXT for anything but the most sound of business reasons. He pointed to Jobs and the reassembled Macintosh crew and declared that given their past success "in terms of a start-up company, it's one that carries the least risk of any I've seen in 25 years in the computer industry"[111] (or calling upon a classic Texan simile on another occasion, Perot suggested that investing in the Apple veterans at NeXT was like drilling right next to "a producing well").[112] Industry analysts remained skeptical, however.[113] Richard Shaffer, the dean of technology stock-watchers, could only shake his head in disbelief at the $126 million valuation of NeXT to which Perot had acquiesced. Shaffer said, "At that kind of valuation, by the usual rules, it should not only have a finished product, it should be shipping and it should be selling at a rate of $20 million or $30 million a year."[114]

Clearly, Perot was *not* applying the usual rules. Another rather obvious reason that he invested in NeXT with such equanimity was that he was less interested in the money than in the invigorating association with a group of young, smart people. He did not use the phrase *thirtysomething* but he implicitly saw NeXT in terms of its providing a youthful tonic. "It is kind of fun," he said, "when you've been around as long as I have to watch these young guys in their 30s."[115] Like Jobs, Perot liked to brag to others with proprietary pride about the collective smarts of NeXT employees, exemplified by Bud Tribble's double degrees in medicine and neurophysiology. Moreover, Perot shared with the NeXT group an interest in improving education, and he was taken by the democratizing potential of a scholar's workstation such as the one that Jobs painted for him, a machine that could make available to students throughout the country the best professors at the leading universities, whose courses could be distilled into special software that could be distributed on NeXT computers to the smallest liberal arts school, endowment or no. This was the sort of revolution that could enlist even a prim patriot like Perot, who at that point was at loose ends himself, having surrendered his personal stake in EDS to GM the year before, and having not yet started a new computer-services company, Perot Systems. Jobs was the personal-computer insurgents' chief propagandist, and Perot was ready to follow him wherever the future would be created.[116] Investing in NeXT was like purchasing a front-row seat for the revolution.

A NeXT crusade appealed to Perot's patriotism, too. Jobs was determined to manufacture his new computer on American soil, demonstrating to all doubters that U.S. manufacturers could hold their own against Japanese competition. This jibed perfectly with Perot's own campaign to awaken complacent U.S. industry to the Japanese threat. He often cited the fact that scrap steel and wastepaper were the principal U.S. exports shipped to Japan out of the New York port; they returned as automobiles and as cardboard boxes containing consumer electronics. We were being reduced, Perot lamented, to scrap salesmen.[117] Keeping manufacturing in the United States was essential; if Americans weren't able to make what they invented, "we might as well start learning Japanese."[118] Steve Jobs could stand as the exemplar of a renascent U.S. industry, showing that Americans could match the Japanese with equal strength in manufacturing. The image that Perot painted of Jobs, however, was a curious amalgam of Perot's favorite artist, Norman Rockwell, and socialist realism. One thinks of the anonymous revolutionary posters with the oversized Proletarian Hero standing in the center, staring at some unseen threat off to the side. Hands and work clothes blackened by oil and grime; face set with steely determination; a bodybuilder's oversized musculature. What Perot imagined was a distinctively American variation on the motif— instead of a proletarian Iron Man, we would have multimillionaire Jobs, who was the closest thing we *could* have in the age of electronics to a dirt-under-the-nails paragon, an industrial leader for the Pepsi generation, someone whose example should shame his unprincipled peers, the best and the brightest who were headed to Wall Street to pursue the quick buck.[119]

Just as socialist realism was anything but realistic, so too the image that Perot had of Jobs was idealized almost beyond recognition. This was another important, if less known, reason why Perot chose to invest in NeXT. His image of Jobs was of a boy genius whose family had literally stepped from a Norman Rockwell painting. Here is Perot addressing the National Press Club:

> I'm going to close with a brief story about one interesting experience I've had. A young man, so bright they let him sit in the engineering classes at Stanford in high school, so poor he couldn't afford to go to college—working in his garage at night, playing with computer chips, which was his hobby, his dad came in one day, who—his dad looks like a character out of a Norman Rockwell painting—and said, "Steve, either make something you can sell or go get a job." Sixty days later, in a wooden box that his dad made for him, the first Apple computer was created. And this high school graduate literally changed the world.[120]

At the risk of appearing churlish, we might point out a couple of the more glaring inaccuracies in Perot's thumbnail biography. Jobs held only a high school diploma not because he was too poor to go to college but because he lacked the motivation to complete studies that he had started; Reed, an expensive private college in Oregon where he began and aborted his college career, was not the only college available to a California high school graduate like Jobs. And it was the other Steve, Steve Wozniak, who built that first Apple computer and who is unaccountably missing from this picture. Or what are we to make of Perot's description of the impression that Jobs had made upon him in "The Entrepreneurs": "smart, modest, and not on any kind of an ego trip"? Steve Jobs, modest? Able to contain his ego? Not even his closest friends would make such claims on his behalf. Or what about Perot's summary of Jobs's vanquishing the evil giant: "This young man went up against IBM in a capital-intensive business and ate 'em alive."[121] What happened to the instant success of the IBM Personal Computer when introduced in 1981 and the blow it dealt to Apple? Who ate whom alive? Or how could we join Perot in paying obeisance to Jobs's business sagacity, the equivalent of what Perot called "50 years of business experience," when we now can look back and see that Jobs had committed the most dunderheaded blunder in modern finance: he sold off most of his Apple stock in 1985, at its absolute nadir, instead of holding on for two more years, in which time it increased in value *eightfold*.

It is worth lingering for a moment on just how costly Jobs's impatience was. Jobs had somehow convinced himself that Apple could not survive without him. He told David Bunnell, the founding publisher of a Macintosh magazine, that Apple would fail and that he had sold all but one share of his Apple stock (the one remaining share ensured that he could continue to get stockholder reports and watch Apple's impending self-destruction).[122] Jobs's disposition of his Apple stock, in fact, was not effected with the dramatic flourish that Jobs spoke of. Publicly available Securities and Exchange Commission records show that the liquidation of many of his shares proceeded in steps over a few months during the middle and latter portions of 1985. However, local legend does not do justice to the enormity of the fortune that Jobs lost by this sell-off on the eve of the dramatic climb of Apple stock. Among venture capitalists it was rumored that Jobs had left $300 million on the table. This figure may seen too large to be credible but SEC filings show that, in fact, $300 million was too low. The arithmetic is a matter of public record, and the actual figure is nearly $700 million in paper losses that could be attributed to the timing of his sale.* NeXT would have to be very, *very* successful, if Jobs were to simply recoup what one might say he lost by liquidating his Apple holdings at an inopportune time.

One final contributing reason for Perot's interest in NeXT in 1986 should be mentioned, and it is the most intriguing of all the

---

*Jobs sold 4.028 million shares in 1985, netting about $70.5 million, allowing for a gentle climb in share prices during the course of this period. If he had held on through 1987, after a two-for-one stock split and the peak price that was reached in the fall of that year, those original four million-some shares, presplit, would have fetched $481,346,000 or something in the vicinity. That means that just the publicly visible pile of chips that Jobs left on the table was about $411 million. In addition, if beyond public view Jobs did indeed sell his remaining shares of Apple stock in early 1986, we should add a stack of chips worth $275 million to the pile left on the table as well.

reasons because at the time it was not widely known: Perot regretted that he had not bought Microsoft from Bill Gates in 1979 when it was still a small start-up. Gates, who turned twenty-four that year, had been invited to Perot's Dallas offices to chat about the possibility of selling. Years later, the two men would recall different figures that Gates suggested—Gates remembered asking between $6 million and $15 million, and Perot remembered a much higher range, between $40 and $60 million. Even at the highest figure, hindsight showed the purchase still would have been a bargain for Perot. In 1986, when Microsoft went public, the valuation of the company quickly passed the $1 billion mark. The opportunity that Perot missed in 1979 owed partly to Gates's lack of interest in selling, and partly to the prudence of Perot and his advisers like Mort Meyerson. Gates wanted much more than Perot was willing to pay; "we did not have the leap of faith," as Meyerson put it. Perot would later call his failure to pursue the deal one of the biggest business mistakes he had ever made. He insisted that it was not the lost billions he mourned (by 1992, when Perot launched his presidential campaign, Microsoft's valuation passed $20 billion and Gates's personal net worth was about double that of Perot's), but rather it was not being able to watch at close hand Gates and Microsoft make business history. He lost "an opportunity to buy a ringside seat." The lesson he drew from this was that there are moments in business when caution should be thrown to the wind: "I should've just said, 'Now Bill, you set the price, and I'll take it.' "[123]

The story of the abortive discussion in 1979 between Gates and Perot became publicly known only many years later, but it puts an entirely new light on Perot's willingness in late 1986 to place Steve Jobs and the fledgling NeXT under his protective wing. If anyone was a candidate to repeat the feat of Bill Gates at Microsoft, it would seem to have been Jobs. No wonder, then, that Perot was happy to accept whatever terms Jobs offered; when Jobs demanded a "leap of faith," Perot, mindful of what had happened in 1979 with Gates, did not hesitate this time. But the influence of the earlier episode involving Gates was not visible to others, who could only see Perot embracing Jobs and the NeXT crew. A simple syllogism led to the public placing faith in NeXT on the basis of Perot's reassuring presence: Ross Perot is a billionaire; one does not become a billionaire without possessing the capacity to make the shrewdest of business judgments; Steve Jobs and NeXT apparently passed the muster of the eagle eyes of the billionaire and his team of crack accountants; ergo, Steve Jobs and his new company indeed must have the right stuff. Ross Perot said so.

Just as Perot saw what he wished to see in Jobs, so too the public saw what they wished to see in Perot. A good part of his appeal was his lack of pretension. He would say, for example, that "really, really bright people" have difficulty delegating their authority because they know they could do the job better themselves. But "for people like me, who are average, it's different; Oh, I've got an ego and all that, but I know I need help."[124] When Perot would say something like this, one's estimation of his business acumen would soar because even while he was affecting a lack of extraordinary intelligence, he was explaining a business precept that the supposedly "really bright people" would never be able to grasp (Jobs, for example, was notoriously unable to delegate). Yet it would be a mistake to read too much into Perot as a business philosopher. Though the world wanted to hear him explain the secrets, and though he himself would try to make some type of inductive sense of his success, he was no more able to articulate its essence than anyone else. When reporters would press him for its sources, he would dutifully recite what he was expected to: growing up in the Great Depression in Texarkana; the formative start of his business career delivering newspapers to poor neighborhoods; learning leadership at the Naval Academy; the fabled sales career at IBM; and so on. Once, after going through the recitation still another time, he made a revealing confession, which makes him less omniscient (but at the same time his candor makes him much more likable):

"It's just a blend of all that, I guess. You see, I don't know where it comes from, but everybody asks me, so I try to create a story."[125]

Such confessions are not generally welcomed; as a society, we much prefer to leave intact our preferred image of Perot, the Businessperson's Businessperson, the Great Wizard of Oz who has all the answers, not the little man standing behind the curtain. Even when the man pulls the curtain open and waves hello to us, we do not want to see him. A similar story of a daisy-chain of wishful thinking can be told about the role of the other NeXT coinvestors, Stanford and Carnegie-Mellon universities. Other colleges and universities assumed that Stanford and CMU had done due diligence and that NeXT's financial fundamentals must have passed muster as solid. Critics outside of higher education assumed that the numbers were so attractive, in fact, that the two universities were willing to prostitute themselves, selling their good names for the sake of an investment opportunity. A *New York Times* editorial led the attack: "Oscar Wilde could resist everything except temptation. University presidents, it seems, can resist everything except money."[126] Everyone was equally wrong, however; the university investments had virtually nothing to do with money at all, and everything to do with the magical spell conjured by the auras of Jobs and Perot.

University investments in risky start-up firms were not without some precedents; beginning in the early 1970s, many schools had diversified their endowment investments and had placed a portion of their assets in venture capital funds, which hold interests in a portfolio of companies. Direct investment in a single company was much rarer, though a famous and very early example of an exception that had paid off quite handsomely was that of Grinnell College's eagerness to invest in the new company of its alumnus Robert Noyce, the engineering genius who was a cofounder of Intel. The $300,000 that Grinnell invested had multiplied in value more than 30 times, almost doubling the college's endowment.[127] But even if regarded as a risky long shot, an investment in NeXT, based on the terms that Jobs offered for a piece of the action, still did not make sense, at least on the basis of the balance sheet. At Stanford, after the due diligence, which had included a review of the NeXT financials by venture capitalists consulted specially on the matter, the university investment staff wanted to pass. But Jobs had something on his side that was far more important than good numbers: he had the support of the university president. Donald Kennedy enjoyed having Steve Jobs as his personal friend and being consulted like a father figure. Kennedy overrode the staff's objections to the deal and went ahead. At Carnegie-Mellon, Jobs called upon the support of its top two administrators: Richard Cyert, the president, who saw investment in NeXT as an opportunity to announce loudly to the world his university's intention to lead in computer-related fields, and Pat Crecine, the senior vice-president for academic affairs, who was also a fatherlike personal friend of Jobs. At both universities, then, Jobs's cultivation of friendships with those in high places was instrumental. So too was the reassuring presence of Perot; universities were no less resistant to the magical presence of a billionaire than anyone else.

In early 1987, at a celebratory dinner at the Stanford faculty club, bringing together all parties to the completed deal—Perot, Jobs, NeXT employees, and representatives of the two universities—Jobs thanked John Nathan ("the only man we would have let into the bedroom") for making the film that Jobs credited for bringing Perot to NeXT. (Let public relations directors around the country take note from this history lesson: open up the company, and the exposure might lead, in unpredictable ways, to a billionaire with open checkbook appearing on your doorstep.) The dinner was a moment of dizzy optimism: NeXT had a great mission, serving education; it had Jobs, who had the magic touch that had given the world the Apple II and Macintosh computers; it had a link to the best minds of two of the most computer-intensive universities in the country; and it had Ross Perot, who brought not only money but also a supervisory presence, the businessperson who always had his feet planted firmly on the ground. He would make sure that Jobs and his crew did not drift off track. He had ridden herd on General Motors until he was paid generously to take his criticism elsewhere, and he could serve as the loyal opposition at NeXT in a nonadversarial environment. Perot himself encouraged such assumptions: he told the press that his role would be like the sand in an oyster that makes a pearl. He laughed, adding, "This is going to be hell on the oyster."[128]

But in fact he was not hell on the oyster. He was too much of a fan to be hard on his young heroes. Perot took one seat on a newly formed board of directors for NeXT. A second seat was taken by Pat Crecine, the CMU administrator, who could not say enough good about Jobs, about Crecine's "real envy of someone with so much chutzpah and talent."[129] And the third seat was taken by Jobs himself. This threesome constituted the only independent oversight that the company would have. Jobs had purposely arranged matters this way. The incorporation laws required that he have three directors, and so that is what he had, no more,[130] and he had ciphers for the two spots that were not occupied by himself. Perot's acquiescence to Jobs when the two held differing views was at odds with Perot's public persona as the Terror of the Boardroom. How ironic that he would sit on a board that functioned precisely like the "pet rock" he had mocked the GM board for resembling. But given his nonfinancial motivation for investing in NeXT, it is perfectly comprehensible. He flew in for the quarterly board meetings, or often could not make the meeting, so had an associate attend as his proxy or conferred with the other two board members by phone. He could ask good questions of Jobs and the NeXT executive staff. But he had convinced himself so thoroughly of their gifted touch, it was not possible for Perot to ever be the unsentimental auditor that the public outside the company assumed him to be. Later, the testimonials of NeXT's cofounders, intended to promote Perot's desirability as a presidential candidate, inadvertently revealed just how passive a role he had chosen for himself while on the NeXT board. Bud Tribble, for example, recalled how Perot would always ask NeXT employees "What can I do to help you?" and would always defer to them: "You guys are the experts." He deferred to Jobs, too. Susan Barnes, intending to show how smoothly Perot got along with others, said that Perot would preface a dissenting comment with reassurance to Jobs like this: "Steve, you have my proxy and you can vote whatever way you want but have you ever considered . . ."[131] Such deference made for good relations between Perot and Jobs, but at the same time it deprived Jobs and his company of the leadership that Perot could have contributed, and which outsiders mistakenly assumed he was providing. Perhaps Jobs indeed *had* been right to assume that investing in NeXT was a privilege, and that he had chosen the investors rather than the other way around. Jobs enjoyed the prerogatives of an absolute monarchy in all respects but name.

In the long run, however, Jobs would have been much better off if he had not been so skilled in packing the small board with respectful friends, if he had instead permitted a healthy bit of sand in the oyster. By bringing Perot and then the two universities aboard, Jobs had averted a financial crack-up, but the sudden infusion of money, without contingencies, without real oversight, without forcing Jobs to share management responsibilities with those better suited to day-to-day operations, meant that Jobs felt free to return to the carefree days of the founding, when the company *felt* much richer than it prudently should have. Having a billionaire investor made it harder than ever for NeXT to manage its affairs well. It was natural for Jobs and the NeXT employees to assume that if this round of financing was depleted, surely Perot would pony up more. In 1987, NeXT was saddled with the same curse it had begun with, too rich for its own good. And oblivious, to boot.

Tunnel Vision

I
f customers chose computers the same way that they went about
choosing sofas or lamps or curtains, Steve Jobs's obsessive
concern with the appearance of the NeXT computer would
have paid off in handsome sales when the machine was eventually
ready for unveiling. From the inception of NeXT, Jobs was unstint-
ing in spending time and money on the appearance of the machine.
Every aesthetic detail was to be perfect, even in the interior of the
computer, right down to expensive plating to be used on interior
screws that would be out of sight of the curious shopper. Jobs
reserved to himself the task of judging when the state of perfection
was achieved, and no detail was too minute to be immune from his
personal verdict (including the choice of plating on those interior
screws). His vision of the computer was of pure form, worshiped
on its own terms, detached from function; the ego poured into
perfectly shaped metal.

Jobs was captivated by the idea of using a cube-shaped box to
house the computer's electronic innards, and like other ideas that
he embraced, no amount of contrary reasoning could force him to
loosen his grip. He had convinced himself that the Cube would

make a powerful statement in the market, that it would grab attention by its novelty, that it would convey elegance. Each edge of the cube, he decreed, would be exactly one foot long, for no other reason than its sweet defiance of the dictates of engineering. The motherboard and other components that would go into the box would have to conform to the outer skin, not the other way around. One foot, by one foot, by one foot. The dimensions were elegant in simplicity, but the computer cases made by competitors were becoming ever smaller, and NeXT was heading against the flow of the mainstream.

Jobs was emboldened to press on by enlisting the support of Hartmut Esslinger, the industrial designer with whom he had worked at Apple. Jobs hired Esslinger's design firm, *frogdesign* (like Rand, Esslinger liked to tinker with upper and lower case), to work out the details of the Cube. The fee was never disclosed, but it appears to have been, like the one paid to Rand, generous in the extreme, and included a provision that Rand too had sought and even he had not succeeded in securing: in addition to the initial fee, NeXT was to pay a royalty on every computer sold. Unfortunately for NeXT, Esslinger was rather like Jobs, an aesthete who was used to being indulged; other clients kept his profligate preferences in check, but Jobs gave Esslinger carte blanche on specifications. Bean counters in accounting were not to interfere with the Artist At Work. With a client like Jobs willing to pay whatever it cost, Esslinger proceeded to design a machine that was aesthetically striking but would prove to be a nightmare to manufacture. (NeXT employees heard that Esslinger was kept on a retainer of tens of thousands of dollars a month for years; if true, this meant that the costs to NeXT of the Esslinger consultancy were ongoing in another form besides the problems with the Cube itself.) Jobs and Esslinger were oblivious to the possibility that NeXT's prospective customers would be more interested in what the computer could *do* than in how its sleek shape gave it claim to a place in the Smithsonian. Most important of all, the Cube needed to be offered at a competitive price, yet the very details that comprised its perfect appearance were chosen without heed to costs.

Ballooning costs began with Jobs's insistence on using cast magnesium for the Cube. Magnesium is a relatively plentiful material used in such things as flashbulbs, precision instruments, and fireworks. It had two attributes that convinced Jobs that it would be the perfect material for the outer case. It is strong, and would give a sense of solidity when a customer pushed on it, unlike the pliable give that a plastic case yielded. And it provides electromagnetic shielding that would contain radio frequency interference, a requirement for Federal Communications Commission licensing for computers to be used in homes. At the time, computers more powerful than personal computers had yet to be engineered in such a way as to secure FCC approval for the home; Jobs wanted his new machine, which he was describing as a "personal mainframe," to be the first, and magnesium would be a great help. These positive attributes of magnesium were matched by some drawbacks, however. Other computer manufacturers had avoided using it for the most part because it was a difficult material to work with, extremely flammable and hard to cast. When injected into a mold, magnesium solidifies quickly, much faster than plastic, leading to a high incidence of air bubbles, voids, and other defects.

Esslinger made the difficult into the near-impossible by specifying that the NeXT Cube was to be a cube in an absolute, literal sense, a cube perfect enough to please Plato. No fudging, no cheating; the mold in which it would be cast, Esslinger said, must not have the slightest draft, that is, angle. This stipulation created problems that were costly to solve. Regardless of the material used when casting, a slight angle in the side walls of the mold helps when it is being removed. Think of baking a cake in a ring-shaped mold pan and how an angle to the sides helps when flipping the pan off. In industrial casting, a similar taper in the sides of a mold, even as slight as a quarter of a degree, is used to facilitate removal. But Esslinger called for zero-draft casting of the Cube. Special molds had to be created that consisted of separate panels for each face of the Cube, each panel built in such a way as to explode outward—simultaneously—when the casting was completed. The cost of the molds alone was $650,000, and a nationwide search was required before a specialty metals shop in Chicago was located that had the expertise to do such tricky casting.

Jobs specified that the magnesium cubes were to be painted a particular shade of black with a low-gloss finish (identical to the black on the tone arm of a stereo turntable that he thought was perfect). The casting process, by its nature, however, would leave a thin protruding line wherever the edges of the various mold faces met; these parting lines had to be sanded off before the paint could be applied. At first, they were sanded by a human worker, who had to be skilled and careful; if the hand-held machine sander dipped even slightly, it would leave a circular mark on the side of the cube, marring perfection and condemning it to the junk heap. Deciding to automate the sanding process, NeXT purchased for its subcontractor a computerized sanding machine to replace the human worker. This $150,000 machine did nothing but remove the cosmetic imperfections left by the mold on the sides of the case.

Painting the NeXT Cube black would set it apart from the omnipresent beige that had come to be a de facto standard for the cases of personal computers. It would also make it difficult, however, to manufacture blemish-free computers. The low-gloss paint did not adhere evenly to the flat surface of the Cube, and it did not hide imperfections well either. Ross Perot, upon hearing of NeXT's difficulties with the paint, suggested that NeXT call upon the paint experts at General Motors and provided an introduction. Although GM rebuffed NeXT's plea to take on responsibility for painting NeXT's Cubes, the more experienced company could explain why it was that NeXT engineers were having so much trouble with the paint: black, because of its pigment content, is the color least able to hide flaws (which is why Detroit reserves black for the cars that have the fewest body defects). The black paint that NeXT was using was so temperamental that it could not even stand up to the gentle chafing of a plastic bag wrapped around the computer when it was shipped in a box padded with styrofoam. All of these tribulations during development work on the Cube could have been an education for Jobs, an opportunity to learn and make adjustments as work proceeded. But he refused to pay heed. When underlings protested that specifications for the Cube contradicted the laws of physics, Jobs would wave the objections away. Anything less than implementation to the last perfect jot was not good enough. Costs were not of primary concern, and so the cost of manufacturing and finishing a single Cube case turned out to be higher than NeXT's original estimates by a factor of ten.

Costs escalated well beyond initial projections on all other fronts, too, yet Jobs could not be swayed from adjusting his course in the slightest. On the inside, his most senior managers always acceded to Jobs on technology choices, just as they did on other matters. They, as well as the other NeXT employees, calmed themselves with bromides. Working for a start-up was a risky proposition by definition, they reminded themselves. If they did not have the stomach for risk, they would not be there in the first place. Jobs told them that they were the smartest group of employees Jobs had ever had (of course, considering the fact that he had only been at Apple before NeXT, this meant the smartest out of a grand total of two groups), or alternatively the smartest group *on the planet* (a bit larger set of candidates). If manufacturing problems arose, they would simply have to work harder and *think* their way to solutions.

NeXT paid its outside advisers well to adopt a similar attitude of insouciance. Jobs favored engineering consultants who were delighted to be paid for designing the near-impossible. David Kelley Design, a firm which had done earlier work for Apple and was hired to do the mechanical engineering for the NeXT Cube, was set to work to solve problems like building invisible torsion bars into the stand upon which the monitor would rest. The equivalent of six human years of labor was invested in just the designs for the mechanical engineering of the Cube and its monitor. It was work that after the Cube's unveiling would win David Kelley Design professional accolades from peers, just as *frogdesign*'s work would. They had no reason to complain. So when the consultants worked out the stratospheric costs for manufacturing the Cube to specification and passed the estimates on to Jobs, the outsiders assumed, just like the insiders, that Steve Jobs, Mr. Walking History, must know what he was doing when he said he could find a way later to whittle the costs down.

The single most expensive, and easily the most unwise, commitment that Jobs made and would not budge from was the decision to manufacture the NeXT computer in-house, with its own state-of-the-art automated factory. At the very beginning, Jobs had a more pragmatic plan: NeXT would subcontract all of the work out and reserve for itself only the final assembly and the testing of the machines, which would be done on the first floor of its small Palo Alto office. (He even imagined that NeXT could become a billion-dollar company with only a hundred employees in this modest space.) But in 1986, Jobs changed his mind, and decided that he wanted NeXT to do its own manufacturing, and nothing less than the most advanced automation would suffice. He wanted to set new standards of quality and keep control in-house. He wanted to make a patriotic statement that cost-effective manufacturing could be done on American soil (which turned out to be a pitch perfectly suited for Ross Perot). He would later crow, "The neatest thing that I love about NeXT is that it's not made in Osaka."[132] He was also obsessed with secrecy, and by keeping manufacturing within the company he could better guard against breaches, as if a company's most potent competitive weapon is the element of surprise. And he wanted to use his factory as a marketing tool. He compared the appeal of the NeXT computer to the appeal of purchasing a BMW. He explained to employees: "If you're going to buy a great sports car, what's the best way to do it? You fly to Europe, go to the factory, and buy it there." Jobs imagined that future customers would do the same, and fly to California so that they could watch the particular computer that they had ordered go through the assembly line.

The decision to build an automated manufacturing plant, in addition to simultaneously designing new hardware and new software, led to an enormous drain of attention and money. The investment in its own factory would also prove costly over the long term in another sense, by creating a vested interest in computer hardware that would make it much more difficult for NeXT to evaluate objectively the wisdom of continuing to market its own hardware instead of focusing on what would become its real strength, software. At the time of the decision, however, Jobs was most fascinated by the minutia of electronics design. The heart of computer manufacturing is the semiconductor chips and fiberglass circuit board upon which they are mounted. Jobs latched on to the motto "Integrate on silicon, not on fiberglass" and directed his engineers to design custom chips that combined the functions of many other chips, available off-the-shelf, into one large integrated circuit, thus reducing the number of chips that would have to be mounted. A laudable idea in theory, but a questionable one when time was critically short and the company lacked other products that it could market and generate cash with in the meantime. Moreover, Jobs's decision that NeXT should do its own board-stuffing, that is, soldering the various electronic components onto the circuit board, made no sense financially. This was the sort of work that dozens of Silicon Valley firms did full-time, as subcontractors, able to capture economies of scale that individual small computer companies like NeXT, or even medium-sized companies, could never capture on their own. Even the huge vertically integrated computer behemoths like IBM and Digital Equipment would soon enough realize that even *they* should not do all of their own manufacturing. Here again we find Jobs moving in the opposite direction from everyone else. Misled by Ross Perot's endorsement—Perot knew a lot about services but little about manufacturing, other than the unique problems of the mega-billion-dollar dinosaur, General Motors—Jobs plunged ahead on a course that was financial folly.

For a factory, NeXT needed more space. Jobs's first impulse was characteristic: demanding that the rest of the world move to accommodate him. He tried and failed to get the tenants of the adjacent buildings booted (his neighbors, the U.S. Geological Survey, had occupied their offices long before NeXT moved next door and were not amused). He next attempted to evict the recalcitrant USGS by personally calling Senator Alan Cranston and enlisting the muscle of the senator in Washington to effect what Jobs wanted done in California. Cranston did not understand the importance of this matter to the welfare of the republic. The USGS was permitted to stay where it was, and Jobs had to look elsewhere. He finally settled on space in Fremont, across the San Francisco Bay. Jobs and Susan Barnes liked to joke privately that they were bound to be successful at NeXT because when they had been at Apple they already had made all the mistakes to be made. The NeXT factory, however, replicated the same mistakes that Jobs had made when building and overseeing a highly automated Macintosh factory a few years earlier. Machines were purchased, installed, and pulled out on Jobs's whim; color schemes received more attention than costs. All the assembly-line machines and robots at NeXT's plant had to be repainted to match, just as Jobs had insisted at the Macintosh factory. He went further, however, demanding that the machines and robots be reengineered, no matter what the cost, so that the circuit-board assembly line moved boards from the right to the left, instead of the industry-standard from left to right. (He insisted on right-to-left so that his future pilgrimatic customers, standing in an overlooking balcony, could better see the procession of boards, but Jobs never used the factory as a marketing tool as he had planned; the factory would remain closed and out of sight to all but the specially invited.) With the bright lighting and white walls of an art gallery, special floor tiles, glass blocks in a lobby (built, torn down, then built again, on Jobs's orders), a one-of-a-kind staircase, black leather seats in the lobby that cost $20,000 each, and designer bathroom fixtures, the NeXT factory was ready for a cover spread in *Architectural Digest*. (It had everything but a place to hang one's coat—closets or wall hooks were forbidden by the interior designer because they would mar the desired look of the place—so coats were draped wherever a projecting edge could be found.)

One wishes that the splendor of the NeXT factory could serve as a successful model for others. Why should factory workers in the late twentieth century continue to labor, as most of the remaining few do, in the crepuscular gloom of the early nineteenth century mill? The Jobs-designed factory obliterated the difference in white-collar/blue-collar work environments found everywhere else; NeXT factory employees in Fremont worked amidst luxury equal to what the employees in the Palo Alto office enjoyed. The Fremont factory, however, lacked two important things: a financial rationale and human workers (nonsentient robots were capable of many things but enjoying the dazzling aesthetics was not one of them). Jobs most certainly did *not* learn from mistakes at Apple because he had never been held accountable for his whimsical management of the Macintosh factory. No one there really knew how much it cost; and as long as the cash flow from the Apple II's had remained strong, it did not seem to matter to anyone, either. The Macintosh factory thus was not nearly as well-proven a model to carry over to NeXT as Jobs assumed.

Fatally attracted to novelty for its own sake, Jobs savored his NeXT factory for the ways it differed from the rest of industrial America rather than for how it advanced the superordinate goal of making a scholar's workstation. The typical American electronics factory was filled with many workers, poorly paid, mostly female and often minority. The highly automated NeXT factory, in contrast, had almost no workers; those few it had were mostly highly paid white males with advanced graduate degrees. But Jobs's personal fascination with manufacturing and the fun he derived from having a group of bright hardware engineers on hand distorted his business judgment. Instead of making decisions on the basis of how best to build cost-effectively a computer in small volume that would find future customer acceptance, Jobs preferred to count the noses of his degreed trophies like game that had been bagged; NeXT bragged at one point that seventy percent of its manufacturing staff had Ph.D.'s when factory workers at other companies would have difficulty mustering seventy percent who had high school diplomas.[133] To entice the best engineers, Jobs said, NeXT had to provide advanced manufacturing that pushed out to "the edge of the envelope,"[134] and in-house manufacturing provided these engineers with, in effect, their very own wind tunnel to have fun with. This was a strange game to play, confusing status anxiety and business analysis. Jobs acted like a lonely rich kid on a junior high school playground, inviting the popular in-crowd over to his house with the best collection of compact discs as the enticement.

None of the five cofounders who had come with Jobs from Apple were manufacturing managers, so in July 1986 Jobs went back to Apple and recruited Linda Wilkin as a "late founder" who would assume the post of manufacturing manager at NeXT. (Jobs could be playful and still remain somewhat serious when he presented new employees like Wilkin with the formal letter outlining the terms of employment, at the end of which the recipient was to sign, certifying "I accept this insanely great offer.") Wilkin had no difficulty catching the utopian drift of the other cofounders. NeXT was building its manufacturing system from scratch and Wilkin, quoted in a company brochure, was delighted that "we have the chance to do it right the first time."[135]

By the fall of 1986, however, NeXT employees could see that they were losing the battle against time. John Nathan's filming had captured a drop in morale between the time of the fall 1985 and early 1986 company retreats, and if he had been on hand for the fall 1986 retreat, he would have seen that morale had plunged much more, as by then it was clear that NeXT was not going to come even close to meeting its original deadline of delivering a finished machine by spring 1987. Jobs dubbed the September 1986 retreat "In The Middle," telling his assembled employees that they were at a point where no one could remember clearly what university customers had said they wanted, and it was still too early to see exactly what it was NeXT was going to end up producing. He likened his employees' position to standing in the middle of a tunnel: "You can't see the light at the entrance or the end."[136] Their uneasiness was understandable, but he warned them that they had to trust their original instincts and him, their leader; otherwise, "if you get confused and change directions, you can bump into a lot of walls."[137]

The tunnel metaphor was absurdly self-imposed: if NeXT had lost track of what its university customers wanted, nothing prevented NeXT from going back out and conferring with them again, as it had done in the cross-country canvassing at the time of the company's founding. It would not have meant bumping into a lot of walls. It would have meant running a risk, however, of hearing some distressing news. By 1986, leaders in academic computing were saying that $3,000—the target price for the NeXT computer—was too high a price for a student computer, that it should not exceed *$1,000* if it was to be universally affordable, and if, to keep its price low, it had to be less powerful than state-of-the-art technology permitted, then so be it.[138] Instead of paying heed, Jobs tried to make the recalcitrant outer world go away and instructed his NeXT troops to pay attention to him, think of tunnels, and keep marching forward.

Everyone that surrounded Jobs told him that his tunnel vision was brilliant. John Nathan, for example, provided a panegyric, admiring Jobs's insulation from self-doubt: "Steve Jobs doesn't sit around short-circuiting his effectiveness by wondering if he's on the right course."[139] Ross Perot added more flattery, saying, with self-deprecating politesse, that Jobs was "a lot smarter than I am," but the two men did share a knack for "tunnel vision," a talent for locking on to things that Perot credited as a defining attribute of successful people.[140] Jobs himself could wax philosophical, when invited to do so, about the acuity of tunnel vision that explicitly ignored what customers wanted. In October 1986, at a roundtable discussion of American entrepreneurs televised by closed-circuit to Merrill Lynch offices, Jobs advised the would-be entrepreneurs in his audience that if they too were to start a technology company, they should not go out and do market research. At the *best* companies, "the few people that are starting the company *are* your market."[141] In other words, whatever pleases NeXT will please everyone else, too. With solipsism as one's guiding philosophy, why indeed should one bother to consult one's intended customers about the wisdom of following the original course?

On the technical front, however, the ambition of Jobs's plans led to additional disappointments, as deadlines continued to slip. The pressure was especially intense on the chip designers, who, under Jobs's orders, were trying to pack the maximum number of microscopic electronic switches possible on a special chip called a gate array. Every time they neared a final design, Jobs would order them to add additional functions to the chip, which would mean much rearranging, leading to still more rearranging, as changes in one portion of the chip cascaded outward. Whenever Jobs asked how long it would take them to finish their designs, they silently suspected it would take a year of seven-days-a-week effort, but they also knew that that answer would not be acceptable to Jobs, so they always said, one more month. The ruse could work for only so long, however. At the next company retreat, in January 1987, Jobs led the company in making the hapless designers the focus of a humiliating public lashing, carrying out what some horrified observers described as a "gang rape." Screaming at the head of the chip design team, "Do you realize you're killing our company?" Jobs transferred responsibility for delays to his underlings and then smeared them with his contempt. Not much thanks for working eighteen-hour days for the previous year. The other NeXT employees witnessed this bloody spectacle and drew the appropriate conclusions. From then on, no one dared to be the one who would deliver the bad news. But Jobs continued nevertheless to pick off single lambs from the flock for ritualized slaughter. The selected victims could expect no help from their comrades, either. The others either watched in tight-lipped silence, or joined in the attack themselves.

Outside of his company, when asked about his business philosophy, Jobs never talked about the cannibalistic aspect of his management style at NeXT. But eating his own and spitting them out was more than a cruel habit that was hidden from public sight, a habit that he admitted he had when confronted in 1987 by most of his employees who had assembled to demand that the rites of humiliation end. (He promised he would do better; the employees were divided into teams that met regularly for six weeks to propose solutions; Jobs received the proposals, the teams were dispersed, and he resumed as he had done before.) It devastated his own company in ways no one fully appreciated at the time. Take the two chip designers, for example, who were the chosen victims of ritualized slaughter at the company retreat in early 1987. They were not fired—despite his temper, Jobs infrequently fired employees—but they were hardly in a state of mind that left them highly motivated to push on in their thankless task. They left shortly thereafter of their own volition, as many others would. But their departure was extremely costly to NeXT in terms of time lost in the transition; their project was complex, and it took months before the designers who inherited it were able to reach the level of familiarity that the original two had had when they left. This was time that the company could not afford to squander, especially considering that so many of the company's subsequent difficulties stemmed from the late delivery of the computer. Trace the tardiness back to 1987, and one sees that the history of NeXT could have been markedly different if it had not been for Jobs's merciless hounding of several key designers.

Early 1987 was also when Linda Wilkin, the "late founder" hired to manage manufacturing, left NeXT, less than a year after joining the company. Hers is an unusual case—first, because she

was actually fired, and second, because she later sued NeXT for
$110 million in damages for wrongful termination.[142] The details
surrounding her departure also set her apart from others who left
NeXT, who were more clearly the victims of Jobs venting his own
frustrations upon others. In Wilkin's case, it is hard to see her
rationale for claiming rights to damages. Court documents showed
that Jobs first had demoted her, ostensibly because of her failure to
fill one position below her (filled, that is, with a candidate that Jobs
accepted; he rejected all that Wilkin had nominated). He offered
her the same salary but demanded that she return a portion of her
NeXT stock; it was when she refused to turn over her stock at its
original value as her contract entitled NeXT to demand, and instead
insisted on a far higher valuation (based on what Ross Perot had
been willing to pay), that he fired her. Whether additional issues,
related to gender or personality (she was the one member of the
senior staff who would poke a finger in Jobs's face and challenge
him), were the primary reasons for the split is difficult to determine.
But when she began at NeXT, Wilkin had had to sign, in addition
to "the insanely great offer," the other piece of paper demanded of
new employees, even "late founders," which stated clearly that "my
employment by NeXT is terminable at will at any time by me or
NeXT." The "at will" clause does not leave a fired employee with
much of a basis to cry foul.

The Wilkin case required two trials. The first one ended in a
mistrial when the presiding judge intemperately told her lawyer "to
cut the bullshit" within the hearing of jurors (an interesting vignette
of American jurisprudence at work);[143] the second trial (with a new
judge) ended swiftly when the judge tossed her suit out even before
NeXT had to present its defense. Before going to trial, Wilkin had
turned down a succession of offers from NeXT to settle the case
out-of-court for as much as $675,000. Holding out for the
$1,500,000 her lawyer had convinced her would be awarded by a
jury, she went to trial, only to end up losing with an ignominious
judgment of $11,700 assessed against her for the nuisance suit.[144]

For Jobs, the lesson that he learned from this annoyance was to redouble his own inclination to destroy documents and guard against the possibility of invasive subpoenas from similar suits, an inclination instilled by Apple's suit against NeXT, which had given outsiders the right to collect NeXT's internal documents. It was standing company policy at NeXT that any file that had not been accessed within the most recent thirty days was to be purged, though it was not followed consistently by the rank-and-file.

Before Wilkin had left NeXT, she had boasted of the manufacturing system that they were building, one that would employ a just-in-time delivery system from suppliers and would produce zero-defects. But in the same breath she also had added an incongruously picayune detail, that "we've got it figured out down to how we seal the shipping boxes."[145] There NeXT was, some two years away, it would turn out, from producing a completed hardware and software system to put *into* the boxes, and the head of manufacturing was proud of knowing how the boxes would be sealed. In this respect, Wilkin was mirroring the same inability to sort out the important problems from the less important as her bête noire, Jobs himself. The difference, in the case of Jobs, was that sycophants praised him constantly for his ability to zoom instantaneously from grand strategy to the smallest detail. They colluded with him in treating as a unique strength what was in fact a grievous inability to allocate his attention rationally. In "The Entrepreneurs" television show, Jobs enumerates in a soliloquy all of the difficulties of starting NeXT, and what is most striking about it is how oblivious he is to what he is saying, as if he thinks that we too would agree that "figuring out how you're going to get [the product] to the marketplace" deserves no more attention than "doing a part number system" or "getting a little kitchen setup." It all came rushing out in an undifferentiated stream—choosing a product to make placed side by side with choosing a coffeemaker—because that was exactly how he managed NeXT. Where else would even the signs on the restrooms be deemed worthy of custom work? (The replacements were not in conformance with state law, however, so employees had to play a little cat-and-mouse game, taking the customized signs down and putting the old signs back up temporarily, whenever a state inspection seemed imminent.)

If Jobs had been willing to delegate to others the decisions about the restroom signs and the coffeemakers and the plating of interior screws and such, he would have had more time to attend to matters of larger import, such as what needed to be done in order to deliver a finished computer that would meet the promised $3,000 target. Instead, he made numerous seemingly little decisions about the Cube, favoring the addition, not the deletion, of features, most of which, singly, were technically defensible, even if risky, but cumulatively made the machine an odd duck, placing it well beyond the bounds of industry standards, and well above its intended price. The Cube became an example for future textbooks of what is called in the industry "creeping elegance." Jobs wanted to make a statement that his machine was a different machine, but he made *everything* different, and expected that his customers would be delighted. Why? Because he and his engineers were. And because the same formula of screw-industry-standards-we'll-build-for-ourselves had worked so well for the Macintosh.

One particular decision, however, added dramatically to the cost of the machine and at the same time relegated the machine to isolation far from the mainstream: Jobs decided that his Cube would use a new, then still-unfinished technology, an erasable magneto-optical disk. Using an intense laser to heat minute areas of the disk, in tandem with use of a standard magnetic field, the optical disk, as it was referred to in shorthand, offered the promise of holding much more digital information in a given space than ordinary recording media. In the past the technology had suffered from a major shortcoming: once the digital 0's and 1's had been inscribed, they could not be changed or erased. But Canon, a Japanese electronics company, had promised NeXT that it could have a more advanced, erasable version of the disk ready in time for the machine's introduction. Jobs was emboldened to order his engineers to plan that the optical disk would be the *only* medium for moving programs and data in and out of the NeXT computer and the *only* medium for storing data within. His staff, however, was uncertain whether the cost could be brought down sufficiently or the optical drive's poky speed increased sufficiently to make it viable. They thought it would be prudent to also include a floppy disk drive, which would use proven technology and standard inexpensive disks that were widely available. The additional cost of adding a floppy drive would have been a trivial sum compared to what was going to be spent on the optical drive, but Jobs refused to accede to his engineers' wishes. It was not a matter of money; it was a matter of making a statement. To Jobs, the floppy disks that everybody else used were the technology of the past. By shunning them, and putting all of his bets on the optical disk, he would show everyone the technology of the future and be hailed for his foresight.

Though Jobs would speak of what he was doing at NeXT in nationalistic terms, describing his company as an example of how Japanese techniques could be used by Americans to regain a competitive position in manufacturing, he was blind to how much he was departing, in fact, from the Japanese model that he thought he was emulating. A Japanese manufacturer would begin, as NeXT began, by identifying who were the intended customers, and it would determine, again as NeXT had at its beginning, what price point would be acceptable to the customers. Then the Japanese would figure out how to manufacture the product for that price, doing whatever it took, including dropping features, to keep to the price point. Here NeXT failed to follow. Jobs, when faced with a technical choice at NeXT, always favored what he thought would be the technology of the future, at an unknown but high price, over the mundane technology of the present that would help keep the price of the Cube down within sight at least of the original $3,000 price point.

While work on the machine proceeded, Jobs approached Fallon

McElligott, an advertising agency in Minneapolis, to work up ideas for the first ad campaign. It was a good choice for a public figure who still was dogged by images of the barefooted bohemian, dating back to the early 1970s. Fallon McElligott was the agency that had become well-known for its *Rolling Stone* campaign begun in 1985, in which print advertisements contrasted the Perception of the magazine as the refuge of a long-haired hippie with the Reality, illustrated by a well-groomed yuppie. Over six months, Fallon McElligott pitched two separate campaigns to NeXT, neither of which pleased Jobs, and the talks ended (the agency's internal autopsy described its work with NeXT as fun, "a wild bronco ride," and its own proposals to NeXT as "too right-brain"). But before the two companies parted, the agency tried to get Jobs to pay attention to the importance of the price point and to give some thought to the student customers who were not already enthusiastic Steve Jobs supporters. What would NeXT's message be for the mildly skeptical mind? How could you move somebody from skepticism to interest to enthusiasm? Jobs was not interested in such questions. When the agency queried Jobs about his marketing plan, so that the advertising campaign could be appropriately fitted to it, it was clear that Jobs had not given much thought to it; the closest approximation to a plan was the assumption that Dan'l Lewin and his golden Rolodex would round up the usual suspects in higher-education computing, just as had happened for the Macintosh.

Once Jobs had decided on his course, he saw himself as the point man, leading skittish troops down through the darkness of the tunnel. He did not want to hear anyone broach the question of creeping elegance, whether NeXT employee, or advertising agency on probation, or his own future customer, a select group of whom were invited by Dan'l Lewin to join what NeXT called its advisory board, which first met in November 1986. The plan was to gather representatives of leading college campuses a couple of times a year and solicit their thoughts about the gestating computer. Despite initial enthusiasm, advisory board members discovered that the computer design was basically set and there was little room for change, other than in convincing NeXT to give more thought (and ultimately not nearly enough) to how the NeXT machines would be connected to networks of other machines. No one from NeXT was interested in what the academic advisers thought about the untested optical disk (the board was extremely skeptical) or the absence of a floppy drive (it vainly pleaded that NeXT reconsider and include such a drive). As for advice about pricing, the board grew increasingly concerned as it watched the estimated price climb. NeXT attempted to contain the academics' anxiety by concealing what the real price was going to be; Lewin, when asked, would explain to his old friends that the number had yet to be determined, but then Jobs would pipe up and pluck a price out of the air that was well below where it actually was, hoping that some miracle in the interim would permit NeXT to meet the figure that he had just promised.

The NeXT advisory board members were sworn to secrecy and the rest of the academic community remained in the dark about what was afoot at NeXT. Publicly, Jobs continued to maintain that he was listening closely to the concerns of universities and that he was aware that campus demands for a powerful personal computer had grown since the proposal for a 3M machine had been first floated. He told college computer administrators at the 1986 Educom meeting: "We've been hearing that you want a lot more [speed and power and] I guess it should come as no surprise, you still want it for $3,000."[146] Jobs said that NeXT would not be able to quite meet the $3,000 goal, but the final price would be close. These were words of reassurance and attentiveness while work on the Cube moved forward. But when by the fall of 1987, two years after its founding, NeXT still did not have a computer prototype that it was willing to show its intended customers, the academics began unhappy mumbling, feeling that their willingness to give a new entrant a chance was going to end badly. An influential administrator at Berkeley, Raymond Neff, predicted that if Jobs priced his new computer even above $2,000, NeXT would encounter "plenty of resistance."[147] At the 1987 meeting of Educom, NeXT kept details of the Cube hidden and instead distributed a beautifully printed eighteen-page brochure about the NeXT logo. Academics, accustomed to the mean penny-pinching of nonprofit organizations, economizing that Jobs no longer could even imagine, were not a good choice of audience for telling in such lengthy form the tale of the $100,000 logo. Conference-goers gleefully took the NeXT brochures over to the booths of competitors, where NeXT's insensitive *faux pas* became the butt of jokes.

Any reasonable future hope for NeXT would have flickered out completely at that meeting of Educom, were it not for Ross Perot riding to the rescue with a speech that saved the day. Jobs, in typical fashion, had spared no expense in providing an invited group of his future university customers with an evening of highbrow diversion. An art museum provided tony ambience, a string quartet provided music, and Ross Perot provided rousing optimism, which Stanford's Michael Carter called "the greatest locker-room speech I've ever heard." Perot told his audience that he, like they, was often asked why the NeXT computer was not yet shipping. "What's going on with these boys?" Wall Street analysts wanted to know. Well, Perot allowed, if he were in charge, he'd surely be shipping the product, but he was not like these boys, perfectionists who were not going to ship anything until it was perfect. This was fine; he admired them for it. Perot did not look concerned at all. He winked, "What are you worried about anyway, that Steve and I are going to run out of money?" The audience laughed and let out a collective sigh of relief. NeXT should have, too, because Perot's pep talk bought the company badly needed time when the university community had run out of patience.

Still, patience has limits, as NeXT's shock troops in marketing discovered as they made the rounds of colleges in 1988, when the announced date for the introduction of the machine was put off again and again. At first, NeXT representatives had been received with warmth; the academic community was so thirsty for news about NeXT that it was glad just to meet with representatives of the company in the flesh. But because Jobs wanted to build up a heightened sense of public anticipation prior to the introduction, NeXT employees could not disclose any details about the machine, a restriction that rendered their presentations vacuous. "We have talked to you about what you need, and here is what we've heard you say," the pitch would go. All generalities, steering clear of any details about what the NeXT machine would actually be like or what it would cost. NeXT marketing representatives on tour were the ones in the trenches who had to confront angry audiences that would stalk out of presentations to protest the smoke and mirrors and the absence of content.

The NeXT advisory board members were the only academics who were privy to the details before the introduction, and Jobs expected this group, the company's closest allies in the university community, to make a good showing in placing advance orders that could be announced on the day of the introduction, establishing the same credibility as the announcement of Apple University Consortium orders had given the Macintosh on the day of its introduction. But Jobs's tunnel vision had prevented him from seeing that NeXT would not, *could* not, repeat the Macintosh recipe. In 1988, unlike 1984, universities and students alike owned lots of personal computers, which presented NeXT with a problem of displacement that Apple had not faced earlier. Jobs's earlier progeny was too successful—the advantage of primogeniture—making it difficult for the later sibling to find a place in the world.

One parallel that could be drawn between the NeXT and the Macintosh was technical. Advisory board members could see that the NeXT Cube, like the first version of the Macintosh, was going to be painfully underpowered, in the sense that its microprocessor was too slow to handle all that was going to be asked of it. In the case of the Macintosh, universities had been indulgent; the software was so superior that shortcomings in the hardware could be forgiven. This time, however, they would be less forbearing because there were alternatives now: NeXT software could be compared to the Macintosh's (the Macintosh never had to go up against the Macintosh at *its* introduction), and for those who wanted blinding speed in their computers, the NeXT hardware would not stand up well to comparison with machines that were just becoming affordable then, based on a relatively new kind of microprocessor now on the scene: something called RISC, for Reduced Instruction Set Computing. This area may seem technically arcane, but its implications have affected the business of computing profoundly; adoption of RISC has turned out to be the least *risk*y course for increasing computer performance, so a short mini-course in RISC and related matters is in order.

Developed in the mid-1970s by IBM researchers led by John Cocke, RISC was initially received skeptically by the fraternity of computer scientists. It was not immediately clear that a RISC microprocessor could perform calculations any faster than the conventional microprocessor based on Complex Instruction Set Computing, or CISC. The two kinds of microprocessors accepted varying numbers of recognizable instructions. With RISC, the computer uses a small number of simple commands, *many times*, to perform a given calculation, and with CISC, the computer uses a large number of complex commands, in dramatically fewer combinations, to get the same job done; common sense would suggest that this would be a wash, and the experts thought so too. But by the mid-1980s, even the skeptics could see that RISC offered performance gains that CISC could not, and its relatively simpler design permitted cheaper manufacturing and more rapid development of successive generations.

NeXT had the misfortune to face the question of what microprocessor it should incorporate in the design of its computer just at that historical moment when the computer world was about to embrace RISC but had not quite done so. Neither Jobs nor his principal hardware advisor, Rich Page, were much interested in pursuing the RISC option, either by developing their own design in-house or by purchasing a RISC chip from an outside supplier like Fairchild, which Jobs dismissed because of what he regarded as too high a price. In contrast, from Motorola, with whom he had a close business relationship from his days at Apple, Jobs was able to get a great package deal on a three-chip set which included a CISC microprocessor. When at Apple, Jobs had wangled a better price from Motorola for its chips than what competitors paid, and he continued the tradition. Page told NeXT staff members that the price that Jobs had agreed to pay Motorola for each microprocessor for the NeXT Cube was even less than what Motorola's own internal divisions paid to the mother company.

The decision to take Motorola's latest CISC chip, a decision that seemed to Jobs to have been a great bargain in 1986, was viewed two years later in a different light by advisory board members, who were not privy to the details of NeXT's special pricing arrangements with Motorola. All they saw before them was a CISC-based NeXT Cube that at birth was going to be well behind the leading edge defined by RISC, and most distressing of all, the NeXT Cube was going to cost academics far more than the original $3,000, and far, far more than the $1,000 that had made the Macintosh a campus hit: the price of a NeXT had ballooned to almost $7,000, and even that would be for a stripped-down configuration. And this at a time when funding for higher education had begun to contract and less money for computers would be available.

The NeXT advisory board gulped when they got the bad news about the price at a meeting on the eve of the Cube's introduction. This was not the machine they had asked for; this was not the machine Jobs had promised them, either. One member, referring to Jobs's promise at Educom two years earlier to bring in a price "close" to $3,000, warned that the higher ed community would regard the promise as broken: "Doubling the price? Maybe that's your definition of 'close,' but it's not mine." It was too late at this point, however, to get the price lowered. Now board members had to demonstrate their fealty to the NeXT cause by announcing their advance orders. For those who had not realized it before, it was clear then that as far as Jobs and NeXT were concerned, the real function of the board was not as an advisory body so much as a prestigious marketing arm for NeXT, packed with the leading names in campus computing. At the somber pre-introduction meeting, NeXT executives had to extract orders from the group, and they came as slowly as stubborn molars that resist the dentist's pliers. There was no attempt to line up $2 million commitments as Apple had done; NeXT was open to whatever numbers schools were willing to pledge. But even under pressure, the advisory board could not muster orders for more than a handful of machines—total. Jobs was stunned. His best customer prospects were unwilling to commit. (Actually, it was worse than he saw: privately, some of the campus representatives were overheard by NeXT employees saying that they had no intention of honoring the numbers that had been forced out of them under duress, knowing full well that NeXT would not be so foolish as to punish its own customers.)

Jobs should have realized then that he had a major problem on his hands, one that should have received his full attention. If any contingency could have arisen that might have forced him to rethink his plan of offering what *he* regarded as the proper revolutionary leap in computing, damn the cost, this should have been it. That the chariness of his *own* advisory board did not provoke a crisis at NeXT is readily explained, however: at that moment it seemed that NeXT would not need to find its own customers because it knew, though the rest of the world did not, that it had captured the single largest customer of them all, International Business Machines. With IBM, the biggest bully on the block, as its ally, and flush with a fresh infusion of cash from its deal, NeXT was full of swagger.

Like other boosts to NeXT's company morale that employees self-mockingly called "sugar highs," the IBM deal originated in Jobs's wheeling and dealing with the exalted. At first glance, it might appear that NeXT, a tiny start-up, was extremely fortunate to have for its chief executive officer a celebrity, someone who could be invited in 1987 to a birthday party for *Washington Post* publisher Katharine Graham, someone with panache, who upon meeting (with Malcolm Forbes providing the introduction) the chief executive officer of IBM, John Akers, would without invitation give free advice about how IBM should change course. It happened that Akers was interested in hearing what Jobs had to say about the shortcomings of software from Bill Gates's Microsoft and the not-yet-publicly revealed wonders in software that Jobs's own NeXT engineers were brewing. A few weeks later, Akers invited Jobs and Bud Tribble to make a presentation at IBM headquarters and Jobs made an exception to his blackout policy and divulged details ("Hey, these are senior executives," he reasoned, "they're not going to run back to their computers and start programming.")[148] The meeting went well, and Akers turned over the task of negotiating rights to NeXT software to Bill Lowe, the executive who had been the original father of the project that became the IBM personal computer.

But Jobs's verve was also attached to his prickliness, and negotiations, which extended over months, almost failed on a number of occasions when Jobs would threaten to end the talks. For securing the rights to the software, IBM was willing to pay NeXT about $60 million—the exact figure has never been disclosed—yet the more interest that IBM displayed, the more ambivalent Jobs became about having IBM as a partner. Fearing that IBM could crush NeXT at will, Jobs wanted to keep IBM at a distance; at the same time he wanted to pull IBM in as a partner. NeXT's head of sales, Todd Rulon-Miller, laughed nervously when he described to his staff how Jobs played "a game of chicken with the largest data processing company in the world." Jobs would storm out of negotiations, throwing up his hands in disgust about proposed colors or titles or other matters that would seem trivial to the others, but which were sufficient to incense Jobs. He would announce, "It's not worth it"; the whole deal was off. Dan'l Lewin earned the gratitude of the IBM negotiators for being the one who would calm Jobs on these occasions with a whispered conference in the hallway. After a few minutes, Jobs would return to the table, explaining, "That's not an issue anymore." Even when the deal had been agreed to in all of its particulars, Jobs refused to consider a contract that ran any longer than two pages. When a copy of the long contract drafted by IBM lawyers arrived, Jobs dropped it without reading it, and delivered to IBM headquarters the criticism that his own employees had learned to dread, "You didn't get it." IBM, acting as if *it* was the company that had not yet released a first product to date, and *NeXT* was the company with $60 billion in annual revenues, uncomplainingly did exactly as Jobs wished, tearing up its draft of the contract and inviting Jobs to draft his own version.[149]

Such is reality distortion at work. But even when Jobs got his way, and Akers and Lowe at the top of IBM had signed off, implementation by the grunts at the lower levels lay ahead, and follow-through was not Jobs's strong suit. As far as he was concerned, IBM was now his, providing a protective cape of invulnerability around NeXT's diminutive shoulders. It was such a coup to have the world's largest computer company eating out of one's own hand that NeXT's future seemed assured, customers or no. By the time the sugar high of the IBM deal faded, the next high would have arrived, the long-awaited day of the Cube's introduction. It was easy to think only about the good news of signing Perot and IBM, and of the imminent arrival of more good news. Jobs had told the company that the giant semiconductor company Motorola, from whom NeXT obtained its microprocessor, had come to NeXT asking if it could invest in the company, and only conflicts with its other customers like Apple stood in the way. And Japan's Canon had also sought out NeXT, offering to pay $15 to $20 million just for the privilege of selling NeXT computers in Asia. NeXT was too busy to absorb so many promising developments. With multibillion-dollar companies coming on bended knee like so many vassal states paying homage to the Mighty Kingdom of NeXT, it was only natural that Jobs and his staff would not be inclined to pay much attention to some problems that also presented themselves at the time, such as the rebellious noises coming from NeXT's best customer prospects. Or the related news, which NeXT had been studiously avoiding, of what the competition was up to.

Sundry Competition

S teve Jobs had difficulty figuring out how to position the machine he was building. Would it be best to describe it as a personal computer? If so, the NeXT would be larger than the competition; with the Cube, oversized monitor, and many megabytes of memory, it would be a personal computer on steroids. Unfortunately, its power came at a price, and it would be much more expensive than its closest competition in the personal-computer world, the Macintosh. Alternatively, the NeXT machine could also be described as a *workstation*, the brawny, speedy machine that scientists and engineers used for calculation-intensive tasks and which were designed to work well in networks. Against other workstations, the Cube would be priced attractively, but then again, in this realm, it would be regarded as slow and underpowered when measured against the competition. The Cube ran the risk of ending up in a netherworld, too pricey to belong with personal computers and too anemic to belong with workstations. Jobs decided to try to finesse this by thinking of his machine as a never-seen-before hybrid, what he called a *personal workstation*, providing the ease-of-use of a personal computer and the power of a workstation. It was a beguiling idea that neatly ignored the reality that it would be too expensive to be a stand-alone personal computer and too technically deficient to be an attractive workstation. By positioning his machine as a personal workstation, Jobs would in effect double his competition: he not only would be taking on all of the personal computer world, the Apples, IBMs, and all the rest, but also all of the workstation world, too. It was like purposely whacking two hornet's nests instead of one.

Foremost among the workstation manufacturers was a company called Sun Microsystems, based in Mountain View, California, not far from NeXT, which had a devoted following in the very market that was NeXT's target, universities. (It was also the manufacturer of the workstations that NeXT's own engineers used to design the hardware and software for NeXT's first computer.) Sun had a bit of a head start on NeXT. It had been founded in 1982, and had grown from $8 million in sales by the close of its first fiscal year in 1983 to $115 million by the end of its third, in 1985, the time of NeXT's founding. At this level, one could imagine that a newly born rival like NeXT could still catch up. But while NeXT worked as fast as it could to ready its own machine, Sun continued to grow: by the time that NeXT was ready to unveil the Cube in 1988, Sun had passed the $1 billion point in annual sales. It happened that quickly. And it was precisely because of Sun's phenomenal growth that Jobs had changed his original plan of running NeXT as a small company and decided that NeXT would have to be a billion-dollar company, too, to be a player.

Sun's sales continued to hurtle upward with depressing speed. Within nine years of its founding, Sun had crossed the $3 billion mark (it had taken IBM fifty years to achieve the same feat). In an indirect way, Sun's success after 1985 could be attributed to the spur of not knowing precisely what Steve Jobs was cooking up at NeXT. In other ways, Sun's success can be explained by how Sun was managed so differently than Jobs's NeXT. In comparing the two Silicon Valley companies, one sees striking contrasts, belying the East Coast notion of a monolithic West Coast culture.

The Sun variant deserves more attention that it has received. Measured by most any yardstick one could choose, Sun was one of the most successful stories of the 1980s for all of industrial America. We Americans pay great attention, for example, to the validation given by listing in the Fortune 500. Sun made the list a mere six years after its founding, one of the most rapid ascents ever. We also love a story of youthful success. Sun should grab our attention on this score, too. The four founders of Sun were born in late 1954 or, like Jobs, in 1955. And though the computer industry pays little attention, we might also add that here is an instructive example of how liberal immigration policies made possible a story of a job-creating business wonder. Three of Sun's five most important early principals—the four founders and its executive vice-president—were foreign-born, immigrating from India, Germany, and France. In Sun we have the makings of a terrific tale, which by now should be a part of American folklore. Yet its story is relatively unknown because its founders are not obsessively self-aggrandizing like Steve Jobs (or Lee Iacocca or Donald Trump) and because they freely share credit among themselves, which means there is no single Herculean hero. The relative obscurity of Sun Microsystems outside of the computer industry tells us that we like our inspirational stories to have a single heroic protagonist, not the complications of several, and we pay most attention to those who scream for it.

A contrarian view is a useful corrective. The more that Jobs clamors for credit for his achievements or attempts to shed responsibility for poor decisions that would detract from his persona of the boy genius with the golden touch, the more reluctant the observer is to accede. In the opposite direction, the more that Sun's principal executives downplay their personal contributions, attribute success to pure luck, and avoid the limelight, the more intriguing they are.

In history, the modest ones should not be shunted aside by the shrill.

The most modest of the four Sun cofounders is Andy Bechtolsheim, brilliant and methodical, the engineer's engineer, who is ill-at-ease in public and holds his six-foot-four-inch frame shyly, as if he somehow could make himself inconspicuous.[150] Though he has become famous in his native home, Bavarian Germany, as the local boy who made good, he remains happily unknown here in the United States. He was headed for an academic career, working on a Ph.D. in electrical engineering and computer science at Stanford University, when he built the machine that would become the prototype for the Sun workstation. Unlike Jobs, whose own college career was short and whose most recent familiarity with developments on campus was gleaned at Olympian altitude, meeting with a college president or a stray Nobel laureate, Bechtolsheim knew the research university with the intimacy of a resident, whose study at Stanford was preceded by an M.S. from Carnegie-Mellon, the other powerhouse in computer science. This was a tremendous advantage. From everyday contact, Bechtolsheim knew how research universities actually ran and what kinds of problems researchers attacked with computers. He knew that what universities needed most desperately was an inexpensive machine that could run a set of basic computer system commands called Unix.

Nothing about the Unix operating system is inviting. Its arcane commands are terse to the point of abstruseness. If one should want to see a list of documents that are stored in the computer and the dates that they were last changed, one must type *ls -l*; to show what documents are awaiting their turn at the printer, one types *lpq*; to stop a program that is already running, one types *kill* and appends the *PID*, the "process identifier." These are the easy commands; becoming comfortable with Unix requires familiarity with other esoteric nomenclature, like *dot files, shell variables, pipes, aliases,* and many more. If bewildered, one cannot expect much help from

Unix experts; they have little patience for questions from innocent novitiates and are likely to respond with a curt acronym, RTFM (*Read the fucking manual*). For a person who wants to use a computer for no more than simple everyday tasks like writing a letter, there would be no reason to go through the pain of learning Unix. But for computer programmers and other scientists working in industrial and university research laboratories, who did not mind the difficulties of learning its obscure secrets, Unix was embraced for several good reasons: it was first developed at Bell Laboratories in 1969 and subsequently made available for a nominal licensing fee from the parent company AT&T; after being rewritten in the early 1970s, it was the first truly portable operating system, easily adapted to run on computers made by different manufacturers; it worked well on networks of computers and provided multitasking, the ability to run several programs simultaneously. Much beloved in the dark den of university research labs, but elsewhere unknown and unlovable, who would have guessed in the early 1980s that Unix would be an essential part of the story of how Andy Bechtolsheim changed from mild-mannered graduate student to mild-mannered millionaire?

While a student at Stanford, Bechtolsheim had spent two summers, in 1979 and 1980, working at—Xerox PARC. But where Steve Jobs had been impressed by the snazzy multiple windows, the mouse, and the programming language found on the machines at PARC, Bechtolsheim had been most deeply impressed by something entirely different: At PARC, everyone had their very own *powerful* computer. Instead of being given dumb terminals, connected to one central mainframe or minicomputer, each person had on the desktop a fire-breathing powerhouse whose processing power was not shared with anybody else, yet all were networked together, which made sharing files and printers extremely convenient. Bechtolsheim realized that this kind of machine, a workstation, was exactly what universities needed, for students and faculty alike. In 1981, while a graduate student, he drew up a design for a machine for the

Stanford University Network (hence, *Sun*) that would use inexpensive off-the-shelf parts and would run Unix software. This was an unorthodox formula at the time. Other computer manufacturers used proprietary chips, which they had designed themselves, and for which they could charge a premium because they were not available from alternative sources. They also required that purchasers lease the proprietary software that made the computer run.

Bechtolsheim gives the U.S. government credit for helping to pave the way for the Sun machine. In the late 1970s, the Defense Advanced Research Projects Agency (DARPA), which funded a great deal of university-based research, had decided that it wanted its far-flung academic researchers to be able to exchange computer data and to adapt newly available hardware to existing software. This was impossible so long as everyone was dependent upon the computers of the Digital Equipment Company, then the dominant machine. Digital regarded the operating system that ran on its popular VAX computers to be proprietary and would not release the source code that would allow university researchers to tinker with it on their own and customize it to their individual needs. Consequently, the federal government poured a couple of million dollars into a research project at Berkeley to rework the then-obscure Unix code, bringing it up-to-date with the new technical requirements of the day, and to make it—and the source code— available to anyone who wanted it, providing a nonproprietary alternative. How fitting that Berkeley would be the place to carry out such a communistic mission, and how ironic that the U.S. government would be the sponsor. Still more ironic, this project and others like it could be said to have strengthened, not weakened, the American economy. DARPA spending in computer science at Berkeley and Stanford led directly to the founding of several companies that spun off from the universities—not just Sun Microsystems, but also Silicon Graphics, which is another computer workstation manufacturer, MIPS, a computer chip manufacturer later absorbed into Silicon Graphics, and several others, whose combined market value by the early 1990s was well over $10 billion, a net return to the larger economy of many multiples of the government's original investment. Amidst the rhetoric that one hears in Silicon Valley about the need not to tamper with Free Enterprise, it is refreshing to hear Bechtolsheim's dissenting voice. He looks back at the origins of Sun not as the story of entrepreneurial genius but rather as the outcome of this government-funded research. He could design and build a new computer himself only because he did not have to come up with millions of dollars to create the software needed for an operating system. He could use Berkeley Unix, which the government had already paid for.

In 1981, Bechtolsheim at Stanford bolted together about twenty new machines, and word of his accomplishment quickly spread throughout the university community. Everybody wanted one, but Bechtolsheim had his studies to attend to, and did not want to be bothered. He came up with what he thought was a perfect solution: he would license the design to other companies for $10,000, providing them with the printed-circuit board layout, schematics, parts lists, everything that they would need to assemble the machines themselves. They would put the machines together and distribute them; he would earn a royalty; academic colleagues would get inexpensive machines; everybody would be happy. The plan flopped, however. No large computer manufacturer was interested in licensing such a machine, for the same very good reason that the academics could not wait to get hold of the machines: there was nothing proprietary embodied in the design, hence no premium could be charged well beyond the actual cost of assembling ordinary parts. Eight small companies took out licenses from Bechtolsheim, but they all had difficulty manufacturing the boards that were the heart of the machine. After six months, none of the licensees had succeeded in making and selling machines, and it looked as if the commercial history of the Sun machine would end there.

It was at this point, in early 1982, that Bechtolsheim happened to receive a call from a Stanford MBA graduate, Vinod Khosla, who had just left a company he had helped found that made a specialized workstation for computer-aided engineering. Khosla was interested in the idea of building a versatile general-purpose machine such as Bechtolsheim's, but he explained, when Bechtolsheim offered him the standard license, that he wanted "the goose that laid the golden egg, not the golden egg." At first, Bechtolsheim declined Khosla's invitation to be a cofounder in the new company that Khosla proposed; Bechtolsheim wanted to finish his Ph.D. But Khosla made a persuasive case that they would be able to secure venture capital funding and soon realize Bechtolsheim's desire to make the Sun machine as widely available as demand called for. They put together a plan in Bechtolsheim's Stanford office, and over a hamburger at McDonald's recruited a third founder, Scott McNealy, friend and roommate of Khosla and also a Class of 1980 MBA graduate at Stanford, who would direct manufacturing. Their pitch was this: Workstations then available on the market, which were used primarily for computer-aided design, cost $20,000 to $200,000, a price too high for companies to provide each engineer individually with a machine. The principal competition was Apollo, an East Coast company that offered a workstation for about $25,000 and was based, as all the rest were, on proprietary components. The Sun founders said they could manufacture a comparable machine for fifty to seventy percent less than the competition, which would bring the retail price for their machines down to the $10,000 to $20,000 range. It was a compelling difference, and made the idea of one-engineer/one-machine realistic. The trio quickly got start-up venture funding just as Khosla had predicted.

Here at its inception, Sun's history is different than NeXT's: Sun's business plan stood on its own merits. The founders did not corral a sugar daddy like Ross Perot based on television profiles or rest on past laurels, because they had none to speak of. Nor did they coast with the complacent knowledge that one among them had untapped millions like Steve Jobs did. They not only had to sell their vision to flinty outsiders who were anything but sentimental, they also had to make their venture profitable as fast as possible, before their funds were exhausted. Sun Microsystems was incorporated in late February 1982; by May, the Sun 1 was shipping; by August the company was profitable. (Compare this with NeXT's later record of taking three years to bring out its first machine and going seven years without a single profitable quarter.)

Khosla set out to recruit executives from the major computer companies but had difficulty. Looking back, years later, he was excessively modest: "When you're twenty-six years old, look like a little kid, talk with a funny accent and have just two people in your company, you don't get very far." But he did recruit another twenty-six-year-old, Bill Joy, lured from a Ph.D. program at Berkeley. Joy looked the part of a Berkeley graduate student, with a rounded crown of long curly hair, beard, and glasses. It was a coup for Sun to hire Joy, who had been the principal designer behind the Berkeley version of Unix, which was the version Sun had decided to use on its machines. Joy was the software prodigy as Bechtolsheim was the hardware prodigy; Khosla and McNealy supplied expertise in finance and manufacturing. Soon, an experienced computer-industry veteran, French-born Bernard Lacroute, hired away from Digital Equipment Corporation, provided ballast as the executive vice-president.

Sun adopted a style of spending that was diametrically opposite to that of NeXT: it gloried in taking tightfistedness to extremes. Sun's leased space was simple industrial-grade; the furniture, purchased from a surplus warehouse; potted plants were used to cover up stains in the carpet. As at NeXT, a major early expenditure was spending for a company logo, but Sun spent $3,000, not $100,000, and it was done by art students, not a Paul Rand. When marketing consultants suggested that the logo color be changed from orange to blue, and that it be rotated 45 degrees, McNealy did not take the designer's instructions nearly as seriously as Steve Jobs. He had the sales staff continue to use the business cards that had already been printed with the Sun logo aligned squarely with the card; to adhere to the new tilted design, he told them to hand the cards out at an angle.[151]

Of the two founders who were strongest on the business side, it would be McNealy who played an ongoing crucial role (Khosla resigned in 1984, partly due to conflicts with the board, and partly due to having achieved the vow he had made as a young man of retiring by the age of thirty). Upon Khosla's departure, McNealy was appointed president of the company by the Sun board of directors, who were initially tentative about the appointment of another twenty-nine-year-old to the position of CEO, when, by that point, Sun appeared to need seasoned executive leadership. The company had blasted through the sales targets of its initial business plan and was well beyond the start-up stage. As unlikely as it may have seemed, McNealy proved to be a good choice, for reasons that again bear comparison with Steve Jobs.

Jobs likes to think of himself as an artiste, an unfulfilled poet who could just as well have ended up on Paris's Left Bank,[152] but McNealy is the artiste's worst nightmare: the anti-intellectual jock. Asked in 1992 what he would do on a perfect day, McNealy answered, "Start off with 18 holes of golf, play a hockey game, play some tennis, take a nap, have a big dinner, see the Sharks [a professional hockey team] play, and then go have some beers with my best friends."[153] On another occasion, he was asked for his favorite book; his reply, *How to Putt Like the Pros*. (Contrast this also with Bill Gates, whose favorite reading is found in *The Economist* and *Scientific American*.) When a Stanford alumni magazine asked him about what he had learned as an MBA student, McNealy emphasized what he had *not* learned, such as that "in some situations the right answer is the best answer, the wrong answer is the second best answer, and no answer is the worst answer." He warned against the temptation to "sit and analyze and absolutely miss the boat."[154] His professors might call this Management-by-Viscera.

McNealy never pursued the highest grades *per se* when in college, but rather had his own goal of what he called maximizing-GPA-per-hour-invested, which made him the self-described most *effective* student on campus. He reasoned that even if he were to receive all C's in his classes, if he "didn't spend a nanosecond working, I might actually win, because then I could go off and play on the golf team, tennis team, or do whatever I needed to do and be much broader and have a much more interesting life."[155]

McNealy is more complicated, however, than he would like us to believe. His love of sports is genuine, and surely no other CEO of a Fortune 500 company plays center twice a week on a local hockey team, as McNealy does. But he has to work hard to explain away the facts that detract from his preferred persona of the average Joe who got lucky. If one points out that he did get a perfect math score on the Scholastic Aptitude Test, that he did go to Harvard as an undergraduate, and that he did go to Stanford for graduate school, he insists on directing attention to his lower score on the verbal portion of the SAT ("They called me the illiterate genius: I could think real good but I couldn't talk real good")[156] and how he was rebuffed in his first attempts to get into business school at Harvard and Stanford and had worked in the interim as a foreman in a truck-hood factory in Ohio. In his telling, the worst part of the Ohio factory experience was that after working two months of fourteen-hour days, he was hospitalized with hepatitis, an ordeal of "no beer for six weeks."[157] This semiserious invention of himself as Animal House denizen is lent more credence by a face that makes him look even younger than he is.

Complications arise also when considering McNealy's upbringing: born to privilege but driven to shed all visible signs of it. His father, William McNealy, was vice-chairman of American Motors Corporation; Iacocca used to visit the house; the younger McNealy could call upon Don Peterson, the president of Ford, for a letter of recommendation for Stanford Business School. But he apparently left home with an instinctual attraction to melding with the masses, and he could still profess awe when an opportunity arose to meet the CEO of a competitor or supplier. There is no visible sign of insincerity when he would say, "It's a big kick in the pants to get to meet all these people. I feel totally blown away sometimes."[158] In contrast, Steve Jobs, who had never had famous figures visiting his family's household, upon becoming a celebrity himself, would approach the opportunities to mix with the famous (and the beautiful) with a palpable air of entitlement.

When McNealy's shares in Sun Microsystems made him a multimillionaire bachelor by the age of thirty, he could not name much that he had bought with his money, other than a large-screen television set to watch hockey and football, and the occasional new hockey stick, which, he allowed, set him back $15 each.[159] (One extravagance was spending $90,000 in 1987 on a four-day golf tournament for friends, honoring an earlier promise that if he were ever to be successful, he would throw a good party.)[160] For his own personal car, he eschewed the Porsche Carreras favored by his Sun colleagues, and took pride in his loyalty to "Good 'ol Deeeetroit iron." Despite a background in which, he joked, he had been born with a "platinum spoon" in his mouth, he gloried in being cheap. At the beginning of the company's history, when their modest single building had no facilities, frugality dictated that he and other employees sneak showers at offices of another company next door; the tradition of keeping expenses as low as possible continued even as the company became a multibillion-dollar success—McNealy insisted, for example, that all Sun employees, himself included, fly coach, unless taking a redeye flight that gave the company an extra day of work. On McNealy's desk was a name tag that identified his title as Chairman and Cheap Operator.[161] Perhaps Jobs and McNealy should be seen as playing out roles dictated by their class backgrounds: Steve Jobs, who grew up in a working-class home, was careless with the money of his company, both at Apple and at NeXT, the classic behavior of the arriviste; Scott McNealy, a preppy in the true sense of the word, as graduate of Cranbrook, a prep academy outside of Detroit, was thrifty to the other extreme, displaying the aversion to ostentation found in those born to privilege.

The family connection to the automotive industry accounts for McNealy's choosing an unorthodox field for an MBA: manufacturing. He had decided that the only *real* jobs were designing, making, or selling products; anything else was superfluous, and he wanted to find work again as a factory foreman. He discovered, however, that the factory job that he had found after graduation with a BA from Harvard was virtually impossible to secure as a newly minted Stanford MBA. When he knocked on doors, he was treated like "a Ph.D. looking for a job in a gas station." No one wanted him to work on the plant floor; every company he spoke with wanted him to work in the strategy area, which he described with dripping sarcasm: "That way I could just *think* about how other people should work on the plant floor." His first employer, FMC, hired him on condition that he initially agree to work in "corporate manufacturing strategy" before he got his wish to work in real plant management. He later moved to Onyx, a small computer manufacturer, where he got his wish to work in manufacturing management, and it was from this modest position that he joined Sun at Khosla's invitation. Yet, for all his passion for manufacturing, he remained much more clear-sighted about its costs than Jobs, and had outside contractors do the board-stuffing and assembly of Sun computers when he saw that doing so would save cash and permit Sun to concentrate its own resources on hardware and software design. Even as a multibillion-dollar company, at one point Sun relied so completely on outside firms that no Sun employees actually touched its bestselling machines: the computer was manufactured by a contract assembler, then shipped directly to the customer by a contract shipper.[162] This was the antithesis of Steve Jobs's approach to manufacturing.

McNealy never tried to paint a picture of himself as a godlike visionary. He could talk, without embarrassment, about the first business venture he had started with Khosla, when he was still working at Onyx. The two had started a company called The Data Dump, which they hoped would provide a chain of word-processing centers for students near universities. It bombed, taking with it the personal investments of the two young men and the $75,000 that they had rounded up from other investors.[163] Once Sun had become a multibillion-dollar company, when McNealy was asked to explain the sources of his success at Sun, he drew a distinction between those who had achieved a great deal over a long period of time, such as Ken Olsen, the patriarch of Digital Equipment Corporation, whose longevity in the top position (1957–1992) made clear that luck alone was not responsible, and others, such as himself, whose success came so suddenly. McNealy did not mention Jobs by name but alluded to him by saying, "Any of my peer group who tells you otherwise—just think about them and think about how lucky they were to be at the right place at the right time."[164]

If McNealy's apparent lack of personal pretension, and his insistence on happenstance in his own success at Sun, seems too thick to be credible, consider how the company's products, the workstations themselves, are unpretentious. The Sun machines have not always boasted the fastest speed or leadership in technology. Instead, the consistency of their appeal is better explained by Sun's offering a combination of reasonably good performance for a comparatively low price, and the open philosophy of Unix software, which meant that customers did not have to lock themselves into one manufacturer's proprietary software standards. For customers of large computers, buying a particular brand of computer was not unlike choosing a marriage partner: if one were to decide later to leave the chosen partner, the cost would be very high—in the case of computers because of the tremendous investment in software that would run only on that one kind of machine. If customers bought a Sun machine, however, and later decided they wanted to switch to another Unix computer, they would be able to move their software easily. That was the beauty of Unix. Even though Sun began as a start-up company up against not just the established computer giants like IBM and Digital, but also the workstation leader Apollo, still, despite its insignificant size, it offered something that none of the others did, which was the peace of mind that purchase of machines today would not impose an expensive penalty if one were to make a different choice tomorrow. Large corporate customers, normally leery of start-ups, nevertheless regarded Sun computers as a "safe buy" precisely because of Sun's adopting open standards instead of protecting proprietary secrets.[165] Sun shared source code; it made its young "Twinkie eaters," the engineers, available to anyone who stopped by Sun offices.[166] The company offered a personality that resembled McNealy's own definition of himself as a "a fast ball down the middle, nothing fancy, nothing tricky."[167]

The computer industry did not pay much attention to what Sun was up to in its early years. The most attention the company received each year was shortly after April Fool's Day, when the rest of Silicon Valley wanted to hear what pranks Sun's engineers had devised to torment the senior executives. The tradition apparently started when one April First an employee had swapped pictures of family members that were found on desks with pictures of nudes (a life-sized figure was pinned to the back of McNealy's door) and discovered that the switch went unnoticed in some cases for quite a while; one jinxed representative of the company held a number of meetings in his office with vendors while remaining unaware of the new photographs that greeted his visitors. Succeeding years produced a series of stunts: Office in Pond, Car in Office, Car in Pond, and then, the one logical permutation remaining, Pond in Office (actually, a pond flanked by sand traps that were built the night before in McNealy's office). These would appear to be the antics of idle minds at a Caltech or MIT, the stuff of adolescents, not adults. Anticipating such an impression, McNealy did not shirk from it but reveled in it; he put himself in a company video titled "Never Grow Up." But in fact the same prankish impulses appear, it seems, wherever one finds collections of engineers, including the manufacturing engineers at NeXT (who on occasion doctored, without the victims' knowledge, the photographs of colleagues that automatically accompanied their outgoing electronic mail messages). The difference was that Jobs could not abide any practical jokes; he had a zero-tolerance policy for "unprofessional" behavior that distracted attention from the official company focus and he "went nonlinear" in anger when he heard about plans afoot among the engineers to hire a stripper for a surprise birthday party that they were conspiring to arrange at the factory. Sun saluted pursuit of fun for catharsis, as ritual on April Fool's Day, as spontaneous inspiration on other occasions, and in weekly beer busts in its early years when the number of employees was still manageable. Its culture acquired a public image as a raucous campus party that McNealy could always be relied upon to join (the image was far overblown—a company does not grow from zero to $1 billion in revenues in record time by staging a nonstop Bacchanalia for its employees). Jobs, in contrast, stamped out incipient distractions conjured by the engineers and kept his company quiet as a cloister.

In Sun's first years, when Jobs was still at Apple, McNealy and Bechtolsheim had tried to interest him a number of times in producing a computer that would run Unix software. They told him that Unix was beloved by universities, and sent him a Sun machine to try out for himself. Jobs had reacted scornfully, telling them that Sun would never amount to anything more than a $40 million company, while Apple was capturing the large volume in the mainstream desktop computer market. Jobs told Sun that they might as well quit.[168] Sun's workstation and minicomputer competitors did not pay much attention either. In 1984, Apollo had about forty percent of the workstation market, and Sun, only seventeen percent. Even in 1985, stock analysts projected that Sun would do no better than fourth place in market share by 1990 because IBM and Digital would weigh in with strong workstation entries,[169] and Sun was deemed to have "untested" management while Apollo was "deep with veterans."[170]

Few noticed that Sun had been able to grow one hundred percent *per quarter* without advertising, even though its competitors advertised heavily. Its nonproprietary Unix computers were so strikingly different from the alternatives that Sun did not have to seek out customers; the customers came to it. Its larger competitors later realized how compelling the Sun philosophy was, including the need to cooperate with technology leaders instead of trying to invent everything on one's own. Bill Joy articulated the idea that those companies that try to do it all, those who were vertically integrated, would inevitably fall behind.[171] Time would prove him correct.

Time would also reveal what analysts in the mid-1980s did not see, the collective strength of the senior managers at Sun, each of whom complemented the others' strengths, while all sharing a keen sense of market trends. The division of labor accorded Bechtolsheim and Joy responsibility for setting the company's technical directions, and McNealy and Lacroute were responsible for directing business operations. Just as they believed that no single company would have the resources to be a technology leader in all areas, so too they believed that no human manager could possibly do all things equally well, staying current with the latest developments in hardware *and* software *and* meeting with stock analysts *and* worrying about manufacturing *and* doing the myriad other tasks required in running a company. There is only so much time and so much attention that can be given to any single item, "only so much bandwidth," as everyone says in the computer industry. At Sun, the limited bandwidth of mortals led to decision-making power being pushed downward.

Yet even though formally released from mundane business concerns, Bechtolsheim and Joy kept closely abreast of commercial currents outside the company, which informed their technical decisions. For example, Bechtolsheim, the person who on paper was the hardware specialist, commanded an encyclopedic knowledge of competitor's sales figures. Here again, McNealy's lack of pretension served him well, permitting him to harness a number of good people as a reasonably well-functioning team instead of tying the company's fortunes to the perspicacity of a single founder's vision. He ascribed his willingness to "stay out of everybody's way" to his lack of experience and explained half-jokingly that if the others would not make the hard decision, he would threaten to do so for them, "and that always scared them into making it."[172] Once a decision was made, however, McNealy was well-known for executing it well. He also was rough on his competitors in public speeches, displaying the unapologetic style of a hockey player who loved to bang opponents against the glass. His antagonistic taunts led Silicon Valley journalists to quip that Sun did not have competitors, it had *enemies*. McNealy knew that the rest of the computer industry would delight in Sun crashing: "There is definitely a crew waiting at the end of the runway and they are not there waiting for the plane to land."[173]

In 1985, when NeXT was founded, no one had any inkling that brassy, unpretentious Sun, lacking any identifiably unique technical distinction, whose technology was either licensed from others or licensed *to* others, would lead what would become a revolution in the computer world, in which large corporations began to unplug their mainframes and replace them with networks of speedy workstations such as Sun's or less powerful personal computers. The Sun machine embodied the same philosophy of open standards that the IBM personal computer had pioneered, making it possible for software to run on the machines of many different manufacturers. This was especially so in the first half of the 1980s, before competition arose at the top layer of software, where Unix customers increasingly had their choice among incompatible "graphical user interfaces." In the world of personal computers based on the microprocessor family that launched the original IBM PC, these problems of software compatibility did not exist, which was one of the reasons that the PC portion of the computer industry continued to grow and grow.

Steve Jobs of course had no personal tie to the revolution wrought by the IBM personal computer; his answer to the IBM PC, the

Macintosh, embodied the older notion of proprietary software and a single manufacturer of the hardware. It should not be surprising, then, that when building the NeXT, he would again choose not to adopt a dominant software standard for graphical display but rather go his own proprietary way. NeXT would find itself paddling against a strong current that was rushing toward standards, however. NeXT would also be hobbled by an organizational culture that was weak in the areas in which Sun was strong: NeXT did not have the cross-checking safeguards of truly shared leadership; it did not know how to operate without expensive frills; its most senior technical leaders did not pay close attention to market realities, as the company prized technological leadership above all else; once NeXT's first product was ready, its marketing leaders would look to elaborately staged media events to carry its marketing message to prospective customers, and not to word-of-mouth testimonials bubbling up from the grassroots.

These weaknesses at NeXT were not visible, however, until after the Cube was unveiled in October 1988. Precisely because no one on the outside was permitted to view what the company was building on the inside without being sworn to secrecy, NeXT looked much more formidable than it otherwise would have. In January 1987, Andy Bechtolsheim, concerned that NeXT would soon release a competitively lethal machine, wrote a thirteen-page memo urging that Sun build a new, powerful, yet inexpensive machine designed especially for the university market. The machine was given the code name "Campus." Bechtolsheim thought that universities were on the verge of purchasing thousands of workstations, and Sun would be left behind without its own relatively inexpensive computer based on RISC technology, which seemed to him to be a superior design. Sun was far ahead of most of the computer industry in realizing that RISC technology was the wave of the future, and it had defied conventional wisdom in 1984 by deciding to develop its own RISC chip and license it widely as an alternative standard rather than continue to use the more complicated CISC chips supplied by the large semiconductor companies.[174] But in 1987 Sun was using its RISC chip only in its high-end machines, called servers, which cost $50,000 and were used as the heart of networks that served many workstations. Bechtolsheim proposed to design a low-end, inexpensive workstation around the same RISC chip.

Bechtolsheim's proposal was turned down, in an interesting instance when the shared-leadership model at Sun led to a most unwise decision. The other senior managers were not immediately receptive because the company had moved up-scale in its marketing focus, away from its roots as the manufacturer of no-frills workstations. It was doing fabulously well selling big, expensive, high-margin servers. The others did not see what Bechtolsheim saw, that market momentum even in the Unix world was quietly shifting toward small desktop machines and that the only way to survive in the future would be by adopting a "volume strategy," selling as many inexpensive machines as possible. Unable to persuade the others of the pressing urgency of the matter, Bechtolsheim decided to start his own company to pursue Campus on his own since Sun would not let him do it. Bechtolsheim owned Sun stock valued at over $26 million[175] when it had gone public the year before, and though he continued to live just as he had before, he and Joy renting a small house in Palo Alto, he could afford to draw down $200,000 to rent office space and set up a new venture, called Unisun. Upon his departure from Sun he did *not* sell his shares in pique; nor did he install himself as CEO and all-powerful potentate. He persuaded Vinod Khosla to serve as president, and gave himself the position of chief of engineering. He left Sun on amicable terms and offered it the opportunity to invest in the new company then or later. Sun passed on the invitation for the moment.

Three months later, after Bechtolsheim had a rough design to show to his old company, Sun decided that it was a good idea after all, and offered to buy Unisun outright and fold it into the parent company. Bechtolsheim, who was interested in getting his computer built, not in making a second fortune, agreed to the terms that Sun proposed, which were simply to reimburse him for the money spent on the project while off on his own. Moreover, Sun insisted that Bechtolsheim hire for his Campus group only those Sun engineers who were otherwise going to quit the company. The condition suited Bechtolsheim because his team of fifteen was composed of those who were most frustrated by the complacency that had crept into Sun as the company enjoyed one success after another.

Bechtolsheim was worried that NeXT would first conquer universities, then the world. He had no concrete picture in advance of what the NeXT computer would be, but he was convinced that the new Sun machine needed to be made as small as possible, ideally the size of a pizza box. In his passionate attention to small details, Bechtolsheim resembled Steve Jobs. They differed in that Bechtolsheim knew that the perfectionist impulse is not the manifestation of greatness but a compulsion that needs to be reined in. Unlike Jobs, Bechtolsheim periodically yielded, aware of how costly it was to pursue hundred-percent perfection instead of settling for ninety-nine percent of the goal; the last degree was always the most costly portion by far. Like Jobs, Bechtolsheim had difficulty furnishing his house because he could never find furniture that he liked,[176] but at work Bechtolsheim paid attention to what the competition was doing and was willing to compromise his own standards in order to stay close to what the rest of the world wanted. Even if compromise on a particular detail was so galling that he refused to give his imprimatur, he did not override decisions just because he was a founder of the company. When development of the Campus machine was moved back to Sun, his engineers told him that the case housing the computer would have to be widened by three millimeters in order to accommodate all of the electronic guts that he had specified. Believing that Sun's culture had become too dominated by "big boxes," and determined that his new machine not incrementally end up like the others, Bechtolsheim refused to agree to the additional three millimeters. But the more junior division head of manufacturing overruled him, and the enlarged dimensions prevailed.[177]

What most distinguished Sun's senior managers from Steve Jobs was the awareness at Sun of the pervasiveness of trade-offs in life. McNealy, for example, had a sharp sense of how decisions about making new computers always demanded choices, between cost and performance, between compatibility and innovation, between ease-of-use and sophistication.[178] The NeXT culture was infused with a utopianism that declared that trade-offs were an illusion, the result of lack of vision. As Sun's soon-to-be competitor, NeXT seemed most potent a threat when its own machine was still hidden behind the veil, and all that could be seen were wisps of fog that enshrouded the company. What magic would Jobs conjure up? Even unbelievers could not ward off a chill of wonder; maybe NeXT would indeed somehow manage to break free of the exasperating trade-offs between which everyone else had to choose. One could not find a more hardheaded group of realists than the managers at Sun, yet even they felt the need to defensively launch work on a machine that might be able to compete with whatever miraculous wonder popped out of NeXT. Sun did not have enough time, however, to have the machine that would be its answer to NeXT ready by the time NeXT was finally ready to introduce its machine. When the long-awaited moment for NeXT arrived in October 1988, NeXT would be able to command the undivided attention of the computer world. No one watched with greater interest than Sun.

The Unveiling

N o other group of 180 people in the computer industry could begin to match the collective hold on the world's attention that the employees of little NeXT, Inc., commanded on the day of the Cube's introduction, October 12, 1988. Steve Jobs and his minions had succeeded masterfully in stoking outside expectations by keeping details secret, creating a hunger for scraps of advance information that the press described as a "feeding frenzy."[179] On the eve of the big day, computer industry pundit Stewart Alsop addressed an open letter to Steve Jobs in his newsletter, begging for an evaluation machine. Alsop admitted he was pandering in an embarrassing fashion but Jobs had "managed to achieve the one thing that no manufacturer has been able to achieve since I started the newsletter in 1985—to make me want a machine that's incompatible with the ones I currently use."[180] This was before Alsop, and all the slavering others, had even gotten a chance to see the machine, let alone touch one.

Forty-five hundred invitations to the event were sent out to selected friends, well-wishers, and power brokers like Alsop. Two hours before doors were opened, hundreds of the invitees were already lined up. "It's like I'm six years old, it's Christmas Eve, and I know I'm getting a train set in the morning," said one anonymous arrival who claimed he was unable to sleep the previous night due to the excitement.[181] Advance hyperbole reached its zenith when Richard Smolan, the photographer who had created the *Day in the Life* books, explained his reason for taking a redeye flight from the East Coast the previous night so that he could attend: "Missing this would be like missing Thomas Edison unveil the phonograph. I don't want to tell my grandchildren I was invited but didn't go."[182] So many representatives of the press sought admittance to the hallowed site of the unveiling, Davies Symphony Hall in San Francisco, that access had to be restricted to a pool of selected newspaper photographers and television cameramen.[183] One can see why, when a NeXT marketing person called *The Wall Street Journal* to inquire about purchasing space for an advertisement to accompany the unveiling, the *Journal* quipped, "Why bother?"[184]

For NeXT employees, the weeks immediately prior to the unveiling had passed in a hyperkinetic, sleepless blur, as they attended to the myriad details of a show that would befit a company the size of IBM, and most demandingly of all, would befit the increasingly irascible Jobs, the perfectionist who already had a reputation as the preeminent showman of the industry. At the rehearsals, Jobs huddled with his coterie of sycophants, who yelped their approval of the boss like the supporting cast in a bad Broadway comedy about Madison Avenue. When a practice slide was projected on the screen, Jobs said: "I really like that green," and his assistants quickly added, "Great green, great green."[185]

For help with staging and design, Jobs hired George Coates, a local theater director whose work mixed postmodern stage drama with other art forms and unusual lighting. Jobs had wanted to stage a visual extravaganza that would top his legendary product introductions at Apple, but Coates showed him that it would be impossible to do so in the symphony hall. When Coates failed to convince Jobs that it would be best to move—Jobs wanted above all else the best possible acoustics so that he could demonstrate his computer's sound capabilities to good effect—Coates worked out an austere, spare look instead for the stage design and lighting. Against a black backdrop, the audience would see a vase of flowers, an unknown object hidden by a black shroud, and a solitary figure. It would be uncrowded to an extreme, a display of loud subtlety.

More difficult was readying the computer itself for the demonstration. Neither the operating system software nor the programs that would be used in the demonstration were close to being finished. A measure of the shaky state of the software at that point is provided by noting that the system software would not be ready for public release, it would turn out, until one year later. NeXT software engineers worked feverishly to try to stabilize at least parts of the programs, but software in such a buggy state behaves in anything but predictable fashion. To get through the demonstration, Jobs would be walking across a marshy bog of unknown software perils. At any step, the program could freeze, requiring that the machine be turned off, then restarted. This would be a nightmare in a demonstration such as this, with the whole world's eyes focused on the big-screen projection of the NeXT computer monitor. Jobs had to run through the demonstration without giving any hint of the rickety state of the software. With the auditorium full, the lights were dimmed, and at 9:39, while in the wings his crew had gathered and chanted a good-luck mantra, "Please don't fuck up, please don't fuck up,"[186] Jobs strode out onto the stage with hands folded prayerfully before his face:

[Applause] I think I speak for everybody at NeXT, saying it's great to be back. [Applause] . . . I think together we're going to experience one of those times that occurs once or twice in a decade of computing, a time when a new architecture is rolled out that is really going to change the future of computing. And we've worked on this for three years. It's turned out [pronounced slowly for emphasis] *in-cre-di-bly* great. . . .

This would be Jobs's show. Only two other people would appear on the stage during the three-hour presentation, and that only briefly. By looking at highlights of his spiel with the detachment that passage of time provides, we can admire its rhetorical ingenuity and identify the claims that did and did not bear up subsequently. It is not possible, however, to re-create the atmosphere in the auditorium that day and his listeners' willingness to rely upon affect instead of analysis. In the darkened room that day, he was the mesmerist, they the willing subjects.

He began with a compact lecture that served to give NeXT the locomotive power of History. Professor Jobs explained that "computer architectures" possessed a ten-year life expectancy. (A preliminary note about terms: For those not familiar with the ubiquitous use of the word in computer jargon, *architecture* here translates roughly into "a hardware design that has a software standard incompatible with other computers".) A computer that was truly "revolutionary," by its very nature, could not run existing software. It was entirely new software, for the new "architecture," that Jobs thought would distinguish the NeXT computer from the rest. What he was blithely saying was that individuals and companies needed to throw away their software investments of many billions of dollars, as well as the investment of time that had been required to learn and feel comfortable with the software, and everyone should be glad to have the opportunity to start all over.

[Jobs points to an image of a wave, rising and falling, projected on the large screen.] Now that starts to get going, the computer takes off, and around year five it reaches its architectural peak, and then it goes into what you might call a glide slope. Now that doesn't mean its unit volume sales peak, but it does mean that the architecture is everything it's ever going to be, at that point.

Jobs led the audience through personal computer history, pointing out how well the model fit: first there had been the best-selling

Apple II, which had reached its technical peak in 1982; then the IBM Personal Computer had come along and peaked in 1986; followed by the Macintosh, which in 1988 he said possessed an elusive quality he called "momentum," which was manifested by "new, aggressive, hot" software being written for it first. He did not linger long on the discordant fact that the second-wave IBM PC and its compatible cousins, which by then supposedly had been eclipsed technically by the third-wave Macintosh, displayed anything but slackened momentum, as defined by volume of sales. But Jobs was in a rush to develop a self-serving prediction about the Macintosh—it was about to "peak" and would soon be in decline. This would pave the way for Jobs to employ more powerful workstations and "make the fourth wave, going into the nineties."

The Jobs model made the NeXT decision to ride a fourth wave seem natural and ineluctable. What the model failed to take into account, however, was that Wave Four, if indeed there was going to be one at all, would have a different shape than, say Wave One or Wave Two, because the presence of preceding waves affected what would follow. Suppose, for example, that Wave Two, the IBM personal computer standard, grew into a fearsome tsunami, climbing off the chart? Wave Four would not have nearly the same chance to grow placidly that Wave One had had back in the ancient days pre–IBM PC.

Jobs provided his audience no time to think about his pat historical model, however. He was already invoking the prestige of university friends to solidify the sense that the NeXT was not just surfing on the next historical Big One, but that it was also obeying the dictates of computer-savvy academics:

. . . How do we define this fourth wave? What we did was collaborate with a group of people that are probably the most diverse and demanding group of computer users in the world, and that's higher education, but [it is also] the place where most of the world's computer invention has sprung from over the last twenty years.

Reading from an ad that he had placed that day in *The Wall Street Journal* "that I suppose you could say is our manifesto," Jobs said:

> . . . We collaborated with the leaders in educational computing, from research universities, such as Stanford and Carnegie-Mellon, liberal arts schools like Vassar and Reed, as well as state universities, from California, to Michigan, to Maryland. We asked them not for their list of specifications, but for a list of their dreams; not to extend what computers have been, but to imagine what they could be. Only then did we begin to develop the NeXT computer.

Quoting from an unnamed university "advisor," Jobs told the audience that the NeXT computer had been described as more than a mere tool; it had been hailed as a "partner in thought."

This is inspirational stuff. It steers well clear of the terrestrial pull of "specifications" and the limits of price points; Jobs would reserve mention of price for the very end of the day's presentation. His description of higher education as an undiscovered market made colleges and universities appear to have wallets that bulged like those of corporations. When he asked, Who exactly is higher education? the answer to his question was crisp and impressive. Three thousand colleges and universities in the United States alone. Over 45,000 departments. Over 600,000 faculty members. Over 12 million students. Don't underestimate the size of these institutions, he warned. The annual budget of a Stanford was $750 million; a University of Michigan, over a billion. His conclusion: "These are Fortune 500 companies disguised by another name."

The audience laughed indulgently at his witticism, but this depiction, ignoring the budget constraints that these institutions faced, was fantastical. Jobs proceeded to talk about everything but price when paraphrasing what faculty and students were clamoring for in their collective requests to NeXT: Give us an open architecture. Give us what the early personal computers had. And we don't want big, hot, and noisy workstations. Give us machines that are small, cool, and quiet. It was curious that he would talk about the request to make the NeXT "open"; in fact, the NeXT machine would attract criticism for being anything but open. Jobs was so adamant about not including floppy disk drives that he even forbade *other* companies from selling drives to his customers. Such an attitude was the antithesis of that of IBM, which had encouraged other companies to make accessories for its machine, an attitude that greatly helped the IBM Personal Computer gain rapid acceptance. It is also strange that Jobs would emphasize the need to make his workstation small, cool, and quiet when the Cube would turn out to be quite large and its optical disk drive quite noisy. He moved on quickly to the problem of traffic congestion that afflicts computer designs; a nice *thirtysomething* sense of humor surfaced when he reviewed how NeXT designers had addressed the problem of bottlenecks when too much data tries to go in and out of the central processor at once:

> Before we raced off and solved this problem in our own way—we're in our early thirties now—we asked, Has anybody else solved this problem?

Displaying a picture of a giant mainframe computer, which was greeted by laughter and applause, Jobs admitted that the solution already was in hand, in the design of older mainframes. "What we realized," Jobs said, was that "higher ed wants a personal mainframe."

The talk about fast input-output, however, did not turn out to help NeXT sell the Cube because the optical disk was the big bottleneck, and for that the special input-output chips upon which Jobs lavished praise could not help. Just as any stereo salesperson loves to point out that any audio system is only as good as its weakest component ("sir, you'll be very happy with this new amplifier, but may I recommend that you upgrade your speakers, too"), so too is the speed of a computer system constrained by the speed of each individual component. As long as Jobs insisted on using the annoyingly slow optical disk, the "throughput" speeds of the other, faster components would all be rendered irrelevant. Jobs bragged about his custom chips (the same ones that had delayed the Cube's introduction so grievously), and during the presentation, he could assert that their performance was "staggering." But afterward, Jobs would have to drop this portion of his road-show spiel because the "staggering" performance was not actually visible to prospective customers. And they cared much less about the number of integrated circuits that the NeXT used—forty-five, Jobs proudly said, about half the number used in fast personal computers—than about the availability of familiar software packages like the prosaic spreadsheet.

The explication of the hardware continued. The three separate processors manufactured by Motorola were lovingly introduced, with much attention given to a special kind of chip called a DSP, a digital signal processor, whose capabilities were also "staggering." The digital signal processor, he said, was going to bring us revolutions in electronic music and computer voice recognition, making imminent the arrival of a computer to which one could give commands simply by speaking to it. Similar chips could be purchased for installation in other personal computers, but only as an add-on gizmo. Jobs explained again why he chose to include as standard these expensive specialty chips like signal processors and number-crunching math coprocessors: It was the only way to induce software developers to write software that would take advantage of these features. Developers wrote only for the "lowest common denominator," and if a DSP chip was available only as an expensive option, developers would ignore it.

You are bound in by your lowest common denominator. *This* is our lowest common denominator: a one-foot square board containing the entire system. [Applause] The most aggressive use of surface-mount technology in the industry. Let me take you through it. [Points out the various chips and components and ports.] [Applause] [Holding the board sacerdotally in his hands] I hope you get a chance to look at this a little later; it's the most beautiful printed circuit board I've ever seen in my life. [Applause]

The audience went along with his rapturous tribute but it was another one of those moments where one had to be physically present in order to experience the emotion. In bright daylight, a circuit board, even the "most beautiful" circuit board, is, well, just a circuit board. Purchasers of new computers are unlikely to gush on, as Jobs did, about the aesthetics of the interior boards. He also was proud that the computers were built "completely untouched by human hands" in NeXT's automated factory.

Up to this point, the audience still had not been given a chance to actually see anything more finished than the circuit board. Jobs let the suspense continue a bit longer and yielded the stage to a short film about the NeXT factory, "The Machine That Builds Machines," that the company had had produced for the occasion (for several hundred thousand dollars). Robots stuffed the moving circuit boards, the boards took a dip into a silvery bath of molten solder, and an unseen narrator intoned praise with a dramatic deep bass voice that made it sound as if NeXT had somehow arrived at the new millennium twelve years before everyone else.

Still not yet time to actually unveil the computer on stage. More disquisition on decisions that NeXT had made. Should the NeXT computer be housed in a tall, upright box, what was called a "tower" in computer parlance, that would sit beneath the desk, freeing space up on the desktop for the monitor and keyboard? How many slots for expansion boards should it provide? What kind of power cord? Jobs had an audience that was happy with whatever he chose to tell them; when he claimed that his computer was "extremely easy to manufacture and to service," a baldly disingenuous statement we know now, the audience had no idea that it could have been otherwise. All they knew was what he told them and what he permitted them to see.

> So now we've got a complete system. It's been designed from the start to be a complete system. You've listened to me talk about it for about forty minutes now. What I'd like to do is have the first computer of the nineties show you itself. [Applause; music; the machine itself is unveiled; more applause.]

Before he dismissed his audience for an intermission, Jobs drew attention to the feature that he clearly was most proud of, yet was the very feature that would prove to be a technical disaster:

> We haven't talked about mass storage. We thought, what should we have for mass storage? And we looked at floppies. The problem is that floppies are pretty small, and every time we want to update our system, it seemed crazy to us to ship fifty, seventy-five floppy disks. And the more we looked at it, the more we realized that floppies were a technology of the seventies. . . . So two years ago, we made a decision. We saw some new technology and we made a decision to *risk our company* [pronounced slowly for emphasis] that we could pull it off and bring it to market about four years before anybody thought possible. And we've done it. The NeXT Computer is the first computer in the world to ship with read-write erasable optical technology storage. [Extended applause]

Each optical disk, he explained, held 250 megabytes [million-bytes], capacious indeed when compared with floppy disks that then stored only 1.4 megabytes each. But storage capacity was only one of several features by which the optical disk would be judged. The speed with which one could read or write to it was important, and how the optical disk compared to others in this regard Jobs chose to leave unmentioned. He was not unaware of the problem; he simply assumed that improved technology would soon solve it. Unfortunately, a small company he secretly had been talking with about a solution never came through with the promised fix.

The cost of the optical disk cartridge was also important, and here Jobs with bravura transformed what should have been a liability into an apparent asset: each optical disk would cost $50, he announced, and the way he said it made it seem as if this was an extremely low price. Compared to what it cost NeXT's Japanese supplier, Canon, to produce, this was indeed low; in fact, the Canon representatives in the audience had not known beforehand what price Jobs would sell their optical disks for, and when they heard "$50" and converted the figure into yen, they were aghast as they realized that Jobs had promised to sell them *below Canon's cost*. Compared to the price of regular magnetic floppy disks, which could be purchased for about a dollar or less, the optical disk was a far more expensive proposition. Later, analysts would voice some discomfort with the price, and software companies, who were most directly affected, would soon yowl in protest, but at the time of the initial announcement, the auditorium of shills applauded in rapturous innocence. Only a nonstudent like Jobs could so completely swing wide of imagining what would be on the minds of real college students:

> So as we move into the 1990s we really can take our entire world in our backpack, pop it out of the computer, run across campus, run across town, run across the country, and pop it into another computer, and have everything we've probably ever done in our lives with us. [Applause]

No, the world-in-a-backpack would rank much lower than other more prosaic considerations, such as cost. The Jobs vision of using one's one-disk *oeuvre* on cross-country trips was also dependent upon everyone else buying a NeXT machine, too, since the NeXT optical disks would not work in any other kind of computer. Jobs had no practical feel for what college students would want. Prior to the introduction, he had been momentarily infatuated with bundling an encyclopedia in electronic form, too. "It's only going to cost us another five bucks," Jobs had exulted. One of the rare NeXT employees who would successfully challenge him (and who not coincidentally left NeXT after a short stint) criticized the idea: "Steve, geez, I never once looked at an encyclopedia as a college student, but then you wouldn't know that since you never really did it." Jobs was silent; for whatever reason, the encyclopedia was not included.

The time for intermission had arrived, and Jobs invited his audience "to see firsthand what we're doing" by proceeding to the lobby to examine for themselves the machines, the optical disks, and the printed circuit boards. Anyone who headed for the lobby with the impression that the Cube was available for keyboard pounding was soon disappointed. The *firsthand* experience that Jobs had promised was the privilege of viewing the machines at a safe remove behind velvet ropes. The software was far too buggy to permit anyone to test it. Jobs kept the instability of the software well hidden, and when the audience was gathered again and he asked, "So what'd you think?" he was bathed in appreciative applause.

Jobs boasted of many "revolutionary" features in the Cube's design, but with the passage of time, it would be seen that most were not so revolutionary, or were easily copied, or were not such a good idea in the first place. The one exception, the one feature introduced that day amidst the many, that turned out to have enduring value was the new operating system that NeXT had designed, called NeXTSTEP. Or perhaps we should say, was at that moment in the process of being designed, given its appalling state of incompleteness. The purpose of the software was to make life as easy for software developers as the Macintosh had for computer users. This was accorded a high priority for NeXT because "our market doesn't want to take six months to write a program; they want a statistics program for next Thursday's statistics class."

The solution, he explained, was to provide a "revolutionary" new program called Interface Builder, whose lineage, though he did not credit it, could be traced to preceding work at small, obscure software shops, like ExperTelligence, or further back, to Xerox

PARC in the 1970s, or still further back to university-based software research, which developed systems that permitted programmers to use and reuse prewritten software modules called objects. Interface Builder provided objects that expedited the design of the look of a screen, the task that Jobs claimed, with his customary tendency to exaggerate, occupied ninety percent of the programmer's time. One can see, however, if ninety percent of a programming project could be reduced to virtually no time at all, thanks to his Interface Builder, why Jobs would expect a multitude of new programs to appear for his Cube in short order.

> Now what I'd like to do now is do some live demos for you. . . . I'd like to remind you of the first two laws of demo'ing. [Some laughter] First law of demos is that demos will always crash. And the second law of demos is that their probability of crashing goes up with the number of people watching. [More laughter and applause] So if something goes wrong today, have some compassion for the demo-er.

Here, in public he was the very picture of charm. It should be noted that this very same person, when watching a demonstration performed by a member of his staff in the privacy of his company offices, would rip out the entrails of anyone who permitted any imperfection, let alone a software crash, to mar the performance.

While the audience watched on the large-screen projection overhead, Jobs gave an introductory tour. Here is where the files were listed; there is where one moves files for deletion (a swirling black hole that swallowed up the picture of the discarded file). Only a machine that was intended for a university market would feature what Jobs used: an illustration of a gas molecule. The connection to academe was made more explicit when Jobs brought on the stage Richard Crandall, a physics professor from Reed College who had been working the past year for NeXT as an Education Fellow, to "help guide us to make sure we're really on track, in terms of making this computer everything that higher education wants."

From his presentation, it is easy to see why Crandall was encouraged to write nifty little demonstrations of the easy-to-program power of the new NeXT software. From the same presentation, it is also easy to see why Crandall was a poor choice for NeXT if the company insisted upon impressment of one single person to represent all of the diverse computing needs of higher education. Crandall was too immersed in his own corner of science to be able to communicate well with the rest of the scholarly community. What came out was a breathless stream of words, larded heavily with partisan praise. Here is a swatch of his running commentary that day while he demonstrated how easily his NeXT program could display complex molecules:

> I love to watch this one rotate. Let me tell you now that no other system has what this system has, which is, something called Mathematica, which I use to draw a quantum wave function plot for this. And I have a quantum wave function object and the method to solve this earlier equation, which solves, you know, the quantum mechanics. And I got what I wanted here, yes. I got this graph from Mathematica—Mathematica is a ten-person-year program, and I just linked to it within my application. It's a piece of cake. So you can see here this quantum wave function, with sort of six little mountain peaks—I'm taking advantage of enormously deep software that I didn't have to write. [Applause]

Crandall closed his presentation by tapping with his hand a microphone that was connected to the NeXT and then calling up a program that simulated an oscilloscope on the computer screen, which transformed the sound of the tapping into a wavy line. This, Crandall impishly explained, was the sound of one hand clapping.

"It's people like Richard that we're making this thing for," said Jobs after Crandall departed. Of course Jobs liked to think of Crandall as the typical prospective customer—Crandall accepted the NeXT machine just as Jobs wanted it to be seen, as the ultimate Swiss Army knife for academics. One should be willing to move mountains in order to get hold of such a machine, hang the cost. Crandall gave Jobs hope for strong sales when he was confronted with the discouraging resistance of the rest of NeXT's academic advisory board to making large-scale commitments on behalf of their home institutions. The Crandalls, however, could not form much of a commercial base for NeXT because there would be too few academics who could afford to say: price is not an issue.

Following Crandall's one-hand clapping, Jobs extended the demonstration of the NeXT's impressive sound capability. "It's great to read things in books," he said, "but sometimes hearing them in a person's own voice is far more moving." The audience heard selections from Martin Luther King's "I Have a Dream" speech, John F. Kennedy's "Ask Not What Your Country Can Do for You," a NASA voice transcript, "The Eagle Has Landed." Jobs also showed the audience how the electronic mail system that NeXT had designed permitted one to attach a recording of one's own voice to a message. Jobs leaned into a microphone:

> "Hi, this is Steve, sending a message on a pretty historic day from Davies Symphony Hall, San Francisco. Let's get a round of applause in it too." [Obliging applause] And of course we can edit that if we want to. [Replays the message]

One wonders if Jobs had scripted this scrap of grandiose pretension—"a pretty historic day"—or if it was blurted spontaneously in the excitement of the moment. In any case, when describing the ease with which NeXT's special multimedia mail could be sent round the world, Jobs did not explain that the recipients also had to have NeXT machines in order to be able to replay such messages. Buying a NeXT for its unique electronic mail would be like buying the AT&T videophone, reintroduced in 1992 after a long hiatus after its World's Fair debut in 1964: it was all but useless unless others bought in too.

We believe that one of the most important things in the first half of the 90s is the concept of the digital library. In other words, using our mass storage and some remarkable new software that we've written at NeXT, we can get the knowledge of civilization at our fingertips. And what we've done is we have made the first real digital book. There has not been an advancement in the state of the art of printed book technology since Gutenberg.

Here we go again, with the thundering pronouncements of historical significance. It was nice that NeXT had licensed the rights to *Webster's Collegiate Dictionary*, *The Oxford Dictionary of Quotations*, and the Oxford edition of Shakespeare's works. But these would turn out to be throwaways, a highbrow version of gimme-caps, willingly accepted but insufficient to influence a decision to purchase. Again, no one at the time questioned Jobs's assertion that his digital library would be an epochal breakthrough, or the tacit assumption that such reference works would be available exclusively on the NeXT computer (these, as well as many more, soon were available from the competition, too). But the sagacity of Jobs's commercial judgment was not uppermost in the minds of his audience that day at Davies Symphony Hall. He was too charming for impertinent doubts to creep in:

So let me show you a few things. First thing I'd like to do is show you what we consider to be the first really good digital book, which is Webster's. And I can turn off and on a thesaurus here. I'll leave it on. And a word that's sometimes used to describe me is "mercurial." [Appreciative laughter] So I decided I'd look it up the other day. And here's what [I found]. "Of or relating to, or born under the planet Mercury." I think the third one is the one they mean: "Characterized by unpredictable changeableness of mood." [Appreciative laughter] If we scroll down the thesaurus, though, we see that the antonym is "saturnine." We go, well what's that? By simply double-clicking on it, we immediately look that up in the dictionary, and here it is: "Cold and steady in moods, slow to act or change, of a gloomy or surly disposition." I don't think "mercurial" is so bad after all. [Applause]

The host could not only poke fun at his reputation, he also could show hip and literary touches:

> We also have the entire works of Bob Dylan on line. I'm not sure we can ship this. [Appreciative laughter] Let's find out what Dylan has to say about "love." Thirty-seven things about love, that's probably pretty good, starting with the "Wedding Song." So I think you understand the potential here. There's, oh, a wonderful book, *The Oxford Dictionary of Quotations*—there's a wonderful quote in this, with the word breakfast in it. Lewis Carroll. *Oxford Dictionary of Quotations*. About twenty-five of them. Notice I have, by the way, smooth scrolling in this whole system, I can just work down— Lewis Carroll: "Why, sometimes I've believed as many as six impossible things before breakfast." [Laughter, applause]

Jobs reserved his greatest enthusiasm for the musical capabilities of his machine, its ability, helped by the digital signal processor, to create music with the ease of a synthesizer, based on what Jobs called "pure mathematics." This was why he had insisted on a symphony hall for the Cube's coming-out party. Selections from three separate pieces—for harpsichord, strings, and Indonesian gamelan—filled the auditorium, all generated by the computer from formulas. A dazzling capability that time would show had an astounding lack of appeal outside of university music departments.

The end of the presentation was near, and it was time to talk about price. Jobs handled the delicate matter of breaking what should have been received as disappointing news by a long running start, reviewing for the audience all of the software that would be bundled along with the hardware. Jobs appraised the mail program, digital library, word processor, and the mathematical, artificial intelligence, and other software included in the price to be worth "thousands and thousands of dollars." So that made it appear that the lucky purchaser of a NeXT would be getting a steal:

Scott McNealy of Sun Microsystems. *(© 1993 Doug Menuez/Reportáge)*

Steve Jobs and Bill Gates, together at Jobs's home in 1991, in a temporary moment of amity. By the next year, Jobs was loudly attacking "the Microsoft monopoly." *George Lange/Outline Press)*

The floor of one of the exhibition halls at the Fall '92 Comdex. *(Comdex)*

We're going to be charging higher education a single price of
$6,500. [Extended applause] Our breakthrough printer that every-
one seems to want in their office—we are going to charge I think
an outstandingly great price: $2,000. [Applause]

Jobs announced that for those who wished to supplement the storage
capabilities of the optical disk drives with conventional hard drives,
"unprecedented" pricing would permit customers to pay a mere
$2,000 or $4,000 in addition. More applause followed.

The joke that had circulated in Silicon Valley before this event
alluded to the late Reverend Jim Jones and Jonestown, predicting
that if Jobs set a cup of grape Kool-Aid in front of every seat, the
audience would drink it down without question.[187] It turned out
not to be so funny because the audience enthusiastically applauded
the news that a basic machine and printer, equipped with a hard
disk (a necessity, it would turn out, because the optical disk was so
slow) would cost over $10,000. For a computer that could not
display color. This did not bear much correspondence to the promised price point of $3,000. And the prospective buyer had no choice
about accepting the bundle in its entirety; one could not unbundle
that software worth "thousands and thousands of dollars" to reduce
the price. Jobs insisted: all or nothing. He also had to deliver the
bad news about the incomplete state of the basic operating system
software, but with his glib handling, the implications of the news
made no apparent impression on the Kool-Aid besotted audience.
Keep in mind that the initial public release of software is named,
by convention, version 1.0, and subsequent improvements proceed
from there. NeXT, however, was still a ways from even getting to
the starting release:

Now we're starting to roll this system out early in November of this
year. And we have a 0.8 software release, which is rolling out to
software developers through the rest of this calendar year. Early
next year, we will have our 0.9 release, which is for software

developers and aggressive end-users. [Appreciative laughter] And some time during Q2 [the second quarter of] next year, we have release 1.0, which should reach perfection and be usable by everybody.

One could say that the unveiling was premature, given that the machines themselves would not be shipped until the next month and the software that would make them usable was not promised for another six months (and would not actually be delivered for another year). But one could also say that Jobs had no choice: he could not wait for the completion of the system, he had to pretend that it was all-but-done to prevent the total defection of his loyal university friends, whose patience had already been stretched far enough by the three years of waiting. To stay in business, he had to dissemble. He handled his task of breaking the news with such aplomb that his audience was gulled into thinking that the work was done when it had not been. Even the incomplete state of the factory had been successfully hidden in the NeXT film. The hard black exterior of the Cube would serve as placeholder, while NeXT would scramble to make good on what it had just promised for the interior.

Playing the recorded voices of well-wishers from the software companies that NeXT had worked with, Jobs appeared to be anything but a lonely prophet; he was leading a crowd of the best and brightest in the whole industry. He had more good news that gave to NeXT the sense of invincibility:

> There's one last relationship that we've been very fortunate to form over the last year, and I need to tell you about it today. [IBM-NeXT logos shown on an onstage screen] It's true. [Applause]

Jobs announced that he had licensed NeXTSTEP to IBM, which would allow the software that ran on NeXT computers to also run on top of IBM's Unix software. He did not specify which IBM machines would run NeXTSTEP, but the unfocused image was of the two companies, hand in hand, offering an attractive pairing for prospective customers and software developers alike. Exhilarated, Jobs declared that music "strikes closest to the soul" and closed the unveiling by introducing a violinist from the San Francisco Symphony orchestra, who played Bach's A Minor Violin Concerto in duet with the NeXT Computer.

It seemed a triumphant ending to a virtuoso performance, and the audience thunderously applauded. This was a genteel form of crowd hysteria, something of a rarity in business outside of Wall Street trading pits or Mary Kay Cosmetics sales conventions. It would have sounded like caviling to point out that the duet was a novelty act, worlds away from the needs of most of this computer's intended users. But Ross Perot, as caught up in the magic of the moment as anyone, would later refer to the incongruous image of human violinist tapping bow against the computer's central processor unit, then a beautiful outpouring of mathematically synthesized music, as the crowning moment of a day that showed the world "what being first and best is all about." Jobs had gotten through the demonstration without tripping a software lock-up, a feat of luck as well as skill. But in Perot's lyrical retelling, before the National Press Club the next month, what Jobs had accomplished that day was breathtakingly brave and tantamount to the impossible: running a software demonstration live, before a stern "who's who of Silicon Valley" (Perot ignored the obvious loyalty to be found among the carefully chosen invitees). Yet, the lone man on the stage, Perot said, had converted his audience into screaming fans, "going nuts" as if they were at a Michael Jackson concert.[188]

Perot's fondness for the mythic is well known, so it is not surprising that he got carried away. It is much more difficult to understand how the press corps, which did not have the vested interest that Perot did in mythologizing Steve Jobs, was no less carried away. At the press conference that followed the introduction, Jobs was in complete control, batting easy questions from a gallery of press fans. When challenged by an impertinent question that did not answer itself, such as why did the unveiling come so much later than he had once predicted, he had a ready answer: His computer was not late, it was "five years ahead of its time." The press laughed appreciatively. When asked how many machines he hoped to produce, Jobs said that NeXT could make a lot but "probably not enough." More chuckles. Wes Smith, a reporter for *The Chicago Tribune* who was not on a regular Silicon Valley beat, was aghast at the way that the few reporters who asked tough questions of Jobs were snarled at and mocked by their own journalistic brethren, while Jobs brushed them aside. Smith, surveying the easy softballs that the press were lobbing Jobs, wistfully said, "Sam Donaldson would rip his lungs out."[189] Jobs was so giddy with his success that he failed to see how flip he would sound when he gave a one-word answer to a perfectly fair question. Jobs was asked what he would tell those who wanted one of his computers but who were not in higher education. He said simply, "Enroll."

When the press repaired back to their offices, they forgave Jobs even for the worst of transgressions—an austere luncheon (mineral water and cream-cheese-and-sprouts croissants). Aside from a few dissenting voices that were drowned out by the majority, the press gave the newly unveiled NeXT extremely positive coverage. Stewart Alsop led the way, predicting that with its "sexy machine" NeXT would be able to get 25,000 people to come out of the woodwork to purchase it in the upcoming eighteen months. Allowing the universities to retain a small percentage for their trouble, this would mean that NeXT would gross about $150 million within a year and a half. Alsop was joined in his enthusiastic reception by the one person whose influence in the personal computer industry approached his, Richard Shaffer, publisher of a rival newsletter. His word was even more persuasive than Alsop's because he claimed he had approached the NeXT as a skeptic. "I arrived a nonbeliever," Shaffer said, "and I came away a convert."[190] Others stood up and confessed to conversion, too. NeXT had both a good machine and good marketing strategy, added Clare Fleig, director of International Technology Group. Michael Murphy, editor of *California Technology Stock Letter*, predicted that NeXT would sell 50,000 machines in the first two years, earning $300 million in revenue.[191] An editor at *Macuser* magazine predicted exuberantly, if not a bit facetiously, that "this machine will replace sex."[192] How could the unveiling and the attendant free publicity have been any more favorable to NeXT? For a moment, NeXT shimmered in luminous brightness. The Fourth Wave was its to ride into the future.

The coital image that NeXT had summoned was apt, at least as applied to the company: the orgasmic climax at Davies Hall was sweet, but ephemeral.

Scholars and Dollars

U topian hopes of transforming education with new technology can be found long before Steve Jobs bestowed the NeXT Cube upon the world in 1988. We might pick, at random, the ill-fated words of earlier prognosticators who were just as certain as Jobs that *their* historical moment was the eve of revolution, too. It was none other than Jobs's own hero, Thomas Edison, for example, who had declared in 1913 that "books will soon be obsolete in the schools," displaced by the far more efficient medium of "motion pictures," which instruct "through the eye."[193] Not only film, but also radio, and then television, also had their moments of apparent bright promise too. Each was hailed upon its introduction as the harbinger of extraordinary changes in education, the wave of the future, the end of the printed textbook—and each subsequently failed to have much of an educational impact.[194]

The pattern continued when computers and education were matched in the 1960s. With universities and colleges such as MIT, the University of Michigan, and Dartmouth leading the way, American higher education was, for a brief historical moment, caught up in a blinding vision of computer-based revolution. Beginning with an experimental exclusively computer-taught course in geometry offered at MIT in 1961,[195] a number of schools by the mid-1960s had developed hundreds of courses that at least incorporated computer exercises (*Time* magazine referred to "The New B.M.O.Cs: Big Machines on Campus").[196] When a new branch of the University of California was established in 1965 at Irvine, it was given a special charter from the state legislature to pioneer in computer-based teaching; "Computer U," as UC-Irvine was dubbed, possessed its first computer before it actually had a campus upon which to place it.[197] At about the same time, a new college in Michigan purposely built its library in such a way as to accommodate only a few thousand books, leaving room for the new media of the audiovisual and computer age. "It's not that we don't like books," said the architect, "it's just that they aren't the best way to transmit information anymore."[198] Jobs was too young to have any personal memories of this earlier period, and by temperament he had no interest in learning retrospectively about the distant archeological past of the pre-Apple era. This was unfortunate because he might have done things at NeXT a bit differently if he had paid attention to the history of computers and revolutionary delusions found on campuses twenty-five years earlier.

NeXT offered its Cube to colleges and universities as the ideal base upon which to construct an electronic adjunct to the human instructor. This was precisely the desideratum of the 1960s, a computer tutor which could provide individualized instruction tailored to each student. The idea that computers could democratize the education formerly enjoyed by the elite was an attractive one that was elucidated by professors[199] and popularized in magazines for general readers. *Redbook* told readers that though Prince Charles of England had his own tutor, and so too had America's own Franklin D. Roosevelt, now computers would make it possible for every student to have the same knowledgeable and sensitive attention based on individual needs as royalty, English and American, had enjoyed.[200] *McCalls* took the idea a step further and spoke of how the advent of computers on campuses meant that soon "the average man could be as productive as today's near-genius" (*McCalls* surely intended "average *man*" to be inclusive of women, too).[201] Robert Tschirgi, the dean of planning for the University of California system, predicted that college students, after graduation, would have fonder nostalgic memories for their "computer-tutor," which would always be "reactive, facile, responsive," than those preceding generations had had for "inanimate, unresponsive" books.[202]

Some saw computers not as mere adjuncts to professors but as their cost-efficient replacements. "Goodbye Teacher" was the much-quoted title of one article of the period, written in seriousness by a behavioral psychologist, Fred Keller.[203] Such talk alarmed those not yet converted, and made things more difficult for moderate reformers. A more diplomatic tack was to present computer-aided instruction as supplementary aid, nothing more, and as a happy synthesis of the ultramodern and the classically revered: this most modern of technology was nothing more than the replication and diffusion of the master teachers of ancient Greece. Computer administrators shrewdly picked classical references for new computer systems: the one at the University of Illinois was called PLATO, a euphonious acronym for Programmed Logic for Automatic Teaching Operations. (The soothing association with classical antiquity continued subsequently, with Stanford's SOCRATES and MIT's ATHENA.) Who would dare impugn the worthiness of such a teaching tool? Only hidebound classics scholars who disavowed any similarity between mechanistic training and the cherished Socratic tutorial. One such critic was Maxwell Goldberg, an offended humanities professor from Pennsylvania State, who in 1969 said, "If Socrates himself heard what is being hailed in his name, he would rise from the dead—only to call for another cup of hemlock."[204]

The most ambitious threat to traditional college instruction was the program bearing the most traditional of names, Illinois's PLATO, which began in 1960 as a jerry-built system using a discarded $10 television set, a keyboard that had only sixteen keys, and real photographic slides which required a human technician in another room to pick out and display them in front of a computer scanner before they appeared on the screen.[205] From these modest beginnings, the system grew into a giant assembly of programs that, as soon as time-sharing became technically feasible, enabled the full computerization of more than 150 courses (completely automated, without humans supplying slides), whose topics by the late 1970s ranged from Swahili to rocketry (though not to Plato).[206]

What makes the fate of PLATO particularly germane to the later story of NeXT is the wealthy backing that it enjoyed from the private sector. The Minneapolis-based Control Data Corporation, which had supplied the university with an older mainframe computer rent-free,[207] took over ownership of PLATO in 1977, agreeing to pay the University of Illinois royalties on courses that had already been developed. Control Data proceeded to invest large sums of money in the program, expanding its offerings and attempting to market the courses to higher education as well as to all other schools, from elementary to vocational. The company's efforts were met with almost complete indifference. But it took years, and by the company's own admission, some $900 million (actually, a figure that for various reasons should be viewed as conservative since it covered costs only up to 1980), before Control Data realized the enormity of the disaster.[208] William Norris, who by virtue of his sainted status as company founder had ultimate authority to persist in trying to make PLATO profitable in the face of overwhelming contrary evidence, was at last ushered into retirement by the Control Data board. Why did PLATO have virtually nothing to show for nearly a billion dollars—that is, nothing that the real world was interested in paying for? PLATO was based on the idea that colleges and universities would be glad to rent computer terminals connected via phone lines to large mainframe computers at Control Data offices, where the PLATO software actually resided. In the 1960s, this idea had been tenable; in the late 1970s, when Apple and other companies were offering truly *personal* computers for sale outright at less than the $1,100 it could cost an institution to rent one PLATO terminal for one month, the idea of centralized computer instruction was dead. Dead forever, only it took Control Data years to realize the sea change that had taken place.

Now, at this point in the narrative of PLATO's sad demise, it might seem that there are few parallels to be drawn with what happened to NeXT when it offered the Cube to higher education at the end of the 1980s. The NeXT was a freestanding machine for sale; there were no leased lines to NeXT headquarters that were part of the cost. In its physical size, its microprocessor guts, and the look of its screen, the NeXT would seem to be closest in its lineage to the Macintosh, and certainly the personal connection that the NeXT founders and many of the early employees had with the Mac reinforced the feeling at NeXT that if one had to point to a historical precedent—and this was done only reluctantly since the Cube was regarded as *de novo*—the Macintosh was the obvious choice. Yet, despite the apparent similarities, one could suggest that the NeXT upon its introduction was not so close to the Macintosh, and in fact bore many similarities to the ancestor no one would want to claim, PLATO. Here are the reasons:

The NeXT was too expensive to be affordable for a student; it was up to the institution, not the students and their parents, to purchase, just as leasing PLATO was an institutional decision. With the NeXT following the Macintosh, this was retrograde marketing in the age of the personal computer. Just as one of the few PLATO users was quoted in 1979 as saying that PLATO was "the Cadillac in a market where a Chevy will do,"[209] so too, ten years later, prospective NeXT purchasers wondered why they needed to buy the most advanced personal computer on the market, one which, with memory expansion and the large hard disk would cost $17,000 (not including a year's service contract, which would be another

$1,600).[210] Such pricing bore no resemblance to the $1,000-a-pop marketing on campuses of the first Macintoshes.

Related to the fact that the NeXT could be afforded only by institutions, not students, was another problem: the NeXT was a throwback to the ancient days of PLATO time-sharing in that students did not have computers actually in their dorm rooms. Rather, they had no choice but to go to a centralized computer center, or public clusters (often called "laboratories" even if ninety percent of the students used the "labs" for word processing, not playing in the virtual DNA wet-lab that Steve Jobs envisaged). When PLATO was first conceived in the 1960s, students had no choice; but when Control Data began to try to market PLATO in the late 1970s, students could opt for personal-computer alternatives; ten years later, NeXT marketing was a full epoch behind the times, trying to sell universities on a machine whose costliness dictated an unwelcome return to leave-the-dorm computing.

If NeXT's obtuseness seems inexplicable, consider one more similarity that can be noted between the NeXT Cube and the PLATO terminal: in both cases, the sponsoring companies were led by company presidents who were contrarians who would go to any length to avoid following in the path of others. It was William Norris of Control Data who said "Whenever I see everybody going south, I have a great compulsion to go north"[211] but the sentiment runs deeply in Jobs, too. The aversion to others went well beyond business calculations; it was a compulsion that took no account of the merits of the case or of occasions when compromise would have been best. Moreover, both men shared a conviction that there was no need to do much marketing because the technology would sell itself. It was William Norris of Control Data in 1979, but it could just as well have been Steve Jobs in 1988, who said: "You don't need any fancy market research; you know the market is there."[212] For Jobs, the ripe opportunity that he had seen in the higher education market was too obvious to need proof or analysis. Large universities had oodles of money, like Fortune 500 companies; he had their dream computer; what else needed to be said?

The NeXT Cube flopped, just as PLATO had flopped. From the perspective of the universities, the NeXT was not really a personal computer, it was a workstation, and this market was not nearly as big as Jobs had assumed. At the time of the Cube's introduction, Staples Information, a market research firm, speculatively undertook on its own a study of the university workstation market, the sort of spadework that NeXT never bothered with. The Staples study concluded that given its hardware and software limitations, such as the lack of color and the unfinished operating system software, the NeXT Cube would not be welcomed in the engineering and computer science departments, where workstation spending was greatest. They already had workstations in place that they were happy with; as an engineering professor at Berkeley told the market researchers, "We will not be replacing our 700 Sun workstations." And the remaining university market, given the price of the NeXT Cube, constituted at best a $140-million-a-year market for low-end workstations.[213] This meant that even if NeXT were somehow able to achieve one-hundred-percent market share, it would remain a small company, a shadow of the billion-dollars-a-year firm that Jobs said was necessary for survival. The grandiose overestimate of the education market was hardly new: in 1966, two decades earlier, American business had rushed into expensive schemes to make a buck in education with computer-aided instruction, committing a similar error of latching upon the seemingly fat numbers in education budgets and disregarding the fact that most spending went for salaries and brick-and-mortar construction.[214]

Jobs thought that with Dan'l Lewin as his head of sales, all of Lewin's university administrator friends from the Apple University Consortium could be relied upon to serve as NeXT pioneers, just as they had done with the Macintosh. This time, it should have gone even better because the relationships were already in place; Lewin would not have to take a campus administrator like Drexel's

Brian Hawkins out to dinner ten times before he earned his trust. NeXT managers liked to think of this as the "leveraged model"— *leveraged* was a perennial favorite in the NeXT lexicon, a term that meant getting a lot for a small amount of investment either in human or financial resources. NeXT would be able to benefit at modest marginal cost from the investment that Apple had earlier spent on building relationships with the influential leaders in academic computing. But not only was the old academic crew disappointed by the NeXT machine and its pricing, it was also relatively powerless to influence the decisions of the individual university departments that decided which workstations best suited their needs. Trying to sell to tens of thousands of balkanized departments turned out to have absolutely nothing to do with a *leveraged* model. NeXT faced the insuperable problem of having to spend a lot of money dispersed across a bewildering number of academic fields in order to generate extremely modest sales.

It should not have come as such a surprise to Jobs, Lewin, and the NeXT marketing crew. The relatively smooth success of the Macintosh prevented them from seeing that they were not playing the same game of selling personal computers this time, but instead were playing a very different game of selling computers to institutions, which had very different rules. Rule Number One was, institutions expect generous donations in equipment. IBM and Digital Equipment long before had established the tradition, and it had paid off handsomely for them as each generation of students entered the work force looking for opportunities to stay with the same manufacturer upon whose machine they had cut their computing teeth. Students who had been trained on the VAX minicomputer that Digital shrewdly donated to universities in large numbers were said to have been *VAXinated*. When the newcomers like Sun Microsystems appeared, they too followed the tradition with discounts and donations; in 1988 university researchers could buy Sun workstations at about fifty percent below list price,[215] not counting outright donations Sun made to university laboratories. Even Apple had a grants program for universities in addition to the discounts it offered to the various categories of favored university customers. But NeXT, holding to what it believed was a matter of equity, refused to extend donations, reasoning that the company could not make equally generous donations to all schools, and it refused to provide volume discounts, too, reasoning that such discounts would give larger schools an unfair advantage over smaller ones. NeXT would make no exceptions: everyone had to pay list price.

Such obstinacy did not go down well among the skinflints of academe. Dartmouth bragged that it always told computer vendors, "We never pay list price," but Carnegie-Mellon went even further, boasting, "We never pay for anything."[216] The University of California at Berkeley received gratis so much computer equipment that much of it went underutilized; one donated workstation discovered in a faculty member's office was used exclusively as a space heater because its circuitry generated considerable heat. The university had to decree that henceforth there would be no more "hardware dumping" permitted and the university would accept as donations only equipment that worked well with its existing machines.[217] University officials would trade tips among themselves about how to extract the most advantageous terms from computer vendors; as Patricia Skarulis, an administrator for Duke, advised peers at a computer conference, "Everything is up for grabs; you can negotiate any type of contract."[218] But this was conspicuously not true in the case of NeXT, which declared itself to be above the fray. College music departments immediately embraced the Cube, but the inflexible pricing made it all but impossible for NeXT to sell more than a few machines elsewhere. To pay list price, with no compensatory donations, for a black-and-white machine that by design did not connect easily to the other computers that campuses already had—and on top of all that still had a buggy, incomplete operating system—did not present an attractive proposition to colleges and universities. The wonder is that Jobs and his company could have thought that its dismal reception would be otherwise.

What NeXT was trying to sell was really nothing more than a "beta" machine. In computer industry parlance, "alpha" testing of a product is done internally in the company, and is then followed by confidential "beta" testing among selected customers, who are asked to identify the bugs that need to be eliminated before the computer is sold to the general public. Universities were often included among beta testers, but it was done as a favor to the vendor in exchange for getting an early peek at the product. Even though the university did not have to pay, in the eyes of some academics it was still seen as an unfair bargain in which universities gave more than they received. At the time of the Cube's introduction, Ronald Weissman, a computer administrator at the University of Maryland at College Park, denounced the practice of universities serving as beta-testers because it seemed to be mostly a marketing ploy by computer companies who sought the blessing of prestigious names. The NeXT Cube was not officially called a beta machine, of course, but in truth that is what it was, and until the NeXT Cube arrived, no computer vendor previously had had the audacity to try to *charge* customers for performing the favor of prerelease debugging. Viewed in this light, NeXT accomplished something quite miraculous: as a member of the NeXT advisory board said in late 1989 as intended comfort to Max Henry, one of NeXT's senior sales managers, "NeXT sold more beta product at full list price to universities than any vendor in history." It is curious that Weissman, the one who at the time of the Cube's unveiling was uncomfortable with what he saw as a trend toward overly cozy relationships between the private interests of computer vendors and the public interests of higher education, soon resigned his academic position and joined NeXT to head higher education marketing.

One, and only one, college was willing to bet heavily on the NeXT Cube: Allegheny College, a small liberal-arts school in Meadville, Pennsylvania. It was in part a ploy to attract national attention in the same calculating way that Drexel University had bet early on the Macintosh. But times had changed too much; the novelty of personal computers and workstations had long faded; Allegheny received scant attention. An indication of just how more expensive the NeXT was compared to the Macintosh can be seen by the small numbers of Cubes that were purchased: a year after the Cube had been introduced, Allegheny owned only twenty-two machines (which still put it ahead of MIT's twenty).[219] The number would grow in the years that followed but even much later, in the fall of 1992, when Allegheny had 150 NeXT machines, the number was a fraction of the number of workstations a NeXT competitor like Sun had on its leading campuses, let alone the comparative numbers of the less expensive personal computers. NeXT officials, always eager to assume the best of possible outcomes, had been certain in 1989 that Allegheny would soon have in place 650 machines, enough to provide a ratio of one machine for every three students. Allegheny remained loyal to NeXT—once it had started with self-promoting fanfare and parlayed its decision into attracting $1 million in outside contributions,[220] how could it change in midcourse? Allegheny faculty developed computer-based exercises as supplements to courses in many fields: chemistry, biology, philosophy, English, physics, mathematics, geology, and religious studies, reminiscent of the rich offerings of old PLATO software. Yet the NeXT machines, like PLATO leases, were too expensive; other schools as latecomers could not secure $1 million in grants like the pioneering Allegheny did; even orders at Allegheny fell short of providing the sales that NeXT had thought it would receive.

Allegheny, like NeXT, was swimming against the tide, shouldering the burden of paying for computing services when other campuses had long since realized that students and their parents could ease the financial load on the institution, thanks to the advent of student purchase of their own personal computers. Allegheny's NeXT machines were available in public clusters, an arrangement which Joel Smith, the director of academic computing, claimed pleased the students because it freed them from the distractions of the dorm room and provided an opportunity for collaborative learning. The real test, however, was how many other schools chose to follow the Allegheny model in which campus computing services were exclusively centralized, and the 1,800 students had to share 150 machines. The model harked back to a time preceding the pioneering days at PARC and its call for one-person/one-computer; it was as if personal computers had never been invented. The Allegheny model also recalled the past in its reliance on a costly support staff, the two-and-a-half to three-and-a-half full-time programmers who were needed to help the faculty write programs for their classes. By the measure of how many other institutions followed, Allegheny failed miserably, remaining the only one among the more than 3,000 colleges and universities that organized networks of NeXTs as a central component of their computing services.

Other colleges and universities dabbled with NeXT machines (and some campuses represented on the NeXT advisory board purchased machines out of an impulse that would be described as charitable). One of the Ivy League schools that was most willing to give NeXT a chance was Cornell, which put thirty-odd machines into a university laboratory. Poor performance and problems with the software led to enormous complaints from students. And when Jobs toured the laboratory to commemorate its opening and met with academics who were working on developing course-related software for the NeXT Cubes, he offended his hosts by criticizing the work of each person he met. When he expressed puzzlement that the computer-science department was apparently not excited about his marvelous new machine, a group of computer-science faculty got together with him and explained what they needed, such as more power, more memory, and certain software packages that were not yet available. Jobs did not listen; instead, he told *them* what they needed, which was the NeXT Cube as it was and the software that it came bundled with. After this inauspicious beginning with NeXT, Cornell faculty stuck to the Sun laboratory that was next door. Eventually, Cornell shut the NeXT laboratory permanently, an outcome that must be explained not just by the larger forces working against NeXT in a crowded marketplace but also as still another example, found in so many instances, of arrogance alienating the very people who were most inclined to give their support to the NeXT experiment.

If you think of NeXT as a workstation, then NeXT's abysmal sales record on campuses can be seen in its poor penetration of engineering and computer science departments. Sun Microsystems, following Willie Sutton's famous answer about why he robbed banks, had gone to those departments because that was where the money was. And by the time Jobs showed up with his underpowered, black-and-white Cube, loaded with software that would most interest the humanities, it would be impossible to get a serious hearing. If you think of NeXT as a very expensive personal computer, and you think of the much less expensive and much more complete alternatives, then NeXT's poor record in the other departments needs no comment. The NeXT machine, instead of being the hybrid that Jobs had envisioned of a "personal workstation," was more of a confused hermaphrodite of uncertain identity, shunned by both personal-computer and workstation worlds.

By the end of 1988, NeXT employees had to absorb the news that few in higher education were willing to buy their machine. It was a shock to most people. Yet there were pockets of the company, most notably at the top, where an optimistic outlook prevailed if by no other force than sheer will. The NeXT factory was turning out machines at the paltry rate of about 400 *a month*, but Randy Heffner, the head of manufacturing, passed on word that the factory needed to ramp up to a pace of producing *10,000* Cubes a month. Nothing had changed, the sales remained stuck at a plateau that required a microscope to see, but Jobs and the senior leadership were convinced that the company's prospects were about to brighten and they wanted to be ready. A shift in strategy was in the works.

"More companies die of indigestion than from starvation"[221] had been Jobs's cocky explanation at the time of the Cube's unveiling of his decision to restrict NeXT sales to colleges and universities.

As a general business proposition about start-up businesses, his aphorism is utterly wrong, and his own company was a typical illustration (if indigestion from too much business was risked by anybody it was at archrival Sun Microsystems). The only aspect that was unusual about the starved state of NeXT was its resembling anorexia nervosa; so much of it was self-inflicted. Sugar daddy Perot or no, the company was not viable if it could not produce sales. So it was that only seven months after the Davies Hall announcements, NeXT abandoned its policy of selling to educators only. In March 1989, with a lavish press event and fanfare, NeXT announced that it had completed a deal with the nation's largest computer retailer, Businessland, which gave Businessland rights to sell to the noneducation market.

Many of NeXT's campus supporters howled that they were being abandoned. NeXT's new relationship with Businessland, a giant monolith whose bread-and-butter business was selling ordinary personal computers to the suits of corporate America, seemed antithetical to the image that NeXT had cultivated earlier, of single-minded devotion to effecting a revolution in teaching and learning. Some critics of NeXT claimed that this had been the plan all along, that higher education had never been intended as the only market, that Jobs had always intended to use college campuses merely as a transitory testing ground before he moved on to the real target, the commercial computer market.

The outside speculation about a master plan was not off the mark. Even before the Cube had been introduced at Davies Hall, NeXT was actively talking with Businessland, which expressed an interest in signing a three-year deal to sell 100,000 machines, which would be worth at retail a billion dollars. The negotiations were conducted in strict secrecy, however, and the public was led to believe that NeXT would be selling only to higher education. But NeXT's change in marketing strategy should not be seen as an act of treachery: the university representatives who sat on the NeXT advisory board had realized that the company would not be viable if it stuck to selling only to higher education. Potential software developers would remain uninterested in writing software for the NeXT machine if the company continued to restrict its own sales to the college market, which was notorious for being chintzy and tolerant of piracy, the illegal copying of programs without payment. If NeXT failed to attract software developers, the NeXT Cube would be of little use to anyone, on or off campus. Selling to a broader base of customers would also help to keep the special prices for higher education relatively low; the other customers could help subsidize, in essence, the NeXT computers sold to universities. Higher education urged NeXT to go ahead and expand distribution beyond colleges and universities, with its blessing.

The selection of Businessland as the new partner may have dismayed some of the NeXT loyalists who were protective of the company's purity, but if NeXT were to strike a deal with any commercial computer dealer, Businessland, by virtue of its dominating size, appeared to be the perfect choice. Here was a company that exuded success. Founded in 1982, by 1989 it had grown from one store to more than a hundred. Sales had climbed in a steep curve: $44 million in 1983; $157 million in 1984; $351 million in 1985, and upward, without pause, passing the billion-dollar mark in 1988. For NeXT, a partnership with Businessland offered instant access to the customers that had made Businessland the largest computer dealer. One might be tempted to think also that the partnership offered NeXT the happy prospect of a close relationship with a tutelary company that had shown the way in reaching the billion-dollar mark in short order, the goal that NeXT had set for itself. But NeXT did not think of itself as a junior partner with anybody. Though tiny, and with sales all but nonexistent, NeXT regarded itself as coequal with Businessland: NeXT was the best in what it did, designing and building machines for the nineties, and it would now have as its partner the computer dealer that was the best at what *it* did, moving computer boxes in high volume onto the desktops of customers.

Both companies also seemed well-matched in each having at their helm a single person who ruled with unchallenged powers. Steve Jobs's counterpart at Businessland was David Norman, an older man seasoned by earlier ventures and an uneven business record. He was not as skilled as Jobs at working a large crowd, but he was extremely persuasive when talking one-on-one with business associates or Wall Street analysts. As the only founder remaining at Businessland by 1989, Norman had played an important role in the company's growth, by attracting early investment from venture capitalists, and later, by keeping Wall Street supplied with cheery news about the company's earnings and prospects. Like Jobs's, his temper was feared by subordinates; like Jobs, he drove ruthlessly hard bargains with vendors and business partners; like Jobs, he waged a relentless war to prevent the release of any information about the company that he did not approve of; like Jobs, his ability to focus on one goal, to the exclusion of all else, was often compared to a laser beam. In 1989, Norman was chairman, president, and chief executive officer of Businessland, which meant that the fortunes of the company, like the fortunes of NeXT, remained bound to the perspicacity of a single founder.

Norman was a generic entrepreneur, with a fine sense of spotting business opportunities. He was not a computer maven, however; the industry that he was in was incidental. He saw, before others did, that Businessland could cultivate relationships with Fortune 500 companies to build up enormous volume (the large accounts drove hard bargains so profits were more elusive), and it was Norman who directed the transformation of Businessland's earliest stores, intended to serve small-and medium-sized downtown businesses, into a new function, as the home base for an outbound sales force that paid calls on the very largest companies. He was good at building revenue, but he knew little about the underlying technology that was contained in the boxes that moved through his stores in ever increasing volume.

Aware of his own technical limitations, Norman relied upon the counsel of Enzo Torresi, another founder and a true technologist. But as Torresi withdrew from active engagement in the affairs of the company, eventually leaving in 1988, Norman increasingly relied upon the technical judgments of Kevin Compton, one of Torresi's lieutenants who became a kind of technologist to the king. Compton was young, technically savvy, full of conviction that his opinions were correct, and incapable of saying no to those with higher status. He had joined the company in 1986 when Businessland had purchased the Kansas City company where he had written accounting and construction-industry programs. His initial Businessland position was the lowly one of answering the phone in the department that provided technical support for accounting packages and for the computer networks that tied computers together. Within a few months, however, he had been promoted to head of the department; a year later, he was head of all of technical services; and three years later, he was vice-president of what had by then become a billion-dollar company.

This heady ascension from answering the phones to a vice-president's title was capped by Norman asking Compton to serve as his eyes and ears, chartering him to find the best products for the future. Norman attached only one condition: Businessland would have to be given exclusive rights to sell whatever products were chosen. For Norman, insisting upon exclusivity and denying competitors the right to distribute the best new products would ensure that Businessland would remain on top. Kevin Compton's job was to find the newest hot items and place a secure Businessland lock upon them.

Businessland was fully aware of its commanding power in the computer world. It had the largest sales volume, the most desirable customers, the best corporate contacts, the most prestigious product lines. Businessland did not have to go to prospective vendors; the vendors came to Businessland. As soon as Norman put out word that his company was interested in expanding beyond its standard line and was interested in carrying a Unix computer, all of the

Unix vendors knocked on Businessland's door in supplication. Sun Microsystems, as the leading Unix workstation manufacturer, would have been perhaps the most logical choice, but after extensive discussions, Sun turned Businessland down, balking at the requirement to assign exclusive retail distribution rights to Businessland. Sun's withdrawal opened an opportunity for NeXT, but as is often the case in business, Businessland's selection process bore more of a resemblance to the serendipity of a roulette wheel, or the personal connections detailed in a Liz Smith gossip column, than it did to the economists' ethereal model of rational choice.

A Texan millionaire named Billy Ladin, one of Apple's favorite longtime dealers and an old friend of Steve Jobs, served as the matchmaker between Jobs and Businessland's Kevin Compton. Ladin was the owner of a chain of retail computer stores called ComputerCraft, based in Houston, which were purchased by Businessland in July 1988. At the time it seemed to be a deal beneficial to both parties: Ladin was able to cash out with a stock swap worth about $24 million, and Businessland acquired a profitable chain that gave it access to the small businesses and individual purchasers that it had abandoned in the past. In retrospect, it was a deal that represented a coup for Ladin, and a complete disaster for Businessland. Almost as soon as the deal was completed, ComputerCraft stores began losing money and entered a tailspin from which they never recovered before crashing. Industry cynics compared Ladin's sale of his chain to Businessland to the sale of a horse that had just expired but had not yet hit the ground.

This would be visible to Businessland only later. In the summer of 1988, Ladin enjoyed the enormous respect of Businessland, and when Ladin suggested to Kevin Compton that Businessland should consider the still-under-wraps NeXT computer for its Unix slot, Compton was willing to listen. Especially when he heard rumors that IBM had licensed NeXT technology. He called Bill Lowe at IBM to confirm the rumors, and Lowe was allowed to say IBM was indeed interested. This was a clincher for Compton, who promptly arranged for Jobs to give a demo for Dave Norman and himself. It is a wonderful example of how successful NeXT was in the art of bootstrapping itself upward by using one partner to bring in the next. The IBM connection impressed Businessland, helping to bring it into partnership with NeXT. Never mind that IBM's interest originated in the same kind of high-level introduction at the top. And never mind that IBM had not yet agreed to a license at that point. Its expression of interest was sufficient to lend legitimacy to NeXT, and IBM's hedged interest helped bring Businessland in, then the Businessland deal in turn helped land other partners. This is why businesspeople are so fond of talking about the importance of "leveraging." No one did it better than Jobs at NeXT.

When Compton and Norman arrived at NeXT, Jobs presented the slide show that was being readied for the October unveiling of the Cube. He brought out the printed circuit board that was the heart of the computer. He answered questions. And then, just as at the unveiling, after a lengthy prologue, the machine itself was brought into the room and unveiled. For Compton, it was love at first sight. Jobs worked on Norman, too, and the courtship was continued at later meetings.

Businessland was invited to the unveiling in Davies Hall, and a few days later Jobs took Compton through the NeXT lab, pointing out products that were in the works, including a color machine (which, unfortunately, would turn out not to be ready for two more years). For Compton, the personal attention that Jobs was devoting to their relationship was unexpected, flattering, exhilarating.

Compton was concerned, however, about the commitment of IBM to NeXT. He had noticed that at the Davies Hall introduction, the only appearance IBM made was in the form of the one slide thrown up at the last minute. In December and January, Compton continued to press IBM for assurance of their commitment; their reply was consistent—they planned to do something with the NeXT software on the IBM workstation. Still vague, but sufficiently reassuring nevertheless. Meanwhile, Compton got to spend time with Jobs, and not coincidentally a Businessland deal with NeXT beckoned with increasing pull.

Norman also drew closer to Jobs as the informal talks progressed in late 1988 and early 1989. Norman and Jobs, two legendary masters of the effective sales pitch, each sold the other grandiose promises that the other wanted to hear. Jobs sold Norman on the idea of the NeXT machine as the defining "fourth-wave" personal computer, which would produce large revenues quickly because software for the machine could be written so easily and would appear without the usual time lag. Norman, in turn, pitched Businessland as the organization that had the advanced technical staff that could handle the demands of networking Unix computers. This was folie à deux. Their assumptions were open to challenge, if they had been interested in hearing anything but dulcet chimes. Software for the NeXT machine would hardly appear quickly, especially given the still unfinished state of the underlying system software. Nor would Unix networking be anything as simple as the networking that Businessland had experience in, stringing together less powerful personal computers. Norman's technical staff knew better, but Norman, like Jobs, chose to believe what he wanted to believe.

In February 1989, Norman had a new, urgent reason to add NeXT to the Businessland offerings: one of his most important existing computer lines, Compaq, decided to drop Businessland completely and immediately. It was a remarkable decision on Compaq's part, to sever its relationship with the leading computer dealer, the dealer that had sold no less than $150 million of its product the previous year. But that was part of the problem: Businessland knew that it had inordinate power over a company such as Compaq and it used that knowledge to press for "special adjustments," that is, preferential discounts given to no other dealer. IBM and Apple reluctantly acceded to Businessland's demands, but Compaq resisted and threatened to withdraw. Norman refused to budge, and called the bluff. What followed was a surprise. Suddenly, Compaq was gone.

Of the two, Compaq seemed to industry observers to be hurt far more than Businessland. Stewart Alsop in his newsletter argued that Businessland had a broad selection of products from other computer companies from which to choose a replacement. Brand loyalty to Compaq or any other single computer line did not exist, Alsop said.[222] Despite such assurances from outside observers, Norman knew that he had at least a problem of transition on his hands. While he made arrangements for replacing Compaq with another personal-computer line, he had to make up for the loss of revenue during the interim. Now, the NeXT looked more attractive than ever. By adding a high-priced workstation that was about to set the office world on fire—both Norman and Compton were convinced that Unix machines were poised to move beyond the lab benches of scientists and engineers and onto the desks of mainstream corporations—the NeXT machine would provide a new, large revenue stream, just what Businessland needed while it fiddled with the broken pipes left by Compaq's abrupt departure. Moreover, Norman had another reason to close a deal with Jobs: NeXT was willing to accept the condition that Sun would not—granting exclusive distribution rights to Businessland.

The very next month, Lilliputian NeXT (1988 revenue, negligible) and Brobdingnagian Businessland (1988 revenue, $1.03 billion) held a lavish press conference announcing their new deal (Jobs, insisting on building a special sound stage and backdrop for the announcement, spent in one week what the company had allocated for marketing expenditures for the entire upcoming year). Well-wishers thought it was a perfect marriage. Richard Shaffer, another newsletter publisher, regarded NeXT as better positioned than all other Unix companies, including Sun, because now NeXT had "the best sales force in the market" working on its behalf.[223] NeXT would not have to spend tens of millions of its own limited resources on advertising, promotion, training its own sales force, and maintaining a large technical-service group. Instead, it could use the resources of the far larger Businessland. This was NeXT's "highly leveraged model" working perfectly. Alsop praised Businessland for "having stomach," first, for its gutsy showdown with Compaq, and second, now, with its willingness to take a chance on a new product with new technology.[224] Businessland was deemed equally fortunate to have landed its new partner. Dan Bricklin, software don and occasional pundit, pointed out Businessland's gain: "For Businessland, it's like being able to put a Maserati on the showroom floor."[225]

In the giddiness of the moment, David Norman made an improbable prediction. He told the press, "NeXT revenues will be as much over the next twelve months as Compaq was over the last twelve months. Compaq business was about $150 million."[226] It was an astonishing prediction because it assumed that the NeXT would literally become an overnight success, even though it was still not really completed, let alone tested in real market conditions. The prediction also assumed that customers would purchase a pricey machine. The base price of the NeXT sold by Businessland was set at $9,995, substantially higher than the price charged to higher-education customers, and a price that would be firm—no discounts. Depending on what options customers chose beyond the basic machine, Norman's prediction of sales of $150 million translated into the sale of 10,000 to 15,000 machines, which was still only one-tenth the number that the NeXT factory was revving up to produce. Newsletter publisher Richard Shaffer was no less susceptible to feverish predictions. He declared, "NeXT was a shabby little start-up, and now it's a $100 million company. There is no way Businessland can't reach its goal of 10,000 computers."[227]

This was emotional conjuring, not rational planning, and NeXT led the way. On the day that the Businessland deal was signed, senior executives from Businessland joined with those at NeXT at a celebratory dinner that Jobs hosted at his house. Toasts were offered by the two CEOs. First, Norman spoke, offering the sort of speech that he was best at, addressing a small group, speaking graciously of the great partnership that had been formed and of looking forward to working with NeXT. Jobs followed, standing up and clicking glasses with Norman. His toast was a battle cry: "Let's go kick the shit out of some people."

When the elite units of the Businessland troops were assembled in Florida the next month, the room was pumped full of the same kind of combustible expectations. The occasion was the meeting of Businessland's "100 Percent Club," the salespeople who had exceeded their annual quotas. Kevin Compton came on the stage to address the group, and he presented a dry outline of some general technology issues facing the industry. He was interrupted by a voice that came over the loudspeaker: "You know, I don't necessarily agree with you." Compton spoke out to the unseen voice: "I'm vice-president of advanced systems here and that's my job, who are you?" The godlike voice answered, "I'm Steve Jobs." The Businessland sales people screamed deliriously. It had all been set up by prior arrangement, with Jobs calling from California and Compton serving as foil. When the crowd quieted enough for Jobs to be heard, he told them how excited he was about joining with Businessland and how NeXT would become an enormous company, too. The bedlam that followed the conversation was described by one attendee this way: "Picture grown, smart adults, standing on their chairs, screaming, they were so excited." It was a transcendent moment. "We had NeXT. Man, it was like a perfect world."

Hollywood

With the passage of time, it is increasingly difficult to recall what Steve Jobs was like in the early days of Apple, before the success of the company made him appear a marketing genius to us, and to himself. But before the task is rendered impossible, it may be useful to reach back in time and note what has now been forgotten: the image of Jobs as the master marketer was itself a product of less well-known master marketers, Regis McKenna and Jay Chiat, the public relations and advertising powers, respectively, behind the success of early Apple. It was they who were inspired to present the two founding Steves to the public as a perfectly matched pair. Wozniak, being the technically more proficient, was assigned the role of the technology prodigy. Jobs loved the technology with the heart of a techie, but being by far the more articulate of the two, he was assigned the role of the marketing prodigy. Over time, however, Jobs came to see himself as McKenna and Chiat had positioned him, as the marketing boy wonder, forgetting that it was an identity that began as a form of sophisticated public-relations hype, devised by others.

By the time he founded NeXT, Jobs had no doubts about his

marketing prowess, and he carried two convictions born of his experience: good technology will sell itself, and the best way to inform the marketplace of the arrival of good technology was through loud, publicity-generating events. The introduction of the NeXT Cube at Davies Hall had been the logical successor to the legendary introduction of the Apple Macintosh, and the proclamations that attended the announcement of the NeXT partnership with Businessland continued the tradition of making as big a splash as possible. For the early NeXT employees, many of whom had only worked at Apple previously, Event Marketing was the only kind of marketing they had any acquaintance with. It meant a succession of ego-gratifying adrenaline rushes, when the bright lights of the press would shine upon them for the event of the season. As small as NeXT was in terms of sales or number of employees, it remained a company of disproportionate interest that, thanks to Jobs, could get what seemed to be the whole world to pay attention to it.

The big event announcing the Businessland deal was followed by more of the same, in dispersed form, as NeXT and Businessland took the show on the road and held "seminars" introducing the Cube in twelve cities at a cost of about $2 million. The events featured the presence of a true celebrity, Steve Jobs, and a true mystery, the NeXT Cube, and drew large crowds everywhere from the Midwest heartland to Wall Street.

NeXT's reliance upon Event Marketing was diametrically opposite to the approach that Sun Microsystems had used. Without a celebrity, without advertising, without much attention from the press, Sun had built itself up by word of mouth, early customers serving as the references that secured new accounts. Sun's territorial success had been hard-won by its direct-sales infantry who inched forward trench by trench without the help of bright flares or the press. If reporters knocked on Sun's door, it was more often than not simply to collect a provocative comment from Scott McNealy about Sun's competition, not about Sun. In February 1989, before the NeXT-Businessland announcement, McNealy, when asked what he thought of the NeXT Cube, obligingly answered with a quotable quote: "My favorite stereo computer to rock on with your bad self. More seriously, it's the wrong operating system, the wrong processor, and the wrong price."[228] McNealy was not singling NeXT out for special attention; he was equally polite when asked what he thought about Apple's Macintoshes, which he praised faintly as "a great typewriter replacement" (Allan Loren, then president of Apple USA, replied in kind by commenting about McNealy's claim that the Sun workstation was easy to use: "If you really believe you're going to have tens of millions of people working with Unix all day long, then I want to get some of the stuff you're smoking."[229]

Even when Sun had the opportunity to do a little crowing of its own, it could not summon the press the way NeXT could. Shortly after NeXT made its announcement with Businessland, Sun introduced the machine originally conceived by Andy Bechtolsheim to meet the NeXT Cube head-on. Sun named it the SPARCstation. In terms of size and price, it was smaller than the Cube and was closer to the top-of-the-line Macintosh, but it had a RISC microprocessor that blazed at speeds many times faster than the other machines.[230] The announcement did not get anything like the attention that Jobs had secured for NeXT. Wall Street analysts doubted that the SPARCstation could win office sales,[231] and the announcement did not seem as important as the news that Sun's most formidable workstation competitor, Apollo, was bought and merged with the workstation division of another competitor, Hewlett-Packard. While NeXT celebrated its partnership with the leading computer retailer, the future looked troubled for Sun.

In the late spring, the outlook for Sun turned from bad to worse. Two senior executives, one of whom was Bernard Lacroute, abruptly quit; the company lost control of its own internal computer system and had to shut down manufacturing for five weeks, and the quarter ended with the first loss the company had ever experienced.[232] For a computer company to suffer from a breakdown of computers was especially embarrassing; the press wondered aloud about the cobbler's children having no shoes.[233] Sun tried to explain that none of the computers involved in the snafu were Sun workstations; the problems had arisen when the company switched from a Hewlett-Packard minicomputer to a larger mainframe computer that was needed when the company had passed the one-billion-dollar mark in sales.[234] The old system was prematurely decommissioned before the new one was fully ready; in the meantime, a torrent of orders had come in for older Sun products whose prices had been slashed to clear the way for the new SPARCstations. At one dark moment, a three-foot stack of sales orders awaited entry into Sun's computer database; until they were properly recorded, the company had no idea which models to manufacture. Austin Mayer, a Sun executive, conceded, "We had to guess what was in there, and we guessed wrong."[235]

With the reporters hovering like vultures, McNealy defensively pointed to other contributing problems: introducing five new product lines in one quarter, building a new manufacturing facility in Scotland, expanding the technical support organization. He put the best face on the quarter's loss by claiming to be flattered by the attention because "you hit 47 straight home runs, it's going to be newsworthy when you strike out your next time at bat."[236] Wall Street was unimpressed by the explanations, and Sun's stock lost fifty percent of its value.

What the press, industry analysts, and the general public at the time did not see—what even the rest of Sun did not see—was that Sun's SPARCstation group, which had forecast immediate heavy demand for its new workstation, had guessed correctly. The reason the introduction of the SPARCstation was a contributor to Sun's crisis of 1989 was because it was spontaneously successful, even without much support from Sun's own marketing forces, whose forecasts for the machine's sales had been much more modest. The avalanche of orders for the SPARCstation caught Sun's manufacturing division unprepared and short of critical components supplied by outside firms. This is that rarity of "indigestion" that Steve Jobs had said he was guarding against when he initially restricted sales of the NeXT Cube to higher education only. By looking at Sun and what happened after the inauspicious launch of the SPARCstation, we must conclude that indigestion is a minor malady that soon passes. Orders for the SPARCstation passed everyone's most optimistic predictions, manufacturing returned to normal operation, Sun returned to profitability the next quarter and completed the fiscal year following the fiasco of 1989 with sales of $1.77 billion, a robust sixty-eight-percent increase over the previous year. Public awareness of the success of the new SPARCstation was slower, but perhaps that worked to Sun's long-term advantage because it meant the continued growth of its workstation business was based on a solid foundation, won solely by hand-to-hand combat in the presence of technically savvy workstation customers who compared the Sun machine to the competition, undistracted by media hoopla or marketeer contrivance. The SPARCstation had to be both powerful and attractively priced to fare so well.

If the public was slow to notice the hidden strength of Sun's unadorned grassroots approach to expanding its customer base, it was also slow to notice the hidden weaknesses that lay intrinsically in NeXT's Event Marketing and the launch of its new relationship with Businessland. If the traveling seminars that brought people out to see Steve Jobs and the NeXT Cube evoked more than Oooh and Ahhh from the crowds, if they had induced the attendees to reach for their checkbooks, the NeXT Cube would have gotten off to a fine start. But the demonstrations did not end with prospective customers stepping forward to become actual customers. To understand why this was so, consider the impulsivity that is required of the customer in Event Marketing. If you go to a circus or a rock concert, you may in the excitement of the moment impulsively buy a $10 souvenir doodad or T-shirt without undue concern about value. But if you went to a demonstration of a NeXT Cube, even if Steve Jobs himself performed the honors, the $10,000 price would prevent you from being transported to a similar state of impulsive consumption. Jobs could not understand this because at his own company, office purchase of a single personal computer was treated for accounting purposes as an ordinary expense, accomplished as easily as buying a box of pencils; at other companies, however, the purchase of even one single machine became a bureaucratic matter, the acquisition of a capital asset, which required an approval process, review by more than one person, and engaged the budgeting authority of the organization. The problem that NeXT and Businessland faced was that once the marks left the big tent without reaching into their wallets, they did not return. They— or their supervisors who wielded financial control—had too many questions for which there were no adequate answers in the harsh glare of daylight.

To begin with, it was plainly evident that the NeXT Cube was far from finished. Jobs had successfully kept the bugs in the operating system from public view when he was at Davies Hall, but he and his associates could not do so when out on the road. Even though the NeXT software team worked feverishly during late 1988 and 1989 to complete the work on the system, they reconciled themselves early on to the fact that there would still be many bugs in the final release; what they concentrated their attention on, in the time that they had before NeXT could wait no longer and would have to declare the system complete, was to track down what the NeXT staff called, appropriately, "showstoppers," the catastrophic bugs that froze the screen, held up printing, caused a loss of data, or incapacitated a network. Their progress in this quest was visible in the interim releases. By April 1989, an outside programmer who was at work developing new software for the NeXT enthused that "today, it crashes once every thirty minutes; two weeks ago, it crashed every thirty seconds; that's a logarithmic pace of improvement."[237] But customers took little solace from the rate of improvement as long as the remaining bugs pulled the system down frequently. In May, two NeXT machines crashed as Jobs was performing a demonstration before a group of 800 software industry executives in San Diego.[238] Similar public embarrassments continued on through the summer. The few in the higher education community who had purchased a NeXT Cube were a hardy bunch who liked to dig into the bowels of computer code and try to fix bugs themselves or devise *workaround*s, as they are called. The corporate customers of Businessland, however, did not take the same hobbyist pleasure in bit twiddling. Understandably, they were reluctant to take on the task of completing the basic operating system on their own in order to have a functioning machine.

Businessland customers were also different from NeXT's academic customers in their software requirements. They had little need of the software that was bundled with the NeXT Cube, which allowed them to render three-dimensional models of molecules, or to write artificial intelligence routines in an esoteric language named LISP, or to *blast* through Shakespeare, to use the Jobsian phrase. Instead, they wanted a database program. None was available. They wanted a computer-aided design program. None was available. They wanted a good word-processing program, with more features than the rudimentary one that came with the machine. None was available. They wanted a spreadsheet, like Lotus 1-2-3. None was available. At a seminar in Akron, Ohio, an enthusiastic Businessland salesperson tried to pitch the program Mathematica—which performed polynomial factorization and other symbolic math for advanced university courses—as an all-purpose business tool that would be a dandy spreadsheet, too. But this did not wash; the business audience needed to do budgets, not calculus. The only program that ran on the NeXT that was not bundled with it was a program for publishing book-length documents, called Framemaker. It had a steep learning curve, was not well-suited for writing letters or short reports, and its behavior was flighty because it could not be fully polished until the underlying layer, the operating system, was first finished by NeXT.

Without software to do the practical work of the office, the NeXT was quite useless. The initially curious would walk away after looking more closely at the Cubes, muttering that NeXT could give the machines away and people would still not want them. Curiously, NeXT and Businessland management acted as if the opposite held true, that customers would not hesitate to pay whatever price was asked. A Businessland newsletter directed at its sales representatives captures the presumption of inelastic demand:

> Businessland Super Stars! How would you like a product: for which You had NO competition (think of that); You Sell at List; Boasting State of the Art Technology; Has Excellent Name Recognition; Creates Big Commissions; Has Excellent Availability; You do have that product today; it is the NeXT Cube!
>
> The Opportunity for selling this user friendly workstation is Enormous. Our projected sales for NeXT will ramp up very quickly. As a field representative you want to make sure that you get your fair share of this revenue! If not, you are working too hard!

To illustrate, the company showed how one Cube, starting with a base price of $9,995, bundled with the printer, a hard-disk drive, service contracts, optical disks, and a miscellany of extras, would run $21,519. The Businessland representative would have to sell eight IBM personal computers or fifteen low-end Macintoshes to earn an equivalent commission.

The optimism that emanated from Dave Norman's office at the top of Businessland radiated downward through the organization, obscuring the twin problems of the shortage of practical software and the high price compared to other personal computers. If the announcement in March of the NeXT-Businessland deal had been followed by a hiatus in the stream of Big Events, the two companies may have been more willing to address the clear negative signals that potential customers issued during the sales seminars that spring. But there was no hiatus: just a few months later, in June 1989, NeXT employees experienced another sugar high when Japan's Canon, NeXT's supplier of the optical disk drive and the key component of its printer, agreed to purchase a 16.67 percent share in NeXT for an even $100 million. NeXT celebrated the good fortune that had again come its way and that added further validation that the company was indeed on the right track (Canon did extract a promise from Jobs that he would hire a chief operating officer, but it would take three years before Jobs would make good on it). Businessland also celebrated what they read as validation of their own decision to sell the NeXT Cubes. Jobs told *The Wall Street Journal* that NeXT was so flush with cash that a good portion of it would probably end up in an idle bank account.[239] This was not dissembling—that would come later when the money was exhausted—but rather an expression of just how miraculously well-funded NeXT had come to be. Jobs also used the Canon coup to return to IBM in the fall of 1989 and renegotiate the licensing agreement, doubling the rate that had been agreed upon earlier. IBM was as gullible as anyone and read the same augury of certain success from the arrival of Canon as NeXT chose to.

In one stroke, NeXT now had a nominal market value of $600 million dollars. Jobs, who after the reshuffling of equity held fifty percent of NeXT shares, now had a stake that had a pro forma value of $300 million. This was a feat without precedent, given that the company had only two hundred some employees, and no revenue to speak of. Even Sun Microsystems could not begin to boast of anything comparable: When Sun had gone public in January 1986, its market value was $430 million but it had already logged almost $200 million in sales by that point.[240]

Steve Jobs and NeXT employees had an obvious vested interest in choosing to see the Canon investment as reflection of the worth of what they were doing, and the other NeXT partners, like Perot, Businessland, and IBM, also had their own reasons to see the investment as confirmation of their own business acumen. What is not so easily explained is why outside observers also went along with the most sanguine interpretation, without pausing to wonder about the sagacity of the Japanese in their rush to pay large sums of money for certain U.S. properties in the heady days of the late 1980s, before the Tokyo economic bubble burst. The evenness of the figure that Canon paid—$100 million—for the equity stake and for exclusive distribution rights in Asia for the NeXT Cube is a clue that Canon's interest in NeXT was arrived at by amorphous "strategic" considerations, not by crunching any hard numbers. Its kin would be the megadeals that drew the Japanese to Hollywood, Sony to Columbia Pictures, and Matsushita to MCA, and no matter what inflated price the Japanese were willing to pay, Americans assumed that the infallible Japanese knew what they were doing. The editorial pages in the United States were filled with hand-wringing about the threat to American interests posed by these investments, and NeXT employees, too, in internal discussions about the proposed Canon deal, worried that accepting the investment would mean a reversal of Steve Jobs's declarations in earlier years that Americans should stand up to the Japanese. Now, in 1989, Jobs rationalized his accommodation with the former enemy by telling his employees that the Canon deal would allow NeXT, an American company with American technology, to infiltrate the Asian market, striking a patriotic counterblow to the powers with whom we had the largest trade deficit. The discussion of threatened American interests did not address another possibility: that the Japanese were caught up, for reasons particular to that hysteria-tinged moment in their own financial history, in an ill-considered buying spree abroad that they would later rue.

In the summer of 1989, however, the Japanese seemed possessed of unerring business judgment, a juggernaut that could not be stopped, and the vote of confidence in NeXT represented by the $100 million infused everyone connected with NeXT with sunny confidence that success was imminent. Businessland sent hundreds of its sales representatives and systems engineers through a training program to acclimate their staff technically to the Cube. NeXT provided engineers to serve as trainers; they plunged enthusiastically into the task, turning what had been twelve-hour days into double-shifts, maintaining their work assignments at NeXT by day and their training assignments for Businessland at night. Separately, Businessland arranged for additional sales training and pep talks for its staff, such as Demo-rama competitions held to see who could perform the most polished demonstration of the Cube. "Socratic Selling Skills" were also impressed upon the staff with the help of an outside consultant, who encouraged the Businessland sales reps to dispense with the conventional pitch to customers. Instead of making a sales call to explain in canned cadences the wonders of the computer, how it would save the customer money, improve productivity, and enhance competitiveness, the Businessland representative was to sell by *listening*, Socratically drawing out the customer's concerns with a skein of gentle questions, each responding to the preceding reply. Once the interrogation was accomplished, the NeXT Cube could then be pitched as the protean answer for every challenge. (This brings to mind the Penn State professor who in the early years of computer-aided education in the 1960s had been so alarmed by the invocation of the hallowed name of Socrates, but that was a premature alarm: *this* is when Socrates would rise from the dead to ask for another cup of hemlock.)

Businessland readied promotional paraphernalia—coffee cups, pens, sales literature. All had to be approved by Jobs personally, and this proved to be difficult. As of July 1989, after NeXT had been selling its Cube for nine months, and now had Businessland and Canon selling it, too, the company had yet to issue a single fact sheet or brochure. Jobs had been displeased by every draft that his marketing staff had attempted, so nothing at all had been issued; reprints of reviews that appeared in the press were used as a stopgap. Finally, a brochure passed Jobs's muster: it was a two-dimensional reproduction of the Cube, in the full scale of twelve by twelve inches. Jobs of course did not stint: it cost $1 each to print and Jobs had 200,000 copies printed (unfortunately, when NeXT ran a prominent advertisement in *The Wall Street Journal* and was deluged with thousands of requests for the brochure, the company belatedly discovered that its odd dimensions rendered all available envelopes useless; no brochures could be sent out until NeXT received a special order of envelopes that had to be hastily manufactured just for them; another surprise awaited the company when it dropped them off at the post office at last and discovered that their special brochures meant special postage, too). The Businessland staff followed NeXT's example and spent lavishly, too. Marching to Norman's orders of preparing to sell $150 million of NeXT Cubes in one year, Businessland calculated the necessary amount of promotional material that would be required to achieve such volume and lay in the necessarily large inventories of materials, as well as the Cubes themselves.

On the eve of the completion of the operating system in September, NeXT and Businessland drew encouragement from a sign that customers were at last on the verge of actually buying the NeXT computer. Serious negotiations were underway for the first significant purchase of NeXT Cubes by a nonacademic customer, the William Morris Agency in Beverly Hills and New York, whose founding stretched back to the previous century. The betrothal of the venerable talent agency and the upstart NeXT was an affair entirely apropos of the Hollywood setting. The two new partners gazed less at each other than at the photographers whom the twosome most sought to impress by linking arms with each other. William Morris, popularly known as the place where ambitious college graduates entered in the lowly mail room, to pay their dues and fight their way up to the exalted position of talent agent, had fallen on hard times in recent years. Its own agents had defected and formed the hugely successful rival, Creative Artists Agency. William Morris had lost many of its clients and had difficulties attracting new ones, having now acquired an image of stodginess; it increasingly depended on income from its real estate investments.[241] The agency wanted to shake off its image of being stuck in the past, and when it heard that the now larger rival agencies were considering major purchases of Macintoshes, an opportunity for public one-upmanship presented itself. William Morris would buy the *post-Macintosh* machine, the NeXT, and become au courant in one stroke.

NeXT also was excited by what a sale to William Morris would do for its own position in the public mind. The conservative image that William Morris sought to shed was precisely what was most valuable to NeXT—the association with the oldest talent agency would help to dispel lingering doubts in the corporate world about NeXT's youth. NeXT Cubes at William Morris could serve as a showcase of what the machine could do in a nontechnical business setting. The agency, by the nature of the work, was skilled in handling the media and attracting attention that was disproportionate to its size, just as NeXT was. A sale of several hundred machines to a company in the Fortune 500 would not generate nearly the attention that such a sale would to the William Morris Agency. The very way the two companies began their negotiations also made them comfortable with each other: the agency insisted on speaking with no one at Businessland or NeXT but Steve Jobs, and when this could not be achieved by conventional channels, it was achieved by employing celebrity connections. "Deal with the people at the top" was the credo at William Morris, which was perfectly suited to the style of Steve Jobs.

The interest of the William Morris Agency, Jobs told his staff, was validation of his laissez-faire marketing strategy, firing buckshot indiscriminately at the entire business world and seeing what customers stepped forward. See, he reasoned, if we had targeted specific areas, we never would have picked talent agencies as a bloc of customers we should pursue, and we never would have gotten this opportunity. He believed that the market for the NeXT computer was in the process of being created by the invisible customers like William Morris, who sought out NeXT instead of NeXT seeking out them. Jobs was determined that the talks with William Morris end successfully, and he was even willing to do what he had sworn he would not: he offered a deep discount to secure the sale of 270 machines. To prevent the concession from serving as a precedent for others, NeXT swore the agency to secrecy about the terms and publicly continued to avow no-discounts-for-anyone as non-negotiable policy. So determined was he to make this the flagship site that he gave his personal word that he would "put his butt on the line" to ensure that the agency received full satisfaction from its maverick purchase.[242]

At the time of the talks with NeXT, the William Morris Agency had little acquaintance with computers, other than in its music department, which had plain IBM-compatible personal computers. Contemplating expansion to all departments, the agency had called in outside consultants at Deloitte Touche to serve as lifeguards to make sure the agency did not swim out into technical waters that were way above its head. Most agents and their assistants did not use personal computers, and expressed no wish to do so, so the agency's management had at first asked Deloitte Touche to provide advice about the desirability of installing a large minicomputer connected to terminals that would be on every person's desk. Interestingly, it was someone who freely admitted that he knew nothing about computers, John Burnham, a senior executive who was cohead of the motion picture department at William Morris, who suggested that the agency look at the NeXT because Burnham had "heard it was a hot machine." Mike Simpson, his colleague, took up the suggestion and became a NeXT advocate, but Simpson, despite a reputation as the resident "power user" of personal computers at the agency, had much more enthusiasm than he had expertise. He and his young assistant, Chris Godsick, were completely at sea when they tried to organize the growing thicket of letters that were stored on a hard disk in Simpson's IBM-compatible computer. They had despaired of ever learning how to subdivide the hard disk space into directories and cluster related groups of letters together to make retrieval easy. Simpson's computer was filled with hundreds of unorganized letters stuck in an electronic wilderness, irretrievable. Frustrated, they had thrown up their hands and had reverted to the old-fashioned system of using paper copies kept in easy-to-file paper folders. Simpson, still struggling with the unfriendly commands of the personal-computer era from the early 1980s, pre-Macintosh, was that rare candidate ripe for NeXT proselytizing in the late 1980s: too busy to be willing to learn of easier-to-use, inexpensive alternatives to the computer software he was using, yet at the same time more than willing to spend a lot of money on machines that were touted as the Next Big Thing.

It is fitting that Mike Simpson, a professional merchant of inflated cinematic dreams, would himself be sold on an inflated dream, that of a NeXT computer that would be so easy to use that the telephone-related chaos of a busy agent's life could at last be tamed. Agents received 50 to 200 calls a day, and a senior agent like Simpson could keep four separate phone lines busy simultaneously—talking on one line, while assistants dialed out and readied a call on a second and two incoming calls were placed in a queue. The process was frenzied, accompanied by constant shouts from one person to another to punch the various telephone buttons that would keep the flow of calls rolling without interruption. Simpson was taken by the idea of purchasing NeXT Cubes and adapting a program for maintaining a phone log called Who's Calling?, which was in the process of being finished for the NeXT by Adamation, a small software firm based in Oakland which had decided to gamble its own fortunes on the NeXT Cube. Simpson envisaged much more than maintaining a simple list of phone numbers; the computer could keep other lists, too, of directors and their availability, of singers and actors, and with the multimedia capabilities of the NeXT, the lists could include photographs and swatches of music, as well. Keep in mind, however, that Simpson purchased dream, not reality. When William Morris Agency made its commitment in the late summer of 1989, the NeXT operating system was not yet complete. Who's Calling?, in turn, was unfinished, and the customized software that the agency wanted was nothing more than a wish list.

The agency pressed for guarantees of satisfaction from all of the companies who were involved: from NeXT, from Businessland, which had had the order land in its lap, and from Adamation, which had no say in designing the custom program that the agency wanted but was eager to please its first major customer. The one party that is missing from the list, Deloitte Touche, is a curious absence; after all, it was Deloitte Touche consultants who were hired by the agency for no purpose other than to serve as impartial technical advisers. They were the only ones who did not have a vested stake in pushing the NeXT sale. But Deloitte Touche, arguing that the NeXT hardware and software was new technology, shed any responsibility for the final result. If William Morris Agency wanted to make a loud statement about being on the cutting edge of computers, fine, but Deloitte Touche would not provide the security of the usual guarantees.

The first thirty NeXT Cubes arrived at the agency in October 1989, with the understanding that another 120 would follow in the early part of the next year. It seemed auspicious: this was the first major sale of Cubes for Businessland, it appeared to mark a breakthrough out of the academic ghetto for NeXT, and the agency received some favorable publicity (CNN: "New computer technology is helping some of Hollywood's top star-makers get ahead of the competition. . . ."), though William Morris and NeXT wished it had received still more. What none of the parties involved realized was that William Morris had taken a disastrous step, hopping into a temperamental Formula One racing car without any driving experience. In 1989, the agency was the only major commercial customer of NeXT, and even three years later, in the summer of 1992, it still was the second-largest commercial site of NeXT machines in North America,[243] but instead of inspirational showcase, it was the sinkhole from hell.

Mindful of the importance of milking the most positive publicity from its decision—which by its nature, once made, was all but irrevocable—the agency praised the NeXT to the press and extolled the many benefits that the machines had brought to the office. The press release trumpeted the NeXT network as a "first for the entertainment industry," yet the sort of innovative decision one would expect from an agency whose tradition was "always setting the standard in the industry." With the NeXT software, agents would be able to store and view videos of its entertainment clients on the computer itself.[244] Having a multimedia database at the agent's fingertips would make it possible, no, already *was* making it possible, for the agency to be more effective in representing its clients. In 1991, Mike Simpson, for example, bragged to a magazine interviewer that he could use the special NeXT software to secure a $2 million fee that he sought for a client. When the executive from Warner Brothers protested that the studio had never paid such a sum to a director with two credits going into his third movie, Simpson was at the ready with the contrary facts, thanks to the NeXT computer: "Wait a minute. Two years ago, you gave so and so two-and-a-quarter, so don't tell me that. . . ."[245] This was wonderful testimonial, except for a minor caveat: the multimedia NeXT database *did not exist*. The agency's custom software in fact was not in sufficiently completed form to permit even trial testing until the fall of 1992, or three years after the agency had convinced itself that the unique benefits of the NeXT software would give it an advantage over its competitors.

Aside from the attempt to have a bit of the *frisson* of the new rub off on the old agency, the principal reason for choosing NeXT in 1989 had been the attractions of the customized software, which Steve Jobs had billed as easy to create. The agency had conceived of a complex database with some eight separate modules, each a technical challenge that was the equivalent of a full-fledged stand-alone software program, yet each was expected to work seamlessly with the others. Everyone who did not actually have a role in writing software code said that it was feasible: NeXT and Businessland, who both wanted to clinch the sale and acceded to whatever the agency requested, and Deloitte Touche, who was happy to provide technical specifications without assuming any responsibility for implementation. It fell to Adamation to try to please the many different parties involved. William Morris made the project all the more difficult because of its elaborate concern for security. Still traumatized by the defections of its former agents, who had taken competitively crippling information about the agency's clients with them, the survivors at William Morris were determined to place multiple locks on each item of information in their custom database. Some people would be permitted to look at the client's calendar; others would be allowed to know what the last gig was; fewer would be allowed to see a phone number. The minutes of executive meetings and other sensitive documents were further protected by special tricks that prevented even those who were permitted to read them from being able to print them.

Stretched across a companywide computer network, a database with such restrictions and multiple modules made creation of the custom software a nightmare. Adamation attempted to persuade William Morris to simplify the design, but the agency would not budge and Adamation eventually had to relinquish the job and NeXT itself had to step in to finish it. Even NeXT had its problems and had to abandon two years of work and start completely over in 1991. Trying to keep its flagship account in Hollywood happy, NeXT ended up spending enormous amounts of its own money, diverting its engineers to work on the problems so that the private disaster did not explode into a major public embarrassment. Aside from the considerable resources themselves that NeXT, a small company, had to spend on the William Morris Agency account, the problems were costly too in the sense of distracting NeXT from focusing on other, larger categories of commercial customers. Even if NeXT had been able to follow the William Morris sale with other firms in the same niche, it would have gained little. The world of talent agencies is only so big, and it is too specialized to lead naturally to other business. Hollywood provided glamour but was otherwise a dead end. Strategically speaking, if NeXT's flagship account had been launched with a sale of similar size to, let us say, a nondescript insurance company, NeXT, and its corporate reseller, Businessland, would have been much better off.

The William Morris Agency also proved to be a deadly anomaly for having desks that were still virginally pure, untouched by other makes of personal computers when the first NeXT's arrived in 1989 and 1990. Consequently, agency employees were well behind the rest of corporate America in discovering word processing and electronic mail. Despite all the hoopla about the unique NeXT technology, the NeXT machines at the agency were used mostly for distributing internal memos within the company and for correspondence, functions that did not require $10,000 workstations. In the life of the prosaic office, the capability to include voice annotation languished;[246] agency memos used the same mute text that non-NeXT software used. There were hundreds of internal memos to be read each week; who had the time to *listen* to them? The only thing new about the system was the new manifestation of the old problem of being careful about what one communicated to whom: six employees were summarily fired when their electronic correspondence, which included discussion of their bosses and how best to avoid additional work duties, accidentally was sent to an administrator.[247] The loose lips did not require a NeXT computer, however; any computer in the age of the networked office would have served.

The William Morris Agency was delighted that its computers enabled the Beverly Hills and New York offices to be interconnected, but NeXT had not made it easy for NeXTs to be interconnected to the non-NeXT machines in the music department, so the two networks were separate, unable to talk with each other.[248] William Morris testimonial was all too plainly naive: it did not separate out which benefits derived from computers generically and which from NeXT specifically. The agency also had to overlook the sluggish performance and frequent crashes of its prized NeXT network, which should have been anchored by machines that were especially designed to serve as a central hub, the server, which Sun and other companies made, but NeXT did not. So, because NeXT was the party who decided how the network should be set up, it chose, no surprise, NeXT machines to stand in the place of servers, and network performance suffered as a result. The agency was simply too inexperienced and anomalous to provide an effective success story that would persuade others of the virtues of the NeXT.

As for the original dream of Mike Simpson, of using NeXT computers to track the maelstrom of phone calls that were at the center of office work at the agency, its realization turned out to be elusive. The sophisticated technology of the NeXT Cube, the computer that Steve Jobs described as the first for the Nineties (1990s) was still overwhelmed by the telephone, the technology of the earlier Seventies (1870s). The sheer volume of the calls made it impossible for assistants to take the trouble of entering the information onto the computer screen. It was most convenient to maintain the phone log as it always had been, by writing by hand on paper, using technology no more sophisticated than the spring of a clipboard. If a manual log seemed a waste of Jobs's "personal mainframe" and its digital signal processor and all the rest of the electronic goodies that the NeXT Cube embodied, there was one modest function that the NeXT Cube might have been able to help out with. It could have maintained a list of phone numbers that, with a simple connection to the phone system, would have permitted an agent to dial outgoing phone calls by hitting a single button on the computer. In 1991, the William Morris staff had heard that this marvelous feature, which seemed exotic and desirable in equal measure, was provided on the Macintoshes that rival Creative Artists Agency had. In fact, telephone dialing by computer was a feature that inexpensive, widely available software had provided even primitive IBM compatibles years before. It was only the lack of experience at the agency that made such a simple aid seem so wondrous and unattainable. While the agency waited and waited for its hopelessly ambitious custom program to be completed, it went without the software conveniences that users of other brands of computers had taken for granted long before.

While the graying William Morris Agency tried hard to show the world it was *cool*, the younger, more powerful Creative Artists Agency felt no need to loudly announce its hipness through its computers. It was well ahead of William Morris, having quietly moved from a sprinkling of Macintoshes and dedicated NBI word-processors to an all-Macintosh companywide network even before William Morris held its press conferences claiming to be the industry pioneer. Creative Artists did not make any public announcements about its new system and even when asked, preferred not to discuss internal operations. Its Macintoshes were used in a similar fashion to the NeXT's at William Morris—for word processing and electronic mail—but at a much lower cost per seat and with faster installation of computerized Rolodexes and customized, security-sensitive databases. For Creative Artists Agency, the decision to adopt Macintoshes was not a difficult choice, but the agency was laconic and did not feel as insecure as William Morris did, and so did not fuss and brag. Compared to CAA, William Morris comes across as no more hip than adults adopting teenager slang, talking in too loud a voice and never quite mastering the argot.

When the William Morris Agency made its commitment to purchase NeXT machines in 1989, it did so to a large measure because it knew that NeXT, as a relative newcomer, would take special care with its first major customer, whereas an order for a few hundred machines would be far too small to draw notice from an IBM or an Apple. The agency would need lots of hand-holding, and if Businessland could not accommodate it, the agency knew that it could go directly to NeXT itself. In this respect, the agency was proven correct, and NeXT did extend costly assistance far beyond what would be required in an ordinary arm's-length transaction between buyer and seller. But this is another reason why the initial announcement of the sale of NeXT Cubes to the agency did not create a bandwagon effect: by definition, there can only be one *first* major customer. Subsequent customers have to commit to the machine without being able to invoke the special status of being the first and expecting the unlimited factory support that came with it. The machines would have to stand on their own, and NeXT and Businessland discovered that they could not make any sales without what they referred to in memos as "senior NeXT exposure," that is, the presence of Jobs himself. The competition also noticed the phenomenon. Field sales representatives for Sun found that their smooth progress in working an account would be thrown in turmoil when Jobs would present himself and sway the customer to consider the NeXT. Then Scott McNealy would hear and have to hop a plane to try to sway the customer back. It maddened McNealy: it was only the celebrity of a Steve Jobs that forced him and other senior Sun executives to play in such a contest whose terms put noncelebrities at a disadvantage.

Jobs was without equal in selling himself. At a computer-industry meeting in late 1989 attended by initially hostile, older corporate information-systems people who came from the world of mainframe computers and who possessed no special fondness for the personal-computer revolution, Jobs stole the show. A *Computerworld* columnist provides this description:

> [Jobs] stood up in his dashing Italian suit—a far cry from his jeans-clad Apple days—and flashed his million-dollar smile. You could feel the crowd melt into his hands; after all, the other guys may be industry heavyweights, but this was a real live *celebrity*. . . . Even the skeptics moved forward in their seats when Jobs sat down and demo'd Next. Like Horowitz at the keyboard. . . . When Jobs bounded offstage to thunderous applause, there was a feeling that he could have sold a few computers right there in the hallway. Even the most hard-bitten were moved, at least a little.[249]

Employing Hollywood dazzle as one's primary marketing tool ultimately was not effective, however. A celebrity, like anyone else, can be in only one place at a time, and even an audience that melts during the performance will not follow through impulsively with orders in large volumes for a slow, expensive workstation that lacks software. (At the same industry conference, Bill Gates said that Microsoft had no interest in remedying NeXT's software lacuna: "We're in the business of writing for machines that sell in the millions, so this is not for us.")[250]

Whenever it publicly disclosed its sales, NeXT always did a little more than simply obey the natural instinct to put the best possible face on news; it stretched the truth a bit, sometimes less, sometimes more. In late 1989, for example, the company sought to convey the idea that its expansion into the commercial marketplace had been successful, and that the major purchase of NeXT Cubes from William Morris Agency had been followed by encouraging purchases in the Fortune 500. To achieve the desired effect in the public mind, NeXT's Dan'l Lewin announced that no less than one hundred companies in the Fortune 500 had NeXT Cubes "installed."[251] What he did not explain was that those computers were loaners and evaluation units, and in fact not a single company, in or outside the Fortune 500, had followed the William Morris Agency with a similar purchase. Even the agency's 270 machines were not purchased, as was publicly implied, in a single order; rather, the number represented a commitment to purchase that was spread over the next two years and was not fulfilled until June 1991.

NeXT did not disclose to the public that at the end of 1989, Businessland had sold a grand total of 360 NeXT Cubes. This was painful to absorb, especially for the NeXT employees who had worked at Apple, which sold more than 400,000 Macintoshes in the first year after its introduction. Even when sales of Cubes to higher education were included, the total was so small that NeXT employees looked at the figures and grimly joked that surely the numbers in the charts were expressed in units of thousands and had had three zeros lopped off. It was not the case, however. The NeXT factory had a run rate of fewer than 100 machines a month. Not

100,000, just plain 100. More than four years after its founding, sixteen months after the Cube had been unveiled at Davies Hall, nine months after announcing its partnership with Businessland, six months after receiving the massive investment from Japanese giant Canon, the marketplace was not cooperating with the script that Steve Jobs and his associates had written for themselves.

Roller Coaster

B usinesses, like families, harbor secrets. In some cases, the divergence between public façade and private reality is extreme, and such has been the case of Steve Jobs's NeXT. The official story at any given point since the introduction of the Cube in 1988 has been that NeXT Computer is succeeding; the story that has been kept private has been one of botched strategies and ever widening gaps between NeXT's sales and those of its targeted competitors. One would expect to find that NeXT employees were racked by cognitive dissonance, trying to reconcile the various dualities at NeXT: the optimistic pronouncements and the disappointing sales, the inner conviction that the company had built a superior machine and the outer indications that the public was not interested, the anointment by Jobs of his subordinates as the best and his belittlement of them as the worst that soon followed. To a remarkable extent, however, NeXT employees kept cognitive dissonance to a minimum; they were able to do so by following as much as they could the example of Jobs himself, the master at denying whatever causes anxiety or discomfort.

Here is an example of the duality that Jobs has adroitly managed:

In September 1989, when NeXT still had virtually no sales outside of higher education, Jobs confidently told a different story to the public. He declared that in its penetration of corporate America the NeXT Computer was ahead of the Macintosh at the same point in its history because the NeXT did not have to be snuck in through the back door like the Mac; it was going straight in through the front door. When asked if he had any regrets, would he have done anything differently with the NeXT, he answered with verve that he would not have changed a thing, he was happy with how things had turned out. So at least he said. Internally, the company was receiving lots of signals that the machine was an overpriced, slow, black-and-white computer that needed software, and convincing software developers to gamble on the NeXT machine was proving to be extremely difficult. But publicly, Jobs maintained everything was dandy; in fact, he said, the company was even *ahead* of its own plans to secure software. Every major software developer was writing software for the NeXT, Jobs told the press; Gates's Microsoft was the only holdout.[252] This was a shrewd bluff. If Jobs succeeded in convincing the public that acceptance of NeXT was gathering momentum, then software developers and customers would hurry to hop on the bandwagon, turning what had been phantom into solid reality.

One could easily assemble an album filled with snapshots of similar duality, when NeXT's public pronouncements were wildly at odds with the facts that were privately concealed. What is of most interest, however, is not the simple fact of divergence between hype and truth, but rather the psychological aspect of this tension and the uneasy complicity of NeXT employees and the wider general public in wishful thinking. Steve Jobs is persuasive only because we have our own needs that mesh well with his. As a society, we are desperate for the heroic figure, and if Steve Jobs wields powers of persuasion with few equals, the credit or blame, as you wish, should also fall upon the audience, the other half of the equation that is too often ignored. The fact that *Inc.* magazine would hail

Jobs as "Entrepreneur of the Decade" in early 1989, after the NeXT Computer had been born in a pitiful state of incompletion and flaws, tells us much about ourselves. We crave the authority of an oracle, whose preternatural vision is validated by youth and early success, and Steve Jobs has been glad to play out the oracular role we have offered to him.

A revealing example of the intertwined interests of Jobs's ego and the public's hunger for a business sage is provided in a television show, "Future Forum," that was filmed in June 1989 at the New York Public Library and sponsored by Dow Jones to commemorate the hundredth anniversary of *The Wall Street Journal*. For a discussion of The Future writ large, a panel of international figures from business and politics was assembled, including Donald Peterson, the chairman of Ford Motor Company; Michael Boskin, chairman of the Council of Economic Advisors; Valéry Giscard d'Estaing, former president of France; Kenichi Ohmae, from McKinsey and Company's Tokyo office; and various notables from Great Britain, Hungary, Mexico, Italy, and the then–Soviet Union. The single under-forty representative among this august group was Steve Jobs.

The discussion of the day was launched by the day's host, news anchor Peter Jennings, who asked the panel to think about a fictional company, Creative Motors, where a bright young engineer was thinking about leaving to start his own company. Jennings naturally fixed upon Jobs, the paragon of youthful entrepreneurialism, to bring the engineer to life, and Jobs obliged with many thoughts, which came tumbling out in an unpolished jumble: "I think what you're highlighting is that it only takes—even in a very large corporation—it only takes a few people to make a difference between an Edsel and a Taurus." He jumped abruptly to his home territory of computers. As the American economy shifted increasingly toward "knowledge work," the only difference, he said, between the Taurus and the Edsel, between a winning car design and a failed one, would be the computerized database employed in the design. From this, he said, one could see that economic competition between countries would not be a matter of competing wage rates but rather a matter of competing educational systems. As he spoke, and as Jennings coaxed from him some thoughts about how he had come to start NeXT, the constant motion of Jobs's gestures placed him apart from the other, less animated members of the panel. The hands provided curlicues: fluttering, pointing, pressed together, pulled apart and twisted. Everyone on the panel listened to the Young Man attentively and politely, and Jobs clearly relished the opportunity to hold forth on industrial policy and the Future Fate of the American Economy. He bragged later that year that Robert Mosbacher, the Secretary of Commerce, had asked him for his thoughts on higher education, and he had answered, "The Secretary of Commerce and the Secretary of Education should be the same person."[253]

The idea at the core of Jobs's prescription for reviving America's ailing industrial sector was that the country needed more of those specially gifted individuals, extremely bright and driven, who made all the difference, and who, he told us, started new companies not in pursuit of money or glory but only out of frustration when their ideas were too far ahead of their time. In short, Steve Jobs said the country needed more people like Steve Jobs.

Within the company, the problem of duality appeared in many forms. Consider, for example, Jobs's official theory about managing others and his actual practice. On the public record, Jobs would speak eloquently of how he liked to hire "self-motivated people," whom you point in the general direction of where they are to head and then "get the hell out of their way."[254] In fact, Jobs could not resist doing the opposite of what he prescribed: he reserved all decisions for himself, interceding in every trivial matter. Perhaps Jobs's behavior is best explained by his egoism: if no one else was his equal, then it would be best to have all decisions made by the most competent person available, that is, himself. He believed his grasp of all functional areas of business was as sure as it was intuitive, and he saw himself as the self-taught creator of an entire industry in the same way that Henry Ford and the Wright Brothers had had no formal business background.²⁵⁵ On a hot summer day, during a hike in the Stanford hills with a fellow employee that took them up to a vantage point from which the sprawl of Silicon Valley could be glimpsed beneath the thick smog, Jobs could look out and say, all in apparent seriousness, "I feel responsible for that."

An alternative explanation—favored by some NeXT employees—hypothesizes that Jobs is actually quite insecure, and maintains his own control by keeping his employees in a perpetual state of disequilibrium. Working at NeXT, they would joke, was like being in a V-8 juice advertisement, in which the figures (who have not gotten their vegetables) walk at an impossible tilt. If you tried to stand up straight, Jobs would push you off-center again with a ferocious attack on the quality of the work. It was so predictable that employees learned over time that it was best to show Jobs a preliminary version of whatever was to be placed before him, so that when the work was judged to be "shit" or "brain-damaged," as it always was, revisions could be readied quickly and the rejection was not so painful.

Still, it was difficult for NeXT employees to adjust to the dramatic drop in regard that Jobs had for them once they had begun work at the company (Susan Barnes would sardonically describe Jobs's pattern of behavior as his "seduce-and-abandon mode"). New employees arrived as heroes, the best of the best who had survived the stringent series of interviews, which could extend to five or six separate visits to the company. No one was hired without a manager persuading Jobs that this person was the absolute best person *on the planet* for the job. All offer letters were issued by Jobs himself, and he exercised peremptory challenges, often rejecting a highly praised prospective candidate after a brief encounter. His fatal all-purpose appraisal for the person he rejected would be, "I don't think that person is very bright." Those who managed to survive the process were brought into the company with a grand introduction, presented to their new colleagues with a recitation of their outstanding credentials, their ears ringing with descriptions that placed them as the best in their field. And their youth was hailed, too—Jobs always mentioned age in their introduction to the company, and if he did not already recall a person's exact age, he would ask the employee to state it before the assembled group; though not intended, Jobs's fixation upon youth could make a veteran employee who was a ripe thirty years feel dismayed by her own advanced age when she silently compared herself to the new, younger stars who were regularly introduced, basking in Jobs's praise.

Yet not long after the golden newcomers began work at NeXT, they discovered that Jobs did not like what they were doing, that they could not seem to do anything right. This led, in turn, to a redoubling of effort in a vain attempt to recapture the approbation of Jobs, the person who possessed monopoly control over one's standing. In the internal NeXT lexicon, this pattern of initial hiring hailed as the very best, followed by disparagement as hopelessly incompetent, was referred to by the shorthand phrase "The Hero-Shithead Roller Coaster."

In the binary world of Jobs, you were either *great*, or you were *shit*, and since in his mind no one was as capable as he was, it did not take long for heroes to fall from grace. The more time that you spent in close proximity to Jobs, the sooner the fall; employees called it the Icarus Effect. On at least one occasion, the Icarus Effect transpired within the compass of a single day, when Jobs gave a short talk to a group of new employees as part of their orientation. Afterward, Jobs pulled aside one of his senior managers and told him to dismiss one member of the new group, who had not impressed Jobs as "smart." It was not clear why Jobs's observation of someone who was asked to do nothing but listen to presentations by others yielded insight that had not come during the intensive grilling in interviews earlier. But with excuses and distractions, the manager averted the unsavory task of firing the person on his first day at work.

From a distance, Jobs's *modus operandi* may appear to be an effective means of pushing employees to work their hardest. In his calculation of how to get the most from people, Jobs drew upon the peculiar mathematics favored by football coaches who ask for "110 percent" from their players. The same math was used by Jobs: his theory was that if he asked for 100 percent of what a person could do, he might get something close to 100 percent, but if he demanded 150 percent (one must be imaginative here to guess what that might mean), then he could expect a superhuman frenzy of effort that would result in 120 percent fulfillment, or 20 percent more than he would have gotten if he had not goaded the person to do the impossible. Viewed from a closer vantage point, where employee demoralization is more visible, the operation of such a system is not such a pretty sight. Jobs always exhorted his troops to think of NeXT's struggle as a marathon, but early employees discovered that it was hard to run a marathon while sustaining the pace of a hold-nothing-back sprint. Over time, it was ever more difficult to draw sufficient sustenance from the sugar highs of the major company announcements, to accept the promise of Jobs that "the next six months will make or break us" when the six months passed only to be replaced with a renewed promise that the *next* six months were the ones that would be truly critical, then the next. Many dropped out of the race and left the company. On the day that he resigned, one marketing manager received an electronic mail message from a fellow employee: "Congratulations on figuring out the only way to turn off the treadmill is to walk away." Soon, employees that had been hired later would flag, too, and leave, and then their successors would pass through the same cycle. In-jokes within the company were attempts to ease the pain. Referring to lithium, the drug used to treat the mania of bipolar disorder—NeXT was regarded as a place of "the highest highs and the lowest lows"—NeXT employees would self-mockingly warn each other to avoid too many trips to the "lithium lick." As disillusioned NeXT employees bailed out, most did not receive the sympathetic gesture like the congratulatory note about the treadmill. Those who stayed behind, for their own psychic self-preservation, tended to view those who left as deserters, deserving of no more thought than weaklings who fell by the wayside in combat. Those who left the company were viewed as the "B players" who could not keep up with the "A players" who bravely marched on, until they too collapsed, and fresher troops stepped over them in turn.

Jobs could use his considerable powers to charm as part of the recruitment process, whether he sought employees, suppliers, or customers, but once he had secured what he wanted, he did not exert himself and bother with even simple civilities. In the private meetings at NeXT, well beyond public view, he was the antithesis of charming. The duality of public and private sides to Jobs was impressed upon his employees, who had to reconcile the suave, charismatic, larger-than-life Founder whom the public knew, with the captious, acid-tongued martinet that they saw before them in the flesh—and whose vicinity they quickly learned to stay as far from as possible.

Former employees, looking back upon their experience at NeXT, have spoken lightheartedly of a new business opportunity: opening "detox centers" just for ex-NeXTies, just as there are centers for deprogramming Scientologists and Hare Krishna followers. With its charter mission to serve higher education, NeXT had attracted "the most passionate people outside of a nonprofit," one veteran tells me, looking back wistfully (and then adds, "well, actually NeXT was a nonprofit, too"). Another former believer describes the idealism at NeXT by recalling how employees were so excited about their work when they began that would say to one another with incredulity, "And they're paying us, too!" Not all NeXT employees were so idealistic, and another step in the process of disillusionment for those who were was the moment of discovery that some colleagues had ignored the rhetoric of egalitarianism and material renouncement and had negotiated higher salaries than others with identical qualifications and responsibilities. The materialists were the ones who turned out to have the most longevity at NeXT because they did not pass through the crisis of disillusionment that the idealists inevitably encountered.

Several other former employees have spoken, not so lightheartedly, of NeXT as a "dysfunctional family," dominated by one person who is winsome in public but abusive in private. Like family members in the codependency model who try to reform the family tormentor by being on their best behavior and trying to exert a salutary influence by being perfect, and yet always falling short, so too NeXT employees tried to reform Jobs and make him less cruel. The dysfunctional-family metaphor seemed especially appropriate to one group of six employees who happened to be chatting together one day when they discovered that five out of the six were children of alcoholics. Others spoke of informal polls among their fellow employees at NeXT that had arrived at similar results. There is a danger here of overstating the case and of perpetuating the seemingly endless speculation based on pop psychology that has long made Jobs a central subject (in his early career, Jobs's name would rarely be mentioned without someone explicating the supposed importance of his being an adopted child). Certainly there are no statistically valid data to corroborate the contention that NeXT employees had a higher than average percentage of people who came from such backgrounds. But what is clear is that the theory held explanatory power to some NeXT employees; it gave them a way of understanding why they would subject themselves to Jobs's cruelty and the unusual psychodynamics of their workplace. Their theory was that they had tolerated it, had in fact gone to NeXT in the first place, because NeXT replicated the emotional environment that they personally were most familiar with, that of their own family.

If we return to the idea that NeXT, like Jobs, had a public side and a dissimilar private side, we can understand why Joe Hutsko, one of the employees who had worked for Jobs at Apple, then again at NeXT, told Jobs, upon resigning, that he would continue to respect the fine products that Jobs made. But Hutsko went on to say that he had come to the conclusion that it was much better to use Jobs's computers than to witness the human cost entailed in producing them. He likened his aversion to seeing how it was done to purposefully not watching as piano movers transport a prized instrument. Jobs heard the same message from one departing employee after another, some of whom prepared long letters of resignation, filling pages with suggestions of how the company's culture could be improved, or presenting at their last staff meetings detailed proposals for change. Even as they were leaving in a state of exhaustion and emotional distress, Jobs's employees would muster a last burst of passion in a vain attempt to get Jobs to address the problems that he preferred to ignore. No one had sufficient power to make him listen, however, and the collective force of the combined messages did not register because Jobs could treat each case singly as an instance of "burn-out," a regrettable but unchangeable constant among the less worthy.

No one had the power to make Jobs do anything that he did not want to do, and such had been the case for so long that he had come to accept with equanimity a pathologically distorted vision of the world. Why should there be any limits to the fulfillment of his every impulse? He was a multimillionaire who had been deified while still a young man; and now his post-Apple company was flush with $100 million from Canon. In 1989, when NeXT offices were moved to greatly expanded quarters along the San Francisco Bay in Redwood City, he repeated the extravagances of the founding, only on a grander scale that made the preparations resemble the building of the Taj Mahal. The construction crews were kept at work around the clock, scurrying to implement Jobs's wishes. As the first tenants of the buildings, NeXT was given a generous allowance for the completion of the interiors, but NeXT far exceeded its allotment. This was quite an accomplishment, considering that the buildings were nothing but shells and there was no existing interior that needed to be ripped out before the new design was built in. The only thing that NeXT had to work around were the elevators that came with the building. But even these were too much to accommodate, so to improve the views and clear room for wide staircases, Jobs ordered the elevators removed entirely, despite objections that without them the movement of people in wheelchairs and equipment would be much more difficult. When the construction was completed, a one-of-a-kind staircase—designed by I. M. Pei's firm—appeared to float by invisible means. The dining area featured gray, black, and white marble. Common areas had $2,200 chairs and $10,000 sofas. On every employee's desk was the most expensive phone—$450 each—that Jobs could find. Special high-capacity T-1 phone lines were leased so that every phone within NeXT's scattered locations could be reached with the dialing of only four digits. Jobs ordered that a T-1 line be installed from NeXT to his home, too. When Alex Gray, the NeXT manager responsible for telecommunication services, returned to Jobs's office to report that the line would cost $660 a month, Jobs did not look up from his computer screen when he replied. "I don't care," he said, "I'm rich."

By continuing his obsession with the most picayune operational details, as he had at the founding of NeXT, Jobs maintained for himself an illusory sense that the world was under his control and "quality" the sine qua non, when in fact it was only his immediate surroundings that were his dominion. Outside business partners were always shocked when they got their first intimate glimpse of life at NeXT under Jobs. When a group of reporters accompanied a delegation of Businessland executives on a visit to NeXT's splendid new offices in Redwood City, the visitors, dressed in suits, disembarked from the limousine and were greeted by Jobs in blue jeans and black turtleneck. As he walked with the group toward the entrance, Jobs was called over by the landscaper who was overseeing installation of the sprinkler system. For twenty minutes, while the group waited on the sidewalk, Jobs gave directions to the landscaping crew, pointing out the exact placement of the sprinkler heads.

Having witnessed such a scene, the Businessland representatives should not have been surprised when they discovered that they too would be subjected to the same maniacal focus on the most trivial of details. A NeXT employee happened to see one day that one of the Businessland stores in Palo Alto had painted a NeXT logo on the window without authorization. The transgression was reported to Jobs, who angrily called Businessland's Kevin Compton, who had the unpleasant task of ordering that the sign be washed off. Compton's subordinate was incredulous: "You have to be kidding." No, Compton explained, he was not; the colors were not right and the sign had to go. Could we not redo the colors, using the official NeXT color card, which specified the precise Pantone Matching System shades? This turned out to be acceptable to Jobs, and the sign painter returned to make sure that the "N" in NeXT was "PMS Warm Red U" and the "e" was "PMS Yellow 109U" and so on. All Businessland stores received the color specification card and orders to take care to ensure proper matching. In such fussing, it would be understatement to use the old saw about missing the forest for the trees; this was focusing on *one* branch of *one* tree and pressing one's nose against a patch of bark.

Even NeXT employees, who generally soon became inured to Jobs's obsessive concern about "quality," were not incapable of astonishment. When the Cube was shipping at long last, the NeXT managers in the marketing and sales group discovered that the orders that they had, small though they were, could not be filled by the NeXT factory in Fremont. Burt Cummings, a manager whom Jobs had hired from Apple, was responsible for getting the Cubes sent out and he discovered, when he called the factory, that the problem was the unsatisfactory paint on the magnesium cases that had arrived from the outside supplier. "There're bubbles on it," Cummings was told. "OK, describe how bad these bubbles are." Well, the factory said, it's too hard to describe. After prolonged wrangling, Cummings was told that if he were willing to vouch for their quality, the factory reluctantly would ship the Cubes out.

So Cummings hopped in the car and drove to Fremont to inspect the cases for himself, and discovered that the mischievous bubbles were not visible until a manager from NeXT's Quality Control department brought out a magnifying glass. Cummings was told that the factory's standards for acceptable quality were not a matter for subjective judgment but were spelled out in a rigorous Quality Assurance test specified in the company manual. The lighting for the test, the proper 45-degree angle and distance for observation— all were spelled out in detail. Cummings stretched out his arm to measure the proper distance, adjusted his position to achieve the required angle, and compared side-by-side one case that had flunked the test with one that had passed and he still could not tell any difference. Fine, said Cummings, if a customer is upset with what is visible only under a magnifying glass and demands a new Cube, we'll tell him we'll ship him one in a few months. But now can we please ship these out so customers will at least have something? Looking back on the memory and laughing, Cummings describes such fussiness at NeXT as doing the little things "down to a gnat's ass," while other, more important matters remained out of control.

In January 1989, Jobs had made quality a superordinate concern of the company, beginning with his placement of the term "quality" on his "Deep Shit" list at a company retreat. (This list was separate from the "Good Shit" list of positive milestones; the motif ran through other Jobsian expressions, such as the sublime praise for employees who pleased him: "You've turned shit into gold!") Jobs saw the enormous publicity that Motorola, one of NeXT's principal suppliers, had received the year before when it won the Malcolm Baldrige Award for its Total Quality Management program, and he decided that NeXT should institute a Total Quality Management program and apply for a Baldrige, too. Eva Chen, a TQM expert and a Baldrige examiner herself, was hired to head NeXT's new program. She was an evangelist whose charter was to show that quality issues pertained not just to defect rates in manufacturing but to every department within the company.

At first blush, it would have seemed that NeXT was the perfect candidate for a successful Total Quality Management program. The TQM principles, which had been developed by Americans like Deming and Juran and embraced and legitimated by large Japanese companies, were the subject of numerous management seminars and books in the late 1980s. Steve Jobs, with his hysterical intolerance of anything that he deemed less than the best, appeared to have a head start on most everybody else in the United States. TQM at NeXT would simply be a formalization of what Jobs had intuitively pressed for on his own. So, at least, it had seemed initially. But as Chen and her team of eleven representatives drawn from all departments at NeXT worked on setting up the TQM program, it soon became clear that TQM principles and Jobs's philosophy were antagonistic in many respects. The prophets of TQM preached the importance of making quality the concern of everyone in the company at the grassroots level; Jobs's attitude was, Let's go for the Baldrige! TQM demanded that all aspects of the business be placed under scrutiny; Jobs's approach implicitly said that those matters dear to his own heart, such as aesthetic appearances, were more important than others, such as understanding one's prospective customers. TQM would require that managers solicit and address feedback; Jobs preferred to pick and choose his news, and the messengers who delivered discouraging news were figuratively shot.

At the middle and lower levels of the company, NeXT employees quickly saw that the Total Quality Management program could bring long-desired changes in NeXT, forcing Jobs and his senior staff to pay more attention to the discomforting messages that the outside world was sending to NeXT but which never seemed to reach the inner sanctum. TQM placed emphasis on the importance of trusting and "empowering" subordinates, delegating authority, making incremental improvements as part of a long continual process, all of which were antithetical to Jobs's makeup. Jobs's interest in TQM lasted as long as any shiny object which momentarily caught his eye; it was discarded and forgotten as soon as he came across the next glittering bauble. It was unfortunate because NeXT might have been an interesting test of the appropriateness of TQM principles in a young, struggling company; if, for the fun of conjecture, we assume that Jobs was constitutionally well-suited for a TQM program, there still would have been problems: TQM gobbled up staff resources and entailed measurements and reports and small-group meetings. Should one wait until the company is more established and can more comfortably spare the resources, or should one start early and view it not as a luxury but as one means to *become* well-established? TQM died at NeXT too soon for an answer.

Frustrated that she could not get Jobs's support to implement a proper Total Quality Management program, Eva Chen left NeXT, bringing to a close the short-lived chapter of TQM in NeXT's book. It is a chapter that the company apparently regards with some retrospective misgivings: Chen contacted NeXT in 1991, more than a year after she had resigned from the company, seeking clearance for speaking about Total Quality Management at NeXT. She was threatened by NeXT's lawyers with a lawsuit if she were to say a word. (One must grant that even if its interest in TQM proved fleeting, NeXT obviously has made great strides in a new field, what might be called *TSM*, for Total *Secrecy* Management.)

An application for the Baldrige award was worked up, but it was a document of frothy unreality: NeXT selectively chose what it wished to report, bragging about the low rate of defects in key electronic components, but turning vague when it came to discussing customer satisfaction and market acceptance of the Cube. The application explicated company goals at great length, talking of airy slogans ("At NeXT, the business plan *is* the quality plan") or formulas that the company had devised ("Vision + TQM = Success"). One component of the NeXT mission statement was "to build computers that change the world and that our friends can afford to buy," but the application did not provide an indication of how many friends had demonstrated the affordability of the machine by actually purchasing one. Inadvertently, the document betrayed the self-referential orientation of NeXT, such as in the boast that NeXT employees understood what its customers needed "sometimes better than the customers themselves." The Baldrige examiners were not impressed; NeXT's application did not advance beyond the preliminary round of the competition.

The flirtation with Total Quality Management and the energy diverted to organizing teams of employees to prepare the application for the Baldrige award was costly to NeXT, not because little came of it all but because it delayed for Jobs the moment of reckoning with his mistakes. He had convinced himself that he had set up a *quality* organization that produced a *quality* computer. At the same time, he could not avoid seeing that his intended customers were not nearly as "delighted and surprised" as the company's mission statement said that they were supposed to be, and that sales failed to take off even after the operating system was completed. So the only possible explanation left in his mind was that his new business partner, Businessland, was bungling the task of selling the machine. In the spring of 1989, Businessland had been hailed by NeXT as the very best at what it did; by the fall, Businessland was hopelessly incompetent, inept, incapable of selling without NeXT holding its hand every step of the way. Almost overnight Businessland became the scapegoat for the disappointing sales of the Cube, replicating the course of the hero-shithead roller coaster with which Jobs's own employees were well familiar.

Jobs's personal familiarity with the commercial offices to which Businessland sold computers was all but nonexistent, and certainly no better than his familiarity with the university offices that had been the earlier target. Somehow he had picked up the idea that NeXT would be successful in the commercial market because his company had a "printer strategy" that no one else had. His lectures on the subject to Businessland executives left them puzzled, however; they thought that customers cared more about price issues, or software availability, than about a marketing message that linked a computer and a printer together. Jobs was not concerned about the customer complaints about the slow speed and high cost of the optical disk because he predicted that the $50 disks would soon be available for $20 (what transpired was the opposite: their price rose to their true cost, $150).[256] And perhaps the most unrealistic idea that Jobs had about his intended market was that the NeXT Cube would be the perfect replacement for people who had a desktop crowded with two machines—a Macintosh *and* a Sun workstation. ("Great, that's about five desks," Dan'l Lewin, the cofounder in charge of marketing, would mutter sub rosa whenever Jobs launched his pat speech on the subject.)

This lack of understanding his market can be explained in part by a little secret: Jobs was not much of a computer user himself. One would never guess that the hallowed father of the personal-computer industry and the master of the computer demonstration, on his own, used his machine for processing electronic mail and little else. The computer, which in speeches he often referred to as "the most powerful tool ever invented," was used in his own life for mundane communication, quite like the William Morris Agency singing the praises of its computers while using them for very little other than as mailboxes. And Jobs himself began using electronic mail later rather than earlier, beginning not at Apple but at NeXT. When he was in the mood and found the time to do it himself instead of scribbling a draft on paper for someone else to tinker with on the computer, he would use his machine to write a letter or prepare slides for the occasional talk. But he did not often use a spreadsheet, the most common software found in business offices, of whose needs he believed he had a profound understanding. He did not spend time expanding his own skills, exploring limits, or testing the software of rivals. He remained as technically dependent upon experts when even small hardware or software glitches arose as any lay person. One is not surprised that a John Sculley, Apple's CEO who formerly was a marketeer at Pepsi, relied heavily upon personal technical assistants. But Steve Jobs? And at home as well as at the office? When he was having a problem with his Cube at home on one occasion, Jobs put in an urgent call one weekend to one of his senior managers, who also was expected to be on call as his personal-computer technical assistant. The plea for help reached him when he happened to be traveling in Europe and was able to remotely turn Jobs's balky machine off, then back on, and remedy the problem, using a handy $5,000-a-month telephone line that NeXT leased. A recurring pattern in Jobs's famous computer demonstrations is that they always highlighted technology—such as mathematically produced orchestral sounds or visually impressive collages of images, like Donald Duck and a red Ferrari—without showing what a marketing person would call *solutions*. Jobs had no idea what problems real people faced in a real office.

Jobs increased the pressure on Businessland's Dave Norman to produce sales, and Norman turned the screws on his subordinates. The wisdom embodied in a folk saying popular at the lower levels at NeXT ("Shit rolls downhill") applied now to Businessland, too. When the enticement of generous bonuses failed to produce the desired results, Businessland senior management issued quotas for each store, with the promise that heads would roll if the quotas were not met. Meanwhile, Businessland had to continue to accept fresh shipments of NeXT Cubes in order to fulfill its contract with NeXT and meet the terms required to maintain its exclusive control of distribution. The warehouses filled up with unsold machines. NeXT maintained that this was wholly Businessland's problem and had no sympathy for its plight.

At the very end of 1989, the NeXT-Businessland relationship took a farcical turn. NeXT wanted to unload a final shipment of 1,300 units on Businessland so that it could close its books on the year with the machines recorded as sold (for perspective, remember that Businessland sold fewer than 400 total for the entire year of 1989), and Businessland, for the same reasons, wanted to close *its* books without its inventory becoming even more bloated than it already was. Like hot potatoes, the machines were tossed back and forth, neither company wanting to be stuck with them. Finally, a compromise was reached: NeXT would ship the Cubes out, but Businessland would not receive them until after it had closed its books for 1989. In the meantime, the machines disappeared into accounting limbo, left on the truck with orders to go around the block several times, so to speak, until NeXT and Businessland both got their books closed. For the Businessland managers who were ordered to carry out such legerdemain, this episode brought home the realization that Businessland was in serious trouble.

Steve Jobs had an epiphany at this time, too. Maybe things were not going so well, after all. "Is this the right product?" he asked his senior staff in early January 1990. There was an abundance of indications that the Cube was not succeeding, but Jobs had not been ready to pay attention until this point. Like a dazed survivor of a train that had derailed, he wanted to know, what happened? Lewin, whose close contacts with academic customers had made him painfully aware of how unrealistically expensive the NeXT Cube had turned out to be for them, let alone for Businessland customers who had to pay a still higher price, had been waiting for an opportunity when Jobs would listen, and finally it had arrived. We need to build a new machine, a product for $3,000, Lewin said, naming the same target price that had been on the white board years ago when NeXT was featured on "The Entrepreneurs." Jobs said, okay, let's build it. The other employees were apprised of the new plan at the company retreat held that month at the Hyatt Monterey. As always, Jobs spent money without regard for the vicissitudes of sales: $500,000 was spent on this retreat alone, an impressive sum for a company of fewer than 400 employees whose only product, it seemed in the words of one NeXT manager, could not even be given away. But once again, employees were provided with a new sugar high. The company would redesign the Cube and have a new machine out for the fall. The crash program was to be called *Warp 9*, a speed that lay beyond the possible (Warp 8 was the maximum speed of the starship Enterprise in *Star Trek*), and a reference to the nine months that the company gave itself to reinvent its computer.

A fiscally prudent chief executive officer would have tried to conserve NeXT's cash kitty as the company limped through the interim period until the *next* NeXT was readied. Susan Barnes, in charge of finance, had voiced a heretical thought: since the Cube was not selling, perhaps it would be best for NeXT to shift back to "research-and-development mode," pull the product from the shelves, concentrate on readying the new one, and conserve its money in the meantime. But Jobs would hear nothing of it. He felt it was best to maintain an image of success. NeXT sales representatives were always dogged by questions concerning the "V" word, the company's viability; Jobs sought to provide reassurance that the company was healthy and would be long-lived, by *spending* in the manner of a healthy company. More buildings were leased in Redwood City and Fremont, even though some would remain unoccupied. NeXT's own direct sales force was greatly expanded with an experienced cadre of computer salespeople from Sun, Silicon Graphics, and other sibling companies; the travel-and-entertainment excesses of the staff on the road soon became legend, even at NeXT where the word "excess" was not in anyone's vocabulary and a single month's catering bill for the company's twenty-four-member executive staff ($22 per person each lunch meeting, with the black lunch box, black cutlery, black napkin) one time came to $13,000. NeXT's actual sales figures were kept secret, so Jobs could point to outward appearances and say to the world, "Does this look like a company that is not going to be around?"

Members of the NeXT sales staff, in fact, had abundant reasons to wonder whether they had made a wise decision to join NeXT. They were accustomed to annually earning commissions of $200,000 to $400,000, but at NeXT the commission structure was based on the assumption that NeXT would become an overnight success. The Macintosh veterans remembered that in the first hundred days after its introduction, some 72,000 Macintoshes had been sold,[257] and Jobs had initially predicted that NeXT would sell 40,000 machines immediately just because at least that many people would buy any computer he made, regardless of what it was.[258] Based on these sunny expectations, Jobs originally wanted each NeXT salesperson to bring in $10 to $20 million in sales as an annual quota; Todd Rulon-Miller, NeXT's head of sales, managed to persuade Jobs to lower it to $5 million. Even this was unrealistic, a figure four to five times larger than what other companies at a similar point in their history had expected of their salespeople. After the Cube was released, NeXT's sales representatives soon discovered that a million in annual sales per person was all that could be achieved, which meant that for the first time in their careers they were not meeting their numbers and had to accept the discouraging minimum "draw," paid as an advance against future commissions that never materialized. (The sales staff conducted an informal survey of customers to try to ascertain how many Cubes were sold for no other reason than that it was Steve Jobs's machine, and the best estimate that they arrived at was that only about 100 machines were purchased primarily for that reason.)

Dan'l Lewin did not wait around for the Second Coming of the NeXT computer. He had gone from hero to shithead, having been demoted and stripped of formal marketing responsibility in July 1989 when he told Jobs that NeXT should not make promises to customers that Jobs knew they had no way of keeping. After demoting Lewin, Jobs had taken the marketing post himself. Finally too frustrated to endure the ignominy of impotent figurehead, Lewin resigned in February 1990, becoming the first of the original five NeXT cofounders who would peel off. Lewin's decision to leave could not be attributed to a lack of desire to work at a fragile start-up: he left NeXT to join another small start-up, GO Corporation, which was working on software for computers that used pens instead of keyboards, and from there he would go on to join Kaleida Labs, a brand-new multimedia software company formed by IBM and

Apple. His successive destinations were companies that offered the same blue-sky possibilities as NeXT had, and without the price of suffering at the hands of Steve Jobs.

Employees who stayed at NeXT were treated curiously by Jobs. They were subject to the same tirades and petty humiliations as before, but when it came time for NeXT to perform the semiannual performance appraisals and determine raises, if any, employees were heroes once again. The old days had passed when one was expected as a demonstration of faith to accept a significant pay cut when joining the company. Now NeXT was willing to pay a premium. Barnes's own assistant, a junior accountant hired from a large accounting firm where such positions paid in the mid-twenty-thousand range, was hired at NeXT for $50,000 a year and within two years was making $90,000. The salaries of others climbed in similar fashion. It was dizzying: raises were not merely five or ten percent at a time, they were often five or ten thousand dollars, and since they were given as salary increases, not bonuses, they were permanent. Thanks to company policy, anyone could learn what anyone else made. If a valued employee made noises about leaving, a raise would be awarded on the spot, then everyone else on the same level would demand one, too, ratcheting salary costs upward. All the while the company's operations resulted in losses of millions of dollars a month.

Yet, despite the red ink, despite the belated abandonment of "Field of Dreams" marketing, building a computer with neat technology and assuming that customers would come to *it*, despite instituting a crash program to design a new computer, Jobs maintained a public façade that all was well. Total Secrecy Management permitted Jobs in late January 1990 to tell the press, which had not been told anything about the company retreat that gave birth to Warp 9, that "I'd say we're doing even a little bit better than we expected."[259] The newspapers knew that sales were slow but they had no idea just how bad things were. They were left to wonder about the increase in NeXT employees and the extravagance so visible in NeXT's Redwood City offices. Why is it, the *San Francisco Chronicle* asked Jobs, that NeXT needs 400 employees when it appears to be shipping few computers? Jobs replied that "we're trying to grow a big old oak tree, and if you look under an oak tree, you'll see a root system that's as big as the tree itself; we've been growing our root system." A local newspaper introduced his remarks with a sarcastic preface, "The English language was further enhanced yesterday by Steve Jobs, a master of high-technology marketing."[260]

Instead of disclosing actual sales, Jobs provided the public with tantalizing tidbits of pseudo-news. He was willing to share that NeXT was "in active dialogue with 50 Fortune 500 companies."[261] He could say, as he had been saying the year before, that this time he was going in through the front door of corporate America.[262] And if this did not impress, he had definite glad tidings about the sales that Businessland was winning for NeXT: "We're starting to close some really seriously big deals."[263] Dave Norman, on his part, kept up the brave front and continued to maintain, even in early 1990, that Businessland would sell $100 million worth of NeXT machines within the year.[264] Businessland had invested almost $1.5 million in the last quarter of 1989 in building up a NeXT-specific sales and marketing infrastructure, including a million in advertising, even though the total number of machines it sold in the period was only 150. This meant that Businessland had spent on just infrastructure about $10,000 *per machine sold* beyond the wholesale cost of the machines. The investments were to continue, on the assumption that by the same quarter at the end of 1990, Businessland would be selling at twenty times this rate. But this was nothing but delusional. A publicly traded company like Businessland could not keep its financials private as NeXT could, and a succession of quarterly losses soon revealed that the largest computer chain in the country was not in a state of good health. As Businessland reacted to its worsening financial straits with staff cutbacks and increases in sales goals, its sales representatives found that they had to sell

$150,000 to $175,000 worth of machines in order to make their monthly quotas. Selling the black-and-white NeXT machine, at list price, with all of its performance and software shortcomings, was proving impossible. The sales cycle of the pricey NeXT required months of lobbying a prospective customer, passing through special evaluations, and ending almost always in rejection, or at best, an order for a single machine or two. This was no way to make one's monthly quota. To Ross Perot, who must have been recalling his own fabled accomplishment of meeting his sales quota for an entire year at IBM by January 19,[265] the problem could be easily solved. He told a NeXT manager, "Just get every Businessland salesman to sell one of those a month, and you'd be selling a thousand of them a month." To him, it was merely a simple matter of arithmetic, and NeXT tried to suggest new incentives to achieve the Perot goal of one-sale-per-sales rep. The new incentives were no more effective than the preceding ones.

Despite his public declarations to the contrary, Jobs was far from happy with Businessland; the big corporate sales that he had prematurely claimed thanks to Businessland had never materialized. In the spring of 1990, he vented his anger at a meeting of the Businessland regional vice-presidents, who had presented their estimates of NeXT Cube sales for the next quarter. The estimates were modest and upon hearing them Jobs turned livid and pounded the table for emphasis: "If you can't do better than that, you shouldn't be in sales at all." Norman was as unrealistic as Jobs and authorized creation of a cadre of full-time NeXT sales managers, who were free from the pressures of meeting a set monthly quota. But these efforts failed to produce any better results, and the more resources that Businessland invested in NeXT, the fewer resources it had to salvage sales in its mainstream lines, which were under increasing pressure due to savage price competition in the computer industry. The entire Businessland ship began to sink.

Amazingly, NeXT was able to conceal the extent of its disastrous foray into the commercial marketplace. The International Data

Corporation, the market research firm that provides the most commonly cited sales estimates in the computer industry, estimated that NeXT's total revenues, including sales to higher education, were $74 million for 1990.[266] But the estimate for NeXT was actually too high; NeXT's total revenues turned out to be, by its own disclosure more than a year later, only $28 million for the year. Compare this to rival Sun Microsystem's $2.76 billion for the same period. A year after its single money-losing quarter in 1989 at the time of the introduction of the SPARCstation, Sun was soaring, its market share expanding, the price of its shares doubling from the previous year.[267] Sun boasted of increased inroads in the commercial market that NeXT and Businessland were trying to enter; expanding beyond the engineering and scientific markets, Sun received large orders from Northwest Airlines, Nike, and Mitsubishi Bank.[268] A commitment from Xerox to purchase $200 million of Sun workstations was an interesting moment in contemporary business history: Xerox, the developer at PARC of the first workstation, was now a major purchaser. To keep its growth to a manageable scale, Sun's McNealy discouraged his company's sales representatives from spending time on any sale that was less than $500,000.[269] At the same time that NeXT was struggling to get more than the sad handful of software developers interested in its machines, Sun had the advantage of gathering momentum and in 1990 claimed more than 2,000 software programs were available for Sun machines.[270] Theresa Liu, an analyst at Montgomery Securities in New York, said in July 1990, "You don't want to ever fall in love with a company, but with Sun, you have to stand back and say, 'Wow.' "[271]

The continued explosive growth of its workstation competitors—not just Sun Microsystems, but also IBM, Digital Equipment, and Hewlett-Packard—meant that the time that NeXT lost while it fumbled along, trying to sell the Cube outside of universities, then belatedly realizing that it would have to develop a second-generation computer, put the company at an increasing disadvantage. The passage of time was no less costly if NeXT chose to regard personal computers as its domain, too. If the world had stood still, or even moved at a more sedate pace, NeXT could have rectified its missteps and kept itself in the race. Or, if NeXT had not been so well funded, the company would have perished. Instead, it remained alive, even if its long-term viability remained questionable, and it always, *always*, put on a happy face for the public. One former employee, looking back on NeXT, remembers how he and his colleagues were always waiting for a definite sign from the heavens, indicating whether NeXT would succeed or fail, but the heavenly Green Light or Red Light never revealed itself. NeXT remained in the race, he said, but it was like a three-legged dog: game to compete, but with no possible chance of winning.

Born Again

Y *ou Never Get a Second Chance to Make a First Impression*;
the maxim, old though it is, holds as true in the age of
high-technology as ever. A Steve Jobs could entice the
world to halt for a moment and pay close attention to his NeXT
computer—once, in 1988 when NeXT unveiled the long-awaited
Cube. But it was all but impossible to get the same amount of
attention a second time, even if the product deserved it. In NeXT's
case, its second generation of machines, born from *Warp 9*, would
be a vast improvement over the first; if there was any justice in the
apportionment, the new machines would have received the attention
that had been lavished on the Cube. It was not to be, however.

Jobs did his best to re-create the aura that his company had
enjoyed in 1988. He arranged for another dramatic unveiling in
September 1990, almost exactly two years after the first, again at
Davies Symphony Hall and again before a sympathetic audience of
industry honchos, NeXT employees, and their invited guests. The
night before the event, Jobs hosted a celebratory dinner, which
included rock musician Graham Nash, an owner of a NeXT Cube,
and Ross Perot; the juxtaposition of these two inspired a computer-

industry journalist to compose a paean to Jobs: "Anyone who can seat a veteran of Woodstock and an ultracapitalist at the same table is all right with me—even if he isn't going to bounce the world on its ear again."[272] The praise of Jobs for saving the computer industry from the dull, humorless new-product announcements from the IBMs or Digital Equipments was intended as a compliment. But it unintentionally undermined what Jobs was attempting to do: he did not want praise for being entertaining, he *wanted* to bounce the world on its ear again, to do what even his defenders were saying was now impossible.

For the second performance at Davies Hall, four black machines sat on-stage unattended, like a wall of amplifiers at a rock concert awaiting the entrance of the musicians. The auditorium lights were dimmed and Jobs bounced out from the wings, with a dapper suit and the longish hair worn with the flip at the back. He exuded success: "This is it, the future of NeXT."

Jobs was so eager to succeed that he was even willing to wear a humble persona for the occasion. Privately, on the eve of Unveiling II, he was unrepentant. He had told his employees that the original Cube was not flawed; the problem was that the marketplace was simply not quite ready for its advanced technology like the optical disk.[273] But publicly, at the 1990 unveiling, he acknowledged shortcomings: the NeXT Cube was too slow, too expensive, lacked color and software. He had glad tidings, however. All of these problems were now solved. A new generation of microprocessor from Motorola provided more zip. A newly redesigned, slimmer model, called the NeXTstation, would allow customers to buy a monochrome NeXT computer for half the previous price. Its main unit fit into a slim design that resembled a pizza box, like Sun's SPARCstation that had come out the year before. (Jobs, not wanting to be seen as copying Sun in any particular, insisted that NeXT's *not* be called a pizza box; it was to be called a *slab* instead.) For more money, customers at last could buy a color version of the machine, too; for a lot more money, they could buy a color version with enhanced color capabilities, housed in the venerable Cube that was outfitted with a special compression chip, which permitted the speedy manipulation of large files used when working with graphics, video, or sound files.

As always, Jobs on-stage was the picture of confidence, but the new machines actually were not quite ready. Motorola had fallen way behind schedule in completing work on its new microprocessors, so when Jobs put on his show in September, there were actually too few bug-free chips to go around, leading him to speak an untruth when he was questioned by reporters and said that all of the NeXT machines at Davies Hall used the new, rather than the old, chip.[274] During his demonstration of the new computers on-stage, he had a safety net that was not visible to members of the audience and was not detected by the press: one of the NeXTstations had suffered an untimely, and irreversible, death, shortly before the show was to begin, so a cable had been tucked through a hole on the stage, connecting the monitor that Jobs used to a Cube that sat out of sight; unseen NeXT engineers also were concurrently connected to the other machines on-stage, in case disaster struck. Jobs came perilously close to an embarrassing snafu when he sat down, about to press on the keyboard, momentarily forgetting that a slow screen-locking program first had to be disarmed. A NeXT engineer behind-stage, connected to the same machine, managed to give the critical Unix command *kill -9* and remove the troublesome program just before Jobs brought his fingers down. One must admire the nonchalance of Jobs throughout his performance that day. To emphasize how reliable the system was, Jobs used a refrain after revealing each amazing new feature: ". . . and it just works!" He said it with declarative confidence; one wonders, however, if he silently was as amazed as his audience.

The monochrome versions of the new NeXT machines would not actually be shipped for another six weeks owing to Motorola's problems; the first low-end color versions of the NeXT computers would not go out until the following March; the high-end version, not until the end of May, or eight months later. Even then, purchasers of the high-end color machines, which cost $14,000, had to settle for an empty socket where the compression chip was supposed to be because the outside supplier was not even close to finishing the chip. Customers who purchased these expensive machines were more than a little unhappy when they learned later that the company that was working on the compression chip for NeXT had abandoned the project entirely and NeXT did nothing to redeem its promise that the computer would be retrofitted with high-speed compression. Strictly speaking, it was not NeXT's fault that the chip design of its outside supplier proved flawed, but it might be said that it *was* NeXT's fault for jumping the gun and using a phantom capability to sell machines before it could make good on the announced promises. When Jobs unveiled the new machines based on the new Motorola chip, he had gambled that Motorola would be able to get the final bugs out quickly. That gamble did work out for NeXT and its customers; NeXT beat Apple to market using the new Motorola chip by almost a year. But the compression-chip-that-never-was did not end so happily, and NeXT's most loyal customers, the early adopters of its high-end color machines, were the ones who paid the price. Refunds were not extended to those who felt they had been gulled by false promises.

Compared to a Sun workstation, which was based on the much faster RISC technology, the new NeXT machines were still relatively slow. But compared to Apple's Macintoshes, which were based on the same family of Motorola chips, the NeXT machines were more competitive than they had ever been. When Apple finally brought out the Macintosh Quadra, its own high-end machines built upon the same Motorola chip on which NeXT had fearlessly bet, they were not only comparatively late, they were also more expensive than the low-end NeXT color machine, which itself was still hardly inexpensive, bearing a basic, stripped-down price of $8,000. The one persisting—and fateful—advantage that the most expensive Macintoshes had over the NeXTs was that all Macintoshes could run any of thousands of software packages, software that the NeXT, by design, could not.

Jobs was an unapologetic snob: to make history, he did not want ordinary software on his extraordinary machine, and in his mind Macintosh software now was as ordinary as the IBM-compatible software that he had ridiculed when the Macintosh was in gestation. When software developers approached NeXT about bringing out a NeXT version of existing software that ran on other kinds of computers, Jobs turned them away in almost all cases. Jobs insisted on wholly original programs, written solely for the NeXT; even these often failed to please him. When they were shown to him, his judgments were swift and unmerciful; "that's shit" was his favorite laconic expression. And he had the curious idea that software companies were to court NeXT, rather than the reverse. For example, he told executives from Symantec, one of the larger software companies that specialized in writing programs for the Macintosh, that "we're thinking about having you develop for us." The Symantec executives looked at each other incredulously and asked, "Excuse me?" as if surely they had misheard Jobs; no one could have been so arrogantly oblivious of how courtship should proceed. They, like Microsoft, Borland, and many other major software publishers, chose to pass.

Imprisoned, as we have seen before, by his selective historical memory, Jobs obstinately discouraged the development of any program that was not a likely candidate for becoming the next "killer app," the one software application (or program) unavailable on any other computer that was so indispensable that it would induce customers to buy an entire computer just to have it. It had happened when the first popular spreadsheet, Visicalc, made Jobs's Apple II successful; it had happened again when Lotus's more powerful spreadsheet program, 1-2-3, made the IBM Personal Computer successful; and it had been repeated when Pagemaker, the first affordable desktop publishing program, made the Macintosh successful outside of the higher education market. Jobs held out for a program that would do the same for the NeXT, and at the unveiling of the new NeXTs in 1990, Jobs believed he was introducing the program that would enter the history books like the three others had. It was called Improv, and like two of the three programs that had made new personal-computer standards successful previously, it was a spreadsheet more powerful than its predecessors. Moreover, its parent was Lotus, the software giant that 1-2-3 had built. It seemed that the laws of history ordained that Improv was fated by the gods to be the next big success. It would be what he called his "A-bomb" program, which would blow people away when they got their first glimpse.

No wonder, then, that Jobs was so dismissive of other software possibilities for the NeXT that came to his attention when he knew Improv was in the works. He had personally courted Lotus beginning in October 1988 to get Improv for the NeXT, displaying the persuasiveness that secured for NeXT its other partners whom Jobs had singled out as the chosen ones. When Jobs first heard about Lotus's new spreadsheet program, work was already underway but the program was being written to run on another new operating system that IBM and Microsoft were then jointly working on, called OS/2. Improv was not an improved version of 1-2-3; it was a radical departure from it and its competitors, all of whom used letter-and-number combinations as pointers to locations. In a conventional spreadsheet, for example, rows and columns divide the screen into boxes, rows being assigned letters of the alphabet and columns numbers. A formula to add $2 + 2$ might look something like $B1 + C1$. Improv dispensed with the B1s and C1s and allowed the use of plain English labels in formulas: Receipts $-$ Expenses $=$ Profits. And a given formula did not belong to a particular box, so one could rearrange numbers easily, while keeping intact the recipes for the calculations. This was not possible in the older kind of spreadsheet.

For Jobs, the new Lotus spreadsheet fit perfectly with his vision of securing wholly new software for his computer. For the Lotus programmers, NeXT was attractive because with its object-oriented software development tools, NeXT too seemed to be on the leading edge of new work. And Lotus executives quickly realized that continuing work on what they believed would be the next generation of spreadsheets for the OS/2 system only advanced the interests of Lotus's hated rival, Microsoft, the company that had just displaced it as the largest personal-computer software company. By moving the work over to NeXT, Lotus would be able to jump ahead of Bill Gates, who, Lotus knew, had said he was not interested in writing software for NeXT. It was an especially delicious opportunity because Microsoft had grown fat and happy to a large measure because it had written software for the Macintosh before others had been willing to take the risk; Lotus had been skittish and pulled out of the Mac software market prematurely, and of course by then dearly regretted it. Lotus now had a chance to redeem itself, to leap ahead of the pack and show that it had the same intestinal fortitude as Microsoft.

NeXT also offered Lotus a solution to a conundrum: how to bring out a much improved spreadsheet without at the same time destroying its cash cow, the venerable 1-2-3. Lotus was a $470 million company, but it was still a one-product-wonder; after many disastrous attempts to diversify, it remained dangerously dependent on good old 1-2-3. If it brought out Improv for any of the mainstream computer standards, and Improv succeeded as it seemed certain to, its success would rest upon cannibalization of sales of 1-2-3. But if Lotus were to bring out Improv initially only on the NeXT, but not bring out a version of 1-2-3 for the NeXT as well, this danger could be avoided. Lotus would not face the problem of having to recommend to customers which of its two, very different spreadsheets should be purchased.[275] NeXT, precisely because of its marginal position, was a safe place for Lotus to experiment with an untested prototype without placing its golden 1-2-3 in peril.

These strategic calculations were not simple. It took four months of deliberations before Lotus decided to move its new spreadsheet to NeXT. Jobs naturally was elated when he heard the news. He sent a three-foot-tall bouquet of flowers and viewed the snaring of the new Lotus spreadsheet not just as the A-bomb program that would ensure success, but also as a trophy that validated his company, a trophy that could be shown to all other software developers who were considering the question of whether to write software for the NeXT. If Lotus was willing to bet on NeXT, Jobs would say to the others, what else need be said? There was, as we have seen, much indeed that could have been said about the rather unique position that Lotus was in; its decision did not necessarily have much pertinence to others. But appearances count for so much, and when Jobs gave Lotus a featured position in the program at Davies Hall when he unveiled the new computers, it seemed that NeXT's software worries were now over. Wordperfect also was on hand to demonstrate a NeXT version of its bestselling word-processing software.

This seemed to be a new Steve Jobs, diplomatically sharing the stage with business partners. A display of penitence and humility? Old Testament images came to mind when Lotus's president, Jim Manzi, took the podium and delivered a tongue-in-cheek sermon that began with three "religious" questions: "Why on the NeXT? Why a new spreadsheet? And does Bill Gates really exist?" Manzi said that because of time limitations, he would not be able to address the third question. As for the question of why the choice of NeXT, Manzi answered, "Because God wanted us to." If anyone remained skeptical that NeXT was now blessed as never before, Jobs had more good news at the end of his presentation: he said that he could not mention names, but large corporate customers had seen the new machines and had been duly impressed. He was pleased to announce that NeXT had in hand "15,000 orders, *real* orders, not napkins [upon which were scribbled] intentions to buy." Whoops of surprise and applause filled the auditorium. The believers knew a divine augury when they heard one.

At the end of the program, the crowd was invited to visit the lobby, where the booths of NeXT's software developers were set up. Most were not large software publishers; they were Two Guys in a Garage, too small to spread their bets. Either NeXT succeeded, or they would fail. They had no other software products to fall back on; to them, Lotus's worries about protecting its own existing business, almost $700 million in 1990, could not have been more remote. They also represented places in the United States far from Silicon Valley or Boston. It was the conceit of Silicon Valley that the world is skewed, just as Saul Steinberg's famous map of the United States for a *New Yorker* cover, which left little room for any place but Manhattan. In the Silicon Valley version, the operative word was *hot* and the image, of nested circles: California was the hot state, Silicon Valley, an inner concentric circle, the hottest place within the state, and NeXT, the circle within that, thought of itself as representing the fusionlike temperatures of the hottest company. The booths of NeXT's software developers revealed, however, that Silicon Valley was not the universe. The age of electronics had democratized entrepreneurial geography. In the past, there was no substitute for physical proximity. To be a part of the automobile industry, a small supplier had to be near Detroit; to be part of steel, near Pittsburgh, or Gary, or some other center. Today, however, economic activity in the computer industry has been dispersed; the essential tools are lightweight and easily transportable; communication between scattered locations is quick and inexpensive. Many of the developers linked to NeXT were dispersed: Albuquerque, New Mexico; Wichita, Kansas; Oklahoma City, Oklahoma; Fairfield, Iowa; Ypsalanti, Michigan; Charleston, Illinois; Knoxville, Tennessee; Chevy Chase, Maryland; Tampa, Florida.

Most of NeXT's software developers were starting out for the first time, steering clear of the much more competitive, crowded worlds of the IBM-compatible personal computers and the Macintosh. These worlds remained aloof; experienced developers in them were reluctant to venture out and take their chances on a new software standard like NeXT's. NeXT evangelists were surprised in particular by how conservative the Macintosh crowd was. In late summer of 1990, when Erica Liebman, the editor of the *NeXT Users Journal*, had an opportunity to pitch the NeXT to small software entrepreneurs at a meeting of Macintosh developers, she discovered that her pitch went nowhere. The audience wanted her to guarantee that they could sell x number of units at such-and-such a price, or a minimum of $500,000 a year, a guarantee that she could not make. "Well," they told her, "we're simply not going to develop for the machine, and no one else is either." Liebman was nonplussed: these had been the risk-takers in 1984. She asked herself, "Where can one pick up some pioneers?"[276] The tiny software companies whose programs that NeXT had succeeded in securing, represented in the booths at Davies Hall in September 1990, were there because they were willing to try their chances beyond the pale, where no one else was willing to venture, where the numbers made no business sense. Collectively, they had drawn a lesson from the history of personal computers that gave them encouragement. Alan Cooper, a successful software author who was mulling over which computer standard to write for, put it well when he described the appearance of a new standard as a "great leveler," taking away the otherwise overwhelming advantages that the entrenched, larger software companies had. "Small companies with nothing to lose can move into an area without competition and roll the dice." Cooper believed that as a lone programmer he had "the same chance" to succeed as a Microsoft or Lotus.[277]

Cooper's statement was originally made in 1989 and he was speaking then in general terms, not referring to NeXT in particular. The "leveling" effect was nowhere to be seen a few years later, when later versions of Microsoft's Windows appeared to create another new window of opportunity for the little companies to write new applications. It proved to be illusory—the company that sold the most applications for Windows was none other than Microsoft itself, which reduced opportunities for the smaller developers. But even in 1990, when previous experience made the "leveling" thesis appear plausible, the software developers who bet their money on the NeXT before the unveiling of new machines in 1990 saw an additional reason to be concerned about their bet: Steve Jobs played favorites, which was wonderful for the company chosen, Lotus, but was discouraging to Lotus's competition, like Ashton-Tate, another large software company, which had been working hard on writing an alternative spreadsheet for NeXT. What chance would they have of getting NeXT's customers to purchase the Ashton-Tate product when Jobs promised the Lotus spreadsheet free to all who purchased a new NeXT machine? The mood of the Ashton-Tate staff in the booth was understandably glum, but other software developers in the crowd, though not directly affected by NeXT's decision to bundle the Lotus program with the machine, also felt a chill of doubt and worry: When their programs were ready, would they find that Jobs would do as he was known to do so often, to "barf" on their pride and joy, as one NeXT employee put it?[278] That Jobs would openly favor a competitor in the same category of software? A parent company was not supposed to favor one sibling over the others, and the Lotus deal was disconcerting to NeXT's other software publishers. It was as if the polite theological courtesy that permitted combatants on opposing sides in war to pray to the same God for victory over the other side was suddenly stripped away and God loudly declared one side to be His Favorite. In this light, Lotus president Jim Manzi's biblical jokes at Davies Hall were not so funny.

Despite the hoopla and the impressive demonstration of its capabilities at Davies Hall, Lotus's Improv was no more ready for final release than the new computers that Jobs introduced that day. It took five more months of work before Improv actually shipped. But in the meantime, Ashton-Tate had been so discouraged by Jobs's embracing of the Lotus competition as the "killer" program and his decision to bundle it with the NeXT computer, that the company lost heart. It simply gave up on its own spreadsheet, so plain in comparison to Lotus's Improv, and did not bother to release it (two years later, the company itself gave up entirely and was purchased by another competitor, Borland). With hindsight, we can see that poor Ashton-Tate abandoned its spreadsheet prematurely. When Lotus finally released Improv, most prospective customers shunned it. The problem was not technical; the program fulfilled every claim that Jobs and Lotus had made for it. The problem was the market preference for evolution over revolution. Improv was so unlike conventional spreadsheets that its advantages were difficult to explain. Jeff Anderholm, Improv's marketing manager, later lamented that the program could not be explained well and the best that Lotus could do was say to customers: "You have to see it." This was not, Anderholm knew, an ideal situation. Once NeXT's offer of bundling Improv expired in 1991 and the program had to make its way on its own, sales languished. (And the more conventional spreadsheet originally written for Ashton-Tate would be resurrected by another company, years after it had been aborted because Improv had appeared to make it obsolete.)

Corporate customers, even those who were willing to look at Improv, needed more software. It was too much to ask companies to spend $5,000, the price of an entry-level black-and-white NeXT-station, just to get a spreadsheet. The other software that was available tended to appeal to narrow markets, such as the Satellite Tool Kit—$6,000 for just the software—that allowed a NeXT computer to calculate satellite orbits. David Grady, the NeXT manager who kept track of software for the NeXT, allowed that this program would appeal to only certain constituencies in aerospace and in government, "not exactly the same size market as, say, word processing."[279] Indeed. Corporate buyers didn't want satellite-tracking programs or molecule modelers or medical transcription programs. They did not even want a newfangled kind of spreadsheet. They wanted what they already knew, which was either 1-2-3, which Lotus did not make available for the NeXT, or they wanted 1-2-3's leading competitor, Excel, which happened to be a Microsoft program that Bill Gates had chosen not to rewrite for the NeXT.

An interim patch—a Macintosh emulator that could have enabled a NeXT computer, in essence, to fool the software and permit the Macintosh version of Excel to run—could have been made available, but Jobs had scorned the software developer who offered it to NeXT.

Prospective corporate buyers also wanted to know about NeXT's established customers, the reference accounts where large networks of NeXTs were already installed. They asked Businessland representatives, who had precious little to tell them; William Morris Agency did not seem to impress anybody. In turn, Businessland representatives, when berated by NeXT executives for not selling more machines, would ask NeXT the same question that was asked of Businessland: where had NeXT received large orders in the sales areas that remained under its own direct control, in government or in education? Todd Rulon-Miller, the head of sales, had no choice but to sputter, trying to buy time with tantalizing news of deals that he was never at liberty to name, deals that were always in the works.

These continuing problems hurt Businessland in its efforts to whip up more corporate interest in NeXT. One would have thought that the rebirth of the NeXT product line in the fall of 1990 would provide just the boost that Businessland's discouraged sales representatives needed. But Jobs had created not only new products but also a new marketing strategy to go along with it, and Businessland was no longer the favored partner it had been the previous year, when it was still the "hero" in Jobs's eyes. Not only did Businessland lose its monopoly control of sales to the corporate market, it also was forced to eat the older inventory of NeXT Cubes that was made obsolete overnight by the announcement of the new machines with the faster chips. The standard practice in the industry is for a manufacturer to provide its retailers with a generous rebate for machines that are sitting on shelves or in the back room and whose market value plummets when faster, spiffier machines are announced. NeXT had gotten Businessland to agree to a contract that provided no such protection, however, and Businessland was told by NeXT that if it wanted the older Cubes to be outfitted with the faster Motorola chip, it would have to pay full price. Without a feasible alternative, Businessland disposed of the older NeXT Cubes in a mammoth "fire sale," incurring huge losses in a frenzy to realize whatever cash it could from its investment in the NeXT inventory. Businessland was now tottering.

It never recovered. Only two years after the revelry that had attended the announcement of its deal with NeXT, mighty Businessland was dead, its pathetic carcass purchased for a pittance by the conglomerate JWP, which in turn suffered painful financial indigestion itself when it discovered after the acquisition that accounting tricks had overstated Businessland's value.[280] Businessland's demise must stand as one of the most precipitous collapses of a billion-dollar-plus retail empire in modern business history. In the postmortem report, the business relationship with NeXT was only one among many maladies that did Businessland in. The single most important was Businessland's failure to understand the sea change that was transforming the computer retail industry, as customers, increasingly comfortable with personal computers and requiring less hand-holding, were more price-conscious and reluctant to pay for the comforts of a well-heeled operation like Businessland. One could say, however, that an important reason that Businessland was so slow to recognize the changes underway, and consequently was so slow in responding to the challenge, was that its attention had been diverted by Steve Jobs and NeXT. In retrospect, it is easy to see that the timing could not have been worse for Businessland. At just the historical moment that computer retailing was turned topsy-turvy, when the viability of all conventional high-cost retail computer operations would be cast into doubt, when even the most well-prepared dealer would have been tested sorely to devise timely changes, it was then that Businessland had embraced NeXT, a high-priced, untested quantity that required a large investment to launch. One has to wonder how the dead weight of the NeXT line contributed to Businessland's sudden expiration.

Long before Businessland collapsed, Jobs and company had changed their marketing plan (a practice that happened so often that wags at NeXT would sarcastically ask, What's the market du jour?). *Out* was the large dinosaur of Businessland, *in* would be one hundred small, independent computer dealers, spread across the country, each chosen for its technical expertise, and each to be provided with a measure of exclusivity when selling NeXTs in their immediate environs. Their charter would be to sell NeXTs to small-and medium-sized companies; NeXT reserved the largest accounts for itself, which it would serve with its own direct sales force. NeXT told the dealers that it had selected—as always, in its own mind NeXT did the choosing, not its partners—that NeXT's telemarketing department fielded no less than 1,000 inquiries a week, many of which it had to discard because the prospective deals that involved sales of ten or fewer units were so small and NeXT's own sales staff so limited. These leads the dealers could have.

The first dealer that Jobs recruited was Computer Attic, whose main store was located in downtown Palo Alto, just a few blocks from Jobs's own home. Its four co-owners were young and venture-some; the business had been begun even before there was a store, in 1983, when one of the four had started selling software out of the trunk of a Mazda; operations were moved to a second-story walk-up and authorization to sell Apple Macintoshes had come in 1986; they had done well and expanded to downstairs space, and a second site, and by early 1991 were selling about $20 million of hardware and software annually. A place like Computer Attic could thrive because of the technical expertise of its salespeople, "gear heads." Observers would call NeXT's signing up such independent dealers its "boutique" strategy. In a letter that Jobs sent to formally welcome Computer Attic, he explained that "we chose Computer Attic because you guys care about the same things we do—great computers and satisfied customers." Computer Attic, in turn, was excited—"pumped"—to be on board. If NeXT were to take off anywhere, surely it would be here, in the very heart of Silicon

Valley, in the backyard of NeXT's own headquarters, and across the street from the cafe that Jobs visited frequently to have coffee.

Serendipity soon provided Computer Attic and NeXT with its largest sale in the area, to a tony real estate broker, Alain Pinel Realty, which served the carriage trade and sought to purchase the most sophisticated computers as a way of differentiating its offices from the pack of commoners. The company's president, Helen Pastorino, was in her thirties and possessed the self-assurance that came from having risen from the ranks of star salespeople. She was not technically inclined and not fond of computers, but she was willing to spend whatever was required to replace an almost new network of ordinary IBM-compatible personal computers she had installed six months earlier at a cost of $180,000 and which had proven to be hard to use and overtaxed. She liked to make decisions quickly, and she had no patience for Computer Attic, which was too technical for her taste. She insisted on dealing with NeXT directly, and NeXT did not read her very well. The company said that it would be three weeks before anyone could come out, and the NeXT representative who was dispatched wrote off the possibility of the sale as soon as she discovered that Pastorino did not even know how much the NeXT computers were and that a network of the size she wanted would cost $400,000. When Pastorino asked if NeXT could provide financing, which of course it could not, the NeXT salesperson snapped her briefcase closed and fled.

Pastorino had also talked with a representative from Sun, who had taken her interest more seriously and had made a much better impression. But Stephan Adams of Adamation, who had learned from the William Morris Agency experience the importance of keeping client expectations realistic, had shown her how custom software for a real estate office could be written more easily on the NeXT than on the Sun or other computers, and Sun's own estimates of the costs of writing the software that Pastorino wanted were frightful. Pastorino did not really need financing; her partner at Alain Pinel was a multimillionaire whose net worth, she liked to say, exceeded that of Steve Jobs. She was willing to take on the risk of investing in NeXT machines, even though NeXT itself could not name a single other office in the Bay Area that had installed them. She liked the idea of being a Big Customer in a Small Pond, which would insure that NeXT would take good care of her if problems arose. But for the deal to close, she wanted Jobs himself to be her salesperson. She wanted his personal word that she would be looked after once the sale was complete.

A meeting was arranged at NeXT offices with Jobs and a silent phalanx of assistants from the sales group. Pastorino used the occasion to tell Jobs how hard it had been to get NeXT to take her seriously. She lamented that she had "gone through hell" and "your salespeople have no clue what's going on." Pastorino then saw that some of these same salespeople were present in the room and looking uncomfortable. Could we talk privately? she asked Jobs. Once the room had been emptied, she resumed. She would not pay full price, she said, because she would be assuming a large risk that would depend on NeXT succeeding. And she had not seen any indication that NeXT was going to be able to succeed, other than its technology. Jobs explained that there are three things that make a company fail: capital, technology, or leadership. He implied that NeXT was strong in all three areas, but Pastorino replied, "That's interesting, because I know a company that had the same leadership, the same capital, and about the equivalent of technology that you do at NeXT, and it folded." It was Pixar, which produced advanced software for computer animation, and though it had not actually gone out of business, it had greatly shrunk in size and was barely surviving. Pixar was a good example to use because Pastorino and Jobs both knew the company well: Pastorino, because her husband had worked for Pixar when it entered its unhappy era, and Jobs, because he had purchased the company from George Lucas. Jobs did not want to mount a defense of the leadership of Pixar or of NeXT; instead he maneuvered the conversation on to more pleasant topics by remaining calm and reminding Pastorino that emotion and business should be kept distinct. The two came to an agreement, which included NeXT providing a discount which was not to be revealed. As part of the package, Pastorino secured a little bit of the celebrity capital that only NeXT could offer—Jobs promised to make a personal appearance at the grand opening of Pastorino's new offices in Los Gatos.

The installation at Alain Pinel of 120 machines would be one of the largest commercial sales for NeXT for all of 1991. For NeXT, it seemed to be confirmation that the history of the Mac was surely repeating itself. NeXT need not define a particular market to target; emerging markets would come to it, and from the most unexpected places. Who would have thought in advance that real estate offices would be a promising new market? Jobs and his marketing and sales group would extrapolate amazing sales projections from a surprising sale like Alain Pinel. They would not pause to consider that Alain Pinel Realty was an unusual real estate office, which sold the most expensive homes in one of the priciest residential real estate markets in the country. Real estate offices elsewhere might not have similar budgets for computers and office equipment. Yet, desperate for encouraging news, NeXT seized upon the Alain Pinel sale as the harbinger of roaring sales that lay just ahead. A single sale could be intoxicating; the company confused the notion that anything is possible with the slightly different notion that *everything* is possible. Perhaps the most bizarre expression of this was when NeXT's Ron Weissman, the former academic who would become the strategic marketing wizard for NeXT, said in January 1991 that NeXT would be treating *high schools* as a new market focus that year.[281]

More unexpected good news came from the government sector. NeXT announced sale of an undisclosed number of machines to the Defense Advanced Research Projects Agency (DARPA), and was cheered by additional orders from the federal agencies involved in intelligence gathering and sensitive military work that were even more in the shadows than DARPA, and which NeXT was not allowed to publicly disclose. After an almost two-year process of negotiations, the Los Angeles County Sheriff's Department also placed an order for 130 NeXT machines, with announced plans of adding 200 to 300 more in the near future. A sheriff's department brought to mind the sleepy television world of Andy Griffith's "Mayberry" and did not have the same cachet as a reference account as, say, a Fortune 500 company. But NeXT's public relations spokesperson, Allison Thomas, put the best possible spin on it by explaining that the L.A. department had 13,000 employees, was responsible for law enforcement for more than 2,700 square miles of unincorporated area in the county, and had an annual budget of more than $1 billion (which brings to mind Jobs's earlier attempt to present large universities as $1 billion-plus Fortune 500 companies in disguise). Again, this unanticipated opening in government agencies seemed to validate Jobs's inclination not to worry about which customers might be most interested in his computer. Build It and They Will Come.

Not just the United States but the entire world would be NeXT's oyster. In Europe, NeXT had remained unknown during its earlier incarnations, when higher education and Businessland distribution had been tried. Its delayed arrival in Europe seemed to work to its advantage, however. When NeXT made its debut at the giant CeBit trade show in Hanover, Germany, it did not have to overcome images of failure and disappointment in the public mind. It could start fresh and once again enjoy being the center of attention as it had at the first Davies Hall introduction. At CeBit, which drew 500,000 attendees and was the largest trade show in the world, NeXT had a small booth in an upstairs corner, but it was the talk of the show and was jammed during the entire seven days with curiosity seekers, who could watch on a giant screen a videotape of Steve Jobs introducing the new NeXT machines from the previous fall.[282]

Best of all, the Europeans did not bridle at high prices. Even though the average price for a NeXT system in Europe was about $15,000, German customers would ask a NeXT dealer in Kiehl,

Germany, why the machines were so inexpensive.²⁸³ Soon, NeXT had signed up 100 separate dealers, each pledging to invest $1,000,000 setting up sales, training, and support; investment in inventory was separate.²⁸⁴ In July 1991, the Japanese version of the NeXT operating system was completed and sales in Japan were also expected to take off quickly, even though Canon, NeXT's major investor and its exclusive distributor in Japan, had a potential conflict of interest: it also was the distributor of the two computers that were NeXT's closest rivals, the Macintosh and the Sun workstation. Success for NeXT in the international market could be read in the trendline: in the first three months of 1991, thirty percent of NeXT's sales had gone to Europe and Japan; by midyear, the percentage had jumped to fifty percent. NeXT could exult that the appeal of its computer was worldwide, too large to be contained by the boundaries of old economic geography.

The pleasant daydreams about NeXTs in every office, every classroom, every government agency, every continent, were not as harmless as they might appear to have been. The born-again NeXT, theoretically receptive to all possibilities, did not pay attention to the ties that it had with existing partners. While new markets in high school education and teaching-of-English-as-a-second-language were momentarily attractive, the old market, higher education, felt ignored. Sales representatives no longer made calls, and the number of students whom NeXT hired as part-time "campus consultants" was also reduced. The students were paid only $7 to $9 an hour, but they were also loaned a NeXT Cube, which they could use for demonstrations in their dorm room (loaning the older, slower Cube was unwise economizing on NeXT's part: prospective customers saw a screen that changed painfully slowly). The campus consultants were energetic advocates of the NeXT cause not for the paltry money but because they appreciated the object-oriented wonders of the NeXT software; they were the most enthusiastic evangelists that NeXT had, at any price, and their turnover was low. But Jobs, unhappy with slow NeXT sales on campuses, ordered their numbers slashed, a form of very selective cost-consciousness.

Higher education sales indeed were slow. By the time that Jobs had introduced the new, improved machines of the reborn NeXT, the competition on campuses was all the more entrenched. Jobs had made a presentation at the annual Educom meeting in the fall of 1990, shortly after Unveiling II at Davies Hall and interest in NeXT, at least on the surface, seemed strong. Despite an awkward moment when the new NeXT crashed and had to be replaced in the middle of his demonstration, the NeXT booth was packed most of the time and discussion of the company's future was often heard in the corridors.[285] But the interest proved transitory. At an institution like the University of California at Berkeley, the campus had 3,000 Macintoshes, 7,000 IBM-compatible personal computers, 1,500 Sun workstations—and only 30 NeXTs. By that point, it was simply too expensive for the university administration to support a greatly expanded number of NeXT machines, even if they were faster and cheaper than they had been before; the other computers were not about to be discarded, and they necessarily received higher priority. NeXT's cause was not helped by its adamant refusal, even after its rebirth, to discard its past policy of not dickering about price and not extending equipment donations to universities. One year after the unveiling of the second generation of machines, sales of the machines on campuses languished. Even at its twenty largest university sites, sales for the thirteen months from September 1990 through September 1991 averaged only 134 machines at each campus for the year. The numbers beyond the top twenty dwindled quickly to the low dozens. All of these figures were too pathetic to be publicly disclosed.

Jobs had new personal interests to buoy his spirits. In March 1991, he married Laurene Powell, a Stanford MBA student, the first marriage for both, and in September, the couple welcomed the birth of a son. The initial birth announcement of the unnamed child was at once serious and humorous: "Laurene and I were blessed with a child, a boy, as yet unnamed; new product names are hard. . . ." Later, he would also poke fun at his own sloganeering and say that he and his wife had had their own "little custom app." But get him started expatiating on the joys of fatherhood, and he became all seriousness and no humor, describing the effect of the arrival of his son, soon named Reed, as "sort of like if you never saw green and all of a sudden you have a child and you can see green for the first time; it's much more profound than I ever would have guessed from hearing about it."[286] Jobs also had a teen-aged daughter, for whom he had become an affectionate father, after a messy beginning involving a much younger Jobs, an estranged mother whom Jobs never married, and absence of close communication between the two at the time of their daughter's birth. His son arrived in much different circumstances.

The changes in Jobs's personal life reverberated through NeXT, as spirits at the company were buoyed by the feeling that NeXT was headed confidently for bigger and better things. In the excitement of developing new business relationships, the company failed to nurture its old relationship with IBM, which had licensed the rights to NeXT's operating system for its own new workstation line. Initially, IBM had fallen behind Sun in bringing out a competitively priced workstation built on the Power Chip, a new, fast RISC processor that IBM had developed itself. When IBM finally introduced its machine in February 1990, however, it was well received. In its first year, it accounted for more than $1 billion in sales for IBM,[287] the very figure that NeXT had planned on reaching and was still, five years later, so far from attaining. In only its second year, IBM sold workstations worth *two* billion dollars.[288] But this was accomplished without the help of NeXTSTEP. Once he got his money from IBM, Jobs did not expend any energy keeping his partner happy, a task that became all the more important as his two strongest supporters within IBM, Bill Lowe and Andy Heller, left IBM themselves. Their successors were not as tolerant of Jobs's predilection to lecture IBM on how it should run its business.

IBM's workstation group struggled to adapt NeXTSTEP so that it would run on IBM's own version of Unix software but it was technically difficult, since the underlying software code was a wholly different version. At a NeXT user group meeting on the Stanford campus in October 1990, IBM offered a tantalizing glimpse of the NeXT software running on the IBM workstation. IBM's software engineers had succeeded in making the program stable only recently, and plans for a version for personal computers that IBM had announced would be forthcoming was formally withdrawn, owing to poor performance. The workstation version of the NeXT software would never be released, either.

Jobs's explanation for this failure is self-serving and puts the responsibility solely on IBM. He said that it was IBM that was so obtuse as not to realize the value of NeXT software, to see the "diamond" that they had dropped in the mud and now lay hidden by a "dirt clod."[289] It was IBM, he said, that allowed NeXTSTEP to be lost in the shuffle of constantly changing executives.[290] He did not confront some other pertinent facts: that IBM had invested an enormous amount of resources in the NeXT project, not only in the money it paid NeXT for licensing rights, but also in the opportunity costs it incurred by keeping a team of some of its brightest engineers at work on the NeXT port. IBM paid too dearly to be accused of casualness about NeXT. Jobs also did not address the fact that it was he who refused to provide IBM with the latest version of NeXT's software. Jobs had insisted that NeXT's licensing agreement entitled IBM to use version 1.0 of its operating system, not version 2.0, and IBM would have to pony up more money if it wanted the current version, and even then, the development tools and applications that NeXT would provide would always remain a subset of what NeXT kept for itself.

Jobs was terrified that IBM, with its superior RISC-based workstation hardware, would destroy little NeXT, so he made sure that

IBM's NeXT offering would always be technically behind NeXT's. He told IBM, "I'm not stupid enough to give you everything I have, when you have 27,000 salespeople." In his fear of being dominated, he failed to see that IBM aimed its own workstations, which cost many tens of thousands of dollars each, at a different up-scale market segment than NeXT could. Jobs was myopic and tried to get more money out of IBM when he should have been offering to do whatever he could to help IBM get NeXT software out in the marketplace, allowing both to prosper.

In his recitation of laments about IBM's failure to embrace his NeXTSTEP, Jobs neglects his own contribution to the deterioration of the relationship. A pivotal moment was in 1990, on the eve of the introduction of the second-generation NeXT computers, when IBM assembled 900 of its systems engineers in Dallas so Jobs could personally give a demonstration and make his pitch to the rank-and-file. On the morning of the meeting, Jobs arrived at the airport, where he would be accompanied on the flight to Dallas by one of his senior sales managers, Mark Hayes. Hayes found Jobs at the airport newsstand, dressed in a suit with his backpack on, and approached him with some trepidation: Hayes had learned the night before that the room in which Jobs would give his presentation was so large that two slide projectors would be needed, but Jobs had only one set of slides prepared and would not be happy when he learned of this little hitch. Hayes debated in his own mind whether he should tell Jobs immediately or wait until they had boarded the plane. He decided to tell Jobs straight off, so they could have the time on the plane to plan out how to handle the special logistics of the large auditorium. Upon hearing the news, Jobs was aghast: "Do you mean to tell me that you're going to send me down there to talk to these people without giving me the tools to do my job?" Hayes proposed that Jobs could use the one slide projector, or perhaps another arrangement could be devised. Jobs interrupted, "Mark, I'm really busy. I don't think I'm going to go." And he set off for the terminal exit, ignoring Hayes's entreaties, "But Steve, they're expecting you . . ."

At this point, Hayes barely had time to catch the plane and could not phone ahead. When he arrived in Dallas, the limousine pulled up, ready to greet Steve Jobs, loaded with veggies, Evian spring water, and senior IBM executives. But there was no Jobs. Hayes mumbled an excuse that "something important had come up," but the disappointment was palpable. When he arrived at the conference hall and got up to address the group, the audience thought that Hayes was the prelude to the featured speaker; Hayes saw how crushed they were when they realized that Jobs had not come. His attempts to cover for Jobs's impulsive decision not to attend a gathering that was held for the sole reason of having him present were unsuccessful. An IBM executive later called NeXT's Phil Wilson and conveyed not just his disappointment but his incredulity: "I can't believe Steve did this."

Mark Hayes would always regret that he did not wait until Jobs was safely on the plane that fateful day before he had broached the news about the hitch with the slide projectors. This and other seemingly insignificant encounters between NeXT and IBM took on larger significance retrospectively, as shifts in loyalties and alignments shook the computer industry. In mid-1991, IBM exercised an option that had not occurred to Jobs, or most anyone else: it announced a multifaceted agreement with Apple, to collaborate, among other things, on sharing software technology designed expressly for workstations. The two former enemies set off together to work on a new object-oriented operating system. Now it was Jobs who was left behind, staring forlornly at the receding backs of others. He bravely told the press that the IBM-Apple agreement was actually good news for him because it validated the NeXT's own emphasis on object-orientation in system software. But this was bluster. It should have been him, not Apple's John Sculley, who was walking hand-in-hand with IBM. Other announcements of new alliances in the computer industry made it seem as if everyone was partnering with someone else, while NeXT's agreement with IBM was nothing but a meaningless piece of paper. Despite its head start in finding a powerful ally in IBM, NeXT now was going to end up alone, the odd person out.

Voodoo Economics

Steve Jobs liked to play peekaboo when asked how his company was doing. He kept NeXT well sealed, and as a privately held company it had no legal obligation to disclose its sales or its financial condition. When it suited him, Jobs would reveal a tantalizing factoid about sales or profits, then return to his regime of silence. The announcement of the 15,000 advance orders that he divulged in September 1990, at the time of the introduction of the second-generation machines, is an example of the game that he played with the public. Peekaboo, look at all these new orders! Then the hands closed, and the public could see nothing more.

It was a game of deception, however. The "15,000 orders" were not 15,000 and were not orders. What NeXT had in fact were nonbinding commitments from prospective buyers to buy a little more than 10,000 new machines some time in the future. In most cases, the commitment was based on certain conditions being met, such as having NeXT versions of software finally made available. NeXT had not collected real orders; it had merely conducted an informal poll. The company had asked clients, would you buy our new machines, and the customers had said, well, if such-and-such is available and you do this-and-that, we'd be interested. To expedite the process, Jobs would tell Customer A that Customer B was buying, then would tell Customer B that Customer A was buying. Neither was aware of how their names were being used simultaneously as references to bring in the other party; each would say, oh, if others are in, count us in, too. The number was also based on nonbinding commitments on the part of NeXT's university customers, who were offered the machines at a special never-announced price of $2,995, or almost half off. This spongy agreeability was then transmogrified by Jobs at Davies Hall into "real orders." The public had no idea that he was presenting numbers that were nothing more than vague commitments from customers, which was what he explicitly denied at the time. A year later, when his sales staff investigated just how many of the university commitments turned out to be honored, they discovered that only about fifty percent of the promises had been fulfilled.

Jobs's number games continued on through 1991. In the first three months, NeXT revealed that it had sold 8,000 machines and had abruptly leapt to second place in the category of "professional workstations." This meant that NeXT had vaulted ahead of the major workstation competitors, Hewlett-Packard, Digital, and even IBM; only Sun kept NeXT from jumping into first place. Of course, NeXT's high standing depended on acceptance of NeXT's own peculiar definition of terms. "Professional workstation" was a wholly new category, cooked up by NeXT, and referred to workstation sales outside of scientific and technical laboratories. Neither NeXT's competitors nor the independent market analysts tracked sales in the way that NeXT was claiming to have done, so NeXT's claims could neither be refuted nor corroborated. In the meantime, Jobs secured for NeXT favorable publicity that made the billion-dollar-plus sales of its most immediate competitors, like IBM and Hewlett-Packard, disappear. IBM sold 12,000 workstations that quarter but NeXT only credited it with 1,000 in the "professional workstation" category; Hewlett-Packard had sold 20,000, but received credit for only 3,000 from NeXT.²⁹¹ The ploy worked; the *Los Angeles Times*, for example, ran a flattering story under the headline "NeXT Finding a Place in the Market."²⁹² Jobs was too modest: if he had announced a market segment of "professional workstations painted the color black," he could as justifiably have claimed first place and 100 percent market share.

During this same period, NeXT quietly made its first layoffs, dismantling the Creative Services group that had provided in-house artistic and editorial services. It was extremely costly for a small company like NeXT to have its own creative group, and now Jobs decided that these were services that NeXT could contract out, as needed ("We're going to buy the milk, not own the cow"). It was a painful decision, and he made himself scarce on the last day of work for the laid-off employees, avoiding the awkwardness of having to say goodbye. Consistent with its policy of remaining mum about any information that did not reflect well on the company, NeXT said not a word about the layoffs to the press. The good news about the 8,000 orders for NeXT machines could stand clear of any distractions.

Just before the decision to reduce his company's payroll, Jobs also decided that it was time to drop NeXT's advertising agency, Ammirati & Puris. In 1988, the agency had been recruited with phony numbers: Jobs promised them media billings of $20 million a year, but NeXT was in a position to spend only a tenth that sum. After signing on, and adding staffing to handle the account, it became apparent that the agency was not going to earn the commissions that it had planned on. Jobs wanted the agency to stay on and offered to pay a retainer fee, in exchange for the agency maintaining a staff dedicated to the NeXT account and available at Job's beck and call. It was this arrangement that Jobs had decided to sever in February 1991. But when Steve Gardner, an Ammirati & Puris executive, stopped by NeXT offices and Jobs planned to inform him of the decision, Gardner delivered some news of his own before Jobs could speak. The agency had decided to drop NeXT as a client, at the urging of Nikon, another client of theirs that had recently been signed up and which felt there was an unacceptable conflict of interest between it and NeXT, which was supported by Nikon's Japanese rival, Canon.

Jobs could have felt relief that he was now absolved from having to be the one to cut the ties. But he was so taken aback that it was someone else other than he who had made the decision that instead of feeling relief he felt only fury. At that moment, NeXT owed Ammirati & Puris several hundred thousand dollars, and Jobs swore he was not going to pay it. "But Steve," one of his managers tried to reason with him, "we were going to drop them anyway." Jobs said, "Don't breathe a word to anybody; we can use this to our advantage." NeXT's own attorneys told Jobs that there was no basis on which to refuse to pay, and dilatory payment would only end in a lawsuit. He relented when the specter of negative publicity threatened to impinge upon the positive images about NeXT in the public mind that he had contrived so carefully.

Though NeXT did not release any specific financial data for what it was describing as a triumphant first quarter of 1991, it still got caught in an indiscretion. The sale of 8,000 computers for which it gave itself credit included, it turned out, a large percentage of motherboards, the principal component that goes into computers but which is not synonymous with the computers themselves. Replacement of an old motherboard for a new one permitted a customer to transform the older, slower Cube into a machine comparable to the new NeXTstations. Software developers struggling with the decision whether it made business sense to take a chance on the NeXT needed accurate sales figures; they were not happy when they figured out that NeXT was not being wholly aboveboard about claiming the sales of 8,000 that included an unknown percentage of upgrade boards in the total. NeXT's reputation was not helped when the *San Jose Mercury News*, a local newspaper which was not as gullible as the *Los Angeles Times*, looked into NeXT's press release concerning the 8,000 orders and discovered that these included orders that were being counted twice—many were the same orders included in the batch of 15,000 advance orders announced in the preceding September, and only now being filled in early 1991. NeXT's Todd Rulon-Miller refused to provide more information that would have clarified which orders were left over from the fall and which were genuinely new. All he would say publicly was that the first quarter was the start of "something big."[293]

By then, it was spring 1991 and NeXT executives were soaring with optimism because the preliminary sales figures then coming in pointed to a very strong second quarter. Jobs was emboldened to predict that NeXT would sell 50,000 machines for the year, bringing in $200 to $250 million in revenue.[294] The moment seemed propitious for the company to finally reach a state of profitability. In his internal newsletter, the *SJ Gazette*, Jobs informed his employees that all attention was to be focused on breaking even that quarter: regular staff meetings were postponed, budgets were reduced by ten percent, employee compensation was frozen. It was not sufficient; NeXT remained an overburdened boat with a high level of seawater in its hold, even with the bilge pumps working furiously. In April, the bad news about the failure to achieve profitability had to be delivered to NeXT's small board of directors, and Ross Perot did not take the news well. He interrupted the presentation: "So what you're telling me is the cockpit's on fire and the plane's in a tailspin. So tell me something that I don't know." He dispatched some of his associates to work with Rulon-Miller to try to find ways to lift sales. Canon also dispatched delegations.

The expense of maintaining a state-of-the-art manufacturing facility, ready to build a billion dollars' worth of computers when orders were running in the low millions, became an increasingly sore point of contention between Jobs and the other members of the board. Like the NeXT machine itself, the NeXT factory looked fabulous when being shown off as a "demo," but it did not make much practical sense. For example, "just-in-time manufacturing," for which NeXT had won so many accolades, meant that NeXT assembled computers only when the orders came in, but the orders did not arrive in a smooth flow. The factory would be idle three weeks, with nothing for the workers to do but munch donuts, then in the last week of the month it would be overwhelmed by a rush of orders. The very last week of a quarter was the busiest of all. Since NeXT had to import its monitors, which required a lead of three months for ordering, and now an inventory of color monitors had to be juggled as well as black-and-white monitors, millions of dollars had to be invested in the parts inventory well in advance of orders for NeXT computers, and deciding on the right mix of monitors was a matter of conjecture, not science.

Canon did what it could to make the system work and dispatched a task force of its own experts to work at NeXT for six weeks, helping NeXT back away from the just-in-time ideal. The factory began to assemble the most popular configurations of its machines during slack periods, and waited for actual orders before it assembled the more unusual configurations, which helped to smooth out the work over the course of a quarter. Still, it made no financial sense for NeXT to retain its own manufacturing facility for such low-volume production, and Jobs's favorite argument in favor of keeping manufacturing in-house—achieving the highest quality of manufacturing—had been revealed to be an act of faith that had no foundation. When NeXT, under Canon's guidance, started seriously to collect manufacturing-quality statistics in 1991, it discovered that defect rates were much higher than the company had been claiming, and most disconcerting, the statistics pointed to a trend of deteriorating quality over time. Canon urged Jobs to move manufacturing offshore. Perot sided with Canon, and in a meeting in Redwood City with Jobs in June, exchanged sharp words and resigned from the board. Frustrated though he was, Perot remained calm enough to protect his investment in NeXT and he helped Jobs maintain the public image of All-Is-Well by not disclosing his resignation to the press.

This was a blow, but it was softened by a raid upon the sanctum of Jobs's rival, Bill Gates. Jobs, who had arrogated to himself the responsibility of directing marketing after demoting Dan'l Lewin, had interviewed many individuals to be Lewin's replacement, and more than a year had passed while the position remained vacant and NeXT's marketing drifted. The search had seemed to be at an end when Peter van Cuylenburg, a British-born executive then with Mercury Communications, a British telecommunications firm, had passed Jobs's muster and had accepted the offer to join NeXT, but he withdrew suddenly just as he was about to start work in April. Finally, in May, Jobs hired Mike Slade from Microsoft as NeXT's new director of marketing. He had an impressive track record: it was he who had presided over the marketing of Microsoft's enormously successful spreadsheet Excel. His arrival at NeXT was met with great anticipation, which was dampened somewhat by his performance when introduced to the NeXT staff: it was known that Slade was a millionaire by virtue of his Microsoft stock and someone in the group asked him why he had decided to come to NeXT. Slade told his new colleagues that "Microsoft is a big place, and I think I'd rather be a big fish in a small pond." He gave no indication that he was joking, either.

Slade's message for the troops was that this moment was do-or-die for NeXT (being a newcomer, Slade did not realize that this had been the company theme at any given moment during the preceding six years, too). He believed that the problems with the original Cube had been fixed with the NeXTstations; the problems with Businessland had been fixed with the new distribution channel of independent retailers. There could be no more excuses; it was time for the NeXT computer to make it on its own. And it would have to make it in the workstation market, not in the personal-computer market, where the machines had become an interchangeable, faceless commodity, customers bought solely on the basis of price, and a premium-priced computer like NeXT had no chance of competing with low-priced IBM-compatible clones. In Slade's mind, NeXT's principal competition was Sun.

When the second quarter results were in, Jobs had his public relations firm broadcast the good news: the press release carried the banner headline "Revenues Increase 86% Over First Quarter, NeXT Achieves First $46 Million Quarter." If revenue in the third quarter grew at the same rate, and then the fourth quarter continued the trend, NeXT would easily realize Jobs's prediction of a $250 million year and be headed skyward just like Sun. Privately, however, Jobs and his executive team were distressed to see that the company, despite the dramatic increase in revenue, was losing as much money as ever. Cash flow problems became more sticky, but all out of sight of the public, and out of sight of its own dealers.

The bright optimism of a newly established NeXT dealer based in Minneapolis, Minnesota, named Imaginet, illustrates the contagiousness of NeXT's public optimism. Authorized as an approved NeXT reseller in April 1991, Imaginet was formed by three youthful partners in their twenties who had sold Macintoshes in the past and were excited by NeXT's superior technology, especially in the area of desktop publishing. Imaginet would be a specialized boutique that would sell NeXT computers and the appropriate software in combinations that were tailored for offices that wanted to produce their own publications. Imaginet did not have a retail store; it maintained offices in a downtown office building and made calls on prospective clients at the customers' own offices. It was a focused strategy completely unlike Businessland's attempt to push the NeXT on everybody. The least expensive NeXTstation, at $5,000, though half as costly as the original Cube, was still too expensive to be used as the general-purpose computer to be placed on every office worker's desk. For the same $5,000, a company could buy an IBM-compatible machine for four employees, not just one. But for publishing, a case could be made for investing in a more powerful workstation. By presenting the NeXT expressly as a machine for producing office publications, Imaginet's owners were confident that they would prosper safely above the cost-cutting fray that bedeviled the ordinary computer resellers.

As enthusiastic about the NeXT as they were, Imaginet's owners were realistic about the limitations of available software. Even though NeXT had called itself the perfect "desktop publishing solution," it remained far from perfect as long as it lacked superior graphics software for manipulating and editing pictures and the interconnectivity and page-layout software that permitted pages prepared on the NeXT to be moved over to non-NeXT computers. NeXTs had to coexist peacefully with other makes of computers, and the software that would make that feasible was not yet available. To help tide it through the waiting period, Imaginet also secured authorization from Apple to sell Macintoshes, which were the established standard in desktop publishing.

The one software package that Imaginet and similar dealers most desperately needed for the NeXT was a program called Quark Xpress, which had become the most common page-layout program used to prepare materials for printing. Quark's program precisely arranged all of the elements that comprise a page layout—the columns, the headlines, the illustrations, the fonts, the page headers and footers, and so on. It provided minute calibration of the spacing between lines and individual letters; it handled color photographs with ease; it saved offices money by handling color separations and other prepress tasks that used to be done by professional service bureaus. Quark's format was the single standard used in publishing; competing programs could not be used as a substitute. Quark Xpress was available only on the Macintosh; if it had been made available on the NeXT too, Imaginet's partners would have pursued their original plan to be an exclusively NeXT dealer, without diluting their proselytizing on NeXT's behalf by also selling Macintoshes to pay the bills.

Jobs was not oblivious to the problem. He had long courted Quark, which was based in Denver and headed by Fred Ebrahimi, a strong-willed founder not unlike Jobs himself. On the eve of the introduction of the NeXTstations in 1990, Jobs painted for Ebrahimi and other Quark executives a wildly optimistic estimate of hundreds of thousands of NeXT machines that would be sold in the near future. This was the usual pitch that Jobs made to all prospective software developers. But realizing that NeXT's best hope for survival would be in desktop publishing, and that this area required getting Quark signed on, Jobs went further and made an exception to his rule of not offering software developers money to bring out software programs for the NeXT. He convinced IBM to go in with him and offer Quark $1.5 million; as huge a sum as this was, it would be a bargain for NeXT, given the critical importance of this particular piece of software to the future of NeXT as a company (and given that Ebrahimi had originally demanded $5 million). Quark agreed to the arrangement just before the 1990 announcements at Davies Hall, and near the end of the day's program Jobs briefly announced that Quark Xpress would be "ported" over to the NeXT. The audience did not need to be told the significance of this news, and applauded and cheered as it did for no other announcement that day.

Once the announcement was made, Quark began to have second thoughts about the likely size of the NeXT publishing market. It also began to look into what software tools it could use to help it reuse program code that was used in the Macintosh version of its program. It had the equivalent of 60 person/years of programming invested in its Xpress program; it was not going to abandon this investment and write the NeXT version from scratch with another 60 person/years of programming. A new little company in Menlo Park, California, called Quorum, was preparing software that would help companies like Quark convert code so that a Macintosh program would run on other computers, like the NeXT. But Jobs and his chief software engineer, Bud Tribble, were adamantly opposed to this approach. They wanted Quark to start over with "native" NeXT code, not recycled code from the inferior Macintosh. They were doing everything they could to dissuade Quorum from offering tools for the NeXT, and when they heard of Quark's intentions to reuse Macintosh code, they said many unflattering things about their new partner. Some of these remarks, which made their way back to Denver, were of a personal, stereotyping nature, linking Iranian-born Ebrahimi to "rug merchants." Quark withdrew into silence.

It was up to Jobs to take the initiative to try to restore good relations, but he compounded the insults in the course of ostensibly offering an olive branch to his new business partner. Jobs faxed a letter to Ebrahimi that said, You've heard that I've called you *sleazy*; well, here's the dictionary definition—and there Jobs pasted in the full definition of the word, taken from the Digital Webster whose convenience he had extolled at Davies Hall in 1988 but could never have foreseen would be so handy in this particular situation. Now, Jobs instructed Ebrahimi, return my unanswered phone calls and show me that the definition of sleazy does *not* fit you. Jobs appears to be the only person at NeXT who was surprised when Ebrahimi did not respond to this unusual invitation.

Even without receiving the infamous "sleazy" fax from Jobs, Quark had reason to be concerned about the trustworthiness of NeXT and the sales numbers that it was claiming. When the agreement between the two companies had been worked out to the mutual satisfaction of both parties, the signing was to be a formality. But when the final contract arrived, Quark was surprised to find that a number of provisions had been changed without prior discussion, provisions that were all altered in a direction that was not in Quark's interests. The belated discovery that NeXT was not being clear about which sales were upgrades of motherboards and which were sales of new, complete systems also made Quark uneasy. NeXT's imprudent use of inflated sales figures contributed to the dissolution of NeXT's ties to what was arguably its single most important software partner. There was one last chance to get Quark back on board. In early 1991, *NeXTWORLD* magazine, the quasi-independent magazine that promoted NeXT, begged its readers to show wavering Quark that the masses were desperately waiting for a NeXT version of Quark Xpress. Write letters to Quark and let them know! After a few months had passed, Quark toted up an underwhelming total of ten letters. This confirmed what Quark had suspected, and marked the end of its interest in NeXT. From then on, Quark redirected its energies into producing a Windows version of its software, where the numbers made more sense. And Quorum adapted its tools for recompiling Macintosh software for the benefit of NeXT's competition, first for Sun Microsystems, then for Silicon Graphics.

Imaginet did not know that the Quark deal was irretrievably lost. It proceeded on the assumption that the missing pieces of publishing-related software that the NeXT lacked would soon be filled in. In the meantime, it had to be careful not to oversell what the NeXT could do, lest it ruin its own credibility in the eyes of its prospective customers. Target Stores was one such customer, which happened to be shopping in 1991 for computers that would be used in its art department to prepare the twenty-page color advertising circular that is tucked into the Sunday newspaper. This was that rarity—a virgin corporate site, still without desktop computers because the work had always been sent to an outside firm. Here was the best possible opportunity for NeXT, in which it would not have to push aside Macintoshes, or IBM-compatibles, or Suns. Target was willing to seriously consider NeXT, and Target managers, accompanied by an outside consultant, flew from Minneapolis to Redwood City, California, just to see for themselves what NeXT offered.

NeXT salespeople gave splendid presentations, and a demonstration of NeXTSTEP and object-oriented programming was provided by a person who was identified as Job's personal technician, the next best thing to having the legend himself on hand. The senior Target representative was duly impressed, and told the NeXT staff that he'd buy nothing but NeXTs if he could be shown how an advertising supplement could be prepared on the machine. Some confusion followed. One member of the NeXT staff said that the program Framemaker could be used; other NeXT employees said that Framemaker was not what Target needed. But they had no better alternative to suggest, so the champion of Framemaker sat down and said that he would work on a mock-up. Unfortunately, Framemaker was best-suited for a book-length document that consisted mostly of text; it was not designed optimally for laying out a short, picture- and headline-filled piece of advertising. Time passed and the work proceeded at an agonizingly slow pace. The Target delegation moved on to look at other things in NeXT's offices, stopping by periodically to see how the mock-up was progressing. Finally, after the Target visitors had exhausted every plausible way of killing time and the work was still unfinished, it was clear that the NeXT, even in 1991, was not yet ready to do the work for which it was billed to be perfect.

Imaginet ended up selling two NeXT machines to Target. One was to be used as a network server, the other was to do special effects for headlines. At the same time, it sold Target eighteen Macintoshes, all of which would have been NeXTs, too, if software like Quark Xpress had been available. And an opportunity like that presented by Target was all too rare, a fact that NeXT salespeople did not appreciate. They told Imaginet and the other NeXT dealers that there was an abundance of such offices that had not yet been touched by the desktop-computer revolution. They were wrong. By 1991, in the real world, the sites that remained untouched by the revolution and yet still had funds to buy $5,000-a-pop workstations were all too few. NeXT needed to stop daydreaming and place highest priority on doing what Jobs had resisted from the beginning, making NeXTs work well with other kinds of computers.

Overall, during its first six months in business, Imaginet sold just over sixty computers to various customers, but only ten were NeXTs. Among the independent dealers that NeXT had selling its machines, Imaginet's record was quite good. In Jobs's own home turf, Computer Attic had experienced accelerated growth; its sales jumped to $28 million in 1991 and would almost double the next year, as its Macintosh and IBM-compatible machines flew out the door. But the NeXTs simply could not be budged. The big sale to Alain Pinel turned out to be unique. By late 1991, Computer Attic could find customers for only two or so NeXTs a month, while it sold hundreds of the other kinds of personal computers at the same time. The disparity in the numbers made it difficult to invest capital in keeping an inventory of NeXT software titles on hand, but without the software titles in stock, it was all the more difficult to entice customers to buy the hardware.

The strategy of relying upon boutique dealers was proving to be enormously expensive for NeXT, too. A standard contract stipulated that a dealer, as a condition of signing on, would take twenty-five machines for its inventory. NeXT provided sixty-day terms. But what happened was that upon the expiration of the sixty-days, NeXT did not receive the money that it was due. When NeXT called the overdue account, the dealer would say, "I've got twenty-three in the back room. I can't pay you." Thirty more days would go by. Another call would yield an update, "I've still got twenty; hey, you can have them back." The NeXT staff faced a difficult choice. It could either have the machines returned, adjust the sales figures that already had been recorded as booked, and endure the wrath of Jobs. Or it could let the accounts receivable slide, and continue to hope that real sales, that is, sales of NeXT computers to flesh-and-blood customers, would soon take off, which the remaining optimists at NeXT felt was about to happen, any time.

But the third quarter proved to be a disaster; NeXT's sales fell almost by half. This did not wholly reflect a bizarre drop in the interest of customers, however. Rather, it revealed the misleading nature of the "sales" figure itself, which refers only to NeXT's sales to its distributors. Separate from this is "sell-through," that is, the sale of machines to the customers who are the last element in the distribution chain, the end-users, and this is a figure that NeXT had difficulty obtaining and would not have revealed publicly even if it had accurate numbers. The initial increase in sales that had followed the introduction of the new NeXTstations was in good measure a manifestation of "channel loading," as it is called, when dealers fill their shelves with inventory. The second quarter's impressive results had been boosted when Canon loaded up its inventory of NeXT machines for sale in Japan. Once the shelves were full, NeXT's "sales" had sagged dramatically.

Now NeXT was in a jam: it could not announce the third quarter results without revealing the precipitous drop. Nor could it tinker with the earlier announced sales for the second quarter to reflect the truth that much of the earlier "sales" were uncollectible receivables. Profitability, needless to say, remained elusive. In the meantime, NeXT had to carry the load of more than $10 million in accounts receivable that had built up. In order to survive until sales took off, NeXT used its receivables as collateral to secure short-term loans from a bank. Depending on the degree of risk, NeXT received anywhere from seventy-five to ninety-five percent of the face value of the receivable, due to be paid in sixty days or when the customer repaid NeXT, whichever came first. The interest that NeXT had to pay on these loans came out of margins that were already perilously slim. NeXT became so desperate for cash that it used receivables as small as $1,000 to head off the cash crisis. Payments to NeXT's own suppliers were also put off.

The company that only two years earlier had gotten an injection of $100 million from the Japanese was once again out of money. Perot, before he left, had been extremely unhappy with the way that Jobs had burned through the money as if he, or Canon, or another sugar daddy would always be on hand to bail him out. Perot saw that paradoxically NeXT had been hurt, not helped, by the generous funding it had been given because Jobs had never had to learn how to stick to a budget. "I shouldn't have let you guys have all that money," Perot told the NeXT policy team. "Biggest mistake I made." He was not about to make it again, so NeXT could not get more money from him. Nor could it get more licensing fees from IBM. The only major partner remaining was Canon, and it was faced with an unsavory choice: it could either inject additional capital into NeXT, or watch its $100 million investment land in Chapter 11. Whether NeXT lived or died depended upon what Canon decided to do.

In too deep to shut the cashier's window at this late point, Canon came through with $10 million and averted a disaster. But that money quickly disappeared, so another $10 million had to be put in. NeXT had debtor's leverage which increased each time: the more money Canon invested, the less choice it had to refuse when NeXT knocked again on its door, demanding still more. At the end of 1991, Canon had to provide a third round of emergency capital, another $20 million (and insisted that Jobs pitch in $10 million of his own money, too). In each instance, failure to shovel in cash would have meant NeXT could not have made payroll, yet in each instance, as soon as the money arrived, the spending spigots were opened wide again.

Through it all, NeXT did not say a word about its financial difficulties to the public. Jobs was as beguiling as ever. He told an interviewer that "we were actually pretty lost in terms of who we were as a company" until recently, fumbling with the right mix of technology, distribution, and marketing. Now, Jobs insisted, he'd gotten it right.[295] Jobs spoke excitedly in late 1991 of how NeXT had gone "from zero to a quarter-billion dollars a year in its first year" (a curious statement, given that NeXT's sales would be half of what he was claiming and 1991 was not its first year but rather its sixth).[296] Most brazenly of all, during the second half of 1991, Jobs told the press on at least three different occasions that NeXT had turned profitable, when at the same time, precisely because the company most decidedly was *not* profitable, it was in fact lurching from one financial crisis to another, staving off bankruptcy only with eleventh-hour rescues.[297]

NeXT had blown through more than $250 million of investment capital, and still was in precarious financial shape, far from being sufficiently healthy to take its shares public. Yet in Jobs's view, things were not nearly as dark as his discouraged employees seemed to think. He plucked what he wanted from history, and he found favorable precedents in the sales volumes of both Apple and Sun when they had gone public.[298] He did not adjust for inflation, differences in the saturation of intended markets, or the pesky discrepancy between their profitability and NeXT's sorry financial condition. Jobs told his employees that NeXT was in excellent shape, beating Sun in head-to-head competition. Bad numbers somehow disappeared. One employee who remained impervious to the Jobsian vision, upon leaving one of Jobs's presentations, devised an impromptu song-and-dance in the corridor, chanting, "Voo-doo eco-no-mics, Voo-doo eco-no-mics . . ."

Disillusionment led a number of NeXT employees to resign, including another founder, Susan Barnes. Paradoxically, Jobs's employees had more freedom to leave than Jobs himself did, or at least so he felt at times, when he would tell them he could not imagine doing anything other than what he was doing at NeXT. Poor little rich boy: too young to retire, too restless to retreat to the sedentary life, puttering about the house like Apple cofounder Steve Wozniak, and perhaps most importantly, too insecure about the nature of his earlier success at Apple. The game at NeXT was not of finances but of existential validation, and he had to keep pushing stacks of poker chips from his and Canon's dwindling piles in order to pay the ante and keep playing, all the while maintaining an optimistic outlook, expecting the very next quarter to bring a surge in sales and acclaim. Mona Simpson, Jobs's sister who was raised separately, dedicated her first novel, *Anywhere But Here* (1987), to Jobs and their mother, and chose a quotation from Ralph Waldo Emerson for the epigraph from which the book's title was taken: "There are three wants which can never be satisfied: that of the rich wanting more, that of the sick, wanting something different, and that of the traveler, who says, 'anywhere but here.' " The book is a stunning work of fiction—the narrator and her peripatetic, delusional mother are literally unforgettable characters. The book itself has nothing to do with "the rich wanting more"; the phrase seems to have been included only because it was in the same sentence as the more apposite "anywhere but here." Jobs was enormously proud of his sister's literary achievement; he introduced her at an early company retreat, and kept a shelf in his office filled with copies of *Anywhere But Here*. Yet how curiously apt was the first item in the Emerson epigraph in describing Jobs, the paragon of a rich person incapable of ever being satisfied. The need to prove himself again, however, kept him imprisoned. For Jobs, NeXT *had* to succeed, and anything and everybody was subordinate to that quest.

For a number of his employees, a well-intentioned benefit that the company had provided turned out to be a kind of shackle that imprisoned, too. Leading the *thirtysomething* company, Jobs had made available to all employees the right to borrow up to half of a year's salary, which many took advantage of to make the down payment on a first house. It was an offer that NeXT was financially unable to sustain, and by 1990, loans to employees were capped at a modest $5,000. But for those who took advantage of the half-year-salary-loan while it was available, the employee obtained a four-year note, with a fixed rate of interest based on prevailing rates at the time; for a loan taken in 1988, for example, interest accrued at twelve percent. No payments on either principal or interest were required during the term, however. If one were to resign from NeXT, the loan had to be repaid upon leaving. These terms and conditions were reasonable; the program made it possible for employees to buy homes in the overpriced northern California real estate market, where "starter" homes were priced at $300,000 and up, and first-time home buyers had to round up $60,000 for just a down payment. If a fixed rate of twelve percent came to be seen as too high when interest rates fell, the indebted employee need not worry unduly because the employee's NeXT shares, which served as the collateral for the loan, would soon be publicly traded, Jobs said. Employees began at NeXT with the expectation that Jobs would lead the company to Apple-like success and everyone would eventually become millionaires, making the personal loan an inconsequential burden.

What happened, however, is that not only did interest rates fall, so too did house prices, and the expected explosion of sales for NeXT did not materialize even after the second-generation NeXT-stations were introduced. The years had passed and NeXT was still hemorrhaging money. If an employee looked at the mismatch of modest sales to large operational losses, the numbers were terrifying. But to permit oneself to become disillusioned about NeXT's prospects was not an option if one was carrying a $50,000 note due immediately if one were to leave NeXT. Through no fault of Jobs or NeXT, the personal-loan program had become over time a heavy encumbrance, which restricted job mobility and consequently restricted what employees could allow themselves to think about NeXT and its future. Objectivity was a luxury that many could not afford. They had no choice but to latch on to Jobs's optimism and believe that their NeXT shares soon would be publicly traded; then they could cash out with the financial windfall that would redeem all of the long hours and arduous struggle.

The buoyant spirits were what outsiders saw when they encountered NeXT employees on the street. In 1991, for example, Burt Cummings, a former NeXT employee, ran into a colleague from sales who still worked at NeXT. How are things going? Cummings asked. "Oh, we're kicking ass," he was told. Oh, where? Well, no area in particular, was the reply, but "we're selling more than we've ever sold." Cummings was one of the few people then outside of NeXT who knew exactly how few had been sold in the past, so saying that an unprecedented number of machines were now being sold was not necessarily saying much. He was curious, what was NeXT's basic marketing message now? "Well, we don't know yet, but they're really moving." For Cummings, the encounter served to confirm the continuing power of Jobs's famous "reality distortion field." His friend, who clearly remained under the spell, was not lying to Cummings; he simply could not distinguish reality and unreality.

The public knew nothing other than what Jobs chose to tell it, and he presented a picture of success. When speaking in public about the initial public offering that he planned in 1992 or early 1993, Jobs made the offering appear to be something that NeXT was thinking about only because it was *already* so successful that its own customers on Wall Street were begging Jobs to let them invest in NeXT. He explained that it would be difficult to let one company invest and not the others, so the only fair thing would be to throw the opportunity open to everybody.[299] In his telling, NeXT's only problem was how best to apportion the dowry among a bevy of eager suitors.

It worked beautifully. The press gave the story of NeXT's intentions prominent play, and in so doing, helped make it more likely to come true, adding legitimacy to the idea that NeXT was fit and sound and taking off. It was circular logic—NeXT must be healthy or it would not be talking of an initial public offering, and it would not be talking of an initial public offering if it were not healthy. But in the vacuum of publicly disclosed financial information, it seemed perfectly credible. Last heard from, NeXT had said its sales in the second quarter had jumped dramatically, so presumably the trend had continued through the year, and now Jobs was also saying that the company had become profitable.

The news of an imminent initial public offering refired excitement; it seemed that the rocket ship of entrepreneurial success was about to head off into the wild blue, repeating the history of Apple. With eyes looking skyward, little attention was paid to another announcement that NeXT quietly made two days later: it was reducing its work force by five percent, the first public mention of a layoff. Forty-eight hours earlier, when NeXT announced the plans to go public, reporters had asked NeXT if any layoffs were being contemplated, and the NeXT spokesperson had emphatically denied any such possibility.[300] So it was a bit awkward to turn around so soon and make the announcement of dismissals. But Jobs and his public relations person Allison Thomas blustered their way through. The timing of the layoffs, coming so soon after disclosure of plans to go public, suggested a connection between the two events, but Thomas fell back to her appointed role of denying, denying, denying. "The two events were unrelated," she said with a perfectly straight face.[301] Well, it would seem to an outsider that the idea of an initial public offering was floated intentionally right before the news about the layoffs. Oh, nothing of the sort happened, said Jobs. He claimed to have innocently mentioned the initial public offering in casual remarks to reporters and he professed "surprise" at the attention it had received.[302] The one conclusion that reporters would naturally draw from the news of the layoffs—that NeXT was having financial difficulties—even this the company denied. NeXT was simply "repositioning," Jobs said, and had plenty of cash. In the end, Jobs and Thomas's campaign worked well: the earlier, favorable coverage of NeXT's plans to go public had filled the company's allotted quota of attention that week. Readers were left with the impression that Jobs wanted them to have.

Live by the sword, die by the sword. At the time that NeXT was manipulating numbers to its advantage for the consumption of the general public, NeXT headquarters was itself the victim of manipulated numbers that were being sent from its vice-president in charge of European operations, Theo Wegbrans. The strong "sales" in Europe, which NeXT had reported to the public as its area of greatest success to date, were a phantom, the result of simple channel loading. Dealers that needed four machines ordered fifty, with the encouragement of NeXT's sales staff in Europe. The warehouses began to bulge with unsold NeXT machines, but Wegbrans, when pressed for sell-through reports from NeXT headquarters in California, made up numbers that provided reassurance that all was well.

The truth can be suppressed for only so long, however, and one would hope that Jobs would have learned something from the

European debacle. When his sales managers in Redwood City came across discrepancies between the robust sales that Wegbrans was claiming and the reports from other parties in Europe, Jobs resisted their recommendations that something be done. As the months passed, and the lies that Wegbrans passed on to cover up weak sales became progressively more audacious, Jobs continued to drag his feet. By the time Jobs reluctantly acceded to the advice of his lieutenants and pulled Wegbrans out, the mess had worsened to the point of complete disaster. Without distinguishing between guilty country managers and innocent underlings, NeXT employees were summarily dismissed and stranded en masse; the network of dealers was dismantled; the sumptuous office on the French Riviera that was NeXT's European headquarters—opened only months earlier—was closed. New managers, a new headquarters, a new sales strategy that avoided dealers and rested upon NeXT's own direct sales to customers were installed. Millions of dollars of NeXT's European inventory could not be accounted for after Wegbrans left, but lodging criminal charges would have brought unwanted publicity and exposure of the phantasmagoric empire that NeXT Europe had built. The losses were quietly written off. Let us call it an expensive lesson in the economics of deceit.

Born Again, Again

The original NeXT Cube had been reinvented. The distribution channel had been radically overhauled. Everything that NeXT could imagine needing fixing had been fixed. Yet the company's revenue remained maddeningly mismatched to operating costs, and profitability remained hopelessly out of reach. If it had not been for the fresh infusions of capital from Canon's and Jobs's own pockets, NeXT would have had to close shop. The continued flow of investment funds gave the company time to reconsider who the NeXT computer was supposed to be for, to reformulate the message to be broadcast to prospective customers, to reinvent the company still again and become a *new* New NeXT. Survival seemed to require embracing the Fortune 500.

A few years earlier, Jobs had treated large corporations with open disdain. In 1985, when still at Apple, he had concluded that the reason the Apple Lisa had failed so miserably was because Apple had contracted a bad case of what Jobs called "Fortune 500-itis," forsaking Apple's roots, "selling to people."[303] The marketing of the Macintosh had returned Apple to the education market and noncorporate users. At NeXT, Jobs had vacillated, beginning by selling to the education market, then expanding the pitch to large corporations through the ill-fated partnership with Businessland. Faced with the Fortune 500's disinterest, NeXT had backpedaled away, shifting toward the smaller businesses served by independent computer dealers. But this was not working either. At the prodding of Mike Slade, his new marketing director, Jobs realized that the only customer segment with pockets deep enough to consider purchase of the NeXT computer was the target of the unsuccessful Lisa and Businessland campaigns, the big corporation. For a renewed assault on the impregnable Fortune 500, NeXT needed another make-over to present a more attractive, less haughty picture of itself to its prospective customers.

Having come from Microsoft, Slade brought a more pragmatic sensibility to the inwardly focused NeXT. He did not remain immune to the influence of Jobs and NeXT culture; he repeated some of the old lines of the past, such as Jobs's silly goal of targeting the desks that currently were too crowded with both a Sun workstation and a Macintosh (Slade: "the goal here at NeXT is to put *only one* computer on every desk, instead of three or four").[304] But he was not a passive inheritor of all of the failed marketing of NeXT's past. He pushed Jobs and the company to see that the marketplace had rendered a clear judgment about what NeXT was offering: the NeXT hardware did not much interest anybody—it was the software that set NeXT apart from its competition, particularly the NeXTSTEP software that customers could use to write their own software. Slade believed that NeXT should abandon the fruitless vigil for the arrival of the single program, the "killer app," that would save the company. Instead, NeXT should promote its computer as the perfect machine to write custom applications on. "There is no such thing as a 'killer app' anymore," he said. "The killer app is the custom app."[305]

Jobs liked the new message and by late 1991 was using it wherever he spoke. The phrase that he latched on to and used with dogged consistency was a mouthful of information-systems jargon:

the NeXT computer was ideal for *"mission-critical custom apps."* He never used an abbreviated version or shorthand; he insisted on the full incantation, repeating it many times in each speech—*mission-critical custom apps . . . mission-critical custom apps . . . mission-critical custom apps*—until it grated on the ears. But he was not addressing the layperson. He was going after the special guild within corporate America, the chief information officers and the managers of information systems.

However, the group that he succeeded in reaching did not belong to corporate America—NeXT's best customers, it turned out, were government intelligence agencies. Unfortunately for NeXT, the company could not use them as reference accounts in the campaign to woo the Fortune 500, first, because of the reticence of spies to talk publicly about their work, but also because of their privileged fiscal prerogatives; the budgets of intelligence agencies, free of public scrutiny, permitted purchases of NeXTs without the penny-pinching of commercial customers. Sales to the spy agencies was such a lucrative business that it spawned a necklace of NeXT-related computer consultants in the suburbs surrounding Washington, D.C.[306] NeXT could use other less-secretive government accounts for testimonials, but these were not easily packaged into terms that would be appealing to the Fortune 500. The L.A. County Sheriff's Department, one of NeXT's largest customers in the country, was not a name that carried authority in the corporate world. Worse, after the Rodney King beating case in 1992, the Sheriff's Department was confused in the public mind with the L.A. Police Department, and Jobs labored to keep NeXT untainted by association.[307]

Even if not mixed up in the Rodney King case, in the eyes of some of Jobs's older fans from the days when Apple stood for a countercultural voice, Jobs and NeXT were still guilty of unsavory association with the police and the CIA. Jobs bragged of how the Canadian Mounted Police was the customer that was using the multimedia capabilities of the NeXT to the fullest—"multimedia out the wazoo," Jobs enthused. This was not the same Steve Jobs who had been anguished in 1985 by the discovery that the tactical nuclear weapons under U.S. command in Europe were controlled by his Apple II computers.[308] John Perry Barlow, a writer who shuttled among a number of diverse interests such as composing lyrics for the Grateful Dead and reviewing NeXT products for *NeXTWORLD* magazine, got an interview with Jobs at the moment when NeXT was proclaiming a new marketing direction yet again. Like a ghost from the countercultural past, Barlow put some sharp questions to Jobs, worried, as he told Jobs, that NeXT would find that it would soon come to resemble its market, not its maker. This was what a disillusioned Mitch Kapor had discovered when his company, Lotus, had been corporatized by the influence of *its* customers. Jobs said that he had met a lot of people in corporate America that he wouldn't mind NeXT coming to resemble, like the young group at O'Connor Services, a commodities trading firm in Chicago, which had adopted the NeXT Computer enthusiastically. "They are great; they look like us; they talk like us."[309] The way Jobs spoke of O'Connor was as if he had plucked the example from a large basket of possibilities, but O'Connor in fact was the largest single site of NeXTs in corporate America.[310] O'Connor loved NeXT, and NeXT naturally reciprocated. What about the CIA, Barlow needled? Aren't they one of your biggest customers? Jobs said that he could not comment, which answered Barlow's question.[311]

Barlow was suggesting that NeXT was abandoning the idealistic principles of its founding, but he did not show an awareness of NeXT's predicament: if NeXT did not secure more customers quickly, customers of whatever stripe, politically correct or not, there would be no more NeXT, period. Jobs could not impress upon NeXT partisans like Barlow how dire the situation was without disclosing the awful financial fix that the company was in. Perhaps even if Jobs had been forthcoming about the exigent state of the company's finances, he still would not have received encouragement from the "early adopters," as they are called in the computer industry. In 1991, Ernest Prabhakar, a frequent contributor to an electronic bulletin board that posted news and opinions about NeXT, declared, "I'd rather have a live dream and a dead company than the other way."[312] This was a tricky maneuver for Jobs to direct: he ran the risk of getting stuck in a no-man's-land, not yet acceptable to Fortune 500 corporate types yet viewed as a quisling by the programmers who abhorred the corporation and the technological mediocrity with which it was associated. It was a risk that Jobs had to take, however. To stay put would mean NeXT would perish shortly.

The single most important step that Jobs could take to increase NeXT's attractiveness was to find a replacement licensee for IBM, so that NeXT's strength, its unique software, could be used on computers other than those that NeXT itself made. The computer world had watched as IBM and NeXT drifted apart, without a version of NeXTSTEP for IBM's RISC-based workstations ever making it out of the lab, and the conclusion that computer industry honchos drew from the unhappy union was that NeXT was not serious about loosening its tight control over all aspects of its product. Apple Computer had a policy similar to that of NeXT: if a customer wanted to use the Macintosh operating system, there was only one version available, the one from Apple. And the hardware that would run the Macintosh software could be purchased from only one company, Apple. The marketplace continued to tolerate this policy of Apple's only because so many Macintoshes had been purchased in the earlier years, before Microsoft had succeeded in developing a reasonable software alternative, that the installed base of Macintoshes created a momentum all its own. But this was the singular exception to the rule that a software standard, at the least, had to work with hardware manufactured by more than one company. Customers valued highly the right to move at will among hardware vendors; relative newcomers to the computer industry like NeXT could not expect special dispensation from the rule. Sun Microsystems, for example, whose own strength was hardware, not software, had discovered that in order for its own RISC microprocessor to be fully accepted by its customers, the chip had to be made widely available. So Sun had had to create, in essence, its own competition, licensing the design to chip manufacturers for use in Sun clones that would compete directly against Sun's own workstations. Its customers demanded it.

The lesson in all this was that the age of proprietary technology had ended. A new computer company could not be successful without obeying the demands of the marketplace and giving customers choices among suppliers. If customers had been reluctant to entrust multibillion-dollar Sun with complete control over their interests, in the absence of the moderating influence of competitive alternatives, these same customers were extremely reluctant, understandably, to entrust little NeXT with monopolistic control. NeXT salespeople continually ran into resistance due to questions about the company's viability. Would NeXT be around three or five years hence? As long as NeXT software and hardware were inextricably combined, and only NeXT provided both, then any questions about the company's likely longevity induced queasiness in the prospective corporate customer. NeXT had found some customers in the business world who remained relatively unconcerned, such as the William Morris Agency, which had looked to NeXT for an immediate boost to the agency's public image, or the financial services boutiques, like O'Connor, whose quants—the number-crunching analysts with a gift for mathematics—armed with the hottest computer technology, could whip up new, esoteric financial products and recoup an investment in a short period of time and not worry about long-term obsolescence. A law firm that had taken the plunge professed no concern when NeXT announced the layoffs in 1991; a spokesperson for Marger, Johnson, McCollom & Stolowitz, said, "Frankly, I couldn't care less if they went belly up tomorrow," reasoning that even if NeXT declared bankruptcy, some other company would pick up the NeXT technology. It was simply too good to be abandoned.[313] But for most companies, the risk of owning orphaned machines could not be viewed with such equanimity. The investment that NeXT was asking them to make, in hardware and software provided by only a single source, NeXT, and incompatible with the computers that were already in place, was deemed by most businesses as unacceptably risky.

These facts were visible to everyone at NeXT, except for Jobs and Bud Tribble, who were adamantly opposed to licensing NeXT's software to other companies. As soon as NeXT's partnership with IBM fell apart at the end of 1990, the lower-level NeXT staff took upon itself a lobbying campaign to port the NeXT operating system to IBM-compatible personal computers. Jobs did not want to take a fatal first step toward becoming a software-only house; he wanted to run a *computer* company, and to him that meant retaining complete control over hardware and software. Tribble, the in-house "rocket scientist," had never shown any special business acumen, but nevertheless Jobs treated Tribble's opinions with deference, and Tribble believed that there was no money to be made by selling operating systems. He said that AT&T, which licensed its version of Unix to other companies, did not make any money from it to speak of, and even the example of Microsoft did not impress him. He said that Microsoft profited only by selling application programs that ran on top of the operating system, and not from selling the operating system itself. With Tribble's reasoning to lend support to his own instinctive wish to keep control, Jobs repelled suggestions from other NeXT staff members to license the NeXT software.

In this particular matter, Jobs should not have accepted Tribble's presentation of the facts. Tribble was plain wrong: Microsoft continued to prosper from its high-margin sales of the DOS operating systems and the Windows environment that ran between DOS and applications. In 1991, no less than thirty-six percent of Microsoft's $1.8 billion in revenue came from its operating systems and language software. Its gross margins in its first quarter in fiscal 1993 were an otherworldly eighty-three percent.[314] But Microsoft was not the company that NeXT would best be compared to; no matter how he wished that it was otherwise, Jobs had no realistic hope of displacing Microsoft in the operating-systems business. A more practical comparison would have been to the privately held Santa Cruz Operation, a small company which sold a version of the Unix operating system to businesses that needed Unix for computers built with the same microprocessors as IBM-compatible personal computers. Compared to Microsoft's DOS operating system, the Santa Cruz Operation's Unix was not well-known. But it was used by businesses that needed to write customized software for uncommonly demanding tasks and which permitted the computer user to run many separate programs simultaneously. This was exactly what the NeXT software excelled at. The Santa Cruz Operation had created in this niche a business that generated annual revenues of about $160 million, selling only software; if NeXT were to move into the same niche, it had a chance of competing effectively. But there would be little likelihood of high visibility and glory, of the power to set standards of the mainstream computer industry, let alone the likelihood of collecting billions in revenue annually, like a Microsoft—or like a Steve Jobs in the happier days at Apple. To step in the direction of a specialty Unix software publisher like the obscure Santa Cruz Operation would be to acknowledge that NeXT would remain marginal, not in a business sense, but in a historical sense, which was the fate Jobs most wished to escape.

Despite the stubborn opposition of their boss, Bud Tribble, and *his* boss, Steve Jobs, Tribble's subordinates in the software division, their allies in the sales and marketing organization, even the company's legal counsel, Gary Moore, continued to press upon Jobs the case for expanded licensing. Moore offered three reasons for NeXT to make its software available on other personal computers. It would add more seats, that is, more machines using NeXT software, which would make NeXT a more attractive standard for outside software developers; the more software written for NeXT, the more attractive NeXT's own machines would be in the eyes of customers. Expanded licensing would help remove the image of NeXT as a proprietary company, an image that in the age of Open Systems did not play well. And the licensing, of course, would bring in additional revenue, a benefit that NeXT could hardly afford to ignore.

Porting the NeXT software to the IBM-compatible world required adapting the software for the microprocessor family made by Intel. Overcoming the technical challenges would be greatly eased if Intel supplied assistance and expertise, making it a "friendly" port. An alternative direction that NeXT could have taken would have been to port to Sun's RISC machines, but that would have been a "hostile" port, lacking Sun's support, and thus was deemed much less practical (according to Jobs, Scott McNealy had said that "I'd rather stick needles in my eyes than work with NeXT").[315] Intel microprocessors thus were the prime target, and two NeXT managers, Max Henry and Chris MacAskill, quietly took upon themselves the task of lobbying Intel on NeXT's behalf, out of sight of the still recalcitrant Jobs. When Henry and MacAskill approached Intel, they discovered that the company was immediately interested in getting NeXT software ported to its microprocessors. It had already conducted market research surveys among its customers, trying to find out how "workstations" were defined and why workstations were preferred over personal computers for certain work environments. The research had revealed that large monitors and RISC microprocessors constituted part of popular conceptions of what made some machines *workstations* and others merely personal computers, but it also revealed that certain kinds of software seemed to be available only on workstations and gave those machines an enviable aura. If Intel could persuade NeXT to bring out its software on machines powered by Intel chips, then IBM-compatible machines could be presented as workstations, too. At the urging of the NeXT emissaries, Intel's president, Andy Grove, called Jobs, and the two got along well. Grove's relationship to Jobs would often be likened by Jobs's associates as like a father's, just as other paternal figures in Jobs's business life were: Ross Perot, at least in the early years; George Fisher, head of Motorola; John Warnock, head of Adobe; Pat Crecine, of the academic world. But

Grove and the others would be more accurately described as playing an avuncular role: all were personally nonthreatening to Jobs.

Intel sweetened the proposition for NeXT to port NeXTSTEP by offering to assign two of its own engineers to work at NeXT full-time. Even then, it took six full months of campaigning, including the appeals of Intel's Grove from the outside, and the continued lobbying by lower-level NeXT employees on the inside, before Jobs capitulated in the summer of 1991 and gave his blessing. It was not appreciated at the time, but it would turn out to be arguably the single most important decision that Jobs had made at NeXT; as sales of NeXT's own hardware plummeted that summer, and sputtered through the fall and on into 1992, NeXT's hopes for a reprieve from oblivion shifted increasingly, later desperately, to the Intel project. It would be, as one discouraged NeXT manager put it, "the last arrow in the quiver." Unfortunately, the six months that were required to persuade Jobs to bring out the Intel version of NeXTSTEP cost the company dearly, as its rivals had hardly stood still in the interim. The colossus of Microsoft had made that much more progress in its advance campaign for its new workstation-class operating system, called Windows NT. IBM grew nearer to releasing its own latest version of operating system software for personal computers, OS/2, which was intended to meet Windows and Windows NT head-on (by the end of 1991, IBM was reported to have lavished 1,700 programmers and $850 million on the project).[316] And Sun had used the same time to prepare a move very similar to NeXT's, moving a new version of its own operating system, Solaris, onto IBM-compatible machines.

The ideal place to make the announcement of NeXT's entry into the mainstream personal-computer market would be at Fall Comdex, in Las Vegas, the largest trade show in the U.S. computer industry—the largest trade show in any U.S. industry. NeXT had always held itself aloof from the commoners who flocked to Comdex, dominated as it was by the vendors of IBM-compatible computers. Now, in the fall of 1991, NeXT needed to rub shoulders with the rabble. And by coincidence, Andy Grove was to be the keynote speaker for Comdex that year, and he was more than willing to use the spotlight to introduce the Intel version of NeXTSTEP in his speech. The opportunity had to be passed up, however, because the software was not even close to being in suitable shape for a public demonstration, and NeXT feared that its software would be compared unfavorably to Sun's newly announced Solaris. Jobs decided it would be best to wait until another time, so that Sun could not rain on his parade. NeXT skipped Comdex entirely, but its skittishness proved unnecessary; Sun sent only a small contingent to the show.

More time passed, and finally in January 1992, in San Francisco, NeXT made its new announcements at its own mini–trade show, which it called NeXTWORLD Expo (the first *annual* NeXT-WORLD Expo, it emphasized). Unlike Comdex, in which the podium must be shared with many others, NeXTWORLD Expo was NeXT's own show, and Jobs did not have to yield to allies, enemies, or anyone else; *he* of course got to present the keynote speech. The audience was greeted with news of the new directions for NeXT, emphasizing the use of the NeXT computer for writing custom software and the imminent diffusion of NeXT software in the IBM-compatible personal-computer market. The Jobs demonstration included the visually arresting tricks of the two previous shows that he had staged at Davies Hall in 1988 and 1990. This time, in addition to the images of Ferraris and Donald Ducks, there was a rotating three-dimensional model that showed off the Pixar computer-animation technology that was going to be incorporated for the first time into NeXT's own operating system. But an entirely new theme, that of NeXTs working congenially with other kinds of computers, ran through Jobs's talk. One would never have known that his staff had had to forcibly drag him to this new position of genial toleration of computer miscegenation.

Jobs was as enthusiastic about his cause as he ever had been, claiming that NeXTSTEP software tools permitted the creation of new software five to ten times faster than the competition. John Perry Barlow overheard a Macintosh pundit say of Jobs, "If this guy had been born in Alabama, he would have been bigger than Swaggart." But Barlow felt that Jobs in 1992 was less theatrical than he had been before, when the two previous shows had resembled "Albert Speer's staging for the rally at Nuremburg."[317]

Still, Jobs made the improbable seem not only possible but likely: NeXT seemed poised to mow down the workstation competition above it, with its superior capabilities in "mission-critical custom apps," and the personal-computer competition below, with what it was then calling NeXTSTEP 486, the version of the NeXT software that was being readied for IBM-compatibles. The "486" referred to the most advanced chip that Intel then offered for personal computers; for technical reasons, the NeXT software could not be adapted to run on machines that ran 386 or earlier generations of the chip family. The refrain that he had used before, ". . . and it just works. . . ." now made NeXTSTEP 486 seem close to realization. Even when there was a small technical snafu during the show, Jobs never lost his poise. When he was showing how a NeXT workstation could be used to query a database that ran on another company's server, the NeXT machine crashed. Jobs ad-libbed gamely, "That's how you know it was live."

Jobs was so successful in portraying a new NeXT, ready to conquer the world of IBM-compatibles with its software, that he made NeXT's dealers extremely worried that sales of NeXT's own computers, so disappointingly modest, would be undercut by the new availability of NeXT software adapted to hardware that was much less expensive than NeXT's own. NeXT's Todd Rulon-Miller tried to soothe NeXT's dealers in a private meeting, where he told them that the Dell personal computer that NeXT was using to show a prototype of NeXTSTEP 486 was no ordinary box. With the special graphics board, additional memory, and other hardware requirements needed for the NeXT software to run, the Dell computer was a $17,000 monster. Rulon-Miller intended this disclosure to be reassuring: dealers who sold NeXT hardware need not worry that their prices would be higher than Intel-based personal computers sold by others; the NeXT hardware would still be cheaper than the IBM-compatible on steroids needed for NeXTSTEP. But his reassurance was puzzling. Just how many customers would be willing to spend $17,000 on a fully loaded 486 personal computer instead of $2,000 on a more conventionally equipped 486? Rulon-Miller's private message to the dealers contradicted Jobs's message to the public. Either NeXTSTEP would be limited to very expensive 486 machines, or NeXTSTEP would be hugely successful in the personal-computer market; one or the other could be true, but not both simultaneously.

The principal enemy that Jobs identified at NeXTWORLD Expo was Sun Microsystems, whom he described, borrowing the demonology of the Persian Gulf War, as the "mother of all competitors." NeXT was beating Sun "80 percent" of the time, Jobs told his audience (the figure should not be taken as statistical verity; he also spoke casually of a "90 percent" rate of success against Sun[318]). Listening to him, one was tempted to picture two enormous sumo wrestlers, arms locked together in a titanic match. Momentarily forgotten was that NeXT was *not* Sun's closest competitor; it was not even close to being so. But Jobs knew exactly what he was doing by portraying NeXT as the occupant of the number-two position, taking on the number-one company. He had explained to his employees on a number of occasions that if an underdog, trailing the pack, focused on the leader and ignored the others, the public would come to think of it as the closest challenger, which would then become self-fulfilling. When Avis had attacked the supremacy of Hertz in the car rental market, it was not, in fact, number-two as it had claimed. But the advertising worked so well that it was able to climb to the number-two position. NeXT could achieve the same.

Sun was hardly in a position vulnerable to attack from little NeXT. Thanks to the acceleration of the movement to downsize large mainframe computers, "big iron," and move to networks of workstations and servers, such as those Sun offered, the company was perfectly positioned to sustain its vertiginous rate of growth. The attractiveness of relatively inexpensive, but speedy, RISC-based Sun, Hewlett-Packard, and IBM workstations can be understood by the observation of Larry Ellison, president of Oracle Corporation, which published database software: "On my desk I have a $10,000 76 MIPS (millions-of-instructions-per-second) Hewlett-Packard workstation that is attached to a $7 million 50 MIPS IBM mainframe. What's wrong with this picture?"[319] Mainframe and minicomputer sales headed downward, while sales of workstations rose ever higher. In 1991, impervious to the impact of the economic recession that had depressed sales and earnings at many other computer companies, Sun reported, for its fiscal year that ended in June, record sales and profits. A news story offered this testimonial: "It almost seems like Sun Microsystems Inc. is doing business on a different planet."[320] For the year, Sun's revenue had gone from $2.4 billion to $3.2 billion. When Jobs delivered to the NeXTWORLD Expo crowd NeXT's happy news of having achieved sales of $127.5 million in 1991, he understandably did *not* mention that NeXT's total sales in its best year in its six-year history did not begin to match the $800 million that its designated rival had gained at the same time over sales from the previous year. Time had not been kind to NeXT; the gap between its revenues and Sun's was widening. If Sun was a sumo wrestler, then NeXT was a runty kid barely tall enough to kick it in the shins.

Scott McNealy had his own boasts to offer stock analysts as Sun continued to produce amazing numbers. The annual-revenue-per-employee, a favored measure of efficiency in Silicon Valley, increased twenty percent at Sun, reaching a new company record of $258,000. Extensive use of subcontracting and low-cost manufacturing were credited for the figure.[321] NeXT never offered comparable figures for annual-revenue-per-employee, but whether calculated pre- or post-layoffs, NeXT's would have been well below Sun's. McNealy did not pay much attention publicly to Jobs. He preferred to be compared with Bill Gates, whom he called "a very dangerous competitor," adding "there's nothing nicer I can say about someone than that." McNealy saw himself as one who reveled in no-holds-barred competition. On the golf course, when his companion would line up a putt, "I'm thinking with every brain wave: Miss!" In Gates, McNealy saw a kindred spirit. As for Jobs, he damned with faint praise, calling him a "product visionary," but omitting him from the ranks of formidable opponents.[322]

Jobs did not want to be relegated to a place of honor in a historical museum; he wanted to be included in the same fray as McNealy, Gates, and the others, and regarded as an equal. But at the NeXT-WORLD Expo, Jobs encountered the same indifference to the newly repositioned NeXT that he had two years earlier when he introduced the second generation of NeXT machines. Loyal NeXT fans showed up, but the rest of the industry paid little notice. Jobs's attempt to present a newly aggressive NeXT, hungry to enter the mainstream personal-computer market, was hurt by the incomplete nature of the NeXTSTEP 486 software. It was not ready for customers quite yet. It had to wait for a new revision of NeXT's basic operating system to be completed, which Jobs promised by the end of June 1992; NeXTSTEP 486 would be released, he said, by September, nine months after the announcement. The trade press yawned.

Despite the new marketing direction, NeXT in some ways remained much like the old company, self-styled insurgents trying to storm the ramparts of the establishment. In a special twelve-page advertising supplement that it ran in *The Wall Street Journal* to accompany the NeXTWORLD Expo announcements, NeXT invited curious readers to inspect the company and its software: "If you're intrigued by the revolution of object-oriented computing, we invite you to do what any self-respecting revolutionary would do: Come join us in a public demonstration."[323] NeXT's guerrilla tactics included distribution of a video that it had commissioned, showing a NeXT programmer going head-to-head with a Sun programmer, each given an identical assignment, competing to complete the code first. The playing field was far from level, however, and the predictable triumph of the young NeXT programmer was so hokey as to embarrass even NeXT's own partisans when the videotape was discussed on the NeXT-related electronic bulletin boards and in *NeXTWORLD* magazine.[324] Far more satisfying was the way that the NeXT machine was highly praised by an unlikely source, *Sunworld* magazine, which demonstrated its independence from its namesake company by rating the NeXT higher than Sun SPARCstations.[325] NeXT employees seized upon this story with understandable joy, but the story came and went without any tangible effect on the competitive fortunes of the two companies.

The one time that NeXT was able to kick Sun's shins really hard was when Sun made itself vulnerable by prepping its own salespeople about a competitive threat from NeXT. Someone at Sun—it still is not clear whether it was a lone sales manager in the field, as Sun later claimed, or whether it included others who were higher up—composed a memo for Sun's sales representatives that presented a list of arguments that could be used on customers to slow NeXT's inroads. It acknowledged that customers could use NeXTSTEP to write their own programs in a tenth the time and the NeXT machine itself set up easily, out of the box, in a matter of minutes (no one could ever make the same claim about Sun and other Unix computers). To compete with NeXT, Sun sales reps needed to "change the rules of the game" and steer the comparison away from NeXT's strength in comparatively rapid programming. Instead, Sun should emphasize the proprietary nature of the NeXT system; the absence of RISC processors; the small number of software applications that ran on the NeXT; the questions about its financial health. "In a delicate fashion," the memo suggested, "you need to question their viability. Will they be around 3 years from now?"

The memo fell into the hands of a Sun customer who also happened to be a NeXT customer, and was passed on to NeXT's offices in Redwood City, where a lengthy point-by-point response was drafted and distributed widely by NeXT's public relations firm. Much of NeXT's defense was weak or disingenuous. Bridling about Sun's mention of rumors that "Steve Jobs was using his own money to meet last month's payroll," the NeXT statement denied the rumor categorically and asserted that NeXT enjoyed the combined backing of Jobs, Perot, and Canon, "whose combined net worth exceeds $15 billion." This was more voodoo economics and disguised the painfully real financial difficulties that the company continued to endure out of public view. But the contents of Sun's charges and NeXT's responses were less important than the fact that Sun had been caught taking NeXT seriously enough to prepare its salespeople with a plan of counterattack.

For Jobs, this was a delicious moment of triumph. In a letter he addressed to NeXT customers who were sent the entire packet, Jobs said the documents were being widely distributed "so that you can personally see how desperate Sun has become in its fight against NeXT." Jobs also took the occasion to denounce the personal nature of some of Sun's questions about Jobs's management of NeXT ("Do you really want to put your future in Steve Jobs's hands?" was the crudest of several questions that Sun sales representatives were advised to raise when speaking with prospective customers). "This kind of unprofessional 'bullying' from Sun must stop," Jobs fumed in his letter. But in fact it was very welcome bullying because it seemed to mark progress toward Jobs's own goal of being regarded by Sun as a serious challenger. Better to be roughed up a bit than treated as so insignificant as to be beneath contempt.

Characteristically, Jobs and his NeXT employees took the good news and inflated it beyond reason. NeXT thought it had put Sun to rout. The premature celebration at NeXT led to new advertisements that carried the triumphant headlines "NeXT Casts Shadow Over Sun" and "Environmental Study Shows Damaging Effect of Sun." At Sun's own mini–trade show, Sunworld, held in April in Santa Clara, NeXT leased a booth right in the heart of enemy territory. It also displayed its tendentious NeXT vs. Sun videotape on sixteen monitors positioned to greet the show's attendees. On the last day, the trade show sponsor, World Expo Corporation, asked that the monitors be removed because it was "too much of a Sun-bash." The NeXT representative feigned indignation but was delighted. Here again was another big win: "We got to Sun enough that they put pressure to yank it." Maybe, NeXT hoped, it would get some favorable mention in the press again, as had the preceding Sun-NeXT war of memos.

No, the world spun serenely on its old axis, unaffected by what NeXT thought were earthshaking tremors created by its epic battle with Sun. No one other than NeXT seemed to be keeping score, and for all of its supposed victories over Sun, which NeXT liked to think of as a badly wounded giant, NeXT had little tangible to show for them. When Sun announced its financials for its 1992 fiscal year that ended in June, there were no visible wounds. Total revenue had grown to $3.59 billion; Sun's $370 million gain from the previous year[326] exceeded NeXT's total revenue by a factor of three. NeXT, on the other hand, watched its sales go down, not up, in the first quarter of 1992.[327] Profitability continued to elude the company in that quarter, and in the second quarter, too; Jobs vowed that everyone should redouble their efforts in the third quarter, yet again NeXT failed to break even. The volume of sales was too low, even for a slimmer company that had gotten the new religion of P & L's (profit and loss statements).

The boasts of robust sales growth in 1991 that Jobs had made in January 1992 made it embarrassing to talk about NeXT's sales performance in the year that followed. So NeXT delayed disclosing the numbers, procrastinating until the moment when it had better news to offer. In the meantime, NeXT did as it always had done, projecting an image of ascendant success. Todd Rulon-Miller resembled a loyal Stalin-era Communist Party apparatchik who could be counted on to denounce the Party line in the past as flawed and the Party line in the present as correct, no matter how many changes in the line he had survived. He told reporters, "We've cracked the code. We know how to sell these things now."[328] A skeptical observer might have added as a coda, if this were so, where was the proof? When Jobs gave a speech at the annual Hambrecht & Quist Technology Conference, a gathering of investment banking types serving high-technology industries, he avoided talking about financials and instead played on his strength, product demonstrations.[329] The *USA Today* said the audience was "wowed."[330]

Jobs also could put on display, as another element of the newly remade NeXT, a chief operating officer who was someone other than himself, a first in NeXT's seven-year history. After years of delay in conforming to what Canon had asked Jobs to do, in March 1992 Jobs appointed Peter van Cuylenburg as the new company president. Van Cuylenburg had almost come to NeXT the year before, and in the interim he had been passed over when the chief executive position had opened at his company, Mercury Communications.[331] When he arrived at NeXT, he was forty-three years old and had a reputation as someone who could stick to budgets. Jobs described van Cuylenburg as "someone who, if I was about to get run over at a crosswalk, I would feel good about leaving in charge of NeXT."[332] Van Cuylenburg, for his part, showed that he believed in the bright destiny of NeXT as the Billion-Dollar-Company-in-the-Making, which he predicted would happen within three years.[333] This love feast brings to mind the similar exchanges of fealty that had accompanied Jobs's recruitment of John Sculley to Apple. Jobs clearly did not want to run any risk, no matter how small, of a repeat of the personal debacle that had followed his relinquishing control to an older outsider in the earlier instance. This time, at NeXT, Jobs took organizational precautions, placing his new alter ego in a newly created Office of the President—shared with Jobs.

Van Cuylenburg set to work, revising budgets, impressing upon NeXT's staff a novel idea, that budgets should be regarded seriously. He introduced new "metrics," as he liked to call them, for measuring how well budgets were adhered to. At Sun Microsystems, or almost any other business one might name, the practices that van Cuylenburg were introducing were mundane and omnipresent; at NeXT, however, these limits marked a new era, at least in the sense of a more tightly run ship. But van Cuylenburg's new metrics had no direct effect upon the desirability of the NeXT computer in the competitive marketplace that lay beyond NeXT's unworldly white walls. The New NeXT needed NeXTSTEP 486 finished, out the door, widening NeXT's appeal. It was not released in the third quarter of 1992, as had been planned, because of delays in the new release of the underlying NeXT operating system. More delays followed, and NeXTSTEP 486 had to be put off for release in 1993, more than a year after its vaporous announcement at NeXTWORLD Expo. As long as prospective customers had no choice but to buy NeXT's own hardware in order to be able to use NeXT software, they would remain hesitant. NeXT still had not released a RISC-based machine or a multiprocessor machine, which could offer dramatic boosts in performance by harnessing more than one microprocessor; Sun had long had the former, and by the summer, with its new SPARCstation 10 series, now offered the latter in a smallish box suitable for the desktop, too. And when the prices of Intel-based personal computers went into virtual free fall during the summer of 1992—while NeXT's own prices remained unchanged—the price disparity widened. The latest generation of IBM-compatible computers with color could be found for well under $2,000, while the low-end NeXTstation Color machine ran about $9,000. Tiny NeXT could not keep up with the trends in either the workstation or the personal-computer worlds that squeezed it from above and below.

The network of independent computer dealers, which NeXT had just established the year before, began to fall apart as the dealers saw that NeXT could not attract a significant number of customers from off the street, while NeXT's own salespeople landed the few fat accounts that came NeXT's way. By the fall of 1992, the dealer network was in such disarray that NeXT was too embarrassed to publicly disclose a list of its dealers. *NeXTWORLD* magazine tried to put the best face on the situation: "NeXT has dealers. Really, it does. It just doesn't want us to publish a list of them for fear that other manufacturers will try to convert them to competitive products."[334] Readers who sought a name were referred to a telephone number. This stretched the limits of credulity, however: why would a customer be able to call the number and locate one of the mysterious NeXT dealers, while the competition could not?

With van Cuylenburg in place, the new NeXT also tried a different tack when facing the old problem of exhausting its capital. In June, when once again NeXT had run out of money, and once again had to go back to Canon for more, as well as dipping into Jobs's own pockets, van Cuylenburg made a public announcement that turned bad news into good. He said that NeXT had just received a $55 million line of credit from Canon and $10 million from Jobs. This was not to be interpreted as an indication of financial distress. Quite the contrary, van Cuylenburg explained. NeXT did not really *need* the money; it was simply nice to have access to additional capital as NeXT "grew"; he thought that the $65 million was roughly twice the amount that NeXT would need before going public. In any case, whether NeXT used the full amount or not, the financing was presented as a vote of confidence in NeXT, as "the final round of private financing." It would have been more accurate if van Cuylenburg had said that debtor's leverage had once again left Canon little choice but to cough up more money, yet Canon had summoned the courage to deliver conditions and an ultimatum to NeXT, which van Cuylenburg had not mentioned: in order to get the full amount, NeXT would have to meet certain sales milestones, and this rescue was really, *really* the last money that Canon would contribute. NeXT should expect no mercy if it came back to Canon begging for more. After Canon laid down the new law, NeXT's internal battle cry *do-or-die* resonated among its employees.

The tenuousness of NeXT's financial survival did not help morale. In 1992, NeXT suffered an acceleration of resignations, leaving few employees who had been recruited in the idealistic era when NeXT was dedicated solely to changing higher education. At the same time, NeXT also lost some of its key recent recruits, the most prominent being Mike Slade, the vice-president of marketing, who left after only a little more than a year at NeXT. Among the troops, Slade had earned respect after his inauspicious beginning at the company; he had helped NeXT develop a clearer marketing message than it had had before, during Jobs's tenure as the titular head of marketing. In disagreements with Jobs, Slade had proved himself an able combatant, who could give him a good fight. But like Dan'l Lewin, who had been his distant predecessor, Slade was eventually exhausted by working under Jobs, a superior who regarded his own prowess in marketing as surpassing that of anyone else, including his own head of marketing.

Symbolically, the biggest defection that NeXT suffered occurred in the summer of 1992, when Bud Tribble, the founder whose judgment Jobs had relied upon most heavily, resigned abruptly. The resignation alone was not so shocking. Over a period of years, attrition even among founders would be expected. Tribble had married cofounder Susan Barnes during NeXT's early years, and Barnes had resigned in 1991. When Tribble followed her a year later, it was not the fact that he departed so much as it was where he chose to go immediately after leaving NeXT that caused such consternation: he went over to the number-one enemy, the "mother of all competitors," Sun. That hurt. His official statement about his decision was brief; he said that he was joining Sun for the opportunity to work on innovative software environments and "get them on an awful lot of desktops," which left one to infer that he did not believe that NeXT's software was destined for "an awful lot of desktops."[335]

Jobs tried to blunt the negative impact of the news by reassuring the press that Tribble's departure did not indicate fundamental problems at NeXT. He maintained that "things are looking great here." Even without Tribble, "we now have the best team on the planet." Jobs attributed Tribble's unhappiness to his failure to secure a vote of confidence from NeXT's software engineers as prospective general manager of a newly created software division in the company.[336] To allay speculation among reporters that Tribble left because of the company's financial difficulties, NeXT promised that a financial report for the first two quarters of 1992 would be issued in July.[337] (July came and went, then August, September, October. . . . the report did not appear.)

Tribble's resignation did not leave as large a hole as one might have guessed. Jobs's contention that Tribble had been regarded as a poor manager was no exaggeration (even if one is tempted to also add: Steve Jobs is a curious one to point an accusatory finger at others in this regard). Tribble's attendance had been irregular much of the previous year due to illness or leaves of absence, and he was not at the apex of popularity among the members of his staff. The loss of his contribution to NeXT's business direction would arguably be more beneficial to NeXT, as was suggested above in the discussion of Tribble's initial resistance to the idea of adapting NeXT software for IBM-compatible computers. But nevertheless his decamping, which caught Jobs by surprise, and his choice of Sun as his new employer, raised more complicated questions than Jobs addressed when he briskly disposed of the news to control the damage.

One question concerned the intangible damage of a leak of NeXT's future plans to its most powerful competitor. The problem here, as in most cases, concerned information that resides within the cranium of an employee who jumps ship; rarely are actual documents transferred. In the case of Tribble going from NeXT to Sun in 1992, just as in the case of Tribble going from Apple to NeXT seven years earlier in 1985, the most that his former employer could charge was that Tribble *knew* too much. When he had left Apple, the result was a lawsuit, but Jobs was a codefendant in that instance. Now, Jobs found himself in a different role, as the aggrieved party, but given his own history he could hardly press a lawsuit as a plaintiff.

Tribble's move also raised questions about authorship. By 1992, it was abundantly clear that the NeXT computer's primary strength was its software, and if the company was ever to become profitable and grow, it would be due to its software advantage, not due to the hardware world of DSPs and optical disks and "Mainframe on a Chip" and all the rest that Jobs had once touted so enthusiastically. And if any single person deserved credit for bringing NeXT software into being, it was Bud Tribble. When Tribble left NeXT, Jobs wasted no time in revising the historical record, downplaying Tribble's contribution.[338] But a persuasive case could be made on Tribble's behalf, not just at NeXT, but also in the Macintosh group at Apple, where there too it was the software that ultimately had proven to be the greatest strength and it was Tribble who was an instrumental leader of the founding software team. It was a charmed record that Tribble carried with him to Sun, and one can understand why Scott McNealy was happy to add to his team's roster a player who upon retirement was certain to be inducted into the Hall of Fame of software designers. No matter what Tribble actually accomplished at Sun, he at the least brought an inspiring record, and for that alone was a lucky talisman for Sun to possess. It surely is not a coincidence that Bill Gates had recruited from Digital Equipment another Hall of Famer, David Cutler, the legendary designer of the system software that helped make VAX minicomputers so successful, to head up the team working on Windows NT. Even in the abstrusely technical world of operating systems, of massive programs that could consist of three million lines of code, where development requires teams of engineers and extensive collaboration—even here the success of the enterprise seemed dependent upon the contributions of a stellar individual.

And so companies pursue the star in the belief that the right person still makes all the difference, even in a technocratic age. The human eye has difficulty focusing on the group; it prefers the heroic individual. The beneficiary of this predilection has been Steve Jobs himself. If his celebrity had not blurred his own past and present, if others had not been disposed to inscribe upon his persona Midas-like powers, if he had not parlayed his exalted aura to secure $250 million to keep NeXT going, while he struggled to change the company again and again, using second, third, and fourth chances to try to find the elusive formula that would prove he did indeed have the touch, the story of his NeXT venture after Apple would have ended long ago.

Mr. Darwin, Welcome
to Las Vegas

A merican business has long been fond of English cousin Charles Darwin, or at least of a popular approximation of the Darwinian model of natural selection. If the brutality of business competition is assumed to be analogous to the world of biological competition—Lord Alfred Tennyson's famous phrase about nature, "Red in tooth and claw," seems no less apt in describing business—then companies that prevail appear to have the blessing of scientific ordination. The winners are *naturally* selected. Sun's Scott McNealy boiled the Darwinian metaphor down to its most vulgar distillate when he addressed Stanford MBA students in 1992: "You either eat someone for lunch, or you can be lunch."[339]

When Steve Jobs was still at Apple and enjoying a feeling of cosmic triumph, he also invoked Darwinian metaphors. When an interviewer asked him in early 1985 how Jobs felt about older companies that had to scramble to catch up with the younger ones, Jobs said that it was inevitable that the older companies would fail and perish. He explained, "That's why I think death is the most wonderful invention of life. It purges the system of these old models that are obsolete."[340] He was not even thirty years old and could then treat death in business with the same equanimity as death in the world of biology; equanimity was inversely proportional to proximity. But when he no longer found himself perched on the mountaintop, when he was forced to start over, as head of NeXT, a small start-up struggling to climb up on to solid land, his perspective on Darwinian struggle naturally underwent a similarly dramatic change. The prospect that his new company might die could not be accepted so lightly, yet who could be blamed for premature death? NeXT's nearest competitors, Apple, Sun, and Microsoft, were not old enough themselves to fit Jobs's earlier theory that the old must certainly perish to make way for the new. Nor could Jobs continue to talk about winning in business competition as the manifestation of technical superiority; to do so would be to concede too much credit to his larger rivals. Jobs, like everyone else in business, invoked the Darwinian metaphor only when it was convenient for his own purposes.

Darwinian theory does provide powerfully suggestive images. The parallel nature of competition in biology and in business is most striking at the annual Fall Comdex show in Las Vegas, where virtually every company in the personal-computer industry converges for a five-day orgy of demonstrations, sales pitches, and one-upmanship. The show, which began modestly enough in 1979 with only about 150 companies represented, had grown in tandem with the industry itself so that the 1992 show presented booths representing more than 2,000 companies, from A4 Tech, Aadtech Micro Systems, Aamazing Technologies (the length that some companies go to in order to be listed at the head of alphabetical lists is, well, aamazing) to ZSoft, ZyLAB, and ZyXEL.

To speak of *booths* at Comdex is a misnomer; what most companies set up are miniature worlds, each bordered by giant plexiglass dividers and subdivided with partitions into amphitheaters for demonstrations, movie minitheaters, and clusters and rows of kiosks displaying computers. The show has grown so large that it fills up two separate convention centers, attached annexes, and exhibition space at four hotels. The decision about which company gets to exhibit where is determined not by size or influence but by the longevity of the company's appearances at the show. It is a system that is commendably evenhanded—everyone pays the organizers the same rate per square foot, but the selection process penalizes withdrawal so heavily that companies must return each year or forfeit their place in the queue to select their exhibit space.

It is extremely costly for the exhibiting company to come. The show organizers charged $38 per square foot in 1992 for the privilege of setting up a display for the five days (if the show ran year-round, that rate would work out to an annual lease of $2,774 per square foot!). The two companies that occupied the most area were IBM and Microsoft, which leased 35,000 and 32,500 square feet, respectively, which meant that they each paid more than $1.2 million just for the privilege of setting up exhibits for the show. The costs of shipping and installing the exhibits and sending out a phalanx of company representatives to Las Vegas, as well as various ancillary charges, were also burdensome. On the other side, each attendee also paid dearly for the privilege of seeing the displays, anything from $75 for access to exhibits only to $450 for special programs in selected areas such as computer networking or corporate computing. Despite the costs, attendance climbed over the years, growing from 4,000 in 1979 to more than 145,000 in 1992. No other event offered such a convenient vantage point to see the entire personal-computer industry compressed into one place. One irony in the phenomenal growth of Comdex was the old-fashioned nature of the persistent attraction of doing comparison shopping, even though the wares that the industry offered embodied the most sophisticated technology of the moment. Even in an age of advanced telecommunication, no substitute had been found for customers and vendors meeting in the flesh, shaking hands and kicking tires. Veterans of previous Comdex shows invariably complained about the inconveniences and the inhuman scale of the show, yet they came back, haunted by the fear of missing the opportunity to remain current.

With twenty miles of aisles and 1.2 million square feet of exhibit area filled with clamoring vendors, each hell-bent on making a better impression than its competitors, the Comdex show resembled an indoor jungle, and it was certainly no less noisy than a real one. Microphones and sound systems amplified the patter of company representatives who performed continuous demonstrations of software; movies and videos ran continuously; music poured out of speakers everywhere; and above all was the roar of tens of thousands of unamplified human voices combined in one place. In one of the IBM exhibits in the center of this cacophony, at a kiosk which was supposed to show off IBM's new software that permitted an inexpensive personal computer to recognize ordinary human speech, the IBM staff was frustrated when the software failed to perform as it had in the laboratory. When the staff members measured the noise level, the suspected problem was confirmed: the ambient noise was more than 80 decibels, approaching the benchmarks of jet takeoffs and jackhammers.

An IBM or a Microsoft could rise above the noise of the Comdex pandemonium by brute force, by commandeering a wide swath of space within the jungle to permit its message to be heard. Smaller companies used other techniques, such as withholding the unveiling of anticipated new products until the show, ingeniously using advertising space throughout Las Vegas, or aggressively pursuing the attention of the press who covered Comdex (IBM and Microsoft used these techniques, too). Gimmickry was the desperate resort of some: a magician here, an oversized slot-machine dispensing software there, a fashion show with professional female models and laser lights over there. For computer companies that had not come to Comdex before, Las Vegas was not for the faint of heart.

NeXT finally made its first appearance at the Fall 1992 Comdex, and fainthearted is the most charitable way of describing its demeanor upon its moment of entry. The 1992 Comdex show also happened to be the first time that Sun Microsystems made a serious run at garnering the attention of the personal-computer world, and the two companies presented an interesting pair. Given the competitive personality of Scott McNealy, Sun naturally was better prepared to enter the fray than NeXT. Sun leased 4,800 square feet of exhibit space, in which it could show off its new low-priced color workstation, the SPARCclassic, brought out just in time for Comdex. Based on a RISC microprocessor, the Sun machine was priced aggressively at an unheard-of $3,995. Sun flew one hundred of its own people to Las Vegas to help get the word out, and it rented space on the front of the Las Vegas Convention Center where it hung a giant banner that could not escape the attention of everyone who attended. Even though it did not make nearly the same investment at Comdex as IBM, Sun succeeded in making its arrival known.

NeXT did not do so well. Confronted with the universal problem shared by everyone other than IBM and Microsoft, of being swallowed up in the din, NeXT chose to remain aloof, or as a spokesperson put it, NeXT decided it would have been very hard "to rise above the clutter." So instead of leasing exhibit space, it rented a small 600-square foot meeting room, which was located off the beaten track, on the second floor of an annex to an annex. Though NeXT was officially at Comdex, it was there just barely, manifesting the same smug confidence that had plagued its entire history: it did not have to extend itself to meet customers, customers would come to it. Even when it came to setting its hours, NeXT felt compelled to assert its individuality: the other exhibits at the convention center opened five days, beginning at 10:00 each day; NeXT's, four days, beginning at 1:00.

NeXT had no new computer hardware to show, nor had it lowered its prices to make its machines more competitive with the falling prices of Unix workstations, Apple Macintoshes, and IBM-compatible personal computers. Its principal exhibit was a prototype of its NeXTSTEP 486 software that ran on IBM-compatible machines, but which NeXT had to explain would not be ready for release for another eight months. Its principal weapon in hand-to-hand combat with its foes was, as always, its resident celebrity, Steve Jobs.

Jobs was one of five chief executive officers of computer companies who were given separate hours to address a hotel auditorium at different times during the Comdex show. Bill Gates spoke the day before Jobs did, and once again spoke of the virtues of evolutionary improvements, showing new applications that had been devised for Microsoft's Windows. He seemed relaxed and was generous in sharing the stage with others, such as a doctor, a banker, and a school kid, each of whom was invited to show off a particular program. Gates had a favorable comment for every revelation made by his invited guests—"neat," "wow," "that was really super," "that's fantastic," and "that's swell," to note a sampling—but even if the words came off as boyish, the overall effect of the presentations was effective: with the help of imaginative customers, Microsoft software was creating wholly new uses for inexpensive personal computers, whether assembling electronic encyclopedias that used video clips instead of static illustrations, or linking personal computers to files scattered on a bank's larger mainframe computers. (The proceedings were lightened by an occasional extemporaneous touch, as when the banker invited his onstage host, the richest person in America, to open an account at his bank.)

When Steve Jobs had his turn the next day, he was the sole actor on-stage, and he kept things simple. Using his binary cosmology, the world according to Jobs consisted of two entities only—Microsoft and NeXT, "the only serious challenge to Microsoft." Just as he had done before he founded NeXT, when he had reduced the world to an elemental pairing, Apple and IBM, representing innovation and stagnation, good and evil, once again he simplified his business woes into a convenient bogey, Microsoft. When Jobs warned the crowd that "we're in a very precarious position," the "we" referred not to NeXT but to the entire computer industry; everyone, Jobs said, was equally in peril because "whenever monopolies come into play, innovation disappears." He implied that support of NeXT and NeXT's forthcoming 486 software was the *world*'s last hope of keeping the fire of innovation alive, before it was extinguished by the enveloping darkness of Gates's evil empire.

This was a comforting way for Jobs and NeXT to look at their bewildering surroundings, filled with so many competitors in addition to Microsoft. Viewed from a more detached perspective, NeXT did not occupy a role in a morality play, the Good Guy pitted against the villainous Microsoft, or Sun Microsystems, or any of the other protagonists. NeXT lived in a competitive ecology that was as implacably amoral as mountain wilderness; the life and death of individual organisms made no difference to the system.

It would diminish Jobs's own inflated self-image if he were to acknowledge just how small a place he, or any other single person, occupied within the vastness of the ecological system that he had chosen for his ambitions (and standing amidst Comdex, one could not ignore how vast indeed the jungle was). But if Jobs had only been willing to think of the computer industry as an ecological system whose workings resemble the operations of a Darwinian model, he would find other compensations. The recent work of paleontologist Stephen Jay Gould, for example, has extended Darwin's work on evolution to show how the diversity of life forms diminished early in natural history, leaving survivors who were lucky more than they were necessarily the fittest. Gould emphasizes the overlooked importance of contingency: "Little quirks at the outset, occurring for no particular reason, unleash cascades of consequences that make a particular future seem inevitable in retrospect." The disappearance of fundamentally different anatomical types in the explosion of multicellular animal types in the Cambrian period could not have been predicted by properties of the organisms themselves,[341] a sophisticated application of the old adage that timing is everything.

It would seem to apply to the rise and fall of computer companies no less than it does to the Cambrian fossils unearthed in Canada's Burgess Shale. Just as nature locked on to a few anatomical types for the evolution of multicellular organisms, effectively foreclosing other directions, so too one can see the operation of a similar mechanism that makes survival increasingly difficult for a nonstandard challenger in the Darwinian world of computer-industry competition. And NeXT can find some solace in speculation about how much more successful it might have been if certain events, seen as minor at the time, such as the delay in the completion of its first machine, or its decision not to come to Comdex in 1991, had not set in motion adverse "cascades of consequences," to use Gould's expression. NeXT's difficulties were *not* overdetermined by some master script in the heavens.

NeXT could also use evolutionary theory to find comfort in other examples found in the history of technology, such as the contest between steam- and gasoline-powered automobile engines in the early twentieth century. One could argue that the contest between the two was actually much closer than we have come to believe, and was decided more by managerial failings on the part of the Stanley brothers, the most successful of the steam car builders, than by technical shortcomings.[342] Or a more recent example of technological competition would be in the contest between videotape formats: Sony's Beta format, though technically superior, was pushed out by a coalition of companies backing the VHS format for a simple negative reason—it was *not* Sony's. The best technology does not always win.

Recent work in sociobiology tells us that nature is not a sweepstakes involving the simple survival of each individual organism but rather is a different kind of evolutionary game, one in which the perpetuation of genes is primary. The genes may be those of one's own, or they may be those of one's kin, real or fictive (altruism, found in many places in the animal kingdom, is otherwise inexplicable in the crude Darwinism that excludes this possibility). Sociobiology provides us with suggestive ways to think about business as a system rather than as a congeries of individual protozoa. In an essay titled "Why the Reckless Survive," anthropologist Melvin Konner suggests that groups that contain "high-risk" individuals—the type of person who in early times would not have hesitated to snatch a child from a pack of wild dogs or attempt to arrest an approaching wildfire—are more likely as a group to possess collectively "Darwinian fitness" and survive.[343] The high-risk person suffers higher mortality, but the group as a whole benefits, thus increasing the likelihood of perpetuation of the genes.

Here is where NeXT's doleful record cannot be entirely exonerated by the biological metaphor, which is after all a figure of speech, not an explanation. Unlike extinct species whose fate was determined by exogenous shocks or seemingly serendipitous events completely out of their control, the individuals at NeXT were sentient beings equipped with five senses who deliberately made decisions that took them down certain paths and not down others. What should have been an evolutionary blessing, the powers of historical memory, proved especially debilitating for the members of NeXT because they continued to act upon the lessons that they drew from personal experiences in the computer industry in the early 1980s that were a poor guide for navigation in the late 1980s. Everyone pays tribute to the trite observation that we live in times of rapid change, but NeXT's contributors failed to appreciate just how rapid the pace, how swiftly the recipes from their past were rendered obsolete. The only way to avoid falling behind is to pay close attention, which is an imperative that Steve Jobs and his followers felt no need to follow. The world was to pay attention to them, not the reverse. This was deliberate, and not an act of nature, though its effect on NeXT was as calamitous as a new Ice Age would have been.

At his talk at Fall Comdex, Jobs asked his audience to agree with his solipsistic assumption that because NeXT had not been successful, therefore innovation in the computer industry was seriously in peril. He was wrong, however. The evolutionary jungle's most dominant organism, Microsoft, was far from inert. It could boast in late 1992 of offering many of the things that NeXT had unveiled in 1988. In his Comdex talk, Gates spoke of the importance of "visual development" and "object orientation," the very strengths of NeXT's software. New revisions of Microsoft's Visual Basic; the introduction of Microsoft's new easy-to-use database program Access; and voice-annotation capabilities and special soundboards for personal computers further diminished NeXT's claim of offering unique capabilities. NeXT also lost its unique claim to an unconventional spreadsheet program unavailable elsewhere: Lotus moved its Improv to Windows, with new features that made it easier to use than its NeXT version; it also added programming capabilities that its NeXT predecessor lacked.[344] Now it would be Microsoft, not NeXT, which could boast of having the most advanced spreadsheet on the market. Lotus was simply going where the customers were. The NeXT version of Improv had sold in numbers too embarrassing to be revealed; the Windows version, however, helped by a low introductory price, sold 125,000 units in its first month.[345]

We have seen how computer industry ecology already had been influenced by the presence of even a little creature like NeXT: The fear of what early NeXT might produce impelled Sun Microsystems in 1987 to launch the new line of inexpensive workstations that transformed Sun and then the industry. Steve Jobs was fond of invoking the sociobiological metaphor himself. When he had left Apple in 1985, he told a newspaper reporter that he wanted Apple "to remain great" because "my genes are there"[346] (privately, he was not so gracious and the favorable disposition of his genes was rendered secondary to his desire for revenge). A biosystem has many elements, and NeXT, as the self-styled provocateur, has made contributions to the local ecology, regardless of whether NeXT itself benefited.

Still, Jobs and NeXT had not succeeded in coming close to dominating the jungle, or moving out from the shadows of their own history. When Jobs was inducted in 1992 into *Fortune*'s National Business Hall of Fame, he again was the youngster in the group, another instance of precocious accomplishment, but he was singled out for this Hall of Fame because of his work years earlier at Apple, and not because of NeXT.[347] The business community had not demanded the repetition of past success before honoring him; it looked to Jobs as the house philosopher for the personal-computer industry, the one who made everyone feel fortunate to be working at a historically significant moment. The "petrochemical revolution" of one hundred years ago freed mechanical energy, Jobs had said; the information revolution, just begun, frees intellectual energy, and will dwarf the petrochemical revolution in its impact.[348]

The concern about History, about "poking the world" in a lasting way, fit with Jobs's choice of defining his own identity as something other than a businessperson. He was a self-described *toolmaker* or *creative* person, and he tried to use his preoccupation with History as a marketing tool for NeXT, addressing Wall Street analysts, for example, as if he were the Thomas Jefferson of the Age of Technology, declaring "every now and then there needs to be a discontiguous [*sic*] break, and you have to rebuild the world."[349] This was precisely what Bill Gates argued was not necessary now, and certainly most business customers did not leap to embrace the idea of "discontiguous breaks" and the willful obsolescence of past investments. But Jobs always understood that if he were to achieve his obsessive aim of a lasting place in History, he could not settle for the incremental improvements of the Gateses and the rest of the pack of "evolutionary" improvers; he would have to differentiate himself with the bold gesture, as he had done with the Macintosh. He told his NeXT customers, "If you want to jump forward, you really can't service history," referring to the older computers as "history." But he was talking less about his customers' needs than about his own.[350]

Jobs needed NeXT to thrive to assuage his own historical insecurities, a need not shared by his less-famous confederates. As much as they too wanted NeXT to succeed, they came to realize, one by one, that Jobs's psychological desperation was his own problem; no one else had reason to fuse their own personal identity so completely with the company as had Jobs. The Fall Comdex show marked the last event in which Jobs was able to present to the world a façade that all continued to be well at NeXT. Shortly before and after the show, NeXT lost additional waves of senior people who joined Slade and Tribble for greener pastures elsewhere. Among the departees were William Parkhurst, one of the software gurus who was an instrumental designer of NeXTSTEP, and Donna Simonides, who had been in charge of recruiting and keeping happy the outside software developers who wrote for the NeXT software standard. According to Jobs, NeXTSTEP 486 would soon make NeXT a major success, but two of his own senior managers who directly oversaw NeXTSTEP 486's completion and related marketing plans, Bruce Martin and Jeff Spirer, decided to leave NeXT—and join Sun Microsystems. Added to these defections, NeXT's vice-president of sales, Todd Rulon-Miller, who was one of the longest-surviving and most loyal of Jobs's lieutenants at NeXT, and a person whose position in sales presumably permitted him to see the likelihood of Jobs's ambitions being realized in the marketplace, decided that he, too, would not stay.

The high-level resignations continued: In January 1993, Rich Page, the last of the two remaining cofounders with Jobs, tendered his resignation. Page had been the vice-president in charge of hardware, so his departure set off much speculation that NeXT was preparing to stop production of NeXT computers and retreat to selling software only. Jobs and NeXT president Peter van Cuylenburg were unwilling to acknowledge the defeat that such news would reveal, and they needed to stall for time while NeXTSTEP 486 was readied. If their company mishandled the transition, it faced the likelihood that its revenue would quickly plunge literally to zero. At the time of Page's resignation, NeXT was still months away from being able to put a bug-free NeXTSTEP 486 on the market. Its release had been delayed because numerous, serious bugs had been belatedly discovered in the most recent 3.0 version of the original NeXT software upon which NeXTSTEP 486 software would be based. If NeXT revealed at that point that it planned to drop its own computer hardware, prospective customers would not purchase machines that would soon be orphaned.

NeXT continued to say officially that no changes were being planned. Attempting to replace the news about Page with something more positive, NeXT decided to relax a mid-1992 vow of not publicly releasing any financial information about the company until the time of its planned initial public offering and instead issued the sunny press release "NeXT Profitable in Q4 '92," summoning the selective numbers of voodoo economics once again to project the message that all was well. But by changing the boilerplate description of NeXT at the end, describing the company as a producer of software and mentioning nothing about hardware, the release foreshadowed impending change. The extent of change, however, caught everyone by surprise, when the bombshell arrived on Black Tuesday, February 9th, and more than half of Jobs's employees learned that they had lost their jobs.

Perhaps it had been his visit to Comdex that had opened Jobs's eyes to the need to jettison hardware and try to survive as a software-only company. Before Comdex, at an off-site company retreat held in September, Jobs had told his employees that the company's salvation would be a new generation of computers that his company was readying, a long-delayed RISC-based workstation. One of his employees had asked about the importance of NeXTSTEP 486, and Jobs had given it short shrift: it would only appeal to a small market and be sold in limited quantities, he had explained then. Now, in February, the almost completed NeXT RISC Workstation had disappeared, and Jobs had a wholly different pitch. He had seen the future, and its name was software.

In order to make a success of a reinvented company that exclusively sold and licensed high-end operating system software for

Intel-based 486 personal computers made by others, Jobs had to join battle with a dismaying roster of competitors: Gates's Microsoft, which was selling its Windows software at the rate of about a *million* copies a month, and which was readying its Unix-like successor, Windows NT, for release; IBM, which as a corporate entity had experienced unprecedented losses but still had managed to ship a respectable two million copies of its OS/2 software between March 1992 and March 1993[351] (Jobs, when asked in January 1993 by a reporter whether he would be interested in the position of CEO at IBM, was undeterred by his own inability to turn a profit at NeXT and brightly answered "Sure!");[352] networking giant Novell, which had recently committed $350 million to purchase Unix Systems Laboratories from AT&T in order to prepare to meet the impending threat from Microsoft's Windows NT;[353] Sun Microsystems, whose Solaris operating system was soon to arrive on Intel computers; Santa Cruz Operation, whose version of Unix already had a large installed base on such machines; and other competitors were entrenched as well. How could Jobs possibly convince himself that he could do well in the face of such opposition? Simple. By linguistic ingenuity, he made all of these operating systems disappear instantly. NeXTSTEP for Intel, as he rechristened the NeXT-STEP 486 software, belonged to an uncrowded special category, Jobs said, of *object-oriented* operating systems (recall his creation a few years earlier of a new category called *professional workstations* which permitted him to paint out most of Sun's sales). Jobs regarded Windows NT and the others as not even worthy of dismissal. The only competitors that he saw for his NeXTSTEP were Microsoft's Cairo, which would be the successor to Windows NT, and the unnamed software that would eventually be released from Taligent, one of IBM and Apple's joint ventures. Because neither Cairo nor Taligent's software was close to release, NeXT boasted in a *Wall Street Journal* advertisement in February 1993 that "for at least two years, we won't even have a competitor."[354]

By this and other indications at the time of the transformation of

NeXT into a software company, Jobs had failed to learn from his timid visit to Comdex the preceding November that staying aloof is not effective; predators do not disappear simply by closing one's eyes and indulging in vapid wishfulness. NeXT was also a bit premature in advertising in February that "our NeXTSTEP software is here today, already polished and perfected in its third release." It was far from perfected; the infestation of bugs discovered in its third release, after all, had forced the delay in the completion of NeXTSTEP for Intel, which had not even entered beta testing at the time that NeXT ran advertisements announcing that "today, we're letting out" the software that "had been locked in a black box."[355]

It was also difficult to understand why Jobs, after throwing down the gauntlet to Microsoft, IBM, and Apple, would choose that moment of all times, when virtually no experienced managers were still left at NeXT, to oust the one person whose managerial abilities in the eyes of worried NeXT customers still remained credible— Peter van Cuylenburg, NeXT's president and chief operating officer, the one whom Jobs only a year before had said "if I was about to get run over at a crosswalk, I would feel good about leaving in charge of NeXT." Jobs pushed van Cuylenburg out not because Jobs had someone else he wished to appoint as president in van Cuylenburg's place; Jobs simply wanted to become president of the company again himself, in addition to retaining his title of chairman. When Jobs decided to regain complete control without sharing power with anyone, van Cuylenburg was left without a position.[356] After serving loyally as the hatchet man who laid off a majority of NeXT's employees, he discovered that he too was not exempt from the executioner's blade. Why would Jobs isolate himself by eliminating van Cuylenburg, when NeXT had launched a noisy assault upon Microsoft? It appeared that Jobs was preparing for eschatological drama, the resolution of his longstanding rivalry with Bill Gates; it would be just him and Gates, mano a mano.

Jobs's self-imposed isolation inspired a satirical "news report" posted on a nationwide electronic bulletin board by Peter Wayner that poked fun at the resemblance between recent events at NeXT headquarters in Redwood City, California, and the contemporaneous stand-off between police and David Koresh, the religious leader in a compound in Waco, Texas. Reporting that "no progress in negotiations with charismatic cult leader Steve Jobs" had been achieved, fictional authorities were said to be worried that "Jobs will fulfill his own apocalyptic prophecies, a worry reinforced when the loudspeakers carry Jobs's own speeches—typically beginning with a chilling 'I want to welcome you to the Next World.' "[357]

Jobs's isolation was a serious business matter, however. By March 1993, as Microsoft's Windows NT software neared release, even multi-billion-dollar companies like Sun Microsystems, Novell, Hewlett-Packard, and IBM felt inadequate to meet the threat independently. These four, along with the Santa Cruz Operation, joined together in March 1993 to announce an end to their squabbling and a timetable for adopting a common approach in modifying their differing Unix recipes in interfaces, networking, and other areas, so that software applications would share a single "dashboard" and look and work the same on disparate brands of Unix computers. The announcement drew considerable attention.[358] The alliance of bitterly rivalrous companies showed how seriously the rest of the computer industry regarded the competitive threat of Microsoft. And *The Wall Street Journal* noted that NeXT's conspicuous absence in the coalition dealt another "serious blow to the already reeling NeXT." Ed Zander, Sun's software chief, explained that NeXT's software had been considered by the group as a possible joint standard to be adopted, but was passed over in favor of one with a much larger installed base of customers.[359]

Jobs reacted to this unfavorable publicity with explanations that were an admixture of paranoia and sophistry that attempted to convert an apparent setback into a triumph. Addressing the remaining survivalists at NeXT, Jobs said that *The Wall Street Journal* had been duped by Sun's public relations department, which he said had "worked overtime to portray the alliance having Sun at the epicenter" and had used "slander and lies" once again to besmirch NeXT's good name. Do not pay any attention to the story, he reassured his employees. The day's announcements actually represented "a serious victory for NeXT" (it was not easy to grasp his reasoning—why would the fact that the alliance had rejected some software standards offered by rivals, as well as rejecting NeXT's, represent "a serious victory" for NeXT?). In Jobs's view, Sun clearly was "growing more desperate" and was striking out at NeXT because "we represent a real threat to their aspirations to become a major software player."

It was *others* who had been rejected. It was *others* who were scared. It was *others* who were desperate. It was *others* who resorted to slander and lies. With Jobs's dream of the NeXT billion-dollar-company in jeopardy, with only a handful of hardy employees left and his one remaining product still unfinished and unreleased, after spending $250 million of capital and enduring eight long years of red ink to reach this dispiriting point, it should not be surprising that Jobs conjured a demonized *other* world to rally his believers. But this had always been Jobs's predilection; only the names— IBM, then Apple, now Sun and Microsoft—had changed over time. The same script played over and over in his mind: it was the forces of light versus darkness, brilliance versus mediocrity, revolution versus complacency. The bad guys always were threatened by the good guy, always trembled at the thought of the potency of his ideas, always were out to get him. Is such thinking best categorized as a tenacious defensiveness, well-suited to a brutally competitive landscape? Or rather is such thinking better viewed as delusional and disabling, poorly suited to a fight for survival?

If we return to the beginning of the end game, we might say that it was fitting that Las Vegas had served as the host for Comdex, for what turned out to have been NeXT's debut in the wilds of personal computer competition, far from the cloistered safety of its offices or the rented symphony halls. In Las Vegas, NeXT could pretend just like everyone else that one can start fresh with each roll of the dice, unburdened by history. To carry on the fight for survival amidst so many larger competitors, NeXT averted its eyes from the paralyzing facts of Darwinian decimation. As Gould points out, the Latin root of *decimate* means "to take one in ten," referring to groups of Roman soldiers guilty of mutiny or cowardice, among whom one in ten was selected by lot and put to death. The same element of randomness is found in the selection of anatomical plans in nature, but the odds are reversed: *nine* of ten disappear, making survival all the more dear.[360] In Las Vegas, the daily decimation of the hopes of gamblers never appears to tarnish its allure, and in business the same irrational defiance of the odds enables hope to be constantly replenished by ambition. If one was lucky enough to win a jackpot once, one will always hear a nagging whisper, that with another roll of the dice, another spin of the wheel, another pull on the handle, the prize will come again.

Acknowledgments

The notes that follow credit the published sources that were helpful. I wish that I could as easily acknowledge the contributions of the 160 individuals that I interviewed in the course of writing the book, but Silicon Valley remains a place filled with ambivalence about speaking publicly about one's work: the desire to contribute to the collective memory that we will call history is counterbalanced by a powerful corporate ethos that sanctifies silence as golden. I, for one, regard my interviewees' willingness to speak with me and contribute to the historical record to constitute acts of kindness, not indiscretion, but I am respectful of the local culture and here will simply thank them collectively and anonymously.

As I was readying the manuscript for publication, a number of individuals made especially valuable contributions, and I am grateful for the insights of Stephan Adams, David Besemer, Max Henry, Gail Hershatter, Arjen Maarleveld, Laura Snapp, and Greg Stross.

Funding for a portion of the research was provided by the National Endowment for the Humanities and San Jose State University.

Before this book was conceived, Elizabeth Kaplan pulled me dazed from a figurative train wreck, became my agent, and then guided me on the recuperative path that led to this completed work. My editor, Lee Goerner, gently helped me reach the end.

R. S.
March 1993

Notes

Notes to Introduction

1. Allison Thomas Associates, NeXT press release, "NeXT Profitable in Q4 '92," 21 January 1993.
2. "Steve's Gone Soft," *Unix World*, April 1993, p. 43.
3. "Next Inc., Citing Its Workstation Sales, Posts First Quarterly Operating Profit," *Wall Street Journal*, 22 January 1993.
4. "Steve's Gone Soft," *Unix World*, April 1993, p. 43.
5. "Next Axes Hardware," *San Jose Mercury News*, 10 February 1993.
6. "NeXT's Black Box May Be the Next to Go," *Business Week*, 25 January 1993, p. 38.
7. "Co-Founder, More Key Employees Leave Struggling Next," *San Jose Mercury News*, 9 January 1993.
8. "NeXT's Black Box May Be the Next To Go," *Business Week*, 25 January 1993, p. 38.
9. "What Next's Announcement Did Not Say," *San Jose Mercury News*, 27 January 1993.
10. "Next's Sales Are Respectable But Not Sizzling," *San Francisco Chronicle*, 19 January 1993.
11. Allison Thomas Associates, NeXT press release, "NeXT to Become Software Company," 10 February 1993; "Downsizing Trend Going Too Far, Sullivan Says," *Nextworld Extra*, March 1993, p. 10.
12. "Next Inc. to Limit Its Business to Software," *New York Times*, 10 February 1993.
13. Allison Thomas Associates, NeXT press release, "NeXT to Become Software Company," 10 February 1993.
14. "Steve Jobs' NeXT Big Gamble," *Fortune*, 8 February 1993, p. 99.

15. NeXT brochure, "On May 25, NeXT Completes the Most Remarkable Transformation in Recent Years in the Industry," n.d.
16. "Key Officer of Next Inc. Is Resigning," *New York Times*, 17 March 1993; "The 'NextStep' for Next Is Finding a Software Developer," *Infoworld*, 22 March 1993, p. 6.
17. "The Forbes Four Hundred," *Forbes*, 13 September 1982, p. 156.
18. "The Forbes Four Hundred," *Forbes*, 27 October 1986, p. 173.
19. "The Richest People in America," *Forbes*, 21 October 1991, pp. 150, 153, 156.
20. Cited in Mansel G. Blackford, *The Rise of Modern Business in Great Britain, the United States, and Japan* (Chapel Hill: University of North Carolina Press, 1988), p. 59.
21. Brit Hume, "Steve Jobs Pulls Ahead of Microsoft Rival in Race for PC Supremacy," *Washington Post*, 31 October 1988.
22. Hume, "Steve Jobs Pulls Ahead," *Washington Post*.
23. "Next Pulls No Punches," *Computer Reseller News*, 4 December 1989.
24. Reported by *Infoworld*'s Peggy Watt. Quoted in Robert X. Cringely, *Accidental Empires: How the Boys of Silicon Valley Make Their Millions, Battle Foreign Competition, and Still Can't Get a Date* (Reading, Mass.: Addison-Wesley, 1992), p. 311.
25. "IBM's Deal May Hurt Gates," *PC Week*, 24 October 1988, p. 76.
26. "A PC Trailblazer Applies Charisma in the Drive to Bring Out His Next," *Philadelphia Inquirer*, 21 May 1989.
27. "Computer Moguls' Gathering Resembles Potshot Video Game," *Washington Post*, 27 September 1989.
28. Cover, *Forbes*, 19 October 1992.
29. "Gates's Bid to Acquire Art Images for Computers is Coolly Received," *Wall Street Journal*, 11 February 1992.
30. "Jobs and Gates Together," *Fortune*, 26 August 1991, pp. 50–54.
31. Peter C. Wensberg, *Land's Polaroid: A Company and the Man Who Invented It* (Boston: Houghton Mifflin, 1987) pp. 3, 22.
32. Steven Levy, "The Whiz Kids Meet Darth Vader," *Rolling Stone*, 1 March 1984, p. 41.
33. "Playboy Interview: Steven Jobs," *Playboy*, February 1985, p. 2.
34. Joseph Nocera, "The Second Coming of Steven Jobs," *Esquire*, December 1986, p. 94.
35. "Entrepreneur of the Decade," *Inc.*, April 1989, p. 124.

Notes to Chapters

1. "Inside the PARC: The 'Information Addicts,' " *IEEE Spectrum*, October 1985, p. 62.
2. Steven Levy, "Hackers in Paradise," *Rolling Stone*, 15 April 1982, p. 45.
3. "Inside the PARC: The 'Information Addicts,' " *IEEE Spectrum*, October 1985, p. 66.
4. Butler W. Lampson, "Personal Distributed Computing: The Alto and Ethernet

Software," in Adele Goldberg, ed., *A History of Personal Workstations* (New York: ACM Press, 1988), p. 295.

5. Stewart Brand, "Spacewar," *Rolling Stone*, 7 December 1972, p. 54.

6. C. P. Thacker, et al., "Alto: A Personal Computer," in Daniel P. Siewiorek, C. Gordon Bell, and Allen Newell, eds., *Computer Structures: Principles and Examples* (New York: McGraw-Hill, 1982), p. 571.

7. "Participants Discussion for Thacker and Lampson," in Adele Goldberg, ed., *A History of Personal Workstations* (New York: ACM Press, 1988), pp. 342.

8. "Inside the PARC: The 'Information Addicts,' " *IEEE Spectrum*, October 1985, p. 68.

9. "The Lab That Ran Away From Xerox," *Fortune*, 5 September 1983, p. 100.

10. Douglas K. Smith and Robert C. Alexander, *Fumbling the Future: How Xerox Invented, Then Ignored, The First Personal Computer* (New York: William Morrow, 1988), pp. 75–76.

11. Smith and Alexander, *Fumbling the Future*, pp. 147–148.

12. Lampson, "Personal Distributed Computing: The Alto and Ethernet Software," p. 296.

13. "Inside the PARC: The 'Information Addicts,' " *IEEE Spectrum*, October 1985, p. 64.

14. Chuck Thacker, "Personal Distributed Computing: The Alto and Ethernet Hardware," in Adele Goldberg, ed., *A History of Personal Workstations* (New York: ACM Press, 1988), p. 273.

15. Susan Lammers, *Programmers at Work* (Redmond, Washington: Microsoft Press, 1986), pp. 21–22.

16. Lammers, *Programmers at Work*, pp. 20–21.

17. "Inside the PARC: The 'Information Addicts,' " *IEEE Spectrum*, October 1985, p. 75.

18. Jeffrey S. Young, *Steve Jobs: The Journey Is the Reward* (Glenview, IL.: Scott, Foresman, 1988), p. 174.

19. "Inside the PARC: The 'Information Addicts,' " *IEEE Spectrum*, October 1985, p. 72.

20. "Inside the PARC: The 'Information Addicts,' " *IEEE Spectrum*, October 1985, p. 72.

21. "Participants Discussion for Thacker and Lampson," in Adele Goldberg, ed., *A History of Personal Workstations* (New York: ACM Press, 1988), pp. 343–344.

22. "Interview: John Seely Brown," *Computerworld*, 17 August 1992.

23. Young, *Steve Jobs: The Journey Is the Reward*, p. 175.

24. Smith and Alexander, *Fumbling the Future*, p. 242.

25. Adele Goldberg, "The Smalltalk-80 System Release Process," in Glenn Krasner, ed., *Smalltalk-80: Bits of History, Words of Advice* (Reading, MA: Addison-Wesley, 1983), p. 3.

26. "Xerox vs. Apple: Standard 'Dashboard' Is at Issue," *New York Times*, 20 December 1989.

27. "Xerox Suit Against Apple Peters Out," *Macweek*, 15 May 1990, p. 10.

28. "Apple Gets Boost in Copyright Suit," *Wall Street Journal*, 7 March 1991.

29. *Xerox Corporation v. Apple Computer Inc.*, 734 F.Supp 1542 (N.D.Cal. 1990).
30. *Apple Computer, Inc. v. Microsoft Corporation and Hewlett-Packard Company*, 799 F.Supp 1006 (N.D.Cal. 1992).
31. "Partners and Adversaries, Apple and Microsoft Weather Stormy Romance," *Macweek*, 14 March 1989, p. 1.
32. "The Year of the Mouse," *Time*, 31 January 1983, p. 51.
33. "Apple's Lisa Makes a Debut," *New York Times*, 19 January 1983.
34. John Sculley, *Odyssey: Pepsi to Apple . . . A Journey of Adventure, Ideas, and the Future* (New York: Harper and Row, 1987), p. 69.
35. "The Year of the Mouse," *Time*, 31 January 1983, p. 51.
36. "Apple's Lisa Meets a Bad End," *Infoworld*, 3 June 1985, p. 21.
37. "No Sour Tune From Ex-Beatle," *Los Angeles Times*, 23 July 1990.
38. "Former Apple Employee Says He, Not Jobs, Conceived Mac," *San Jose Mercury News*, 1 January 1990.
39. Lammers, *Programmers at Work*, p. 229.
40. John Markoff and Ezra Shapiro, "Macintosh's Other Designers," *Byte*, August 1984, p. 348.
41. Markoff and Shapiro, "Macintosh's Other Designers," p. 350.
42. Lammers, *Programmers at Work*, pp. 229–230.
43. Markoff and Shapiro, "Macintosh's Other Designers," p. 347.
44. Frank Rose, *West of Eden: The End of Innocence at Apple Computer* (New York: Viking Penguin, 1989), p. 49.
45. Markoff and Shapiro, "Macintosh's Other Designers," p. 350.
46. Young, *Steve Jobs: The Journey Is the Reward*, pp. 208–213.
47. Markoff and Shapiro, "Macintosh's Other Designers," p. 355.
48. Markoff and Shapiro, "Macintosh's Other Designers," p. 350.
49. "Apple to Extend Discounts on Its Macintosh Personal Computer to More Colleges," *Chronicle of Higher Education*, 11 April 1984, p. 15.
50. "A Computer on Every Desk," *Byte*, June 1984, p. 184.
51. "Playboy Interview: Steven Jobs," *Playboy*, February 1985, p. 180.
52. "Playboy Interview: Steven Jobs," *Playboy*, February 1985, p. 180.
53. "The Soul of a Not-So-New Machine," *Macweek*, 17 January 1989, p. 52.
54. "Playboy Interview: Steven Jobs," *Playboy*, February 1985, pp. 58, 184.
55. "Jobs Talks About His Rise and Fall," *Newsweek*, 30 September 1985, p. 52.
56. "Jobs Talks About His Rise and Fall," *Newsweek*, 30 September 1985, p. 52.
57. "The Gospel, According to Jobs," *San Jose Mercury News*, 25 September 1985.
58. Rose, *West of Eden* pp. 311–316; Sculley, *Odyssey*, p. 315.
59. Sculley, *Odyssey*, p. 316.
60. *Apple Computer Inc. v. Steven P. Jobs and Richard A. Page*, Superior Court of Santa Clara County, California, filed 23 September 1985.
61. "Steven Jobs Denies He's a Bad Apple," *San Francisco Examiner*, 25 September 1985.
62. Sculley, *Odyssey*, pp. 316–317.
63. "Jobs Talks About His Rise and Fall," *Newsweek*, 30 September 1985, p. 57.
64. "Can Steve Jobs Do It Again?" *New York Times*, 8 November 1987.

65. Paul Rand, *A Designer's Art* (New Haven: Yale University Press, 1985), pp. 233–235.
66. Paul Rand, NeXT brochure, spring 1986.
67. "Steve Jobs: Out for Revenge," *New York Times Magazine*, 6 August 1989, p. 56.
68. "Jobs Asserts Apple Undermined Efforts to Settle Dispute Over His New Venture," *Wall Street Journal*, 25 September 1985.
69. NeXT, Inc., brochure, "If I Have Been Able to See Farther Than Others, It Was Because I Stood on the Shoulders of Giants," n.d., n.p.
70. "The Entrepreneur of the Decade," *Inc.*, April 1989, p. 126.
71. "Valley Squalls: Apple Drags Jobs into Court," *Business Week*, 7 October 1985, p. 36.
72. "Jobs Talks About His Rise and Fall," *Newsweek*, 30 September 1985, p. 52.
73. Loren Baritz, *City on a Hill: A History of Ideas and Myths in America* (New York: John Wiley, 1964), p. 17.
74. "An Apple on Every Desk," *Inc.*, October 1981, p. 50.
75. "Next, Cypress Strive to Be Fair," *San Jose Mercury News*, 11 June 1990.
76. "At Next, Everyone Knows Who Earns How Much," *Fortune*, 26 March 1990, pp. 35–36.
77. "A Conversation with Steve Jobs," *Communications of the ACM*, April 1989, p. 440.
78. Baritz, *City on a Hill*, p. 17.
79. "The Entrepreneur of the Decade," *Inc.*, April 1989, p. 124.
80. Matt Rothman, "A Peek Inside the Black Box," *California Business*, April 1990, p. 34.
81. "Apple Era Behind Him," *Wall Street Journal*, 13 October 1988.
82. "Microsoft," *Business Week*, 24 February 1992, p. 65.
83. Rothman, "A Peek Inside the Black Box," p. 35.
84. "Mach's Main Man," *Nextworld*, Winter 1991, p. 12.
85. "Steve Jobs Comes Back," *Newsweek*, 24 October 1988, p. 49.
86. "Steve Jobs Comes Back," *Newsweek*, 24 October 1988, p. 48.
87. Nicole Biggart, *Charismatic Capitalism: Direct Selling Organizations in America* (Chicago: University of Chicago Press, 1989, p. 133; Edward Shils, "Charisma, Order, and Status," *American Sociological Review* 30, no. 2 (1965): 200–202.
88. Bryan R. Wilson, *The Noble Savages: The Primitive Origins of Charisma and Its Contemporary Survival* (Berkeley and Los Angeles: University of California Press, 1975), p. 7.
89. Rosabeth Moss Kanter, *Commitment and Community: Communes and Utopias in Sociological Perspective* (Cambridge, MA: Harvard University Press, 1972).
90. Paul Ciotti, "Revenge of the Nerds," *California*, July 1982, p. 133.
91. Reinhard Bendix, *Max Weber: An Intellectual Portrait* (Garden City, NY: Doubleday, 1960), pp. 308–309.
92. "Apple Computer," *Infoworld*, 8 March 1982, p. 12; "Playboy Interview: Steven Jobs," *Playboy*, February 1985, p. 174.
93. Nocera, "The Second Coming of Steve Jobs," *Esquire*, p. 92.

94. Michael Meyer, *The Alexander Complex: The Dreams That Drive the Great Businessmen* (New York: Times Books, 1989), p. 50.
95. NeXT brochure, "If I Have Been Able to See Farther Than Others."
96. "The Adventures of Steve Jobs (Cont'd)," *Fortune*, 14 October 1985, p. 124.
97. " 'In Search of Excellence,' on PBS," *New York Times*, 16 January 1985.
98. "A Look at Five Business Heroes, Warts and All," *Chicago Tribune*, 18 December 1986.
99. "Apple Computer, Jobs Settle Dispute," *Infoworld*, 27 January 1986, p. 10; Rose, *West of Eden*, p. 335.
100. "A Conversation with Steve Jobs," *Communications of the ACM*, April 1989, p. 438.
101. "Why Jobs Took on Perot as Investor," *San Francisco Chronicle*, 31 January 1987.
102. " 'The Entrepreneurs,' Documentary on 13," *New York Times*, 5 November 1986.
103. "Perot and Jobs: Who's Next?" *Newsweek*, 9 February 1987, p. 48.
104. "The World According to Ross Perot," *Life*, February 1988, p. 70.
105. "Jobs, Perot Become Unlikely Partners in the Apple Founder's New Concern," *Wall Street Journal*, 2 February 1987.
106. "Perot and Jobs: Who's Next?" *Newsweek*, 9 February 1987, p. 48.
107. "The Idaho Angel on Their Shoulder," *Washington Post*, 12 April 1992.
108. "Angels of Capitalism," *Boston Globe*, 13 November 1990.
109. "The Work of Angels," *Inc.*, September 1989, p. 40.
110. "The Forbes Four Hundred," *Forbes*, 26 October 1987, p. 116.
111. "Computer Venture Confirmed by Perot," *New York Times*, 31 January 1987.
112. "Perot and Jobs: Who's Next?" *Newsweek*, 9 February 1987, p. 48.
113. "Ross Perot Turns into an Angel for Steve Jobs," *Business Week*, 9 February 1987, p. 32.
114. "Computer Industry Wary of Jobs-Perot Alliance," *Washington Post*, 8 February 1987.
115. "Will Steven Jobs' Computer Sell?" *Los Angeles Times*, 23 October 1988.
116. "Jobs, Perot Become Unlikely Partners in the Apple Founder's New Concern," *Wall Street Journal*, 2 February 1987.
117. "The World According to Ross Perot," *Life*, February 1988, p. 70.
118. "Jobs, Perot Become Unlikely Partners in the Apple Founder's New Concern," *Wall Street Journal*, 2 February 1987.
119. "Perot Warns Against U.S. Complacency," *Computerworld*, 12 December 1988, p. 120.
120. Ross Perot, transcript of address at National Press Club, 17 November 1988.
121. "The World According to Ross Perot," *Life*, February 1988, p. 70.
122. David Bunnell, "How Macworld Magazine Made the Macintosh," in Doug Clapp, ed., *The Macintosh Reader* (New York: Random House Electronic Publishing, 1992), p. 63.
123. "I Blew It, Perot Says," *Seattle Times*, 4 June 1992; "Perot's Missed Opportunity," *San Jose Mercury News*, 16 June 1992.
124. "Cowboy Capitalist," *Inc.*, January 1989, p. 60.

125. "Cowboy Capitalist," *Inc.*, January 1989, p. 58.
126. "Pure Knowledge vs. Impure Profit," *New York Times*, 19 September 1988. See also the retort of Richard Cyert, president of Carnegie-Mellon, in his letter, "No Dollar Signs in Researchers' Eyes," *New York Times*, 24 September 1988.
127. Tom Wolfe, "The Tinkerings of Robert Noyce," *Esquire*, December 1983, pp. 364, 373.
128. "Perot and Jobs: Who's Next?" *Newsweek*, 9 February 1987, p. 48.
129. "Georgia Tech's Outspoken President Tackles Atlanta," *Chronicle of Higher Education*, 10 August 1988, p. A3.
130. "Two Universities Join Next as Investors," *San Jose Mercury News*, 31 January 1987.
131. "Working with Perot," *San Francisco Examiner*, 21 June 1992.
132. "Shorter Cycles Make Subcontractors Work Harder," *Electronic Business*, 23 July 1990, p. 37.
133. "How Next Makes Manufacturing Its Quality Cornerstone," *Electronic Business*, 15 October 1990, p. 136.
134. "A Conversation with Steve Jobs," *Communications of the ACM*, April 1989, p. 439.
135. NeXT brochure, "If I Have Been Able . . ."
136. "Exiled From Apple, The Enigmatic Leader Is Back with Next," *Boston Globe*, 4 December 1988.
137. "Steve Jobs: What's Next," *Fortune*, 7 November 1988, p. 16.
138. Steven W. Gilbert and Kenneth C. Green, "New Computing in Higher Education," *Change*, May–June 1986, p. 47.
139. "Coming of Age," *Inc.*, April 1989, p. 39.
140. "The World According to Ross Perot," *Life*, February 1988, p. 70.
141. Merrill Lynch roundtable, 28 October 1986.
142. "Judge Throws Out Lawsuit Over Next Founder's Firing," *San Jose Mercury News*, 9 November 1989.
143. "Mistrial in Next Case," *San Francisco Chronicle*, 13 June 1989.
144. *Linda Wilkin v. Steven P. Jobs and NeXT, Inc.*, Superior Court of Santa Clara County, California, filed 23 October 1987.
145. NeXT brochure, "If I Have Been Able . . ."
146. Steven P. Jobs, "The Future of Computing in Higher Education," *Educom Bulletin*, Spring 1987, p. 7.
147. "Computer Warfare on Campus," *U.S. News and World Report*, 14 September 1987, p. 54.
148. "How Steve Jobs Linked Up With IBM," *Fortune*, 9 October 1989, p. 50.
149. "Steve Jobs—Out for Revenge," *New York Times Magazine*, 6 August 1989.
150. G. Pascal Zachary, "Andy Bechtolsheim and His Demons," *Upside*, October 1990, pp. 60–61.
151. "Stories from the Old Days at Sun," prepared by Sun Microsystems for the company's tenth anniversary.
152. "Snow Jobs by Jobs," *San Francisco Chronicle*, 10 June 1984.
153. "Interview with Scott McNealy," 23 January 1992, Ten Years pamphlet series, Sun Microsystems.

154. "The Sun Rises for the Class of '80," *Stanford GSB*, Winter 1984, p. 27.
155. "A New Ballgame for Sun's Scott McNealy," *Upside*, November–December 1989, p. 50.
156. "Scott McNealy," *Forbes*, 27 May 1991, p. 230.
157. "High Noon for Sun," *Business Week*, 24 July 1989, p. 70.
158. "Scott McNealy," *USA Today*, 19 January 1988.
159. "A New Ballgame for Sun's Scott McNealy," *Upside*, November–December 1989, p. 54.
160. "Scott McNealy," *USA Today*, 19 January 1988.
161. "Sun's Workstation Juggernaut Is Still Barreling," *Los Angeles Times*, 24 November 1991.
162. "High-Tech Firms Find It's Good to Line Up Outside Contractors," *Wall Street Journal*, 29 July 1992.
163. Scott McNealy, personal autobiographical statement, n.d., Sun Microsystems.
164. "A New Ballgame for Sun's Scott McNealy," *Upside*, November–December 1989, p. 53.
165. "Sun Micro: Hot Spot in a Cool Market," *Computer Systems News*, 28 October 1985, p. 67; "Sun's Sizzling Race to the Top," *Fortune* 17 August 1987, p. 90.
166. "Computerdom's Heavenly Brawl," *Fortune*, 4 February 1985, p. 99.
167. "Scott McNealy," *USA Today*, 19 January 1988.
168. "Purely by Design," *Workstation News*, October 1990, p. 37.
169. "Sun Microsystems a Stellar Performer," *San Francisco Chronicle*, 20 October 1986.
170. "Computerdom's Heavenly Brawl," *Fortune*, 4 February 1985, p. 99.
171. "Sun's Sizzling Race to the Top," *Fortune*, 17 August 1987, p. 89.
172. "A New Ballgame for Sun's Scott McNealy," *Upside*, November–December 1989, p. 52.
173. "They Are Not There Waiting for the Plane to Land," *Forbes*, 17 June 1988, p. 50.
174. "The Gospel According to Joy," *New York Times Magazine*, 27 March 1988, p. 32.
175. "Sun's Success Doubly Sweet for Designer," *Wall Street Journal*, 29 May 1990.
176. "Sun's Success Doubly Sweet for Designer," *Wall Street Journal*, 29 May 1990.
177. "Sun's Success Doubly Sweet for Designer," *Wall Street Journal*, 29 May 1990.
178. Transcript of speech given at Siggraph, August 1991.
179. "Secrecy Increases Allure," *Los Angeles Times*, 12 October 1988.
180. "Dear Next: When Can I Get My Machine?" *P.C. Letter*, 11 October 1988, p. 1.
181. "Next Question," *Infoworld*, 17 October 1988, p. 94.
182. "The Next Generation: Stars Trek to S.F." *San Jose Mercury News*, 10 October 1988.
183. "Next Inc. Produces a Gala," *New York Times*, 10 October 1988.
184. "Steve Jobs Comes Back," *Newsweek*, 24 October 1988, p. 46.
185. "Steve Jobs Comes Back," *Newsweek*, 24 October 1988, p. 46.
186. "It's All Right Now," *Upside*, May 1992, p. 38.

187. "The Cult of Steve," *Chicago Tribune*, 23 October 1988.
188. Ross Perot, transcript of address at National Press Club, 17 November 1988.
189. "The Cult of Steve," *Chicago Tribune*, 23 October 1988.
190. "Soul of the Next Machine," *Time*, 24 October 1988, p. 80.
191. "Will Steven Jobs' Computer Sell?" *Los Angeles Times*, 23 October 1988.
192. "Eight Megabytes of Sexual Satisfaction," *San Francisco Examiner*, 16 October 1988.
193. Cited in Paul Saettler, *A History of Instructional Technology* (New York: McGraw-Hill, 1968), p. 98.
194. Larry Cuban, *Teachers and Machines: The Classroom Use of Technology Since 1920* (New York: Teachers College Press, 1986), p. 3.
195. "Teaching by Computer," *Science News Letter*, 14 October 1961, p. 255.
196. "The New B.M.O.Cs: Big Machines on Campus," *Time*, 19 May 1967, p. 98.
197. Sally Ventie Kiester, "It's Student and Computer, One on One," *Change*, January 1978, p. 56.
198. "Dial 'H' For History," *Newsweek*, 2 March 1964, p. 77.
199. Patrick Suppes, "The Uses of Computers in Education," *Scientific American*, September 1966, pp. 207–208.
200. "Teachers Without Tempers," *Redbook*, January 1969, p. 46.
201. "How Computers Will Change Your Life," *McCall's*, May 1965, p. 34.
202. James Ridgeway, "Computer-Tutor," *New Republic*, 4 June 1966, p. 21.
203. Cited in Stephan L. Chorover, "Cautions on Computers in Education," *Byte*, June 1984, p. 224.
204. Maxwell Goldberg, "Technological Mythmaking and Humanities Teaching," *School and Society*, November 1969, p. 425.
205. "Origins of PLATO: A $10 TV Set and the Vision of a Researcher," *Chronicle of Higher Education*, 28 November 1984, p. 23.
206. "Living: Pushbutton Power," *Time*, 20 February 1978, p. 48.
207. James C. Worthy, *William C. Norris: Portrait of a Maverick* (Cambridge, MA: Ballinger, 1987), p. 85.
208. "Use of Computers for Teaching Gains Ground," *Chronicle of Higher Education*, 28 November 1984, p. 23.
209. "A Social Strategy Based on Profits," *Business Week*, 25 June 1979, p. 123.
210. "NeXT on Campus: The Cube Advances," *Macweek*, 11 July 1989, p. 83.
211. Worthy, *William C. Norris*, opening epigraph.
212. "A Social Strategy Based on Profits," *Business Week*, 25 June 1979, p. 123.
213. Staples Information Inc., *The Next Computer: Did Steve Jobs Misread the Market?* (Houston: Staples Information, 1988), pp. 1–11.
214. Ridgeway, "Computer-Tutor," *New Republic*, p. 22.
215. "NeXT's Black Workstation Fighting an Uphill Battle?" *Computer Reseller News*, 24 October 1988, p. 117.
216. "Amid Computer Slump, Computer Sales to Colleges Boom," *Chronicle of Higher Education*, 17 July 1985, p. 12.
217. "At Berkeley, Computers Have to Work—Even If They're Donated," *Chronicle of Higher Education*, 2 April 1986, p. 27.

218. "Vendors Negotiate Everything, Duke University Official Says," *Chronicle of Higher Education*, 22 January 1986, p. 28.
219. "Key Software Completed for 'NeXT' Computer; Tiny Allegheny College, a Big User, Breathes Sigh of Relief," *Chronicle of Higher Education*, 27 September 1989, p. A19.
220. "College Enables Professors to Write Computer Programs with Ease," *Chronicle of Higher Education*, 20 May 1992, p. A16.
221. "Jobs Older, Wiser," *San Francisco Chronicle*, 13 October 1988.
222. "Next Hits the Street," *P.C. Letter*, 28 March 1989.
223. "Businessland to Sell Nexts," *San Francisco Chronicle*, 31 March 1989.
224. "Next Hits the Street," *P.C. Letter*, 28 March 1989.
225. "Battle for the Desktop," *Wall Street Journal*, 31 March 1989.
226. "Businessland Deal Means Next Is No Longer Merely Academic," *San Jose Mercury News*, 31 March 1989.
227. "Businessland Deal Means Next Is No Longer Merely Academic," *San Jose Mercury News*, 31 March 1989.
228. "The World According to Sun Microsystems' CEO," *PC Week*, 6 February 1989, p. 58.
229. "Computer Stars on Collision Course," *New York Times*, 10 March 1989.
230. "Power Station in a Pizza Box," *Time*, 24 April 1989, p. 51.
231. "Can Sun Stand the Heat in the PC Market?" *Business Week*, 24 April 1989, p. 139.
232. "Will Sun Also Rise in the Office Market?" *Business Week*, 21 May 1990, p. 44.
233. "The Cobblers at Sun Make Hammers, Not Shoes," *PC Week*, 19 June 1989, p. 65.
234. "Systems Snafu Stuns Sun," *Computerworld*, 5 June 1989, p. 1.
235. "Life on the Speedway: Many Faces of Growth," *Business Month*, May 1990, p. 42.
236. "A New Ballgame for Sun's Scott McNealy," *Upside*, November–December 1989, p. 47.
237. "NeXT OS Still Has Ground to Cover," *Infoworld*, 10 April 1989, p. 38.
238. "Steve Jobs Banks Next Hopes on IBM Move," *Washington Post*, 3 June 1989.
239. "Canon Purchase of 16.7% Stake in Next Values Jobs's Company At $600 Million," *Wall Street Journal*, 13 June 1989.
240. "Steven Jobs Is Back with Next and Going Strong," *Times Tribune*, 21 June 1989.
241. Frank Rose, "The Case of the Ankling Agents," *Premiere*, August 1991, p. 56; "R.I.P.?" *Los Angeles Magazine*, May 1991, p. 70.
242. "Next's Stature Grows, But Sales Lag," *San Jose Mercury*, 2 May 1990.
243. "Top 40 North American NeXT Sites," *Nextworld*, Summer 1992, p. 28.
244. "William Morris Buys 250 Next Workstations," *Los Angeles Times*, 1 May 1990.
245. "Profile: The Star System," *Nextworld*, March–April 1991, p. 37.
246. "Enterprisewide Multimedia; Not Ready for Prime Time," *Infoworld*, 25 May 1992, p. 48.

247. "Forget Doing Lunch—Hollywood's on E-mail," *New York Times*, 6 September 1992.
248. "NextStep to Integrate Mac, PC LANs," *Infoworld*, 23 December 1991, p. 8.
249. "Writing the Book of Jobs," *Computerworld*, 11 December 1989, p. 107.
250. "Writing the Book of Jobs," *Computerworld*, 11 December 1989, p. 107.
251. "Jobs' Corporate Vision for NeXT Met by Skeptics on Wall Street," *PC Week*, 4 December 1989, p. 6.
252. "Jobs: Poised for NeXT Success," *Macweek*, 19 September 1989, p. S20.
253. "EDUCOM Meet Highlights Networking," *Macweek*, 24 October 1989, p. 6.
254. "A Conversation with Steve Jobs," *Communications of the ACM*, April 1989, p. 440.
255. "Steve Jobs," *Computerworld*, 22 June 1992, p. 8.
256. "Developers Split Over Optical Drive," *Macweek*, 19 September 1989, p. S8.
257. "The Soul of a Not-So-New-Machine," *Macweek*, 17 January 1989, p. 52.
258. Bunnell, "How Macworld Magazine Made the Macintosh," p. 63.
259. "Jobs's New Computer off to a Sluggish Start," *New York Times*, 20 January 1990.
260. "Technobabble Update," *San Francisco Chronicle*, 10 May 1990.
261. "Technobabble Update," *San Francisco Chronicle*, 10 May 1990.
262. "The State of the NeXT Revolution," *Macweek*, 3 April 1990, p. 25.
263. "Performance, Lack of Software Hinder Sales of NeXT Machine," *Macweek*, 3 April 1990, p. 25.
264. "Next to Market Through VAR's," *Computer Reseller News*, 22 January 1990, p. 2.
265. Robert Slater, *Portraits in Silicon* (Cambridge, MA.: MIT Press, 1987), p. 130.
266. "Overall Workstation Industry Growth Slows as Unit Market Prices Drop," *CIMweek*, 11 February 1991.
267. "Sun to Unveil Challenge to Apple, IBM," *San Jose Mercury News*, 23 July 1990.
268. Sun Microsystems, *Annual Report 1990*, p. 5.
269. "Life on the Speedway: Many Faces of Growth," *Business Month*, May 1990, p. 42.
270. Sun Microsystems, *Annual Report 1990*, pp. 5, 9.
271. "Sun to Unveil Challenge to Apple, IBM," *San Jose Mercury News*, 23 July 1990.
272. "Of Sailing Ships and Sales Dips," *Computerworld*, 1 October 1990, p. 111.
273. "Next Pins Hopes on Rollout," *San Jose Mercury News*, 17 September 1990.
274. "Jobs' New Hope," *San Jose Mercury News*, 19 September 1990.
275. "Improv: The Inside Story," *Nextworld*, Fall 1991, p. 35.
276. "Welcome," *Next Users' Journal*, September 1990, p. 1.
277. "Software Can Make or Break Newest Computers," *San Francisco Examiner*, 18 June 1989.
278. "Third-Party Developers Describe 'Spotty' Relations," *Nextworld Extra*, March 1992, p. 4.

279. *The Grady Report*, 4 October 1991.
280. "Businessland Endorses Takeover for $54 Million," *New York Times*, 5 June 1991; "JWP Sees Another Big Loss and Will Sell Unit," *New York Times*, 20 March 1993; "JWP to Shed Information Services Line, Stress Its Core Subcontracting Business," *Wall Street Journal*, 22 March 1993; "JWP to Sell Information Services in Midst of Formidable·Losses," *PC Week*, 29 March 1993, p. 121.
281. "The Legacy Continues," *BANG Newsletter*, Fall 1991, p. 25.
282. "NeXT Goes Global," *Nextworld*, Winter 1991, p. 37.
283. "NeXT Casts Bid in German Workstation Arena," *PC Week*, 18 March 1991, p. 140.
284. "Market Takes Off in Europe," *Nextworld*, Fall 1991, p. 14.
285. "Next's Computer May Now Be a 'Force To Reckon With,' " *Chronicle of Higher Education*, 31 October 1991, p. A11.
286. "Steve Jobs," *Computerworld*, 22 June 1992,, p. 8; "Reinventing NeXT," *Nextworld*, Fall 1992, p. 33.
287. Richard Shaffer, "Here Comes IBM," *Forbes*, 18 February 1991, p. 108.
288. "Andy Heller Against the World," *Unix World*, March 1992, p. 34.
289. "Jobs and Gates Together," *Fortune*, 26 August 1991, p. 54.
290. "IBM, NeXT Reach Impasse on Next Step Port to AIX," *Unix Today*, 14 October 1991, pp. 1, 78.
291. NeXT Press Release, "NeXT Ships 8,000 CPUs in First Quarter," 4 April 1991.
292. "NeXT Finding a Place in the Market," *Los Angeles Times*, 5 April 1990.
293. "We're No. 2—Really," *San Jose Mercury News*, 5 May 1991.
294. "Next Posts Gain in Computer Sales," *New York Times*, 5 May 1991.
295. "Is NeXT Finally Zeroing In on the Right Target?" *Business Week*, 15 April 1991, p. 74.
296. "Can Steven Jobs Perform Miracles, Again?" *Financial Post*, 4 November 1991.
297. "Alliances Validate Next Philosophy," *Infoworld*, 5 August 1991, p. 114; "An Industry Guru, a Top User, and the Firing Line," *Unix Today*, 30 September 1991, p. 13; "The Next Step: Jobs Outlines His Strategy," *Computer Reseller News*, 4 November 1991, p. 3.
298. "The Next Step: Jobs Outlines His Strategy," *Computer Reseller News*, 4 November 1991, p. 3.
299. "Jobs Discloses Next Inc. Plans Public Offering," *Wall Street Journal*, 31 October 1991.
300. "Four Tech Firms Will Lay Off Staff," *San Jose Mercury News*, 2 November 1991.
301. "While Jobs Talks of Public Offering, NeXT Lays Off 5 Percent of Staff," *Macweek*, 12 November 1991, p. 100.
302. "Four Tech Firms Will Lay Off Staff," *San Jose Mercury News*, 2 November 1991.
303. "Playboy Interview: Steve Jobs," *Playboy*, February 1985, p. 54.

304. "Business Buyers Breathe Life into NeXT Computer," *Supercomputer Review*, April 1992, p. 46.
305. "Business Buyers Breathe Life into NeXT Computer," *Supercomputer Review*, April 1992, p. 46.
306. "Black Market," *Nextworld*, Summer 1992, p. 23.
307. "Overheard," *Unix World*, June 1992, p. 18.
308. "Playboy Interview: Steven Jobs," *Playboy*, February 1985, p. 182.
309. John Perry Barlow, "At Last, NeXT Sells the Dream . . . To MIS," *Microtimes*, 22 January 1992, pp. 178–180.
310. "Top 40 North American NeXT Sites," *Nextworld*, Summer 1992, p. 28.
311. Barlow, "At Last, NeXT Sells the Dream," *Microtimes*, p. 180.
312. Posted by Ernest Prabhakar, 9 July 1991.
313. "Next's Layoffs Not Alarming Customers," *Computerworld*, 11 November 1991, p. 45.
314. "Apple's Gross Margins Going Down," *Macweek*, 26 October 1992, p. 38.
315. "Steve Jobs Rouses Rabble at Object World to Hisses and Boos for His Also-Ran Rivals," *Computergram International*, 4 August 1992.
316. "How an IBM Attempt to Regain PC Lead Has Slid into Trouble," *Wall Street Journal*, 2 December 1991.
317. John Perry Barlow, "NeXT in the Real World," *Microtimes*, 17 February 1992, pp. 51–52.
318. Barlow, "NeXT in the Real World," *Microtimes*, p. 57.
319. "Foray into Mainstream for Parallel Computing," *New York Times*, 15 January 1992.
320. "Sun Profits Are Out of the World," *San Jose Mercury News*, 9 August 1991.
321. "Sun Profits Are Out of the World," *San Jose Mercury News*, 9 August 1991.
322. "Scott McNealy," *Computerworld*, 22 June 1992, p. 36.
323. *Wall Street Journal*, 23 January 1992.
324. Dan Ruby, "Petri Dish," *Nextworld*, Summer 1992, p. 3.
325. "Turbo NeXTstation Color Computer," *Sunworld*, March 1992, pp. 51–54.
326. "Sun Microsystems Reports Profit Dropped 43 Percent in Fiscal Fourth Quarter," *Wall Street Journal*, 6 August 1992.
327. "It's All Right Now," *Upside*, May 1992, p. 64.
328. "NeXT Sharpens Sales Focus," *Nextworld Extra*, September 1992, p. 1.
329. "IPO Groundwork Heats Up," *Nextworld Extra*, June 1992, p. 5.
330. "NeXTstep Wows Money Managers," *USA Today*, 28 April 1992.
331. "Van Cuylenburg Quits Cable & Wireless," *The Independent*, 19 March 1992; "Strategy for Next Generation of Workstations," *Financial Times*, 7 July 1992, p. 28.
332. "Next Finds a President in Telephone Industry," *New York Times*, 19 March 1992.
333. "Strategy for Next Generation of Workstations," *Financial Times*, 7 July 1992, p. 28.
334. "Help!" *Nextworld*, Fall 1992, p. 26.
335. "Key Engineer Quits Next Computer to Join Sun," *New York Times*, 3 June 1992.

336. "Another Cog Drops Out of Next Gang," *San Jose Mercury News*, 2 June 1992.
337. "Next Defections Continue, Spurring More Concerns About Firm," *San Jose Mercury News*, 23 June 1992.
338. "Another Cog Drops Out of Next Gang," *San Jose Mercury News*, 2 June 1992.
339. "Rally Tests Entrepreneurial Know-How," *San Jose Mercury News*, 21 May 1992.
340. "Playboy Interview: Steven Jobs," *Playboy*, February 1985, p. 182.
341. Stephen Jay Gould, *Wonderful Life: The Burgess Shale and the Nature of History* (New York: Norton, 1989), pp. 47–68, 232–238, 320–321.
342. George Basalla, *The Evolution of Technology* (Cambridge: Cambridge University Press, 1988), pp. 198–203.
343. Melvin Konner, *Why the Reckless Survive and Other Secrets of Human Nature* (New York: Penguin, 1990), pp. 5–7, 136–138.
344. "Improv: A Better Spreadsheet," *PC Magazine*, 23 February 1993, p. 81.
345. "Lotus Sells 125,000 Units of Improv for Windows in First Month," Business Wire press release, 30 March 1993.
346. "Despite Spat, Apple Remains Jobs' First Love," *San Jose Mercury News*, 23 September 1985.
347. "The National Business Hall of Fame," *Fortune*, 23 March 1992, pp. 114–115.
348. "Playboy Interview: Steven Jobs," *Playboy*, February 1985, p. 50.
349. "Jobs' Corporate Vision for NeXT Met By Skeptics on Wall Street," *PC Week*, 4 December 1989, p. 6.
350. "Steve Jobs Plans Broad Role for Computers," *San Francisco Chronicle*, 9 October 1987.
351. "New IBM Vice President Speaks," *Computer Reseller News*, 29 March 1993.
352. "IBM Plans to Oust John Akers as Chief," *USA Today*, 27 January 1993.
353. "Novell and Unix: A Good Fit," *PC Magazine*, 30 March 1993, p. 99.
354. NeXT advertisement, *Wall Street Journal*, 18 February 1993.
355. NeXT advertisement, *Wall Street Journal*, 18 February 1993.
356. "The 'NextStep' for Next Is Finding a Software Developer," *Infoworld*, 22 March 1993, p. 6.
357. Posted by Peter Wayner, 18 March 1993.
358. "Unix Rivals Unite," *Computerworld*, 22 March 1993, p. 1.
359. "Unix Program's Suppliers Adopt Joint Approach," *Wall Street Journal*, 17 March 1993.
360. Gould, *Wonderful Life*, p. 47.

Index